KILLING FIELDS, LIVING FIELDS

'Among the last missionaries to leave Cambodia when the Khmer Rouge took power and one of the first to return afterwards, Don Cormack is better qualified than anyone to tell the story of the still-young church God has planted there. This heartwrenching, heartwarming narrative prompts tears, prayers, praises and hopes in turn. It is a long time since I read anything so poignant.'

Professor J I Packer
Regent College, Vancouver

'I could not be more enthusiastic about this book. It is Hebrews 11 in the twentieth century, totally absorbing, vividly written, deeply moving and hugely quotable. The tragedy of Cambodia is too little known, but this book goes far beyond information. I would be surprised if it does not become a classic of its kind.'

Rev Eric J Alexander

'The gates of Hell have not prevailed against the faithful ones who were anointed for burial. You cannot read this continuing story of the Cambodian Church without being moved to pray.'

The Most Rev Dr Moses Tay
Archbishop of the Province of South East Asia and
Bishop of Singapore

'Great! At last: a long anticipated account of the Cambodian church from a man who has lived alongside it through stormy years of its history. Rejoice in what the Chief Harvester has done in a long overlooked mission field.'

Dr Michael Griffiths

'A marvellous story of hope and courage, from a near-forgotten country. An attack on 'soft-option' Christianity and an unmistakable call to sacrificial faith.'

Rev Stephen Gaukroger

'What the Jewish people suffered at Auschwitz and Belsen, the Cambodians suffered in the 'concentration camps' of the Killing Fields. Don Cormack paints a remarkable picture that reveals the smile of God's mercy and glory shining through the worst horrors of human depravity, and assuring us that his purposes in the face of Jesus the Messiah can never be snuffed out. Living Fields indeed.'

Rev Ray Lockhart
Vicar, Christ Church, Jerusalem

'More than twenty years on from Pol Pot's Year Zero, the Cambodian nation still bears the physical and psychological scars of prolonged terror and torment. Few people can be as qualified to write about Cambodia with such authority – or to relate such stories with such compassion – as Don Cormack. His gripping narrative has convinced me that this country, which has had more than its fair share of tragedy, is not a land bereft of hope.'

Jonathan Miller
BBC Indo-China correspondent

'In a profoundly moving account, beautifully and intelligently written, Don Cormack's story of the Cambodian church opens our eyes to the extraordinary suffering of God's people, their courageous witness to Christ, remarkable answers to prayer, and the faithfulness of the Lord in whom they trust.

'We Western Christians who know so little about sacrifice and martyrdom urgently need to heed the lessons from this vivid and harrowing account: that the first principle of church growth and missionary fruitfulness is still that which Jesus predicted and exemplified – the seed must die before it bears much fruit.

'Written with integrity and compassion, *Killing Fields, Living Fields* tells a story that we cannot ignore. It is destined to become one of the late twentieth century's most significant accounts of the painful birth of Christian witness, a description of a church with the authentic mark of suffering.

'Twenty-five years after an urgent appeal to British Christians, the harrowing story of the Cambodian church is once again brought to our attention in a moving account of extraordinary suffering yet profound faith. Today we must not ignore the lessons, and the needs, with which this book confronts us. I urge you to read it.'

Jonathan Lamb
Chairman, Keswick Convention, IFES Regional Secretary,
Europe and CIS

Killing Fields, Living Fields stunned me. It is hard to know how to say anything at all about such heroism, such uncompromising faithfulness in the midst of unspeakable suffering.'

Elisabeth Elliot

Killing Fields, Living Fields is a MUST-read. Too many Christians are ill informed about what happened in the past and what is happening around them now, despite media coverage. This book shows the power of God in the lives of the persecuted and marginalised, and affirms the power of the gospel to take root in the most unpromising circumstances.'

Rt Rev Frank Retief
Area Bishop, Church of England in South Africa

'As I read this, I paused every few minutes and sobbed in anger. Amid this great tragedy, the extraordinary power of faith, hope, and love manifests itself – in the lives of a few ordinary Christians. They are my heroes. How I wish all Khmer Rouge leaders would read this book, weep in repentance, and find forgiveness in the Lord Jesus Christ.'

Dr Sorpong Peou
A survivor of the 'killing fields'

PUBLISHING

OMF International works in most East Asian countries, and among East Asian peoples around the world. It was founded by James Hudson Taylor in 1865 as the China Inland Mission. Our overall purpose is to glorify God through the urgent evangelisation of East Asia's billions, and this is reflected in our publishing.

Through our books, booklets, website and quarterly magazine, *East Asia's Billions,* OMF Publishing aims to motivate Christians for world mission, and to equip them for playing a part in it. Publications include:

- contemporary mission issues
- the biblical basis of mission
- the life of faith
- stories and biographies related to God's work in East Asia
- accounts of the growth and development of the Church in Asia
- studies of Asian culture and religion relating to the spiritual needs of her peoples

Visit our website at *www.omf.org*

Addresses for OMF English-speaking centres can be found at the back of this book.

Killing Fields
Living Fields

An unfinished portrait of the
Cambodian Church
—the Church that would not die

DON CORMACK

MONARCH
BOOKS

Mill Hill, London NW7 3SA and Grand Rapids, Michigan

First published by Monarch Books in the UK in 1997,
Concorde House, Grenville Place,
Mill Hill, London, NW7 3SA.

Published in the USA by Monarch Books 2001.

Reprinted 1997, 1998.
Reissued 2000.
Reprinted 2001.

Distributed by:
UK: STL, PO Box 300, Kingstown Broadway, Carlisle,
Cumbria CA3 0QS;
USA: Kregel Publications, PO Box 2607
Grand Rapids, Michigan 49501.

ISBN 1 85424 487 6 (UK)
ISBN 0 8254 6002 6 (USA)

British Library Cataloguing Data
A catalogue record for this book is available
from the British Library.

Cover photo: Kevin Morris

Book design and production for the publishers by
Bookprint Creative Services,
P.O. Box 827, BN21 3YJ, England.
Printed in Great Britain.

Dedicated to
Setha ('Little Brother')
wherever you are …
with affection and gratitude.

CONTENTS

FOREWORD

You are about to read an extraordinary book. I believe it is one of the great Christian books of our time. It is certainly one of the most remarkable books I have ever read. At times I have been unable to see the page for tears and at other times unwilling to turn it over for fear of what I was about to find on the other side.

An entire country turned into one colossal concentration camp. One-and-a-half million men, women and children executed by the Khmer Rouge and huge numbers dying of starvation and disease. In all, perhaps thirty per cent of the Cambodian people and ninety per cent of the young Cambodian Church was wiped out. And yet, in the midst of it all, God; the God who daily bears the pain of a fallen world, at work calling, comforting, rescuing, saving lives that are falling like sparks into the water, like seed into the ground.

So we read too of faith, fortitude, and triumph in the midst of disaster. I shall never forget Don's account of the last days of Phnom Penh as the Khmer Rouge armies surrounded and shelled the city and as the Christians spread over the city preaching to crowds, baptising hundreds, and in Christ's name quite literally 'rescuing the perishing' from the jaws of hell. Most of them paid for such a harvest with their lives but it was a price they were willing to pay and they are honoured in heaven:

> 'These are they who have come out of the great tribulation; they have washed their robes and made them white in the blood of the Lamb. Therefore they are before the throne of God and serve him day and night in his temple; and he who sits on the throne will spread his tent over them. Never again will they thirst. The sun will not beat upon them nor any scorching heat. For the Lamb at the centre of the throne will be their shepherd; he will lead them to springs of living water. And God will wipe away every tear from their eyes.' (Rev 7:14-17)

The early Church, too, was born in conflict. Its leader was the

Prince of Peace, its message called men and women into a kingdom of peace, yet it was rarely left in peace for long. Then, as now, the price for peace with God seemed to be conflict with others. 'In fact,' says the Apostle Paul, 'everyone who wants to live a godly life in Christ Jesus will be persecuted.' (2 Tim 3:12) That has been the experience of Cambodian Christians from the beginning, and if it is not our experience in the comfortable and affluent West we must ask if this is because we have taken the escape route implied in those words. Whenever we speak out boldly for Christ, whenever we counter corruption and challenge the system, whenever we refuse to compromise, we shall be targets of anger and resentment as well as beacons of hope and light. Where we have taken shelter in guilty silence and retreated from the spiritual warfare we are called to wage, we shall never experience or understand the paradoxical words of the Apostle Peter: 'If you are insulted because of the name of Christ, you are blessed, for the Spirit of glory and of God rests on you.' (1 Peter 4:14) These are some of the abiding lessons of this book.

The book is beautifully written, the prose is rich and evocative, the author has an eye for personal details as well as historic events. At times he will move in close to a family or an individual with graphic pen-strokes and vivid local colour, at other times he will succinctly and helpfully summarise a complex political situation or take a wide sweep of events over a large area. All in all he has written a modern Christian classic. It is the *Wild Swans* of Cambodia and the suffering Church. It is a story which, like the Church of Jesus Christ, will never die:

'Then those who feared the Lord talked with each other, and the Lord listened and heard. A scroll of remembrance was written in his presence concerning those who feared the Lord and honoured his name. "They will be mine," says the Lord Almighty, "in the day when I make up my treasured possession."' (Malachi 3:16-17)

The Revd Peter Lewis
Cornerstone Evangelical Church
Nottingham

PREFACE

This book was originally intended to explore the emergence of a new church among Cambodian exiles in refugee camps in Thailand over the years since 1975, when Cambodia fell into communist hands and hundreds of thousands of her people began fleeing their homeland. I found I was unable to do this without looking back to Cambodia during the Khmer Rouge reign of terror (1975-1979) – that fiery crucible, sparks from which ignited revival fires in grim border refugee camps in Thailand. But even the moving story of the church under the Khmer Rouge cannot properly be understood without first examining the preceding five years of great harvest (1970-1975) part of which I witnessed personally in Phnom Penh. That much-prayed-for ingathering would not have been possible but for the tenacious roots which for fifty years before that had persistently pushed deeper into the resistant Cambodian bedrock, through many seasons of sowing with weeping and of long waiting with patience.

Thus we need to trace the history of the Cambodian Protestant church from its humble origins among the hardy rice farmers of north-west Cambodia in the mid-1920s. After this followed decades of near fruitless toil and considerable opposition, culminating in the incredible 1970s, when joyous harvest was juxtaposed with indescribable devastation. Throughout the turbulent 1980s, insecurity and communist rule forced the decimated church underground in Cambodia, drove it across into neighbouring Thailand's crowded refugee camps, and then scattered it across six continents. With the 1990s has come the opportunity for a new beginning, with the restoration in Cambodia of a heady freedom for all. On this final decade of the Millennium, the jury is still out. Others will have to detail this part of the portrait later.

Some have written about the Cambodian church up until the fall of Cambodia to the Khmer Rouge on April 17, 1975, using the reports of missionaries and relief workers. In this book, however, along with personal observations gleaned over more than twenty years, I have attempted to use primarily the testimonies of Cambodian Christians themselves, and to write from their experiences and recollections.

What follows is by no means an exhaustive scholarly history of this remarkable church. Rather, it is a portrait, an unfinished portrait, and a distinctly impressionist perhaps even surreal portrait, of the Cambodian church, interpreted and understood through the lives and testimonies of a number of stalwart, very typical, and in some cases very strategic Cambodian believers and their families. They experienced all the times and seasons, both peaceful and tumultuous, through which the Cambodian Evangelical Church has passed in her short seventy-five year history. Their memories and roots reach back to the first Cambodian Christians in the early 1920s, and their branches extend into the Cambodian church today, inside Cambodia and scattered throughout a world-wide diaspora. Looking through the eyes of these families is like taking a cross-section right through the history of this amazing church.

A portrait thus composed would lack unity and form indeed, and so I have taken the liberty of filling in with broad strokes the background landscape of Cambodian life and culture, and where appropriate, highlighting the images with touches and hues from the experiences and reports of numerous other Cambodians I have known. The result is not a precise photographic representation. This can never be. All recorded history is an interpretation. What emerges is a portrait which I believe depicts authentically with human warmth and colour, when surveyed as a whole from a suitable distance, a true and compelling picture of the historic pilgrimage of this church.

My purpose in writing this account is four-fold. *First*, I have written for the glory of God, to promote righteousness among men and the praise of his Name. 'Let all thy works praise thee, O Lord.' For as we penetrate ever more deeply the mystery of our Christian vocation to be children of God, the Church of Jesus Christ is served. Through these glimpses into the history of the Cambodian church we behold the salvation of God realised in the fabric of human time and space. We behold another part of God's grand design to purchase for himself a people from every tribe and tongue and nation.

Secondly, I wanted to preserve these precious memories primarily for the Cambodian Christians, many of whom live beyond Cambodia's borders, and now since the late 1980s, a growing number of new Christians in Cambodia. Most are unaware of their rich Christian heritage, and the sheer cost to those who preceded them in holding fast the integrity of the gospel. Most of the early Christians are now dead, and almost all the mature leadership perished under the Khmer Rouge. If Cambodian Christians today are aware of the faithfulness, the endurance, and the martyrdom of their spiritual mothers and fathers, I trust this will help keep them from playing fast and loose with the precious and eternal gospel which they have received intact; and which they also are now called upon to live out and pass on to others amid many of the same kinds of testings.

So much of Cambodia has been squandered and destroyed in recent years. The Cambodians are a people cut loose from their physical and spiritual moorings, adrift in uncharted and hazardous seas. But not so the Christians. They have an anchor which holds them fast to their source of life, and a spiritual history which, although relatively short, is filled with a great cloud of witnesses. What could be more relevant to them today, than the realisation that they are part of that glorious and unbroken progress of pilgrims through history, ascending the 'Mountain of the Lord', worshipping as they go. The summons to 'remember' is God's antidote for carelessness and faithless forgetfulness.

Thirdly, I have written to edify fellow believers throughout the world. The Cambodian church may be poor in outward form, but it possesses through the testimony of its members, a spiritual reservoir from which we can all draw living water. Testimony such as this should not be kept 'under a bushel'. It must be shared so that others may be encouraged, comforted, chastened, and led to glorify God for his mighty works of salvation.

And *fourthly*, to study the brief history of the Cambodian church is an instructive exercise, for here we catch glimpses of the sovereign hand of God moving among the Cambodian people. Its relatively short historical backdrop includes raw paganism and spiritual darkness, civil war, imperialism, political intrigue, great power rivalry, corruption, persecution of every kind, atheistic communism and militarism at its most cruel and radical, refugee camps, massive Christian and secular relief, and a world-wide dispersion. It serves as an excellent model for the evaluation and scrutiny of our modern missionary enterprise.

Our quest is to discover the true 'planting of the Lord', those 'oaks of righteousness' who can never be uprooted. But we need also to look honestly and realistically at what has been merely the planting of men in the flesh, thus resulting in wood, hay and straw. Questions must be raised and issues faced as we consider the priorities, attitudes, strategies, methods, motives and styles that have been adopted, all in the name of doing the work of God.

Have we replaced genuine spirituality with activism? Are we anxious to turn out know-how functionaries or men and women who know God, slick entrepreneurs for God in the world's mould or children of God with the mind of Christ? And where do we go from here?

These and numerous other questions suggest themselves as we sift through the history of a church which is the result of modern twentieth-century missionary endeavour, and see just what has survived the flames.

I have struggled within myself about writing some of these things, and have often been tempted to abandon so ambitious and complex a project altogether. I have sought to avoid political and missiological correctness in this age of spiritual slogans and sound bites. There is the risk of being misunderstood by friends, both Cambodians and westerners. It would seem safer to leave much unsaid. Why raise questions in an already confused and troubled situation? However, if we are to be good and faithful servants in God's kingdom, we need to consider how God is planting his church and in humility, evaluate how much more perfectly we can be workers together with him.

Finally, it remains for me to acknowledge my debt of gratitude to those who have laboured with me in prayer and direct participation for so long in the writing of this book. To all our faithful praying friends around the world, thank you for persevering with us through the years, interruptions, difficulties and discouragements. Your encouragements and reminders were a constant rebuke to my often flagging zeal. I say a deep 'Thank you' to my Cambodian brothers and sisters for their patience with me as I interviewed and recorded them, and questioned them relentlessly for every detail. To my wife, Margaret, no amount of thanks could express my gratitude for her seeming endless patience over this project as we packed and unpacked it and hauled it from place to place round and round the world in battered cardboard boxes; for her invaluable advice, her painstaking in typing and retyping the manuscripts, and most of all her godly prayers. The final copy was typed by Paulette Sheard with incredible speed and accuracy. I am grateful for the helpful suggestions of Phyllis Thompson and the gentle encouragement of Julia Cameron, both of OMF. I also wish to take this opportunity to acknowledge and thank those mentors and exemplary senior missionaries I was blessed with over the years. Without their graciousness and patience I would not have gone very far: Denis Lane, John Miller, the late Henry Guinness, the late Dr Pauline Hamilton, Alice Compain, Andrew Way, Canon John Benson and Archbishop Moses Tay of Singapore.

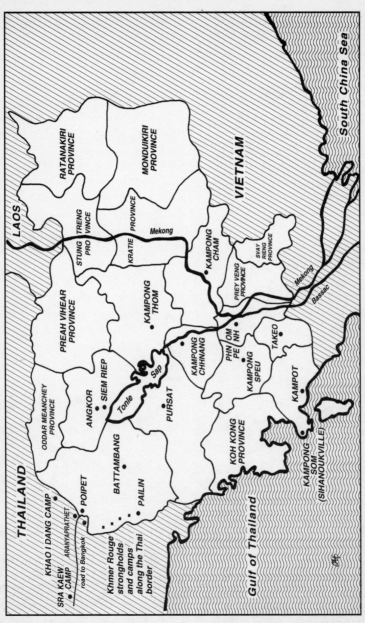

Map of Cambodia and surrounding countries

PROLOGUE

It was just as well that we had talked late into the night, sitting around in the pale flickering glow of a solitary candle, hardly aware of the incessant sound of exploding artillery shells from the city perimeter. As our final day in Phnom Penh dawned sunny and hot as ever, words utterly failed us. One by one the Cambodian Christians whom I had come to love so deeply, had taught, worked and lived with, filed in and out for the last time. Unable to express their hearts, each came silently and pressed his wet face against mine with a deliberate yet slow and gentle inhaling of breath, the Cambodian way of showing affection.

Finally, when all had gone, Setha, 'Little Brother' appeared, standing quietly in the doorway, his head down. He was holding the little potted plant which we had nurtured from a tiny cutting. It was all he had asked for when I shared out my things. He glanced across at me with dark sensitive eyes and a look of gentle melancholy which betrayed a depth of grief beyond words. 'You won't forget us, will you?' he whispered. Then, lingering only momentarily, he turned, picked up a suitcase and led the way down to a waiting *cyclor.*[1]

We were leaving. Suddenly we were leaving Cambodia, leaving behind us a church born out of fifty years of affliction and toil.

Beneath me as the circling aeroplane gained height lay Phnom Penh. From that height, momentarily above the shabbiness, one could imagine her former beauty and charm, her sparkling river

21

front and tree-lined boulevards. But now she was in the throes of death. The tightening noose of the Khmer Rouge pressed in all around her, while from within she was being slowly stifled and crushed by the weight of over two million refugees. Soon she would be a ghost town, her empty streets and looted buildings strewn with litter and corpses, her people sent away to a four-year-long 'gulag'. Closed off and largely ignored by the outside world, the cries of Phnom Penh's stampeding millions would be heard by death's gates alone.

I turned from the plane's cabin window and looked down at the note which had been pushed into our hands by one of the Cambodian Christian leaders as we departed.

Phnom Penh
Feb. 1975

To dear Missionary Friends,

'Where is the Lord God of Elijah?' he (Elisha) cried out. 'And the water parted and Elisha went across!' (2 Kings 2:14). This verse tells us how hard it was for the young man Elisha to be left behind while the old and powerful prophet of the Lord, Elijah, was taken away.

'Where is the Lord God of Elijah?' This is also the cry of the young Khmer church leaders at this moment. Elijah had been sent by God to the Israeli nation during the dark reign of its evil King Ahab. Despite the mighty miracles Elijah had performed, the people had not changed their hearts from sins. Then the time came for Elijah to be taken to heaven and the young Elisha had to carry on the mission during those dark days in Israel. But Elisha's special request of God's power was granted.

'The spirit of Elijah rests upon Elisha. And they went to meet him and greeted him respectfully.' (v15)

Dear friends, do remember us in your prayers as we Khmer Christians are left behind to continue the task in the difficult days ahead. We do need God's greater power and wisdom as Elisha did. Please pray for us and ask God to give us the right words as we boldly tell our agonising people about the Lord, and as we explain to them that his salvation is for them now. May God add many more souls to his young church in the Khmer Republic and let it grow stronger until the day of his return.

Your servant in the Lord,
Taing Chhirc

The cry of the Cambodian church! This was but the beginning of their long agonised cry as they entered the most terrifying trial yet of their painful history. Ninety per cent of the church and virtually all the leaders and pastors, including the writer of this note, would perish.

My mind turned to 'Little Brother', probably hurrying home now through that seething mass, carrying with him the little potted plant. What would become of this young gardener and his two friends? With the severe food shortage, we had allowed them to dig up our lawn and plant vegetables. They had worked hard at it, stripped to the waist, the perspiration gleaming on their backs and soaking the cloth *bandannas* wrapped around their heads. They had dug, chopped and raked at the rocklike, unproductive earth with bare hands, sticks and a couple of simple tools. With all the concern and aspiration of dedicated gardeners they had come daily to splash water over the frail young plants, some of which later succumbed to various pests; others were taken off half-grown by thieves. Nevertheless, after weeks of hard work the three lads had joyfully harvested a good crop of vegetables. Recently Little Brother, Hon and Sophana had begun again to prepare the soil and raise new seedlings.

Then my mind turned to that other vastly more significant garden – the Cambodian church. What would become of all those seedlings amid the ravages of spiritual disease, parasites, and thieves? Would anything survive the impending drought? Plants are such susceptible things in this changing climate. Many of our favourite seedlings and cuttings, lovingly watched over and protected, would be uprooted, while others withered in the scorching heat. But surely some would survive, mature, and bear fruit? And these three young men, typical of many in Cambodia, were becoming experienced gardeners in God's vineyard. Would they labour on? Would there still be gardeners on the watch for more good soil, ready to till, plant and patiently nurture a new crop till harvest time? Many, no doubt, would find themselves alone, afraid, inexperienced and without help. It would be very costly.

With the city of man falling around him, a final hurriedly written letter from 'Little Brother' reached me in Bangkok in neighbouring Thailand. He wrote:

The little plant has died eight days ago, but now I plant new one more … also we are starting to garden again. I hope that my plants will beautifully grow up. Yes, we are happy to tell you our plants are growing, We also found a new piece of land at New Phnom Penh, we have planned to plant some things like potatoes, sugar canes and some vegetables.

God had planted a garden in the difficult unyielding Cambodian soil in infinite love, tenderness, patience, wisdom and perseverance. Men, too, had been busy working in that garden. In the devastation looming, both plantings would soon be clearly revealed.

PART I: 1923-1975

CHAPTER 1

THE FALLOW GROUND

'O land, land, land, hear the word of the Lord!'
(Jeremiah 22:29)

The long tortuous dry season of 1923 was finally at an end. Signs of a new season were all around them as the four men quickened their pace along the dirt lane winding out from the small village of Doentiey, and on down the seven or eight kilometres to the big market town of Battambang in north west Cambodia. They walked with a strong sense of purpose, as though on an errand of considerable importance. On either side sun-baked and cracked rice paddies were softening, and a fresh green hue tinged the brown fields of last year's stubble. They greeted a passing farmer leading his bulky grey water buffalo by a rope through its nose. Over the farmer's right shoulder hung a single furrow wooden plough.

'Where are you going, son?' they asked.

'To awaken the earth, uncle, to awaken the earth.'

Uncle Has and his three companions, Uncle Moeung, Grandfather Pum and Grandfather Bou paused to exchange views with the other farmer. They spoke mainly of the good spring rains and the work of repairing broken-down paddy embankments and preparing special beds for the young rice seedlings. Uncle Has looked out across the waiting fields, a broad expanse of flat farmland dotted with spindly sugar palms suddenly culminating in a languid green tuft mushroomed against the vast azure sky. Here and there makeshift open-sided thatch shelters up on stilts interrupted the landscape, a checkerboard of empty paddies, each surrounded by low earthen dykes about eighteen inches high. Has's dark eyes narrowed and he pointed with his lips towards the bank of great rolling cumulus clouds billowing up on the western horizon.

By early afternoon the sky would turn dark and heavy. Then a fresh wind would sweep across the land, whipping up dead leaves and grass in swirling clouds of red dust till the great wall of the approaching storm overtook it and beat everything back down into the earth, as torrents of cool lashing rain inundated the parched land. After a few hours, the storm would pass and the clean rain-soaked air would reverberate with the croaking of myriads of frogs unseen in the flooded paddies.

The men were determined to reach Battambang before the storm broke. They did pause once more to eat the dry salted fish and rice which their wives had wrapped in a cloth for the journey. Eating time is not the time for talking and so they sat in silence in an open-sided wooden *sala*, or shelter, situated at a place where an old rutted lane led down to a Buddhist temple set back from the road. A few saffron-robed monks, shaven-headed and barefooted, moved noiselessly about the compound. Ubiquitous brown mongrel dogs lazed and scratched in the heat of the late morning sun. The monks had been out at dawn, walking slowly in single file around the nearby villages, their begging bowls clasped in both arms in front of them. On this daily ritual they said nothing, acknowledged no one, looked neither to left nor right, but simply paused momentarily before each home where someone stood with a bowl of rice from which she ladled a portion to each monk. The people greeted the monks with a gesture of high respect – head lowered, palms placed together just in front of the nose. The monks were not really begging, but allowing each person the opportunity to make merit for the future and outweigh the accumulated misdeeds of former lives. Even the ragged little boys who followed the monks were making merit by carrying the containers of surplus rice.

Now it was about time for the festival marking the beginning of the Buddhist Lent which coincided with the wet season. This annual festival began on the first night of the waning moon of the sixth month, according to the Buddhist calendar. There would be a great requiem for all the departed spirits of deceased relatives and ancestors, more merit making, monks chanting the *dharma* or law, candles and incense sticks burned for departed ones. During Lent the monks would be largely confined to the temple in order to study the ancient Buddhist writings. Lent would end when the rains stopped several months later, with yet another great festival, more merit making and so on.

Nothing had changed in Cambodia for centuries. Buddhist monks from Sri Lanka had brought Theravada Buddhism to the great Khmer Brahmin kingdom of Angkor during the fourteenth-century when it was in a state of moral, economic and military collapse. The national conversion to Buddhist tranquillity and passivism thus coincided with the beginning of the disintegration and collapse of this mighty kingdom stretching outwards from its monumental capital of Angkor in north west Cambodia. There, unapproachable priest-kings with names like Jayavarman, Indravarman and Suryavarman had ruled as gods over the vast Khmer empire. What a magnificent city was Angkor with its extensive and richly ornamented temple complexes and highly-developed system of reservoirs for irrigation and rice production. Even now it was a spectacular sight as it lay in ruins waging a new war, not now with its ancient enemies the Thai and the Chams, but with nature, as the relentless jungle growth undermined it, slowly strangling and tearing it apart.

Successive Angkorian kings erected grand and costly temples to honour their divinity, and in so doing drained the nation of its wealth and energy. With the fall of Angkor in the fifteenth century, Cambodia entered into a long dark age of self-destruction and national suicide as three centuries of warring, palace intrigue, treachery, internal feuding and corruption brought Cambodia to the brink of extinction. Cambodia might easily have been swallowed up by neighbouring Vietnam and Thailand in the mid-nineteenth century had the French not annexed it to their Indo-

Chinese colonies in 1863 during the reign of King Ang Duong. Now, in 1923, Cambodia had been a French colony for sixty years.

And so the endless cycle of festivals and merit-making ceremonies continued round and round year by year. Called 'Buddhism', it was in fact an all-embracing synthesis with Brahminism, animism and ancestor worship, all under the inscrutable smile of the Buddha. Everything centred around the Buddhist temple whose influence dominated every community, and permeated every aspect of the social, political, intellectual and spiritual life of the Khmer people. The temple was not there primarily for worship, but for housing the Buddhist idols. It was a place where merit could be made. The very building of it, preferably in a high and difficult location, would afford the builder much merit. It was inconceivable that anyone would question this inexorable system; each sought rather to live in harmony with life's circumstances, passively accepting his fate. Everything had been predetermined by the spontaneous law of *karma*, the law of cause and effect. In this life every person was reaping the fruit of good and bad deeds in past lives, living perpetually in the shadow of past demerits. The hope was to build up sufficient merit to be better off in the next reincarnation, and move a step closer to Nirvana. One would continue to die and be reborn, moving up and down in an all night game of spiritual snakes-and-ladders, through many levels of hell, the world of animals and humans and heaven, until at some distant time, having quelled all desire and 'thirst for life', the cause of suffering, one might gain access to 'Nirvana' – the ultimate state of blissful non-existence.

Thus the seasons came and went, punctuated always by the merit-making festivals, the ploughing, sowing, harvesting, marrying, dying and being reborn in the infinite and impersonal ceaseless cycles of existence, round and round, and round and round. As the familiar Cambodian proverb says: 'The waters rise, the fish eat the ants; the waters fall, the ants eat the fish.' To follow in a different direction or seek to swim against the ebb and flow of this fathomless ocean in which everyone else was drifting and being absorbed was unthinkable, even dangerous.

Uncle Has stared blankly at the temple building before him as the sunlight played crazily on the spangled roof tiles. Heedlessly his jaws opened and closed on the salty fish. He was a Khmer Buddhist rice-farmer, from generations of Khmer Buddhist farmers. If he sensed that he was being beckoned to walk in another unknown way, even to take a few faltering steps upon it, he did not show it. If he had any sense of destiny, that he would mark the beginning of a great watershed in the history of the Cambodian people which two generations later would become a floodtide, it was not apparent as he sat there on his haunches in the coolness of the *sala*.

This *sala* was shaded by a huge spreading tree. The old tree was considered sacred and held in fear and respect lest any offend the spirits which inhabited its roots and branches. No man would dare lay an axe to it lest a terrible tragedy befall him. About its girth was tied a strip of saffron cloth, and various colourful trinkets and other paraphernalia hung about the lower limbs. Half-burned incense sticks and votive candles stuck out from the surface roots where they had been lit and pushed into the ground to appease underground spirits. At the base a little red spirit house stood, like a miniature temple. Offerings of rice and fruits had been placed in little blue-painted china bowls just at the door of the wooden spirit house, but now it had all dried out and some had been spilled by foraging dogs. They had also knocked over a tall container full of charred incense sticks, scattering them among the tattered remains of once beautiful and heavily perfumed garlands woven from orchids and jasmine blossoms.

It was a common enough sight to Uncle Has. Spirit houses were set up outside many homes, in city compounds, outside public buildings, government offices, along the cart tracks, out in fields, under trees and bushes or up on high rocks and hills. Each place had its spirits and some were very formidable, controlling lesser spirits in a given area. It was awareness of these spirits and people's required behaviour towards them that composed everyday religious thought and experience of most rural Khmers. Pure Buddhism with its philosophical attitude to life and its high ascetic demands was little understood and largely irrelevant to the daily practical needs of ordinary people. They had reduced it all down to one simple dictum: 'Do good, get good; do bad, get bad.'

None of these things before him – the Buddhist temple, the spirit tree and everything they represented – stirred any attentiveness within Uncle Has. They struck only a muted chord of passive indifference, and, possibly, an increasing weariness of spirit. They were dry like the blowing chaff, empty like the withering wind which was just now beginning to swirl through the open *sala*. Recognising together this unmistakable sign of the approaching rain, the men exchanged nods and set off again down the road to Battambang. Uncle Has was quieter now, walking alone just ahead of the others who chatted amiably together as they followed him. What was he taking them to see? Why was he setting off for Battambang like this when all the other men in the village were about the routine tasks of ploughing? And what was this nagging restlessness within him which compelled him to go in search of an obscure foreigner who, according to the gossip of those returning from the Battambang market, was teaching some new thing about a living creator God, and something about a man named Jesus dying on a cross for the Cambodian people?

Uncle Has was highly respected in the village. He was a sober sort of a man, reliable, faithful to his one wife, and had raised a good family. People had noticed when he listened so attentively and asked probing questions of the travellers from Battambang before starting out that morning to hear for himself. His companions were perhaps more intrigued by Has's strange curiosity than by any personal desire to meet the tall white stranger and hear his new teaching, this 'Good News' as the wandering pedlars had called it. The fields could wait another day. The rains were only just beginning to soften the hard ground.

The hubbub of buying and selling at Battambang market held little attraction for Uncle Has today. He only smiled and nodded at a few people who called his name, ignoring the calls of the hawkers and the many wares over which people haggled noisily for bargains. With occasional hesitations here and there over directions, he made straight for the place where the teacher was said to have set up a stand with posters and booklets.

Then Has saw him; just as the people had said, a tall foreigner standing right at the edge of the bustling market midst a small crowd of curious listeners and passers-by. The others had seen him too. Bowing low, they apologetically pushed their way past the talkative onlookers standing around on the periphery of the gathering, laughing and chattering together about the speaker's 'big nose', 'light hair' and 'such fair skin'. The four men squatted comfortably down on the ground among those who were listening more intently, just a few metres from where the stranger stood speaking.

At first Has's attention was taken up with the foreigner's build and strange features. The man spoke Cambodian quite well, though with the unmistakable sound of excessive air on his lips the way the white people always did. *He must be a good man as well as a clever one,* thought Has, *talking about God and religion so openly like this.* Then he began to listen more intently to what the teacher was actually saying. As he spoke he was pointing to pictures and diagrams on a chart which showed all mankind as having a sinful nature and so being separated from a holy God. The teacher had explained that this was the one true God of all people, because he was the uncreated Creator of the universe. As he listened, Has found himself nodding in agreement with the statement that everyone he knew, including himself, was imperfect and far from meeting the standard of this great and holy God. Then the teacher indicated a great cross extending down from God to man and linking them together. On the cross was nailed a bleeding man dying in awful agony because, the teacher said, he knew and loved each one of us and sacrificed himself to redeem us from our sin.

From this point on Has understood very little. He was engrossed in the awful portrait of Jesus impaled on that cross. The crowd had surged forward when the teacher uncovered this gruesome spectacle. Some emitted two or three sharp clucking sounds with their tongue, expressing shock at the sight of such a cruel death; others laughed nervously, pointing at the nails which pierced the feet and hands. After that it was hard to concentrate on all the meaning and significance of this event, but Has tried hard to take it all in, squatting there in the early afternoon heat and the cacophony of noise in Battambang's central market.

The foreboding sky, now leaden with lowering clouds, threatened an imminent deluge. Windy blasts swept through the diminishing huddle of listeners. The first few drops fell very gently. Lifting his gaze skyward and commenting on the significance of reading nature's signs, the missionary brought the meeting to a close. Has observed him as he stood there, very still, the wind tugging at his shirt, eyes closed, palms pressed together in front of his face as Cambodians did when greeting a king. Then he began to talk to his God as if he were right there beside him, as one speaking with a friend. Finally, smiling kindly, he handed some leaflets to all the people who remained around him, including Has and his companions, with exhortations to take them home, read them carefully and come again.

Despite the impending storm, Has lingered with further questions, and a desire to examine the posters more closely. The missionary therefore invited the four friends to come back to his home and join in a meal with his family. And so the discussion continued as the skies opened, releasing torrents of rain. They talked over things about which Has had rarely voiced an opinion, though these questions about life and death struck a familiar chord. He was impressed too by the obvious kindness and humility of this man and his wife. As they prepared to leave, backing toward the door with profuse smiles and nods, the missionary took from a cupboard a little book and placed it in Has's hand, pointing out and then underlining certain portions for them to contemplate further. The book was entitled *The Good News according to Luke*. (As yet only a few parts of Scripture had been translated into Khmer.)[1]

The rain had eased up now to occasional light squalls, and inky clouds scudded across the sky between sudden gleams of brilliant sunshine. The hint of a rainbow lingered behind a passing shower. It was already late as they hurried back up the muddy road towards their village. Murky yellowish water filled the potholes and cartwheel tracks. The air was clear and alive, vibrant with the sound of innumerable tiny creatures and water dripping from trembling branches, and the trickling of a thousand rivulets.

One by one kerosene lamps flickered on in the dusky gloom of evening from within the clusters of thatch dwellings along the way. Without stopping the men exchanged a word or two with weary ploughmen returning from their fields, plodding silently along behind their buffaloes on which sat young boys stripped to the waist. All alike were muddied to the knees from guiding the plough round and round waterlogged paddies turning over the heavy brown earth.

Arriving home at last, the four men stopped to splash water over their mud-splattered feet, dipping with a piece of coconut shell into a stone jar standing at the foot of the ladder which led up to the house. All the homes were on stilts so that they would remain dry when the floods came at the height of the rainy season. In the dry season this kept out much of the red dust which billowed across the scorched landscape, as well as the intrusion of various dogs, pigs and chickens which lazed, scratched and rooted under the houses.

Seeing that the men were finally home from their day in the city, several curious neighbours and relatives as well as the Has household itself had gathered to meet them. Normally the conversation would have centred around the latest market prices of this and that or where the best bargains might be found, and always spiced with various pieces of market gossip. But this time Uncle Has had nothing with him for them to examine or inquire the price of, nor any new tales to tell. He simply pulled from his shirt the bundle of leaflets which the missionary had given him and passed them round the inquisitive assembly. As carefully as he could, Has began to relate everything the teacher had said about the living God who had created all things: the land and the sea, the hills and trees, the animals, and finally man, uniquely made in the very image of the Creator himself.

As he talked on, the neighbours began to chatter together and interrupt him. They wanted to know how much money this teacher made, if he had a wife and children, how old he was, why he had really come to Battambang – for money? For women? Politics? When they saw that Has was not interested in satisfying their curiosity but rather intent on continuing to impress this new teaching upon them, some began to grow tired of the discussion. Noisily they excused themselves, calling out to one another and jesting over what they suspected the foreign white man had really come for, or over the disconcertingly sober and uncompromising countenance of their old neighbour.

Now that most of the crowd had departed, Has's wife Pos prepared some rice, vegetables and fish for the men to eat. A small group comprised mostly of family members had remained, and now listened respectfully as Has repeated and explained in greater detail all he had learned that day. Occasionally he would stop and read slowly and deliberately from the booklets and gospels spread before him. Predictably, there was immediate interest when he turned to a picture of Jesus nailed to the cross. Has wished he could remember more of what the teacher had said about this man and the meaning of his death, but he recalled at least that somehow with his blood, Jesus had paid the price to redeem mankind, releasing them from the heavy yoke of sin and death. It was, the teacher had added, rather like what happens after a thief comes and steals your buffalo. The farmer has no choice but to go with money in hand to buy back his own highly valued possession from the thief. But Jesus had paid the price with his own life blood to ransom men from an evil taskmaster called Satan, the source of all evil, who enticed men away from their creator God. What was more, this Jesus had come back to life three days later, proving beyond doubt that he was God – as man.

Has began to feel a little out of his depth, so he decided to read to them the texts which the missionary had underlined. As he did so he became aware of a strong conviction taking root within him, that finally in his hands he held answers to questions and internal longings he had been aware of for many years. And he knew that this new life germinating within him could in no way be kept hidden or contained. Even more awesome was the growing awareness that he was abandoning all he once held secure, and surrendering himself to this crucified and risen Lord Jesus to whom he was being inexorably and yet so blithely drawn...

Unnoticed, just beyond the glow of the single lamp light around which the men were sitting cross-legged and absorbed in conversation, sat a slender woman in her late teens, her hands resting lightly on her rounded stomach as the unborn child stirred within her. Rose was listening intently to all that was being said. Her warm dark eyes, bright with interest, followed every expression and reaction of her husband Koeum, one of her father's most engrossed listeners. He was a good man, different from most of the village men who had other girls and squandered their earnings on gambling and excessive drinking at the festivals and temple fairs which followed each harvest. She had grown to love him increasingly ever since her father, to whom she was devoted, arranged the match. She considered herself a fortunate woman to be a member of this household where the menfolk were not only industrious but kind. Such was her respect for Koeum and her trust in his judgement that she would unhesitatingly follow him anywhere, all the days of her life.

Meanwhile the animated conversation among the men continued as they pored over the verses of Scripture. Like Has, they were fascinated by these strange new truths. One by one, lamps in each of the village dwellings were extinguished. Some young men returning home late noticed a lamp still glowing in the Has household. Emboldened by rice whisky yet fearful of the lurking spirits of the night, they called out loudly to each other. The village dogs prowled in small packs, snarling and barking whenever one encroached on another's territory. But in the home of Uncle Has the light continued to burn, and low voices murmured on into the small hours.

Outside, beyond the sleeping village, the first seedlings were beginning to push their way up out of the mud of silent paddies into the darkness of the night.

CHAPTER 2

THE IMPLANTED SEED

'He who observes the wind will not sow;
and he who regards the clouds will not reap.
As you do not know how the spirit comes to the bones
    in the womb of a woman with child,
so you do not know the work of God
who makes everything.
In the morning sow your seed,
and at evening withhold not your hand;
for you do not know which will prosper,
this or that, or whether both alike will be good.'

(Ecclesiastes 11:4-6)

The village roosters heralded the dawning of a new day, their sensitive little eyes perceiving the first faint streaks of rosy light in the cloudless eastern sky. Rose raised herself on one elbow and reached out for the pull string tied to the hand-woven cloth hammock hanging just above the straw mat where she and Koeum lay. She gave two or three gentle pulls to set the hammock in motion. It began creaking and swinging back and forth, momentarily quieting little Tou who was beginning to stir from his slumbers.

Koeum smiled to himself at the sound of his son's persistent appeals for attention which had ended all hope of further rest. After going through the brief ritual of sitting up cross-legged, then twisting his body and arms sharply to the left and right to crack and limber his stiff joints, he tightened the long cotton *sarong* about his waist, slid across the mat and proudly raised his firstborn out of the hammock. As Rose quickly rolled up the mat and tidied away their corner of the sleeping area in her father's house, Koeum cradled the boy close to his face, sniffing his plump little cheeks, murmuring and chuckling. Expertly, Rose knotted her long thick black hair into a bun high on the back of her head, bent down and lifted the baby from her husband's arms. Then pulling up one side of her plain, loose-fitting blouse she began to nurse the child. At the same time she chattered away to her mother who was rousing the tousled bundle of youngsters sleeping by the back wall furthest from the door.

Outside at the foot of the ladder,[1] Has was squatting beside the stone water jars loudly clearing his nose and throat, splashing water from a dipper onto his face and rubbing it briskly with the other hand. He had been up early, standing out beyond the house near the still mist-laden paddies watching the eastern sky and sniffing the heavy warm moist air of the monsoon. Then he returned to look over the two oxen tethered under the house, motionless but for their incessant cud-chewing.

When Has came in the family gathered to eat, all sitting around the food cross-legged on the polished wooden floor boards, except for the two women who sat to one side, each leaning on her left arm, knees bent back and bare feet tucked carefully out of sight behind them. Without any announcement they all lowered their heads and waited for Has to offer thanks for the simple breakfast, which consisted of rice soup boiled with finely chopped green onions and left-over pieces of chicken from the evening before. All joined in a loud 'amen' then took up the short tin spoons and turned their undivided attention to eating, looking down intently into their bowls, testing each mouthful purposefully, noisily sucking on the bones, and finally rinsing their mouths with fresh rain water drunk from a single dipper which was passed round.

Apart from the brief prayer, everything that was done that morning in the Has household was also going on in all the other village homes. But now Has stood up and walked over to the back wall of the large single room, near to where they all slept on a wide raised platform. From a little wooden shelf nailed respectfully high up above head level he took down a booklet. Then, resuming his place, he slowly and deliberately read a passage of Scripture to the family. This he always did following the morning and evening meal, except that in the evening he would talk to them about what he had read and then someone would pray.

Rose watched her father return the booklet to the shelf, pausing to straighten the precious little pile of pamphlets and brush away a stray cobweb. Not long before, that same shelf had been the home of a small brass idol, a pot of joss sticks and various other objects around which hung little garlands of withering flowers. Right above the shelf a lighter patch in the wall boards still betrayed where a faded picture of the Buddha in a posture of meditation had once hung. It had been there as long as Rose could remember, its brown and brittle edges curled and cracked with age. But now it was gone, and the little shelf had been swept clean to make way for the small pile of well-thumbed Scripture booklets. This had all happened a few weeks earlier when Has, under deep conviction, had risen early from his sleep, removed all the Buddhist and spirit paraphernalia from the house, taken it out into the field and burned it. What would not burn he threw into the stream. No one knew what he had done until morning when the old god shelf, stripped bare, and conspicuous by its emptiness, confronted them.

At that breakfast time Has had explained carefully what his action meant, and together they had prayed for God's presence and protection over their home, now cut off from the influence and power of its former guardian spirits. If Has had any second thoughts or fears over what he had done, they vanished in the all-consuming sense of peace and the indescribable joy which flooded and filled his whole being. They vanished like the grey pre-dawn mist which daily lingered over the paddies till it was melted away by the warm touch of the rising sun.

Emboldened by this new freedom and security, Has felt a strong compulsion to reach out and pull all those around him up from the mire in which he, with new eyes, saw them pathetically stumbling around. He would make his own home the centre of this work. It would become a haven, a meeting place, a church in which the believers could worship and grow in the strength and knowledge of the true God.

Now Rose's thoughts moved on to that unforgettable day when their simple home had been dedicated to be a meeting place for the worship of the living God. The missionary and his wife, now regular visitors to the Has home at Doentiey, had arrived to lead the dedication ceremony with all the new Christians. Besides her mother and father there was faithful old Uncle Moeung, who along with Has took responsibility to organise these regular meetings, and the other two men who had first gone to Battambang in search of 'the new teaching' – frail Grandfather Bou, and the inimitable Grandfather Pum whose weathered old face was creased and wrinkled into a permanent expression of delight from a lifetime of laughing and joking. The only other adult men sitting on the men's side of the room were Koeum, and Uncle Pol who had believed when he first heard the gospel from Has, his older brother. Their wives were there, and at the very front a cluster of excited children sat straight backed, sensing the importance and gravity of the occasion. Their playmates meanwhile, a ragtag of naked and semi-clad village youngsters, hovered expectantly around the doorway. Perched on the upper rungs of the ladder, they peered wide-eyed and open mouthed with that characteristic fixed expression of amazement, at the people gathered inside. Boys jostled for position with girls who clung deftly to younger siblings astride one hip. Both shy and curious, the children were drawn from their play first by the appearance of the white man and woman and then by the new and strange sound of Christian hymn singing. Others had been sent to spy by parents who were either secretly interested in the new teaching, or just looking for more gossip to fuel their fiery tongues.

* * *

Thus one of the first churches in Cambodia was planted among a handful of rice farmers in a remote village in the heart of Battambang province, the richest and most fertile province in all the land. A tiny point of light began to glow in the darkness. It marked the dawning of a new day – the genesis of a new age.

Within days of putting in the plough and sowing the first seed, dark clouds of anger and strong winds of hostility threatened this fresh planting of the Lord. Was it because Has had burned his gods? Was it because of young Rose's defiant refusal to let the local midwives tie strings around Tou's little wrists and ankles as soon as he was born to ward off the evil spirits? Or was it the fact that in the early mornings no one was ever now seen standing outside the Has home with a bowl of rice for the monks? And not one of the family had participated in the great annual ceremony at the village temple to ensure a good harvest. Whatever the cause, almost the entire community rose up in hostility against the Christians. Has had not even set up the customary talisman for the spirits which inhabited his fields nor had he made offerings to them so that in return they might protect and bless the growing rice. By offending the spirits in this way he risked calling down their curse on all the village fields for the entire season.

A passing farmer one day came upon Uncle Has sitting on his haunches on the embankment of one of his paddies, his hands together as if in worship. Drawing closer, the farmer noticed that his eyes were closed and he was talking in everyday Cambodian to some 'invisible spirit' for, as the man told his friends later, he could see no object of worship and Has had nothing in his hands to offer.

Initially all this was regarded as merely a bizarre deviation from the accepted routine, giving the villagers material for jokes and gossip about Uncle Has, his friends and their obsession with the 'foreigners' religion'. But very quickly it came to be viewed as treacherous folly, un-Khmer, which could not be tolerated and which, if allowed to continue, would threaten the very foundation and fabric of their society. The villagers reacted with strident outrage. Evil rumours spread like a dry season bushfire, consuming the whole district around Doentiey. The Christians, it was said, were forming their own sect within the village, holding meetings in which they prayed to 'non-Khmer gods', and maintaining that the idols were not gods at all, and that centuries-old merit-making ceremonies and spirit worship were of no avail, even sinful. Their allegiance was clearly elsewhere. They were traitors to Cambodia.

The Christians tried to explain that their faith was in the living God, the creator of all mankind. But most villagers could not see beyond the fact that it was different and therefore antagonistic towards the ancient Khmer religious belief and conduct, which had been handed down by their ancestors and to which all Khmers unquestioningly conformed. As the hostility spread throughout those early weeks of ploughing and sowing, life became increasingly difficult for the Christians. Stones would crash onto the corrugated tin roof during meetings as mischievous village urchins were encouraged to scamper past the house screaming 'Yesu, Yesu,' laughing loudly as they scuttled away. They relished this newly sanctioned sport of rudeness and disrespect to adults who were caricatured by their parents as village idiots working for a devious and wealthy foreigner who caught little children and sold them into slavery, or even ate them.

People no longer greeted or spoke to Has and his family. The Christians had become virtual outcasts within the community. Their property and fields were frequently vandalised. Fearful of the consequences of being a Christian or being associated with one, some people who had been showing interest now offered lame excuses for no longer attending the meetings, or simply avoided the Christians altogether. But through it all the Christians persevered in living upright lives, and showing no malice in return. They met frequently to encourage and support one another, to pray and study the Scriptures together.

News of all these rumours and disturbances quickly reached the ears of the Buddhist temple abbot and the district chief. This culminated in a delegation led by the village headman, himself a close relative of Uncle Has, being sent to warn the Christian leaders to end this 'waywardness', this 'Jesus religion', and behave like proper and loyal Khmers. The delegation stipulated that all Khmers were Buddhist, and they should only believe the teachings of their own race and not those of a foreigner. About the same time Uncle Moeung, returning from his fields one evening, was surrounded by an angry mob of farmers and cruelly beaten with sticks.

When the district headman saw that the Christians were

determined to continue in their new course, he ordered Has, Moeung and Pum, the Christian leaders, to be arrested and imprisoned as troublemakers, and for conspiring to start an uprising. They would be kept in prison until they turned from their foolishness and stopped believing in this Jesus. Unmoved by all the threats, the three leading men were arrested and thrown into a cell in the district jail. The prison cell was cramped, and almost totally dark except for the small amount of daylight and minimal fresh air which filtered through tiny slats high in the walls. It was also filthy, and the men were plagued constantly by lice. At nighttime their discomfort was compounded by the swarms of mosquitoes which descended on them, and the ceaseless scurrying of rats. From the infected floorboards they one by one contracted scabies, an irritating rash which quickly spread over their bodies making sitting very uncomfortable and sleep almost impossible.

The three men, however, continually refused to relinquish their new faith in God, and kept their spirits up by loudly singing and praying day and night in their dark prison cell. On the meagre diet of a little rice and fish sauce they were becoming thinner and weaker each day. Their bodies were racked by malaria, alternately shivering and then sweating, their gaunt faces yellow with anaemia and grime as the parasites multiplied and fed on their red blood cells.

From time to time the district chief would come and shout to them from outside the prison wall, 'Have you stopped believing in Jesus yet?'

'No,' the men would call back, 'we will never stop believing in Jesus.'

'In that case, you will have to stay there until you die,' the official would shout back in frustration as he strode away.

Back in Doentiey the Christian families waited for news, amazed by the reports of their brothers' adamant refusal to deny the Lord. The wives were never permitted to visit their husbands because they would not give the customary bribe to the guards. For this reason too none of the food they lovingly prepared, or the Christian literature they sent ever reached the prisoners. The missionary from Battambang came also to encourage and pray with the Christians. As they prayed they wept, and their confidence and trust in God increased.

If the believers were amazed by the faith and courage of the three imprisoned men, the prison guards and local villagers were even more impressed. This kind of deep conviction, this unwavering confidence regardless of circumstances or expediency, this vigorous contending for truth against all manner of adversity was unknown to them. A blithe acceptance of fate, some bargaining or pragmatic compromise, a quiet pay off, would have been the normal course of action. But not these three. And most incredible of all, this awesome resolve came from three very ordinary rice farmers like themselves. *Well,* thought some, *even if those Christians aren't altogether mad, the way of Jesus looks singularly arduous and unattractive.*

Still the district chief made his increasingly frequent and desperate visits to the jail, imploring, 'Will you now leave off believing in this Jesus and go free?'

Still the same reply came from within, 'No, we will never stop believing in Jesus.' This was followed by the now familiar singing of *O Happy Day!* and *Hallelujah, Praise the Lord!* As the days passed into weeks, and the weeks into months, it became very clear to all that the three men could not be intimidated into giving up their Christian faith. With time the attitude of the villagers turned ambivalent; Christian bashing lost its novelty and most began to lose interest in the whole affair. A few more perceptive ones secretly came to respect the Christians for their stubborn faith and obvious integrity.

The village leaders, however, continued to be worried by uncomfortable feelings of insecurity and frustration in the face of such dogged belief and non-conformity.

Quite suddenly one morning, the guards opened the prison doors and simply ordered the men to 'Go home.' There was no word of explanation, no mention of charges or apology. Their eyes burning from the bright sunlight and their legs weak from inactivity and malnutrition, the three men stumbled home as quickly as they could. Children shouted the news around the village as the filthy, ragged trio staggered into the waiting arms of their weeping loved ones who had prayed on so patiently. Rose never forgot that day, helping her mother wash the filth and stench from her father's skeletal body, and applying salve to his raw skin. Though the agony of the imprisonment was over, what hurt Rose even more than the physical abuse he had suffered was the humiliation, the constant taunting and ridicule to which he was now subjected almost daily. Even the village urchins and beggars, the drunkards and prostitutes scorned and despised him and the message of salvation he constantly sought to declare to them. Has too found this relentless invective harder to bear than all the days of his imprisonment.

To a greater or lesser degree it would always be that way for any Cambodian bold enough to take a firm stand on the side of the living God. It would be fair to say that being a Christian in Buddhist Cambodia then was as difficult and unimaginable as a Buddhist Englishman in medieval England. Every subsequent decade would see a major wave of opposition against the church, in ever-increasing intensity. The dross would never be permitted to gather for long about the pure gold of this church. The hostility to those early Christians was the pattern, a harbinger of things to come. They would always be a despised minority, misunderstood, a convenient scapegoat for all manner of accusations. They would be betrayed and cast out even by members of their own families. It was always at the hands of their own people that Khmer Christians suffered the most. But in steadfast faith and courage, in childlike trust, Has and the others set another pattern, one for the Cambodian church to follow in all its seasons of persecution and difficulty.

The tumultuous season of the early monsoon, the time for ploughing, breaking up the hard fallow ground, and sowing the precious seed had passed. Rose had taken little Tou and his hammock down under the house to catch the cool and fragrant breezes which now wafted in from the surrounding fields. She crouched beside one of the large wooden stakes on which the house rested, and rhythmically pulled on the hammock string to keep little Tou gently rocking back and forth. As she did so, she gazed out across the flooded paddies lying before her like huge mirrors reflecting the season's beguiling and unpredictable sky. In the distance a squall moved slowly along the horizon, a dark concentration of grey mist creating a great shadow before it.

An overhead cloud briefly masked the full effect of the sun whose persistent rays burst forth instead in long straight shafts of light, fanning out all around the periphery. On the horizon, cumulus white puffs sailed effortlessly eastward in the sea-blue sky, disappearing over the distant line of Cardamom mountains which formed a natural land border with neighbouring Siam. Rose began to whisper the words of a lullaby:

> Sleep little one, sleep my beloved son,
> Don't cry, quietly, quietly,
> Sleep softly, my little one…'

The words drifted on in a prolonged and plaintive moaning, like a kind of dirge, its nasal cadence rising and falling, ebbing and flowing, now words, now a gentle sighing.

Rose was vaguely aware of the steady click-clack, click-clack of a nearby hand loom, the buzzing of persistent flies, and the occasional sound of women's voices calling out to one another across the fields. An uneven line of them was moving slowly backwards across the paddy, each woman bent over at right angles from the waist, clutching a bundle of lush green seedlings freshly pulled from the nearby seed beds. Patiently they toiled, pushing each individual seedling securely into the soft mud, leaving behind straight rows of tender green shoots sticking out above the murky water. Apart from their bare wet legs, the workers were completely covered to protect themselves from the burning sun which beat down mercilessly, reflecting cruelly its blazing yellow orb in the water below.

In the placid water in which they toiled lurked deadly poisonous snakes which came to feed on the frogs. And black leeches stuck fast to the workers' arms and legs, sucking their blood. Unseen too were various crippling parasites which could bore through soles of the labourers' feet and work their way up into the intestines and liver. It was back-breaking indeed, performed almost entirely by the womenfolk in the hottest part of the day.

But the seasoned workers persevered, planting each seedling with little thought to these hazards, because in their mind's eye they saw the harvest which in due time would be gathered in with great joy and celebration.

CHAPTER 3

THE 'SEMINARY'

[Seminary 1. A piece of ground in which plants are sown (or raised from cuttings, etc) to be afterwards transplanted; a seed plot. Obs.]
Oxford English Dictionary

'Does he who ploughs for sowing plough
   continually?
Does he continually open and harrow his ground?
When he has levelled its surface,
Does he not scatter dill, sow cumin,
and put in wheat in rows
and barley in its proper place,
and spelt as the border?
For he is instructed aright;
his God teaches him.'

(Isaiah 28:24-26)

From its source high up in the Tibetan mountains, the mighty Mekong River flows through south China down the western border of land-locked Laos, and then steadily southward over magnificent falls and cataracts. Into the very heartland of Cambodia it courses, right past the majestic capital of Phnom Penh where at a great confluence in front of the old Royal Palace it is joined by another river which flows out from the Tonle Sap, an enormous freshwater lake. In June of every year, with the onset of the flood season, the Mekong, swollen by the melting Himalayan snows at its source as well as the heavy monsoon rains, dramatically reverses the flow of this second river and pushes the torrents of muddy floodwater back up into the shallow Tonle Sap. This large shallow lake then spreads to several times its dry season size, like a great freshwater sea, overflowing into countless tributaries and streams which flow, teeming with fish, across the great central Cambodian plain, leaving in its wake a fertile deposit of silt all across the lowland rice fields. In November about the time of the water festival, as the rains taper off, the lake water reverses its flow again draining eastwards back into the Mekong. From the Phnom Penh waterfront, called the 'Four Faces' because of the four rivers which meet there, the Mekong sends off a branch called the Bassac. Together these two waterways move steadily down through south-eastern Cambodia and across into South Vietnam where, after forming a huge fertile delta, they flow out into the South China Sea.

Historically this rich rice-growing area of South Vietnam watered by the Mekong and the Bassac was called Cochin China. It is the home of several hundred thousand ethnic Khmers known in Cambodia as the Khmer *Kraom* (the Khmers below). They are mostly rice farmers, forming their own communities adjacent to the Cambodian border. Perhaps as a result of being a minority among the aggressive Vietnamese, the Khmer *Kraom* have become a strong and industrious people, providing Cambodia with some of her finest leaders and soldiers. And it was here in this fertile delta in South Vietnam that the very first Cambodians became Christians in the early 1920s, just before the door to Cambodia itself opened to Protestant missionaries in 1923. More receptive to the gospel, these industrious people were to provide the infant church in Cambodia with her first students of the Bible, pastors and evangelists.

In later years the church planted in the motherland would in turn reach back with the gospel to the Khmer *Kraom* outside her borders. And later still, in Cambodia's darkest hour, the Khmer *Kraom* would provide a safe haven for many fleeing from the ravages of the Khmer Rouge. One of the few surviving pastors (pre-1975 trained) of the early church in Cambodia today was himself kept by God among the Khmer *Kraom*, until it was safe for him and his family to return to Phnom Penh following the Vietnamese invasion which drove out the Khmer Rouge in 1979. It is ironic that Vietnam and Thailand, Cambodia's historic enemies, each a source of constant danger to her political security over the centuries, became for the Cambodian church at various times a source of strength and a place of refuge from the threats to her existence within Cambodia.

And so it was also that in God's perfect plan two missionary couples, anxious to enter Cambodia where the biblical gospel had never been clearly proclaimed to the indigenous Cambodian masses, were kept studying the Khmer language and working among the Khmer *Kraom* in South Vietnam, while they continued to cry out to God against Cambodia's closed doors. Vietnamese evangelists and Bible colporteurs also sought to bring the gospel to the Khmer *Kraom*. At that time the only part of God's Word in the Khmer language was Luke and Acts, half an inch thick and hand-written. It was in 1922 in Chau Doc province, bordering Cambodia, one year before the door to Cambodia opened, that significant numbers of Khmer *Kraom* families believed. One such family was that of Mr Prac, in the village of Kapchrook.

Mr Prac was a young farmer whose first wife had died, leaving him with three children. He had remarried and now his new wife Yen had fallen gravely ill with tetanus, shortly before giving birth to daughter Siew. Jaws aching and teeth clenched fast like a vice beneath pinched and shrivelled lips, she lay before the anxious gaze of all her family. The older children took turns at sitting with her and squeezing drops of water wrung from a cloth into her mouth. Knowing nothing of tetanus or its cause, Prac watched in despair, helpless before what he thought to be a demon tormenting his wife's body. They had covered her emaciated frame with layer upon layer of clothes and blankets in order to keep in all the body heat, fearful that the coldness of death might touch her. Her frightened eyes rolled back and forth to her children who were gathered nervously about her, terrified by the sudden seizures which stiffened and arched their mother's body.

'What hideous force is it that writhes and fights within her?' Prac asked himself. Everything he had done had failed. The house had been full of fascinated villagers when the local spirit doctor came to perform healing ceremonies over her. Seven times spirit healers had been called, each time at greater expense, with the promise that this time with a superior power they would drive out the evil thing and bring healing. In elaborate and noisy ceremonies these *kroos* spat and sprayed water from their mouths over Yen's trembling body. Fetishes were tied about her neck, and spirit strings hung from her bony wrists and ankles. Prac had sold off bushels of his precious supply of rice, chicken and ducks. Even their few treasured pieces of gold had gone. All the traditional offerings had been made: a chicken hung impaled on two crossed sticks outside the house, heavily scented joss sticks burned to the spirits within the house, fresh food and flowers were placed daily on the high shelf before the various images, and finally at great expense a whole pig's head was offered in a desperate entreaty to the spirits to ward off the impending doom.

Now the distraught family stood utterly helpless, penniless, and friendless before what everyone recognised to be the inevitable outworking of Yen's bad *karma:* fate would have to take its course. Nothing could alter the inexorable outworking of this law of cause and effect. Some villagers even despised the doomed woman fearing that they too might be contaminated by the Evil which lurked in the Prac household. Yen's breathing became shallower and shallower, at times just a deathly rattle in the back of her throat.

Without speaking, Prac turned miserably away from the wide-eyed children gathered in silent vigil. Wearily he climbed down the ladder, trudged across his neglected fields, and slipped silently into the forest beyond. If he could not save his wife then he must try to save his newborn baby daughter Siew, whose constant pathetic wailing for sustenance drove him out in search of the leaves which when brewed served as an age-old substitute for mother's milk. There in the bush he noticed also the plant from whose root a deadly poison could be made. Not a few men before him had chosen to quietly destroy themselves and all their family by such means in the face of such a fate. But he would never do that. Prac found himself stubbornly resisting the traditional and expected response of passively accepting one's fate like a victim. There must be another answer, if only he could find it. Then as he stood there in the quietness of the forest the chant of *Puok Yesu, Puok Yesu* began to play persistently through Prac's mind – idle words he had heard earlier that day tossed lightly and casually about in the village banter. The 'followers of Jesus' had been about the neighbourhood again, handing out their booklets, drawing crowds of children around them in the shade of a mango tree to hear their stories about the God Jesus. Prac had seen them once while driving his ox-cart full of unhusked rice to the mill. Like most others in the market he paid them only passing attention. He had his religion, the one historic religion of all true Khmer people – he was a Buddhist like his parents and grandparents before him. What did he want with this *preah barang* or Frenchman's god? They were a zealous and tenacious little band though; one had even come over and given him a leaflet which Prac hadn't bothered to read since he, like most villagers, was not in the habit of reading anyway. Later he had used it to roll tobacco leaves in. It made a good smoke for the journey home.

Lingering now in the forest with evening gathering about him, Prac smiled as he recalled the fun the villagers always made of the *Puok Yesu*. They would change the name *Yesu* very slightly to *Yiey Su* meaning 'old Granny Sue'. And yet the Christians, always kind and patient in return, persevered with a determination and confidence which Prac in his present melancholy quite suddenly found very compelling. Turning, he let the stalks of the 'infant milk herb' fall from his hand. He straightened himself, drawing in a long hissing breath through his teeth. He must go to them. Right now, he would set off in search of the *Puok Yesu* and ask them to come to his house and heal his wife.

There was no little stir late that evening in the village of Kapchrook when Mr Prac returned with the *Puok Yesu*, including the white man himself. They were heralded, as always, by dozens of darting shouting village children, and some furiously barking dogs who had met them at the edge of the village. 'It's the *Puok*

Yesu,' the villagers called to one another on seeing the white man
in their midst. Uncharacteristically, Prac spoke to no one but
grimly staring straight ahead, directed the visitors up into his
house. Following close on their heels came the gaggle of excited
youngsters who hoped to hear one of the amazing stories about
Preah Yesu. But there would be no story this time, and the
children withdrew as the Christians gathered in the gloom over by
the back wall around the still form of Mrs Yen. The missionary
and those with him knelt down beside her. Showing obvious
concern over her sorrowful condition, he took her frail hand in his
and in fluent Cambodian language spoke quietly first to her and
then to Mr Prac, who had sat down at a respectful distance with
his children gathered around him in awed silence. The Christians
invited him to tell them all about her sickness and what had
happened subsequently. He did so in great detail, explaining how
he had spent all his money and imploring them to ask *Preah Yesu*
to help his wife.

The stale air in the room hung heavy and oppressive about
them, mingled with the pungent smouldering incense sticks and
the acrid odours of sickness and soiled clothing. The missionary
turned to Mr Prac and, as simply and briefly as he knew how,
explained about the living creator God, and about Jesus, his Son,
the Saviour of all mankind, in whose risen power they were now
going to trust for his wife's healing.

'First,' he asked Mrs Yen gently, 'will you allow me to cut
away all these fetishes and strings tied about your body, and are
you willing to place your faith in Jesus Christ?' Even Prac was
surprised at how quickly she nodded her assent. Her cavernous
eyes, moist with tears which trickled slowly down the hollow
cheeks, stared up at them with a look of fear mingled with
expectation.

The Christians knelt around her, heads bowed, hands clasped
before them in silence. Then one by one they prayed, calling out
to God in the name of Jesus to touch and heal Yen's body and
spirit. They prayed, Prac noticed, using terms of high respect for
God just as if they were in a king's palace, and yet they were
speaking the everyday market language of the Khmers and he

could understand every word of it. This was not at all like the Buddhist monks, who in unison chanted prayers in the ancient Indian language of Pali, quite unintelligible to the uneducated. As they continued to pray, Prac glanced down at his wife. She had closed her eyes and drawn her bony hands up together on her chest; so still, so quiet she lay, as if dead. And yet he felt no fear, but only a deep awareness that somehow this 'Heavenly Father' to whom all these prayers were being spoken was right there in the room with them. He did however feel uneasy, for he was aware that something was missing. Nothing had been given or offered or burned to this unseen 'Heavenly Father', so how could Prac expect anything in return? He then thought at least he should close his eyes too, in order not to offend by his rudeness this great and invisible God who at this very moment was surely watching them all.

Mr Prac heard one of the Christians telling him, 'You can open your eyes now; we have finished praying and will be leaving.' They promised to continue to pray, and return soon. Mrs Yen was resting quietly as they left, her eyes still closed. They told the family not to disturb her, but to remove a few of the heavy blankets.

'And that was all,' Prac told the curious gathering who began to ply him with questions almost before the Christians had walked away from the village, seen off by their faithful following of children.

'How much? How much did they charge?' several kept asking him. *Why, they asked for nothing,* Prac thought aloud, and this perplexed him still more as he turned away from the crowd and climbed the ladder back up into the silent room. He went over and stood watching for a long while his wife sleeping quietly, just as they had left her. Then, rolling out his own mat nearby, he stretched himself wearily upon it and stared blankly up into the bamboo crossbeams and thatch roofing. He felt a sense of relief that finally it was dusk and there was no more to be done for today, and tomorrow was not yet come.

Sleep did not come to Prac as quickly as he had hoped, and Yen's gentle breathing nearby caused him to relive the events of the evening. That indescribable expression of trust deep in his wife's moist eyes; the quiet comforting words of the *Puok Yesu*, so confident and so simple; the plainly spoken prayers to invisible 'Heavenly Father'; and not even a mention of payment. He closed his eyes, placing the palms of his hands together just as he had seen the Christians do earlier, and began speaking to 'Heavenly Father'. He was nervous at first but then the words flowed more easily: his wife…, the children…, little Siew…, the troubles…, the frustrations…, the fears… His prayers went on and on until he drifted into a fitful and restless kind of sleep.

It must have been around midnight when he was suddenly aware of his wife's hand tugging and pulling on his arm. She was awake, trying to say something! He leaned over her and heard the words: 'I can open my mouth, my mouth is open!' Excitedly she pulled his hand to her mouth and he felt her wet tongue against his index finger between her unlocked teeth. Before he could respond, her husky voice was struggling to speak again; 'Heavenly Father' is the true God. We must believe in him. He has opened my mouth.'

'Yes, we will all believe in him now.' Prac heard himself echoing her words in the darkness, and he felt the moist warmth of his wife's tears flowing against his hand.

By first light many had gathered about the Prac home, running up and down the steps to see Yen's freed jaws for themselves. 'He is the true God; he opened my mouth,' she declared to each one. 'We are turning to *Preah Yesu*, for only he could save my life.'

Mrs Yen grew steadily stronger and there was no happier home in the whole village of Kapchrook. Little Siew lived, and within a year had a new brother whom they named Chhorn. Prac dedicated his home to God and opened it up as a meeting place for Christian witness, teaching and Sunday worship for the whole district. The family soon came to know and love other scattered Christians in the area, such as Uncle Chea, Sek, Hock, old Grandfather Ngin, Granny Mien and her two zealous sons Chum and Voich. The handful of early believers among the Khmer *Kraom* were bound together by strong and enduring bonds of Christian love and fellowship. They did not experience the fierce opposition and intimidation that Mr Has and his friends would face inside Cambodia. (This church in South Vietnam continued to spread its roots and grow among the Khmer *Kraom* right up until 1954 when an outbreak of fierce persecution forced them to flee westwards over the border into Cambodia to the province of Takeo.)

While continuing to work among the Khmers in Vietnam, the missionaries and their supporters back home were still with their prayers pushing at the doors of Cambodia itself, held closed by indifferent and sometimes anti-Protestant French colonial officials. Finally, early in 1923, two missionary couples were given permission by the French Resident Superior to enter and work in Cambodia, with these foreboding words, 'The Cambodians are staunch Buddhists. You cannot expect to have any success.' But since those first missionaries were not looking for any 'success' by human art or skill, they moved forward across the border from Vietnam into Cambodia undaunted by such prophecies, in the knowledge that God would in his time give the increase as they faithfully sowed and watered.

One couple, Mr and Mrs Arthur Hammond, remained in Phnom Penh, giving themselves wholly to the formidable task of translating the entire Bible into Cambodian. (This work which began in 1925 would take thirty years of patient endurance before the complete Cambodian Bible was printed in 1954. It was then the 201st language in which the Bible Society had published the entire Bible.) The other couple, Mr and Mrs David Ellison, headed 200 miles further northward to Battambang, Cambodia's second largest city, situated in the heart of the bountiful province of the same name. And so it was that they came to live right beside the busy central market area of the city to pursue a vigorous ministry of evangelism and teaching. Before long a few small house groups had been started in outlying villages, such as the one at Mr Has's home in Doentiey.

Within the first two years, the importance of discipling godly leaders to become pastors and evangelists for this emerging church became imperative. So in 1925, at the missionaries' home in Battambang, a small Bible School, a 'seminary', was started. This strategic little seminary would for exactly fifty years be the ground where all the pastors and leaders of the Khmer Evangelical church would be carefully raised and nurtured before being transplanted one by one out across the provinces of Cambodia to bear fruit.

The first students were five men chosen from the Khmer *Kraom* believers who had moved across to Battambang. They lived upstairs in the two-storey home with the missionaries, who taught them daily and systematically from God's Word. Now more than just Luke and Acts was available – John's Gospel and other New Testament books as well as various gospel tracts and some hymns were being produced through the ongoing translation work in Phnom Penh. These two ministries perfectly complemented each other as literature was provided to meet the demands of the growing body of Bible School students up in Battambang. With expository teaching, careful study of the Khmer Scriptures, grounding in fundamental Christian doctrines and regular practical opportunities to apply these truths through ministry in the various village churches scattered around Battambang, these first students grew strong and resilient. After one year of study, the five men went out for a complete year of itinerant ministry, teaching among the house churches and scattered Christian homes, evangelising, and spreading the newly translated portions and tracts among the people. The seminary became the nucleus around which the Christian outreach gravitated.

Lay leaders too, unable to spend long periods of time away from their fields and families, came for a few months at a time. For these, the school scheduled sessions regulated by the monsoons and the seasons of planting and reaping. Mr Has, for example, having planted his rice would set himself to study for the remainder of the wet season. With the onset of the dry season and the harvest, he cut his rice and then engaged in dry season evangelism in the scattered farming communities around Doentiey.

Another village where a significant number of Christians were settled was Chkae Koun, twenty-eight kilometres north of the city of Battambang. Nearly all these people were economic migrants from among the Cambodian Christian community in South Vietnam. In frontier Battambang the soil was good for rice farming, and as migrants anyway they were more open to change and new ideas.

The Bible School provided a stable centre for administration, fellowship and teaching for the scattered early Christian minority in Cambodia and a place where many young men and women would find believing partners. Here was the cradle of the Cambodian Evangelical Church in the mid 1920s.

And so in evangelistic waves the travelling preachers and colporteurs spread out from the seminary, travelling by foot, bicycle, riverboat and ox-cart up and down the byways of Cambodia, hot and dusty in the dry season, wet and muddy in flood season, reaching out to the villages and small towns all across the land. Within ten years, Christians from the seminary were to be found ministering in eleven of Cambodia's fourteen provinces. However, the majority of house churches and believers were concentrated in the three northern provinces of Battambang, Siem Riep and Kampong Cham.

At the same time as this initial outreach was going on, the Christian community in Battambang was further strengthened by the addition of more Khmer *Kraom* families from South Vietnam. Initially the men came to study at the seminary, but when they saw what a spacious and fertile province Battambang was, good for growing rice and vegetables, some decided to stay. Furthermore, land in this as yet undeveloped region was cheap, and there were few thieves or bandits to contend with. Mr Prac was among this small exodus, leading a group of about twenty families from his village of Kapchrook the several hundred kilometres north west to a new life on the fertile plains of central Battambang. Most of these families were Christians, eager to stay together in a place where they could flourish and grow spiritually. Mr Prac and his extended family settled in the little village of Chendu-Swa, thirty-four kilometres north of Battambang city where the Christian seminary gave opportunity for their young people to study and their older men to receive short-term teaching during the four months between the wet season planting and the harvest.

There was an immediate rapport between the Battambang Christians like Mr Has and the new arrivals. They mutually encouraged and helped each other to the point where no one lacked for anything. Their sons and daughters intermarried, and a strong though small church was formed which became a bastion against the almost ceaseless persecution and ridicule from the community at large.

In Chendu-Swa where the Prac family settled in 1926, the Christians did no work in their fields on Sundays but rather spent the day together or in visiting the sick and needy. About two dozen of them gathered each Lord's day at Uncle Chea's home to worship. Prac and Uncle Sek were the elders assisting their pastor Uncle Chum, whom the Christians helped support with their tithes. Later, Chum and the other men built a small chapel beside his house for the forty or so who now met each week. At the annual Harvest Thanksgiving, the believers would bring one tenth of their rice (perhaps thirty bushels) for the pastor's needs. Little Siew put aside a few coins each week in a cloth bag, one tenth of all the money she made from the eggs her hens laid. Christmas was the season the children loved best, with pageants, gifts, singing, and baptisms out in the nearby river which ran through the rice fields.

In their homes the Christian families maintained a time for family worship, carefully teaching their children the ways of the Lord. Daughter Siew, brother Chhorn and now new baby sister Song were all taught God's word in this way from an early age, until in their late teens they too entered the seminary for more in-depth study. In his spare time, Mr Prac went out evangelising and visiting the other house groups. At Doentiey he met Mr Has, and together they would go out distributing gospel tracts in the market places or, during the wet season, take time to study at the seminary. The church in Mr Has's home had increased to about six families. Rose's husband Koeum would go with his father-in-law on long evangelistic trips, walking over the fields to outlying villages where they would preach in the open air using picture rolls.

One day Koeum and Rose were asked to consider leaving Battambang and go down to Phnom Penh to help in the growing literature and Bible translation work there. Rose struggled for a long time over the decision, for she found it too hard a thing to contemplate leaving her parents and the village where she had always lived since childhood. *Who will care for my mother and father*, she wondered; *surely this is my duty*. But then, as she prayed, she realised that if God were calling her to serve him in Phnom Penh he would take care of all these things. Thoughts about her own happiness and convenience were not worthy of a believer. Yes, she would go to Phnom Penh with her husband and little Tou. Nevertheless she wept as she left her village home, her family and friends. And for quite a while she felt very homesick in the strange city of Phnom Penh with its sophisticated people, grand buildings and temples, and busy streets criss-crossed by a system of canals and waterways. As God had promised to bless obedience, Rose's parents were cared for and she was able to spend many years in fruitful ministry along with her husband, who was helping with the translation of the Bible.

As is generally the case, as the Christian church emerged from the surrounding society, many of those drawn into its embrace were from communities and classes exploited and suffering in the prevailing religious, moral and ethical climate: those suffering from leprosy, the demon-possessed, women, orphans, widows, the very poor, the darker skinned, ex-prisoners, hired labourers and so on. The close-knit Christian community which generally extended out along family and marriage lines, being a ridiculed minority itself, provided a place of real understanding, security and love for all these other social outcasts – marginalised, unwanted and despised. They were irresistibly drawn by the promise of unconditional forgiveness and loving personal acceptance by the living God, the Creator, Sustainer and Saviour of them all. They experienced deliverance from evil spirits and the heavy yoke of slavery to some fickle and impersonal fate; honesty, fidelity and respect within the family of the church; a high moral standard firmly based on unchanging absolutes, freewill acts of charity, and a universality irrespective of persons. All cut across the deep-seated traditional barriers of class, race, sex and culture.

As the bands of eager sowers left the seminary year by year to broadcast the good seed upon what were mostly hard-trodden, rocky and thorn-infested fields, some of it fell into prepared soil where the ploughshares of trial and suffering had already cut deep furrows. One such heart was that of a young lad named Sou. Born to a poor woman who died shortly afterwards, Sou was finally put out of the house by the new woman who had moved in with his father. Like a stray, or as the villagers called after him, 'a crocodile wandering far from the pool', he drifted from place to place working as a hired hand for anyone who would provide him with basic food and shelter. The temporary shelter he found with a grandmother ended abruptly at the age of ten when he was thrown out as a troublemaker because he had begun showing interest in the *Puok Yesu*, attending their children's meetings and coming home singing the Christian choruses he had learned. From then on he wandered from village to village as a beggar, a pathetic waif, sometimes with only a piece of discarded rice sacking for covering, sleeping rough at night, bitten mercilessly by mosquitoes. Like dozens of other unwanted and abandoned children, he gathered wild watercress from the streams or caught a few fish to trade for rice. Those who hired him soon despised him the more when they discovered his liking for the 'white man's god'. At sixteen, with the little money he had earned reaping the previous harvest and some help from the Christians, he attended the seminary for a time of basic teaching and grounding in God's Word. But in 1941 came the Japanese invasion of Cambodia and the internment of all the missionaries in a prison camp. It would be another ten years before he could fulfil his dream of full-time Bible study.

One of the earliest Cambodian evangelists from the seminary was Mr Haum, who frequently preached at the little street chapel at Battambang. On one occasion as he was preaching, along came a Mr Put. He was another of the very poor and hard-pressed country people who wandered from place to place in search of seasonal employment, finding release from his heavy burden of worry in alcohol and opium. Recently he had travelled with his family across from distant Svay Rieng province to Battambang, to work in the deep jungle cutting teak wood and raising a few vegetables. This day he had come to Battambang market to sell some produce and stock up on his supply of opium before heading back into the bush. In fact he had just stepped unsteadily out of the opium den when he was almost immediately confronted by the evangelist and those gathered about him.

Though the words all sounded very new and foreign in his ears, Put found himself strangely drawn to this teacher. Twice he found himself right in the front, at the very edge of the platform on which the evangelist stood, and twice he drew back in embarrassment. Unable to ignore Put's unusual behaviour, on finishing his message, the evangelist immediately reached out his hand to him where he stood with eyes and ears wide open. Eager to know more of the living God and the Saviour Jesus Christ, Put stayed that Sunday night at Haum's home. Only too aware of his need, his addiction and desperate situation, he put his trust in Jesus that very evening. Next day he returned to his camp in the forest and immediately told his wife and children, including his little son Yeah, all he had learned. He read to them from the gospel booklets and encouraged all who listened to believe in Jesus.

Days and weeks passed until one morning, taking a shirt from a nail on the wall, he found a package in the pocket. Startled and surprised, he realised that here folded in a scrap of old newspaper was the opium he had bought that day in Battambang. For all these weeks he had not once even thought of it or craved for it. God had broken its hold over him and released him from a twenty-year-long addiction! Put was overwhelmed with joy and gratitude. He hurried outside and threw the deadly drug into the stream, then he snatched up his old opium pipe from its hiding place and smashed it to pieces. With tears of repentance, Put fell to his knees right there and alone before God confessed all the filth and sin in his meaningless life. In that moment he knew that he must return to Battambang, seek out the Christians and learn more of this great and powerful Deliverer.

For two years Put studied at the seminary, and then with all his family he set off back to his own province of Svay Rieng in eastern Cambodia near the Vietnamese border. Here his home became a centre for Christian meetings and the study of God's Word, with Christians coming from Phnom Penh to help him establish a church. Mr Put brought all his children up to know and fear the living God. His fifth son Yeah was especially attentive, and in the years following World War II and the retreat of the occupying Japanese and Thai forces, Yeah would join other young people like Prac's son Chhorn, Rose's boy Tou, and the outcast Sou at the seminary. They became the new wave of second generation post World War II Christian disciples, some of whom would persevere to become the church's leaders in the exacting sixties and seventies, years of rich harvest, unimaginable suffering and world-wide dispersion.

During those first twenty-five years of church planting in Cambodia, the Bible was completely translated. The seminary was established and proven as a training ground for the pastors and lay leaders of those early scattered village house churches; and a harvest was brought in which, though small, was hardy and enduring. The secret being that each new believer learned the true nature of Christian discipleship.

To be a Christian in Cambodian society was to be a social pariah, misunderstood and ill-treated, a convenient scapegoat for blame and abuse. The Son of God had redeemed them at tremendous personal cost and suffering; Cambodian Christians willing to be entrusted with the ministry of reconciliation were likewise prepared to suffer. The early believers were for the most part rice-farmers, unsophisticated country folk. God chose the 'foolish' and the 'unwise' of Cambodian society to be the foundation stones of his church. It was they who were least inclined to flee to the West, and were best able to endure the rigours of the rural-based communist system in the late 1970s and 1980s. And such are still the tenacious roots and fibre of Cambodian society which survive and endure.

As yet in our account of this church, no Mekong-like floodtide of turning had swept through the Cambodian heartland, backing up and overflowing in life-giving streams into the hinterland. No vast fertile alluvial deposits received the scattered seed, and no monsoon-like downpours of blessing had fallen upon the waiting land. If anything at all was seen rising on the distant horizon over this parched and barren plain, it was but a small cloud in a rainless sky, 'no bigger than a man's hand'. And the question then was, would those who were bent low before it in prayer be able to persevere until the promised deluge came?

CHAPTER 4

THE PESTILENCE, DROUGHT
AND DESTROYER

'What the cutting locust left,
    the swarming locust has eaten.
What the swarming locust has left,
    the hopping locust has eaten,
    and what the hopping locust has left,
    the destroying locust has eaten.'

(Joel 1:4)

Throughout the entire seventy-five year history of the Cambodian Evangelical Church, not a decade has passed without some severe wave of persecution or restriction against the Christians. Sometimes it was a deliberate policy of the governing powers to move against the church as a convenient scapegoat, identifying it with the prevailing enemy in times of political upheaval. For example, the church at one time was accused of being a tool of the American CIA, and at another of being Khmer Rouge communist inspired. While these kinds of politically motivated attacks have been the most cruel and devastating for the church, there has also been the perpetual harassment and hostility from the Cambodian community at large. The fact is that this little church has never feared persecution from the foreign invader so much as from the Cambodian people themselves. Even under the Khmer Rouge reign of terror, when all Cambodians suffered alike, Christians were betrayed into the hands of the communists by fellow

Cambodian neighbours.

More recently in the refugee camps in Thailand, 'progressive', but largely godless westerners working with powerful international political and relief organisations, some in the name of 'Christianity', have also ridiculed and opposed the evangelical church despite the charters and liberal guarantees of rights and freedoms they purport to uphold. Then there have been the humanistic and cynical journalists, snapping around the periphery like jackals, writing their prejudicial and distorted reports about the Christians whom they almost always portray in the negative. And all of this together, further exacerbating the ever present antipathy of the Khmer Buddhists for the Christians whether in Cambodia, in refugee camps, or across the world where hundreds of thousands of Cambodians have been resettled since 1975.

Thus from the time the first Christians appeared preaching the biblical gospel of Jesus Christ, right through over seventy years and eight major political changes in Cambodia down to recent experiences of Cambodian exiles in refugee camps and throughout the world, the preaching of the cross has been considered offensive and they have had to pay the high price of Christian discipleship and counter culture. The church has never sought to adapt its message to suit prevailing and ever-changing philosophical fashion or compromise on its biblical position, despite considerable pressure to do so. It has resolutely and unitedly resisted the temptation to seek peaceful coexistence at the expense of its integrity with the various political and religious giants among whom it dwelt. Every generation of Cambodian Christians wherever they may be, sooner or later, usually sooner, has to face this challenge. Wonderfully, the history of the Cambodian church is full of fine examples of faithfulness, a great cloud of witnesses to which the present divided and troubled generation of Cambodian Christians can look for encouragement.

We have already noted how opposition to the gospel was first manifested back in the early 1920s, when the French colonial rulers and King Sisowath of Cambodia decided together to refuse all permission for Protestant missionaries to enter and work in Cambodia. It is difficult to understand the reason for this, since evangelical missionaries and national churches had long existed in the neighbouring French colony of Vietnam and uncolonised Buddhist Siam as well as in the rest of South East Asia.

'Cambodia has no place for Christian missionaries' was the cry which greeted the earliest attempts to enter Cambodia. This cry has echoed down through the decades right up to the present day, at times reaching almost hysterical proportions. 'No place' to be born, 'no place' to lay his head, 'no place' to be buried, and it seemed in 1922 'no place' in Cambodia. But when the door finally did open into this hostile land, Christ was given a place in the lowly hearts of some of its poorest and humblest inhabitants, the rice-farmers. This too is unchanged in Cambodia today.

In 1928, just five years after permission to enter was so reluctantly given, and only three years after the opening of the Bible School in Battambang, the first political opposition broke out. 'You are operating a clandestine school,' was the official rebuke. The local government was becoming alarmed as the effect of the Bible School began to be felt in the north-west. Those running the school were accused of training spies and troublemakers, and threatened with deportation.

Four years later, in 1932, came a further blow when the new King Monivong published a royal edict forbidding anyone in the kingdom to proselytise Cambodians. This seriously inhibited the spread of the gospel and the growth of the infant church. It was not uncommon for the early believers to be thrown into jail without trial and generally intimidated for becoming Christians, as we saw in the case of Mr Has. In Battambang the pressure was particularly intense, and also for the six or seven house groups in neighbouring Siem Riep province where the king's edict was publicly posted. Several of the young itinerant evangelists from the Bible School were arrested, interrogated and threatened, and others were thrown into jail for continuing to preach the gospel of Christ. One such travelling preacher in the northern province of Kratie was imprisoned and then ordered out of the province. The missionaries too were forced to withdraw from this province where opposition to the gospel was very fierce. Fortunately however, the edicts and various anti-Christian regulations, like most regulations in Cambodia, were not always carried out or adhered to consistently for long periods, and neither were they enforced uniformly across the country. So the Christians usually had times and places of respite during these unpredictable seasons of pestilence, drought and destruction. For them it was a time to learn about patience and importunate prayer.

Buddhism was seen as such an inseparable part of being a Khmer that only a traitor would entertain another system of belief. Neither does a society built on traditional Buddhist philosophy have much place for individual thinking or initiative. The emphasis is on conformity and thus outward tranquillity in all things. Deep pain and longings, however, simmer unseen beneath the passive Buddha-like mask of Cambodia, a face which has led to popular and romantic myths about the exotic Khmers as a peaceful, ever smiling, gentle, pastoral folk. Nothing could be further from the truth. Few people have displayed such cruel violence and divisiveness among themselves, or such a propensity to betrayal, intrigue and self-annihilation as the Khmers. Certainly young Christians disowned by families and friends, despised and abused, were not aware of many gentle, smiling and accepting fellow countrymen.

Problems arose too for the Phnom Penh team working on the translation of the Bible and production of other Christian literature. Permission had to be sought before any booklet or tract could be printed and distributed, and this was often painfully slow in coming, due to hostility, bureaucratic red tape, and corrupt officials waiting for a bribe. Sometimes fault was found with various words used, because they did not imply the supremacy of the Buddha. The word used for 'God', for example, could not explicitly imply that he was the one true God, for that would offend the king and the Buddhist establishment despite the fact that Buddhism has no personal God.

Rose and Koeum, however, with their growing family of six boys and two girls, persevered along with the missionaries and their team of language informants and interpreters. They worshipped together at the one meeting place for the handful of believers there in the capital city. By the late 1930s, despite constant setbacks, considerable progress had been made on all fronts. The New Testament was completed, the Old Testament almost finished, hymns, Bible study books, and gospel tracts had been produced and were now in constant use by the young churches. (Unfortunately after the war the entire Bible had to be rewritten and reprinted, when the Cambodian government revised and standardised the correct meaning and spelling of all Khmer words in the first official dictionary.)

By 1942, with the world at war, Cambodia suddenly found herself firmly under the control of two foreign invaders, the Japanese and the Thai. The occupation forces of the Japanese Imperial Army arrived in strength in 1941, expelling the Vichy French colonial government, and cruelly imprisoning resident expatriates. This included the missionaries who were forced to leave Cambodia or be interned. For the first time in its history the Cambodian church found itself in the midst of political upheaval, under a foreign military power, and bereft of missionaries and the help and spiritual leadership they had provided for the past twenty years. The Christians would now begin to realise that in such times of trouble they must look to God alone. It was a time when they first began to learn to stand on their own feet.

Thailand, ever eager to exploit her neighbour's woes, seized the fertile provinces of Battambang and Siem Riep from a powerless Cambodia. In a deal with the Japanese, the Thai moved quickly into these two northern provinces in the same year. The Cambodian people of Battambang and Siem Riep, about half a million of them, now found themselves under a Thai administration with a programme designed to bring them under the influence of Thai language and customs. The Bible School was forced to close down when Battambang province was ceded to Thailand, and the students returned to their scattered villages where the church continued on quietly in small house groups.

These war years were a most difficult and trying time for all Cambodians who had to endure the humiliation and physical privation of a harsh foreign military occupation and the amputation and colonisation of their most fertile province.

Rose and her eight children were forced to leave Phnom Penh, while her husband tried to maintain order over church and mission property in the capital. She travelled north to seek refuge with her husband's brothers in his former village up near the Tonle Sap. But no refuge was to be found, for her in-laws and the other villagers were hostile to Christians because they refused to participate in the local Buddhist merit-making festivals. So for the whole course of the war Rose lived apart with her children in a small shack raised on stilts, all but cut off from society, an unwanted stranger among her own people. To survive, she needed all her considerable determination and strength of character, and her faith in God's loving kindness and faithfulness.

The family lived together, working hard to raise pigs and chickens, and a few vegetables around the house. Many fruits grow readily and plentifully in Cambodia, and its streams and rivers abound with fish, shellfish and vegetation, all good to eat. From time to time a friendly Chinese neighbour would come by with some rice and a little cash for them. Throughout the entire difficult four-year period, God protected and provided for them all. Even during severe flooding one wet season, when the whole area turned into an enormous lake inundated by the floodwaters of the Tonle Sap, and their vegetables and rice were washed away, the Lord provided for them by way of a small cache of gold and valuables which they discovered washed up among the debris under the house.

Despite all the hardships, it was during these years of scarcity that Rose and her children entered into a new and deeper relationship with God. Every day she would gather her children about her and lead them in prayer and hymn singing. Then she would begin to teach them principles and truths from the copy of God's Word which she always kept with her. On hearing the familiar singing, passers-by would call mockingly up, 'Sing to your Jesus, but does he fill your stomachs?' In spite of this frequent chorus of abuse and scorn, they learned many hymns and Bible stories together, growing as they did so in faith and knowledge of God. Later, all six of Rose's sons would study at the Bible School and go into Christian ministry.

She constantly taught them that, no matter what the village

children said or did, they must never repay evil with evil or abuse with abuse, but rather seek God in prayer for grace and wisdom. Sometimes the villagers would catch the children and try to force them to burn incense sticks to the spirits. When they refused, they would scold them and beat their little hands with sticks, sending them running home crying for their mother. As she comforted them she would impart to them her own great strength and trust in God, and with her children gathered around her, she would sing the choruses they loved.

The situation was much the same in Battambang. Scattered Christian groups, hard pressed and apprehensive, had few trained leaders and no missionaries to help. But they continued at least to maintain short times of worship and Bible reading together as families, or perhaps with a few believing neighbours.

In Chendu Swa little Song, Mr Prac's youngest daughter, struggled within herself as she and all the village children attending the new Thai-language school were expected each morning to turn and face the Buddhist image set up high on the classroom's west wall, and at the given moment bow in obeisance and pay respect to it. Each day as every head obediently turned west to face the teacher standing below the image, he saw in the midst of the rows of upheld little faces a shock of black hair as one head was turned defiantly in the opposite direction. Finally Song was called out by the teacher to account for her disobedience. Unashamedly, she stepped forward and explained her Christian belief to the Thai teacher in front of the whole class. He was too overcome with surprise at meeting such determined belief in a small girl to be angry with her, and so asked like a true Buddhist if she might at least consider facing west with all the other children, for the sake of conformity and appearance. Daughter Song would only consent to this after she had discussed the matter with her father, and he explained that she could look in the idol's direction provided she did not bow to it or worship it in any way.

A few years later, when Song was sixteen, her father was afraid that his attractive and intelligent youngest daughter might be forced like other teenage girls into a liaison with a Thai Buddhist man. So following Khmer custom he arranged a marriage for her with a young Christian man named Ham, the son of one of the Khmer *Kraom* families who had come to Battambang with the Prac family twenty years earlier.

In 1945, following the defeat of Japan and the restoration of full French colonial rule, the Thai were called on by the United Nations to withdraw from Cambodia's provinces of Battambang and Siem Riep. On the ancient Cambodian throne now sat the popular young King Norodom Sihanouk, determined to shake off the colonial yoke and lead a free and independent Cambodia. He even passed an edict assuring freedom of religious belief.

Sihanouk at age eighteen had been put on the throne by the French just prior to the Japanese occupation in 1941. They saw him as a pliable young playboy. The move upset others in the royal household who also had claims to the throne, thus beginning another serious royal feud which would fester for thirty years till 1970 when Prince Sirik Matak joined with General Lon Nol in ousting Sihanouk. In 1975, to Sihanouk's delight, Sirik Matak was executed by the Khmer Rouge. These damaging jealousies and rivalries between Cambodia's royal princes have over the centuries cost Cambodia territory and prestige. Another generation of them continue squabbling to the present day.

Sihanouk, a shrewd political manipulator, connived with the fascist Japanese 'liberators' in 1941 to remove the French colonialists, but this backfired when the Japanese imposed their own direct military rule over the country. Four years later in 1945, he would be welcoming the French back again. Over the next half century this king in the tradition of his Angkorian forbears would ally himself with anything from fascism to Marxism, terrorist to superpower, in order to keep himself in power. The tragic consequence of this man's personal egoism and lust for power is only too obvious in all the political intrigue and chaos of Cambodia today. Unlike Thailand, Cambodia's kings have brought their nation to its knees in every way.

However, his efforts to lead Cambodia towards independence following World War II and indeed the peace and stability of the whole nation were immediately threatened by a new and virulent internal uprising. The *Issaraks* or independence fighters had been encouraged and aided by the retreating Japanese and Thai to fight against King Sihanouk's newly restored Cambodian government. Thailand supported one major faction of the rebellion, rooted in Battambang, which was fighting against the French. Later another faction linked up with the communist Vietminh in neighbouring Vietnam to threaten the Cambodian government itself. Besides being anti-French (though in fact no white person was safe from them), they were like some of today's Cambodian resistance groups in being fanatically nationalistic, with a great hatred towards Christianity. The Khmer Christians were perceived as spies and sympathisers of the hated French, and were expected to show their patriotism by going to the Buddhist temple. Several believers were actually forced to the temples on pain of death. So, while the Japanese and Thai had in general left the church to fend for itself, the Khmer *Issaraks* where they operated posed a direct and dangerous threat to the life of every Christian. With no single leader holding the movement together, they were little more than money hungry bandits, robbers, hostage takers and murderers led by local strong men and thugs. Full independence from France in 1953, however, removed their *raison d'être*.

Much of the rebellion was centred in Battambang province where the rebels engaged in guerrilla warfare, raiding and pillaging the villages and towns from their jungle strongholds. In Battambang, where the Christians were most numerous (both Catholic and Protestant) and lived scattered in isolated villages, they suffered most of all. For seven or eight years following World War II these rural areas were very dangerous for them, particularly at night-time. Though they sought to live normal peaceful lives, they could never be quite sure that they were not being watched by *Issarak* spies or betrayed by vengeful local villagers. 'Let your Jesus help you then,' the villagers would threaten.

In Chendu Swa, Mr Prac and his wife Yen cautiously went on holding meetings in their home each Sunday and visiting and encouraging Christian neighbours and friends. Following the rice harvest and threshing, they set off early one morning in the ox-cart, down the well-worn track leading westward towards the

Baval River and an area of forest and scattered villages called Prey Liew, about fifteen kilometres from Chendu Swa. Into the cart they had loaded a few supplies and several packages of Scriptures and gospel tracts, which they would distribute among the villagers and at the evening evangelistic meeting. After two or three days when they did not return, the family back in Chendu Swa became very worried. Older daughter Siew who by now was married with a two-year-old son, kept up a steady vigil, watching each ox-cart which rumbled down the dusty track. Her anxiety grew as she failed to recognise father's familiar figure at the reins.

Finally, after several days of fruitless inquiries, the fearful news was casually passed to them by an *Issarak* sympathiser in the village. Prac and Yen had been taken by the rebels, accused of being French spies and disseminating poisonous propaganda. The *Issaraks* had a great hatred for Christian literature and destroyed it whenever they found it. All the family was numbed with fear and shock, made worse by the villagers' constantly wagging tongues and gruesome tales declaring that there was no hope and that the Issaraks had already strangled Prac and Yen and abandoned them in the forest. Reports were that altogether thirty people had been captured, and were being held at an *Issarak* jungle stronghold nearby. That night the torn and bloodied blouse of a captured woman was left hanging from a tree in the middle of the village as a warning for all to see. Siew gathered all the relatives and other Christian friends together to pray fervently for her parents' lives.

Meanwhile, at the rebel camp in the forest, Prac and his wife lay bound outside in the leaves. For four days they were questioned and threatened with death. Prac simply explained to his captors the reason for his journey, to spread the 'good news' of the living Saviour God. Eventually they were unbound and permitted to sleep in one of the makeshift bamboo huts. None of the other prisoners were to be seen – they had all already been taken out and brutally murdered. Prac and Yen continued to pray together that they might see their children's faces again, and to tell the men guarding them about the way of true liberty and freedom for the Khmers.

Then, quite unexpectedly, after about a month, while Siew was sitting working under the house in the early morning light, she caught sight of a dishevelled and haggard form stumbling out of the forest beyond the temple and across the fields of stubble towards the house. It was her mother! She had been set free with orders to secure 10,000 *riels*. She was to take 5,000 *riels* to Battambang market to buy various medicines which the rebels badly needed, and then secretly take them to the *Issarak* camp with the other 5,000 *riels* in cash. Without hesitation the family set about selling their recently harvested store of rice, and putting together all the money and valuables they had. No price was too high to redeem their beloved father from the hands of the *Issaraks*. If some feared it might be a trap or that mother was returning to her death, they said nothing but rather sought to fulfil all the demands, trusting God for the outcome. At two o'clock the next morning Yen pulled herself away from the arms of her anxious children and slipped quietly back into the forest as she had come, the medicines wrapped in the long cloth *krama*[1] over her shoulder and the cash tucked securely under the waist of her sarong.

Later that same morning, in faith, the family set off quietly from Chendu Swa. They travelled westward out of the village, taking the same road as their parents had taken weeks earlier. Each kilometre further tested their faith and resolve but they pressed on, walking closely together and speaking very little. Out in front marched Siew, her eyes squinting as she anxiously scanned the horizon for her beloved parents. Suddenly, as they turned a bend in the road, there directly ahead of them they saw mother and father coming slowly towards them. They had been released as promised. For a long while the reunited family wept and embraced, blurting out parts of their mutual ordeal in excited tones only to weep and embrace all over again. Then together at last though all but penniless, for the ransom price had taken almost everything they had, they set off back down the road to Chendu Swa.

They were just crossing a shallow stream when they heard horse's hoofs galloping up the track behind them. Turning round they saw with dismay the rider had a *bandanna* roughly tied around his head. Unmistakably it was an *Issarak*. Speechless, and in a state of shock, they huddled together by the side of the cart track as the man drew up the frothing pony in a cloud of red dust. He was shouting something and waving a package in his right hand. Leaning over he handed it to Mr Prac, yelling, 'Here, we don't want to take your money; take it back.' Prac nervously protested, but the man ignored him and tossing down the package containing the 5,000 *riels*, he turned the pony round and cantered back down the trail and out of sight.

In Chendu Swa the entire village gathered in wonder and amazement about the released prisoners, plying them with ceaseless questions. Prac, rejoicing with his family and the other believers who had come to greet him, lost no opportunity to testify to his miraculous deliverance, and tell of the ransom money he held in his hand, so strangely returned to them in full. Two years later the rebellion flared up again, with looting, burning and pillaging rampant across the land. This time the vulnerable Christian community sought safety in the city of Battambang, taking refuge in the large solid brick house which had formerly served as the mission centre and Bible School. The missionaries, along with other expatriates, had been forced to flee south to Phnom Penh as the *Issaraks* began attacking into the city of Battambang itself. During these night raids on Battambang scores of people were killed including many Catholics, mostly Vietnamese and Chinese. Their mutilated bodies were found strewn about the streets and along the banks of the river. The Christians crowded into the old brick house with all the doors and windows shut tight, and there kept up a prayer vigil through those long terrifying nights during the height of the battle, while the shooting and screaming continued outside.

It was during this terrifying time that the Cambodian church had its first martyrs. One night Elder Eang was caught and murdered by the Issaraks. In the morning the Christians carried his battered body back into the house and buried it in the compound. Another of the early martyrs was Pastor Yan, one of the four men who had been commissioned and ordained back in 1940 just as the war was beginning and the missionaries were leaving. Walking in the footsteps of his Lord and the legions of martyrs since Stephen, he was bold to his last breath in declaring the gospel of salvation through Christ alone, with no thought to his own reputation or safety.

Pastor Yan had been going about his duties as head of the district church committee when he was surrounded one afternoon by a band of angry *Issarak* rebels. They pushed him off his bicycle and began taunting him.

'It's one of the *Puok Yesu*. Why don't you ask your precious Jesus to help you now?' they scoffed as they pushed him over to a freshly dug hole.

Showing no fear, he replied, 'Do what you have to do, but first allow me to pray.' He knelt down beside the open grave, his face radiant with the joy of Christ as he called out, 'Lord Jesus, be with me in this moment.' Then one of the rebels struck him on the back of the head with a cudgel. The pastor fell headlong into the grave where he lay quite still. The attitude of prayer and the indescribable expression of sublime peace and joy on his face remained. As his murderers filled earth into the hole, that death-defying expression was indelibly imprinted on their minds, haunting and troubling them, and prompting them to speak of it to others. Thus the Christians heard the story of how their brother went to be with the Lord. Every one of these martyrs, like the hundreds who would follow in later years, was struck down by their own Khmer people, the very ones whom they loved and longed to see repent and turn from darkness and enter into the light of Jesus Christ.

The troubles continued for several years more, during which the Lord revealed himself strong and powerful on behalf of his Cambodian children in many remarkable ways. They were preserved in times of bloody ambush by day, and raids on their villages by night, in trains derailed by mines and in remote areas where they were surrounded by hostility and contempt. The rebellion came to an end in 1953 when France gave Cambodia her independence, and King Sihanouk granted a general amnesty to surrendering *Issarak* soldiers.

When the missionaries were able to return to Battambang in the late 1940s between the ebb and flow of the rebel movements, they wondered if anything would remain of the planted church and the fruits of the seminary after nearly a decade of such pestilence and destruction. While some had indeed withered and died because they had developed no real roots of their own, and others had perished under the hand of the invader or been carried away by the various 'thieves' who had come to plunder the little garden, there remained a faithful remnant flourishing and growing, more firmly rooted and hardy in their native soil.

The Cambodian Evangelical Church had successfully endured privation, loneliness, intense persecution and even death for the sake of the gospel. The older leaders who remained and a new crop of untried second generation Christians returned to the reopened seminary with a renewed zeal and commitment to be further strengthened and trained for labour in the extremes of the heat, drought and flood of the Cambodian spiritual climate.

In 1949, after twenty-five years in Battambang, the Bible School was moved to the relative safety and convenience of Phnom Penh. At Takmau on the southern outskirts of the capital it reopened (for a further twenty-five year period) on a spacious plot of land along the lush green banks of the Bassac River, there to be watered and fed by the long-awaited late rains.

CHAPTER 5

THE LATE RAINS

> 'Be patient, therefore, brethren, until the
> coming of the Lord. Behold, the farmer waits
> for the precious fruit of the earth, being
> patient over it until it receives the early
> and the late rain.'
>
> (James 5:7)

After the turbulent and harrowing years of World War II and the *Issarak* rebellions came a decade of relative peace and tranquillity (1955-1965), during which the Cambodian church was watered and nourished in a refreshing climate of calm and prosperity. The increase given during this season of 'late rains' was to be seen in every area of church life.

The irrepressible King Sihanouk had led Cambodia to complete independence in 1953 after ninety years of French colonial rule. In 1955, in order to gain real political power, he abdicated the throne and started his own National Socialist party which of course swept to victory given his 'divine' credentials with the rural masses. Then, as political leader, he embarked on an ambitious programme of development in agriculture, public health, industry and education – particularly literacy. In 1954 he had been presented with a specially-bound copy of the recently published Cambodian Bible, and had declared freedom of religion throughout the kingdom, though as yet the Protestant church had been given no official recognition.

The Bible School had reopened at Takmau just south of Phnom Penh, and several more workers had arrived to strengthen the team of missionaries. Then, with the increasing need for Cambodian Christian literature, the Gospel Press of Cambodia was set up in Phnom Penh. Here a growing number of books and tracts were printed as well as magazines, teaching aids and correspondence courses. Christian radio was also introduced into Cambodia at this time, with tapes prepared in Cambodia being sent to FEBC[1] in the Philippines for broadcasting. The church began to broaden its horizons and come into contact with other Asian evangelists and church leaders. It also recognised its missionary responsibility to the thousands of neglected hill tribes people within Cambodia (still virtually unreached when Cambodia fell in 1975) and to the Khmer *Kraom* over the southern border in South Vietnam. Special Christian youth and women's organisations were established to reach out more effectively and involve these people in church life. During this period too, Chinese churches were established in Phnom Penh and Battambang, helped by missionaries from Hong Kong.

From all over Cambodia, the churches were sending some of their choicest young men and women, mostly second generation Christians now, to be discipled at the Bible School. Along with them came other new believers, increasingly from the urban and more educated communities, including former Buddhist monks, soldiers, teachers and business people. Dozens of Bible School students during the fifties and early sixties had to endure as part of their practical training the rigours of the travelling gospel teams, or assisting pastors in isolated and difficult locations. Most were dedicated young men such as old Mr Put's faithful son, Reach Yeah (eventually to become the president of the church); the godly Pastor Chau Uth; missionary to the Khmer *Kraom*, Pastor Siang;[2] the capable Pastor Sen Boun; the internationally recognised Son Sonne; the zealous visionary and martyr, Taing Chhirc; and the faithful Lim Cheong, abandoned by his parents as a lad when he believed. These and others would form the shape of church leadership during the demanding seventies. The few who survived the horrific Khmer Rouge era (1975-1979) when most were cruelly martyred or fled, were among the hard-pressed and sought-after leaders of the decimated and confused underground church inside Cambodia during the Vietnamese occupation of the 1980s and the thinly scattered world-wide church in the Cambodian dispersion.

Among these outstanding young men whom God raised up out of Cambodia's thin soil during this season of the latter rains was one Chan Hom. Like a tender rice seedling he was taken, planted, and nourished in the fields of rural Battambang, where so much of the church was already maturing. Out of these humble beginnings this quiet and gentle man would emerge as one of Cambodia's finest pastors. He was one of only three who was kept 'hidden' by God and preserved during the Khmer Rouge reign of terror. Later, in the aftermath of that fiery crucible and following the Vietnamese invasion in 1978, he further devoted himself to serving the suffering remnant of the Battambang Church. At the same time he also found opportunity to minister quietly to young conscript soldiers of the invading Vietnamese army, who in ones and twos secretly sought him out for spiritual counsel.

In late 1979 Pastor Hom, his family, and little flock made the dangerous journey to the war-torn Thai border and there crossed over into free Thailand as refugees.[3] Here at the huge Khao I Dang camp just inside Thailand, through his exemplary life and testimony and thoughtful Bible teaching, he gave spiritual leadership to thousands of despairing Cambodians crowded into the camps. He later agreed to move to a grim and hostile detention camp for former young Khmer Rouge killer soldiers deeper inside Thailand at Sra Kaew, in order to pastor the church which was emerging even there. He is now persevering in pastoral ministry with the spiritually vulnerable believers among the Cambodian dispersion in the United States.

During the time in the refugee camps, wherever Pastor Hom and his family went, close at hand would be a quiet, partially-sighted old lady being slowly led along by one of the children. This was Rin, Hom's widowed mother and the person who had the most profound influence upon him. Whenever a crowd of neighbours and friends gathered on the porch to talk with the pastor, she could always be seen sitting quietly inside the house, back in the shadows, working patiently at some task with her hands. When her son preached she was usually there squatting close by in the crowd, her *krama* pulled up over her head to shade off the fierce tropical sun or to wipe her watering eyes, often red and painful, for she was now going blind.

From the time I came to know her as a refugee in Thailand, I perceived a deep grief in those silent tears – all the accumulated pain of recent years, of the Khmer Rouge killing time, of the traumatic flight from her homeland midst another civil war, and the loss of virtually everything she had known and cherished. And after entering a new and darkening world since 1980, and being herded about from one crowded noisy camp to another, she thought much about the past. Though blind, she could see back to a time when everything was very clear, and recall how it all began: the call of God on her life when she was just a girl in her parents' home in the village of Kokhmum in central Battambang province.

Each year young Rin would carefully push the yellow corn seeds in straight rows into the prepared soil of her father's garden. When harvest time came, she would go out to cut the ripe cobs off the tall corn stalks and carry them home in her arms, to be roasted over the charcoal fire behind the house. Curiously she would run her little fingers over the rows of smooth waxy kernels. Pressing them to her cheek as she wandered back up the path, she would often ask herself, 'Who made this corn, and the very first seeds from which it grew?' Sometimes, as she gazed out across the vast expanse of fields of gently waving and ripening rice hanging heavy in the ear, a familiar question would taunt her mind, 'What causes the rice to grow and ripen with the regular pattern of the passing seasons?'

Little Rin, troubled by these questions, began to inquire of those about her: 'Where did the sky and the earth come from? Who designed all the many kinds of trees and plants in the forest and formed the blue line of distant mountains beyond? Who thought it all up and arranged it thus and so? And what of the different varieties of animals and living creatures under, on, and above the earth, where did they first come from?'

When the local villagers laughed at her childish curiosity, she turned to the old people of the village for answers. But they just told her legends or made up some fantastic fairy story to amuse her. There was never a real answer, one which completely satisfied her mind. No one had any knowledge of these things, it seemed. Yet what was most perplexing of all was that no one even seemed to share her curiosity, at least not openly. The elders eventually just sighed and ignored her persistent questions about this and that, or why such a thing was the way it was. The honest ones simply exclaimed in exasperation, 'We don't know; no one knows.'

Rin's fertile little mind was unusually fascinated by the various religious objects and idols about the house, the 'gods' and various spirits which inhabited the fields, trees and streams, the eerie talk about the ghosts of dead villagers and the numerous relics and religious pictures to be seen everywhere. Sometimes her old grandfather would carve a tiny image of the Buddha from a molar or bone of a deceased relative. When no one was around Rin would climb up to the god shelf in her parents' home, reach out a trembling hand and touch one of the figures to see if anything would happen to her. Once, in secret, she actually lifted one of the gods down and examined it nervously, wondering to herself, 'Can this little god see me and hear me, and does he know my name? Can he really help me and answer my questions?' Then holding the little statue up before her searching eyes and looking boldly into its tiny carved face she whispered, 'Who made the earth and the sky above, and all the creatures, the trees in the forest and mountains beyond?' Listening intently, she heard only the familiar rustling of the wind in the thatch, and the crickets chirping under the floor. No voice, no fresh insight, nothing entered her mind. The plump and unresponsive figurine only trembled silently with the movement of her nervous little hands.

After that personal encounter with the 'god', Rin unconsciously began to lose her former awe for these inscrutable little images sitting silently on their shelf overhead. They were just something that had to be dusted and kept clean, and have their garlands and offerings changed regularly. Her doubts and questions persisted, but now she kept them to herself, in her heart.

When Rin reached marriageable age, a match was soon arranged by her parents with one of the young men in the village, named Chan. Like Rin, or more likely because of her precocious nature, he too began seeking answers to eternal questions. Following the ancient custom for sons to enter the monkhood for a season in order to gain merit for their aged parents' afterlife, Chan had his head shaved and went through the age-old ceremony of entering the village temple, donning the saffron robes and submitting to the discipline of a Buddhist monk for one entire dry season. He believed that here he might gain some understanding into the unsettling questions lingering in the back of his mind. Perhaps here answers could be found in the study of the ancient Buddhist writings in the Bali language which the older monks studied in the monastery, in the chanting of the sutras, or from the wisdom of the abbot and senior monks, some of whom had been in the temple since childhood. The weeks passed and he learned many deep philosophical ideas, many rules and regulations, but no one could actually tell him what or who was ultimately behind the universe and its ordered laws and patterns so apparent in the world about him. The monks, when pressed, could only reply that there was no answer except the law of cause and effect, the fixed law of *karma*. Besides, he should not be troubling his soul by agonising and questioning in this way, but seek rather to adopt a more passive attitude to the world, and through a process of self-denial live in harmony and oneness with the universe rather than try to fathom it all out. In the monastery Chan was instructed in the mystical secrets of Nirvana and the pathway to the annihilation of his human passions and desires, in a perfect cessation of normal conscious life, a kind of freezing point of perfect and sublime solitude.

To all these things Chan sought seriously to apply himself. This was unusual, because for most of the young village novices their time in the temple was just an ordeal, a ritual to go along with in order to satisfy their parents' desire for merit and security in the life beyond; more immediately, it was something that everybody else did, and it had to be got out of the way before a young man could marry. Like a stint in the army, the religious establishment and Cambodian society required this also of every young man. No one questioned it.

One hot afternoon, as was his custom, Chan had gone out just beyond the tranquil temple compound. Sitting cross-legged on a platform of split bamboo under the shade of a giant mango tree, he was engrossed in deep inner meditation. Suddenly and alarmingly, just as if someone had slapped him across the face, an uncontrollable sense of uneasiness and doubt swept like a huge tidal wave relentlessly through his mind. The old questions, which had almost been anaesthetised, now leaped back to life and were pounding through his head, making it totally impossible for him to concentrate further on emptying his mind and the cessation of striving, no matter how hard he tried. Abandoning then his inner gaze with a movement of his head and a deep sigh he focused his eyes and peered down fixedly at his weathered brown hands. His feet crossed in front of him were broad and flat, calloused by the toil of ploughing the fields. He smelled the fragrance of the warm earth beneath him and remembered he was Chan the farmer. A breeze in the upper air gently stirred the branches of the old tree, and all around he could hear the rustlings of small animals and the fluting of distant bird song emanating from a very real and wonderful world vibrant with life and warmth, movement and feeling. Voices seemed to be calling him back to what he was and where he belonged. At that moment he wanted more than anything else to leap up, throw off the long saffron robe which encumbered him, and fling himself joyfully into the arms of life. And yet the answer for which his pounding heart so ached eluded him still. If to have a passionate thirst for life was sinful for the Buddhist, then he was the chief of sinners, for he could no longer rein in the emotions, the longings, the cry of his heart.

Disorientated and confused, he glanced uneasily around, lifted himself off the bench, and walked slowly back to his cubicle in the novices' quarters. Like Lazarus in the tomb, he had stirred at the sound of a voice calling his name. But as yet the caller's face was unseen and the grave clothes bound him still.

For the remaining weeks, disillusioned and cynical, Chan went through the motions and routines of the monkhood until finally the day came when he could return home.

During the time that her husband Chan had been away in the temple and not permitted even to glance at a woman, Rin had finally found what she had been seeking for so long. A Christian team from nearby Chendu Swa village, out on dry season evangelism, had visited her village of Kokhmum. From God's Word, written in a book in the Cambodian language, they had shown her the answers to her questions; questions which had lain dormant and unresolved in her heart since as a little girl she had carried in the fresh cobs of corn from her father's garden.

Chan appeared very morose when he came home and was not really interested when his excited young wife showed him her gospel booklets and tracts. She thought it would probably be unwise, however, to tell him how she had been praying daily for him while he was at the temple. But he did not forbid her to go to Chendu Swa each week for the Christian meetings, as most husbands would have done, and sometimes he even listened when she explained enthusiastically to him portions of the teaching she was receiving.

Although he continued to work his fields and garden as usual, inside, Chan was feeling empty and rather sceptical about yet another religious system. Something deep in his soul was starving, suffering. Inner desires and eternal yearnings had been aroused, but were as yet unsatisfied. When not working, he avoided excessive company, preferring rather to remain at home, often spending hours lying on his back in a cloth hammock nursing his growing depression and internal bereavement. Devoid of any peace of mind, increasingly disgruntled and introspective, perhaps out of a longing to relate to a divinity more imminent and immediate than the vague and transcendental abstractions of Buddhism, Chan's interest turned increasingly to the spiritism and witchcraft which was rampant all about him. Thus while the winsome Rin grew in strength and security in her Christian faith, her husband sank deeper and deeper into a dark abyss of despair, into a shadowy world dominated by oppressive demons, lurking ghosts and malevolent spirits.

These ancient animistic beliefs and rituals of popular Brahmanism everywhere underlie the veneer of Theravada Buddhism, a relative latecomer to Cambodia. They are a sinister and ugly world of gods and goddesses, ghosts and restless spirits of dead ancestors, casting a long dark shadow over the lives of all the Khmer people. The power from this world is evil, fearful and capricious, and has to be appeased by costly sacrifice and ritual.

Every village has its spirit doctors and mediums who are in touch with this realm and, for a fee, will mediate, foretell the future, heal, exorcise, cast spells, effect protection, make a man virile or a woman desirable or fertile, and provide a host of other services. In truth, it is the real day to day practical and heart religion of most Khmer people. It was to this that Chan now turned, in the hope that he might be able to harness and manipulate its powers to satisfy his personal spiritual needs.

Chan and Rin had four youngsters by this time. Being but poor farmers, they, like many others, were under the constant pressure to provide for a growing family and older dependants. For a family as poor as they were, life could be very precarious. A single illness or sudden injury could spell disaster, and a whole year's crop might have to be sold in the towns to the wealthy tradesmen and money lenders, usually Chinese, to pay off accumulated debts. Such circumstances often forced the bread-winner to hire himself out to others for the meagre wages of a casual farm labourer or city coolie.

It was worrisome therefore for Rin to see Chan spending so much time and money on all kinds of spirit paraphernalia, sacrifices, and the myriad variety of images and fetishes sold by the travelling peddlers who cleverly convinced their buyers of the great power each charm had to protect miraculously, heal or impart good fortune to its owner. Rin watched her husband spend money they could ill afford in accumulating more and more of these amulets. On the one hand he slavishly adhered to the rituals and taboos associated with them, and yet on the other, was increasingly weighed down by a burden of fear and guilt mingled with frustration as each new purchase failed to meet his hopes or satisfy his intense spiritual hunger and agony of soul. He seemed to be searching for a direct path to God.

Then suddenly one evening the volcano within him erupted. Quite inexplicably, in a terrifying fit of hot anger and rage, he gathered up the enormous accumulation of demonic clutter, bundled it outside the house, and cast the whole sordid collection into the stream. All the demon things about the house, the amulets, chains and statuettes, all the pictures of ancient Indian gods and goddesses, the costly pieces of cloth inscribed with inscriptions of various incantations, texts and diagrams, and the pots of half-burned joss sticks, along with all the contents of the god shelf – in an instant Chan destroyed it all. He paused at the water's edge only long enough to throw after it all the strings and fetishes he was furiously tearing away from around his neck, waist and wrists. The task completed, totally exhausted in body and spirit, he slowly and listlessly climbed back up the ladder and threw himself down in the 'naked house', now completely exposed and vulnerable to any demonic attack.

In his anguish of mind he turned to Rin, who was sitting quietly nearby watching him. 'I am unable to bear them any longer,' he groaned, 'I have today abandoned all the guardian spirits and ancestral gods and cast them out of our home. This night I do not know how we shall sleep. I do not know how the offended spirits will now regard us. I do not know what evil they will now rain down upon our heads.' He was in great torment. His face was drawn and haggard, and his eyes red and sunken. Chan felt keenly the accumulated anger of the evil spirits. Their foul and shadowy presence was all around him and he shuddered and cringed deep within himself. His limbs felt heavy and his stomach like a great empty pit.

As the evening drew on and Rin unrolled the sleeping mats, Chan became increasingly restless. He felt 'them' suffocating him, at his throat strangling him, pressing in upon him. He was, it seemed, totally at their mercy. At about midnight he cried aloud, screaming out in agony and protest. He was aware of a strong desire to go quickly and bring fresh joss sticks and burn them about the house to appease the threatening spirits, to make some sacrifice to placate their awful wrath. And yet something restrained him. Better die than live any longer in their bondage.

Then, at about two in the morning, trembling and perspiring all over, Chan raised himself off the floor like a man in great pain and fell to his knees. The sleepless Rin looked on helplessly in fear and then amazement. Slowly, but very deliberately, he raised his tightly gripped hands to full length above his head, opened his mouth and cried out into the night. It was a prayer, the first real God-inspired supplication ever to cross his lips, 'Lord Jesus,' he called the name out several times, as if to be sure he had Christ's full attention. 'Creator of the heaven and the earth, you alone have the power to break asunder these bonds of guilt and despair which blind and imprison me; you alone can save your servant from destruction. Help me, release me, rescue me from the power of these evil forces.' Like the broken prodigal kneeling at the swine trough, he had finally come to his senses. He did not belong in the pig pen, his heavenly Father wanted him home. His heart, burning and thirsting, had been awakened to the love of God. And it was as if he saw with the eye of faith One hurrying down the way towards him with arms outstretched after long watching and waiting.

Formerly, when he had bowed before the idols, there had been a brief, passing sense of relief, but the pain and fear had always returned in greater measure than before. But now, having cried out to the living God, he felt a new power pulsating through him which was at once enervating and invigorating. He was possessed, he knew, by a great peace, by an overwhelming sense of cleanness and an acceptance far beyond his comprehension. He had been set free, forgiven. This he knew beyond doubt.

That night, while he slept long and peacefully, he dreamed that a voice from heaven called out to him: 'Do not fear, they can do nothing.' A new horizon opened out before him which was, it seemed, as limitless as heaven itself.

This was the first night when Hom's father believed and called out in faith to the Lord. His faith, along with that of his wife Rin, grew deeper and stronger until the day he left this world many years later and went home as promised to be with Jesus.

Hom was the sixth of nine children, and born after his parents Chan and Rin had become Christians. Consequently he was spared all the influence of idolatry and spiritism which normally filled the Cambodian home from birth until death. Instead he grew up in a household where God was daily worshipped, thanks were offered before every meal, and the Word of God was taught, loved and obeyed. Every Sunday all work ceased, and they went together as a family with the handful of other nearby believers over to the Christian meeting place at Chendu Swa. Whenever fierce doubts assailed the young boy, his father would take him outside into the fields and point out to him God's creation and handiwork in the vast flying sky overhead, and in the fields and trees about them. 'All these things were made by the Creator, the eternal and living God, the one who was incarnate in the Lord Jesus Christ, the Saviour of all mankind,' Chan would assure his son. 'The Buddha,' he would explain, 'was a teacher, a philosopher, a good man with a nature like ours, searching for understanding and escape from a cruel world. He himself never claimed any more than that.'

In this way, strengthened by his parents' constant teaching and example, Hom grew to adolescence with a deep personal conviction of the truth of the gospel of Christ. Like all the other village youngsters, he studied at the local school and worked hard along with the rest of the family in the rice fields and vegetable gardens. The time that Hom loved best of all, however, was early in the dry season, around November, when the nights are cool and the young men sleep at night under the dazzling starlit canopy, lying on their mats in open-sided thatch shelters erected in the fields to guard the crops and make ready for harvest-time. It was a time of refreshing breezes, rich colours, and fecundity. Here a boy could lie on his back in the shade of an anthill and gaze up at the great circling birds drifting lazily on the thermal currents high up in that fathomless deep blue sky, or listen to the distant crooning of the doves and the drowsy whirring of the cicadas, their cadences endlessly rising and falling. All about him fragrant breezes whispered softly through the shimmering rice, turning it this way and that in constant motion. And with the whole creation about him ready to explode with energy and abundance, Hom's youthful heart knew the Creator of it all, the God of the seasons who sent the early rains to soften the sun-baked fields, who caused the seeds to swell in the earth, burst with life, and send up their bright green shoots, the promise of harvest.

As a lad, Hom loved to watch the drifting clouds, imagining them as giant monsters pursuing one another across the sky, changing shape and tumbling into each other. Then by late afternoon that great grey wall which had been steadily rising across the south western horizon would darken the sky overhead. An exhilarating rush of air would send everyone scurrying for shelter, followed by a brief stillness before the sound of the first heavy drops of rain. With nightfall the stars appeared, first one, then another and another, and before long the whole night sky filled with twinkling points of light arranged in fascinating clusters and formations. Finally, to complete the picture, and like a guest arriving splendidly dressed but late for the party, in would steal the moon, emerging silently from behind the dark trees until finally in place, it seemed to stop, bathing the sky with pale silvery light. Like the seasons it too had its fixed patterns of waxing and waning, rising and falling, and the Cambodian farmers were familiar with them all. Lying there with his father in the open *sala,* wrapped in their blankets, Hom could feel his heart swelling up within him. At times he could have cried out in joy and worship to the Creator of all these things. He perceived that nothing either great or small had arisen by chance or accident, or by its own ability. Everything around him confirmed otherwise, declaring unmistakably to him the existence and power, faithfulness and love of a living God, Hom's God.

It was this keen understanding and appreciation of the creation, learned from his father since boyhood, that was the bedrock on which Hom built his faith and knowledge of God. The mysteries and laws written in the created order around him thrilled and satisfied his soul, and served as a constant reminder of his creatureliness and of the intimate and eternal relationship which existed between him and his Creator. Years later during the dark days of the Khmer Rouge reign of terror when there was virtually no Christian fellowship, no Scriptures, no freedom to worship God, Hom took daily courage and assurance from the abiding covenant written in the creation about him. Thus from a very early age Hom fixed his heart in devotion toward God.

From the age of ten Hom read the Scriptures seriously to himself every day. By the time he was in his teens he had set aside three periods each day for Bible reading and meditation. The Bible was his constant companion. He even took it out into the fields with him, in a small cloth bag slung over his shoulder, as he walked in the freshly turned furrows behind the plough, urging the oxen forward. Then at a convenient point in the ploughing he would call the oxen to halt, squat down beside the wooden plough and pull out the well-thumbed Bible. He always read slowly, aloud to himself, inwardly listening to the sacred words. He read one book at a time from beginning to end. By the age of sixteen he had carefully read the Bible through four times. And even though he did not understand everything he read, he revered every word because he knew that it was God's word to him.

These things, Hom knew, were divine mysteries from the heart of God. Here before him lay God's great design as revealed through the history of his people and the incarnation of his Son. He valued these times above all else, and desired to spend the one life God had given him in serving his Lord. He frequently accompanied his father or one of the Cambodian pastors on the Sunday afternoon evangelistic excursions to other villages, exhorting the people to repent and believe in the living God. Together they would distribute tracts and stop to pray for the sick, troubled and demon-oppressed. But his heart's desire, now as a young man, was to go and study at the Bible School. From the age of seventeen, he began to pray that God would open the way for him to prepare for full time Christian ministry.

At first his father Chan was not enthusiastic about his oldest son going off to Phnom Penh for so long. It could take four or five years, and his strong arms were needed there on the farm to help with the ploughing and harvesting. Hom, however, was not discouraged. He had his Bible, and, for the time being, he would simply have to study it himself. And so during the work breaks, with his arms and legs aching from driving the plough through the heavy clods of earth, Hom would rest his back against a tree and set to studying his Bible with renewed determination, confident that God's hand was upon him. On putting his hand to the plough again his mind was full of what he had read. He would mull it over and compare it with other passages he had read, applying it to himself or working it into a lively exhortation to an imaginary gathering of villagers.

One day Hom decided to ask God for a definite sign of confirmation that he should go to Bible School. Since the weather had been unseasonably dry, he decided to 'put out a fleece' as Gideon had done and pray for rain. In answer to his fervent prayers, the Lord sent a torrential rain for three days which almost flooded the young seedlings.

On another occasion, when his nine-year-old younger sister and he were riding home from church on their bicycles, talking excitedly together, they collided. The little girl lost control of her bicycle and went crashing to the ground, striking her head hard against a rock along the roadside. She lay absolutely still, the colour draining from her face. Hom picked her up and carried her home, but despite all attempts to revive her she remained completely motionless. About an hour later her eyes rolled back and, after a slight rattling of breath deep in her throat, she seemed to stop breathing altogether.

Hom was beside himself with worry and grief. His distraught father clearly held him totally responsible for what had happened, even though Hom had tried to explain the circumstances of the accident. His whole world seemed to have come to an end. All hope of Bible School and serving God had just died along with 'little sister', lying there pale and motionless on the floor before him. Praying and weeping in his anguish before the Lord, Hom suddenly recalled how Elijah had prayed for the dead son of the widow. So, kneeling down beside the silent form of his sister, the young man prayed with all his heart for her life to return. Three hours later, he recalls, the child opened her eyes and began breathing. A little later still, at about five in the evening, she spoke to them. Whether she had actually died or had fallen into a deep coma, we shall never know, but none of the household had any doubt that the child had indeed been returned to them. For Hom, this was yet another sign of God's presence with him for blessing.

Hom worked especially hard that year, ploughing, planting, harvesting and threshing. When all the grain had been gathered up and stored away, Chan told his son that he could go to Bible School following the spring rains and the planting. The day finally came when Hom left his village and, with a few belongings wrapped in a *krama,* boarded the train in Battambang for Phnom Penh and Bible School. He had been studying for only about six months when an urgent telegram arrived. It called him to return home at once as his father had had a serious accident.

With tears of grief and frustration Hom packed his things and prepared to leave on the early morning train north back to Battambang. It was difficult to understand why circumstances should so turn against him. The other young men, his fellow students in the dormitory, prayed with their colleague and tried to comfort him. From the railway station in Battambang, Hom hurried to the church, where he left his belongings with a sympathetic Pastor Haum and then set off for the hospital. There he found his father lying in bed with a broken right shoulder and a deep gash on his forehead. On seeing his father, the tension in Hom's heart began to ease. After attending to his needs he took the local bus north to Kokhmum, where the harvest was in full swing. He found the whole village busy in the fields, sickles in hand, working their way across the fields cutting handful by handful the ripe stalks of rice, and then tying them into sheaves for threshing. Changing into his work clothes, Hom took up a sickle and went out to join his family in the fields.

That evening his mother told him all that had happened. Everything seemed to have gone awry on that fateful day. First, during the afternoon when the women had taken the ox-cart out into the fields where the men were harvesting, the bullocks suddenly became skittish and began fighting against being yoked together. Tossing and thrashing around as if alarmed by some terrible unseen thing, they broke free from the cart shafts and galloped away, trampling down the uncut rice in a neighbour's fields before ending up in a pool beyond the village. Father retrieved and calmed them, brought the cartload of sheaves back to the granary and then decided to spend the night sleeping on the threshing floor in case thieves came to steal his grain.

Late into the night Chan was awakened by the dogs' raucous barking. Holding a lantern and calling aloud he went out to investigate. Almost immediately he was surprised by four armed bandits who threatened him with a gun. They beat him up and pushed him into a pool, leaving him for dead. By the light of an oil lamp his family, alerted by the noise, found him lying in the shallows, his head covered in blood. He was clinging to the wooden pier where the women came to do their morning washing. Unable to accomplish anything until morning they lit a fire, covered him with blankets and sat down beside him.

The news spread quickly. By morning the local spirit doctor and healers came wanting him to drink juice from the red betel nuts which they had chewed and spat out. The family brushed away their offers and haggling over money, and took him instead on a slow and painful bus journey to Battambang where there was a government hospital.

For one whole year Chan was not able to work in the fields and Hom had to stay home in order to help on the farm. That year was a tremendous test of his commitment and trust in God. Despite his own longing to be back at the Bible School, he submitted himself to God's providential overruling, and patiently worked on until his father had fully recovered his strength. As he had always done since a lad, Hom read his Bible daily in the fields. And in August 1960, now aged nineteen, he returned once again to Phnom Penh and Bible School, following the annual planting of the rice seedlings.

Besides working hard at his studies, Hom had to look for part-time work, odd jobs repairing and cleaning, in order to earn his way through Bible School. The various courses were very demanding for a country lad with little formal education. But Hom applied himself with a whole heart because he never forgot that his life had been consecrated to God, and he desired to be well equipped for whatever service God might call him to perform. The Lord was faithful to Hom, encouraging him in frequent times of discouragement and loneliness when he sorely missed his friends and family back in Kokhmum. And Hom in turn was a constant source of strength to his fellow students, many of whom were also good-hearted country people with little money, and often feeling homesick for their families and their fields. Here in the strange and busy city of Phnom Penh the sophisticated townspeople looked down on these sun-darkened uneducated rural folk with their provincial accents.

After five long years of steady work at Bible courses, theology, church history, practical assignments and one year of internship in a rural church situation, Hom graduated from the Bible School in 1965. As was the custom, he received his diploma at the main conference of the Khmer Evangelical Church held every April, about the time of the Cambodia new year. It was held at the Bible School premises at Takmau just outside Phnom Penh, on the shady banks of the Bassac River.

One month later, back in Battambang, Hom married a young woman named Saon. She too had been a student at the Bible School between 1961 and 1965, coming from the village of Kuntreang near the ancient ruins of Angkor in Siem Riep province. Hom had told his parents about his feelings for Saon, and according to custom they had gone to visit her parents in Siem Riep to ask for her hand in marriage to their son. As Saon's parents were also Christians, they were delighted that their daughter should have such a fine Christian husband. Following the wedding, Saon left her home village and went to live with Hom at Kokhmum near his family.

In July 1965, the central committee of the church in Phnom Penh asked Hom if he would move to the busy riverside town of Kampong Cham, about four hundred kilometres south east of Battambang, to assist with the church there. Hom and his young wife travelled down to their new home amid one of the worst flooding seasons to inundate the countryside in years. Many hectares of rice were washed away, a severe setback for the masses of rural Khmer whose livelihood depended on the proceeds of the annual harvest. For some, whose resources were exhausted and who were unable to buy or borrow more seed, it meant bankruptcy.

And for the seedling Cambodian church too, 1965 was a watershed. It marked the end of this fifteen year period of relative calm and growth. The 'latter rains' had now come and gone. Ahead for Hom and Saon and many other Cambodian Christians, full-time workers and lay people alike, loomed a further season of hardship and testing. They were about to be overtaken by another floodtide of opposition.

Once again, they would be forced back on their spiritual resources, as the generation before them had been in 1940, forced to look with the eye of faith away from the devastation wrought by the swirling floodwaters of their enemies foaming about their feet, to their invisible Captain. So many precious seedlings were about to be lost, each one planted with such sweat and toil only to be washed away, their frail roots torn from the good soil or hopelessly submerged in the murky tide without life-giving air. And lest they too be rendered bankrupt by all this ruin and loss, the Christians stretched out their hands in love towards heaven where their treasure was safely kept, and where the eyes of faith of patient farmers could trace the covenantal sign of his faithfulness and promise through the threatening clouds.

And out beyond the troubles of the late 1960s and unseen during the decades of the fifties and sixties, when the faith of men and women like Hom and Saon was striking deep roots in the native Cambodian soil, an insidious and malignant growth was being nurtured thousands of miles away. In the hothouses of Parisian universities, clever young middle-class Cambodians were being fed on the Western ideology of revolutionary Marxism. Soon to be transplanted back into Cambodian soil, these deadly weeds nourished by imported and toxic fertilisers would flourish and spread their poisonous black roots like a blight throughout Cambodia, threatening to choke off all other natural life. The deathly Khmer Rouge, a nascent communist movement, hardly known then, within ten years would be masters of the land, transforming Hom's beloved living fields into killing fields.

CHAPTER 6

THE THINNING

'Every branch of mine that bears no fruit,
he takes away,
And every branch that does bear fruit
he prunes,
that it may bear more fruit.'

(John 15:2)

The 'late rains' of the fifties and early sixties had left little pools of fresh clear water across the otherwise barren landscape. And around these sources of life, healthy new Christian communities began to spring up, growing heavenwards and flourishing under the care of various pastors and lay leaders, the husbandmen who watched over and cultivated them. But it was a hazardous land, still cluttered with stones and clumps of thorny bamboo whose stubborn roots permeated the soil everywhere. Under Prince Norodom Sihanouk the pervading feeling in the Kingdom of Cambodia was still that every true and patriotic Khmer must be a Buddhist. Consequently, throughout the entire period there had been a constant process of thinning, pruning and sifting taking place among the churches. This climaxed in 1965 with a major five-year crackdown against the Christians by the central government in Phnom Penh.

The life of a Cambodian pastor or full-time worker carried with it a heavy load of responsibility. There was not only considerable travelling around, trial enough to test the endurance of the best of them as they visited their small and often widely scattered flocks. But they had constantly to contend with the deadening apathy at every side, and sometimes strong opposition from those whom they sought to introduce to Christ. Also there were all the discouragements of backsliding, immorality, dishonesty, squabbling and lack of genuine self-sacrificial commitment among some of the believers.

Church leaders had no choice but to live simple and frugal lives. They were barely supported by the tithes of their equally poor members, especially in the rural areas. To this was added a small subsidy from the mission society. The mid-fifties were an especially difficult time economically, and with a devalued currency the Cambodian Christian workers were finding themselves hard-pressed to work and raise their own families with no secure income. It was at this time that the foreign mission board announced it was phasing out its monetary aid to the churches in order to encourage them to become self-supporting. This action was received with considerable dismay and reluctance by the Khmer workers and their congregations. For a few difficult and testing years it appeared that practically every worker might be lost to the church, as one by one they left their ministries to accept more lucrative employment elsewhere. Although it was a painful decision, and some might argue a time bomb which should never have been left so long before defusing, the mission stuck to its resolve in the interest of developing a strong and healthy indigenous church, and not one forever tied to the apron strings of the foreign missionary society.

It is little wonder, therefore, that all those who had 'entered the ministry' primarily because they saw it as a secure and respectable career, in which they could always rely on the patronage of wealthy foreigners for support or for other material or social perks, soon became disillusioned with the reality of gruelling and thankless toil with no substantial reward. These were among the first to be thinned out, returning to secular employment or taking up positions with other organisations willing to pay them well enough. The education, social skills and English language they had acquired at the Bible School did open other doors to them. This hireling mentality would continue to plague the church in later years, indeed right up to the present day, but especially with the arrival in the early 1970s of Christian relief organizations and various cults all eager for recruits, workers, and instant 'indigeneity' to impress the homeside support base with half-digested and popular missiological slogans, and willing of course to pay well for the Khmer 'membership'. This patronage syndrome, so entrenched throughout Khmer social, political and military culture, was to become a fundamental weakness in the Cambodian church, stunting its true indigenous growth, distorting its perception of Christian discipleship and service; exposing it to attack and ridicule, and endlessly dividing it by creating all manner of jealousies and misunderstandings within the community of believers.

By 1956, after thirty years of missionary presence, several of the apparently healthy looking plants who had made such impressive bursts of growth above ground, were found to be all but rootless in the stony Cambodian soil. Very soon they began to wilt in the oppressive heat, and vanish like the wind-driven chaff from the threshing floor.

As well as a substantial thinning of mature workers there was also an alarming decline in the number of young people willing to attend Bible School and prepare themselves for ministry. In 1958 the 'seminary' remained completely unsown, with no classes held at the Bible School. So few showed interest in attending. Then in 1959 four young men offered themselves; in 1960 six; in 1961 twelve people; and in 1962 sixteen registered. The severe pruning had cleared the dead wood for other young saplings hidden in the shadows.

For example, when Rose and Koeum's five sons each reached their teens and expressed a desire to study to serve the Lord, their mother strongly impressed upon them if it was fine clothes, human respect and esteem they were seeking, then they would certainly not find it in Christian service in Cambodia. Only those prepared to throw away their own lives and be forgetful of self should consecrate themselves to serve Christ. Later, when Mr

Prac's handsome young son Chhorn asked for Rose's daughter Roeun's hand in marriage at their graduation from Bible School, Rose required first of all from him a commitment to place Christ and his service foremost in the family's life. She was keenly aware of the strong temptations which the church workers were facing, and how young pastors and elders were falling away from serving the Lord because they wanted comfort, prestige and a better salary. Her own white-hot zeal for the kingdom of God was burned upon the hearts of all her children and grandchildren. She always expected to see them put aside all work on a Sunday and be in church together with their family members. Thus, with Chhorn's rather nervous promise to serve the Lord all his life, she consented to the marriage.

But no sooner had Chhorn and Roeun become established in a rural church ministry, and their first children started to arrive, than Chhorn began to neglect his responsibilities at the church and go off into the bush hunting for game which brought a good price at the market. Seeing he could make a comfortable living this way, he retreated further and further from the Christian community, finally moving the whole family back to Chendu Swa where he worked a large and successful banana plantation. Chhorn's heart grew very cold against the Lord and his people, to the point where he even forbade his wife and children to go to the Christian meetings.

On hearing all these things, Rose boarded a plane for the first time in her life. She travelled as quickly as she could from Phnom Penh back to Battambang, to be near her wayward son-in-law, her daughter and the grandchildren. Since she was not really welcome in their home, she would go and sit under the raised house and sing hymns aloud, or talk to the children outside. When Chhorn was in the house she would stand underneath pleading and exhorting him to return to the Lord and to bring his family back into the fellowship of the church. 'The Lord knows you, why don't you recognise him?' she would call up. 'He is coming back soon, don't waste these years away from him.' In the early afternoon when it was quiet and she knew Chhorn was resting inside she would come again to sit under the house and sing hymns. There was one chorus she often chose to sing because sometimes she could just hear him singing quietly along with her under his breath, 'I know the Lord will make a way for me.'

Rose never gave up praying for her son-in-law and imploring him to repent of his stubbornness and turn back to God. Her persistence and importunity continued for over twenty years, until one day early in 1975 just three months before the country fell to the Khmer Rouge, Chhorn finally turned his face once again to God, repented, and was restored to full fellowship in the body of Christ. Soon freedom would be gone and he would be separated from his family for six years, undergoing great suffering and trial. But the Lord had prepared a very special task for Chhorn.

In 1951, about the time Chhorn had begun his shortlived ministry, his youngest sister Song and her husband went to gain more practical experience, part way through their formal Bible School training, working with the church in Rogagong. In this busy town on the Mekong River just north of Phnom Penh, they met with particularly strident opposition and abuse. After only a few months in Rogagong they transferred to Siem Riep to work with Rose's first-born son, Tou. It was during these days that Mr Hin and his family became Christians in the village of Kuntreang in Siem Riep province. His little daughter Saon would become the wife and helpmate of Pastor Hom fifteen years later. But these individuals were exceptions. Very few people were interested in listening to the gospel, and those who did show interest were so widely dispersed that the young workers had to spend much time travelling about the primitive country roads seeking them out and following them up.

In 1952, following this period of internship in Siem Riep, Song and Ham returned to the Bible School at Takmau on the outskirts of Phnom Penh for a final year of study. On graduation they were assigned again to the difficult town of Rogagong, to build up the half dozen or so Christian families who badly needed discipling into a viable church. Ham quickly became discouraged with the arduous work, the lack of response and the painfully slow growth in the church. It seemed to him that there was never enough food, never enough time, and never enough money to live on. He began to complain and to ask the missionaries to increase his monthly salary from eight hundred *riels* to twelve hundred. When this was refused, Ham refused to work for the church any longer. Since he had acquired a good knowledge of English from studying with the foreign missionaries, he soon found a lucrative job at the US Embassy in Phnom Penh.

Song did her best to keep the family together, teaching her four children in the ways of the Lord. But as Ham prospered materially by working with the Americans, increasingly he compromised and forsook the Christian faith, falling more and more into line with the irresponsible, materialistic lifestyle of those around him. In 1960 he took another wife, and five years later abandoned faithful Song and the four children, leaving them utterly destitute. Heartbroken and very lonely, but with her faith unshaken, Song went to help at one of the two Khmer churches in Phnom Penh at that time. It was called Bethlehem Church. Here the office of the central church committee was situated. She began to help out with any task she could, giving herself to the ministry of a faithful Bible woman and servant of all. Her children matured and grew in their faith under the Bible teaching of the Pastor, Sen Boun, who was then president of the national church. Under the Lord's care and provision she lived on happily in Phnom Penh and worked at Bethlehem for ten more years, until 1975 when along with the city's entire population, then swollen to three million people, she would be driven out in that horrifying and notorious forced exodus which was ordered within hours of the Khmer Rouge victory.

Put, the former outcast and wandering orphan who had received so much help from the church all through his tragic youth, had also completed his Bible School training by the early fifties. The missionaries had found him work and subsidised his tuition fees. He was then sent north to Siem Riep to work with Grandfather Chom, one of the elders. They travelled from place to place teaching the local believers, selling Christian literature, and proclaiming the gospel in the market places or among those they found gathered at the communal wells and washing pools of the tiny hamlets which dotted the Cambodian countryside.

Put travelled around Phnom Penh, up the Mekong to the town

of Romeas, and across to areas near the Vietnam border where the infiltrating Viet Minh communists were already making travel in certain areas dangerous, just as in Battambang pockets of Issarak rebels still roamed the countryside. In Kampong Chhnang Province, he walked many miles yet sold so few Christian books, meeting just one Vietnamese Christian family who treated the weary young traveller very kindly. He usually stayed in Christian homes along the way and had just enough money for food. This he supplemented by catching fish with his boyhood skills, and finding edible plants and roots. For a year he stayed in Oudong where there was just one Christian family, but as always numerous children happily gathered to hear the Christian stories. Whenever he travelled to a new town or village it was necessary to visit the local district official and obtain written permission to sell his Christian books. Sometimes he was treated kindly and given directions and assistance, but more often he was greeted with rudeness or indifference. Threats were commonplace. In some places he was driven out of town with stones and abuse, and of course most officers could be moved only by a bribe.

On one occasion, he found himself in Siem Riep with old Chom as his companion, and as he had done so often before, he approached the local district officer to explain his coming and ask for permission to preach and sell his books.

'We are disciples and witnesses of the Lord Jesus,' he explained, 'and wish to teach and sell Christian literature in this area.' The officer's face became suddenly and inexplicably angry, and he immediately drove them out of his office. His secretary, however, who had been present and seen all this, followed the two men outside and invited them to come to his home for the night. After they had eaten with the secretary's family, the two Christians unrolled their mats and prepared for sleep, but before retiring they began to pray together, weeping and pleading before God for the town. Alarmed at the fervency of their prayers the secretary became worried for the safety of his home, fearing the spirits might be offended. So he asked the two men to leave at once.

It was already eight in the evening and pouring with rain when they stepped outside, carrying their few bundles of books and possessions. Having second thoughts, the secretary called after them that they might sleep under the house for the night but must be gone by morning. The morning light found them chilled to the bone, soaking wet and with very little money left. The sodden and pathetic packages of tracts, which they were not allowed to sell and in which it seemed no one was interested anyway, weighed heavily on their shoulders.

Mr Chom returned home after this experience and Put boarded a bus for Battambang. Here his young wife Lida, a grand-daughter of old Granny Mien who had believed thirty years earlier back among the Khmer *Kraom*, was living with her parents. His brief stay with his parents-in-law did little to lift his sagging spirits, and so he returned south to Oudong and on to Phnom Penh, totally dispirited. All along the laboured and dusty bus journey he reflected on the hopelessness of the task before him. No one was the least interested in him, in Jesus, or in his books, and most couldn't read anyway. The power and influence of Buddhism was everywhere, and as the crowded bus rattled along the dirt road he could almost hear Satan laughing and mocking at his futile efforts. 'Why don't you give up? It's a waste of time.' From everything his eye surveyed a chorus echoed back loud and clear, 'Give up, give up, give up...'

He observed the people blithely going about their business, boarding and leaving the bus as it clattered and creaked its way southward. They gossiped, they laughed, they bought and sold, they ate, they slept. They were relaxed, easy going, and content enough. This was the Cambodia the tourists saw and liked so much: peaceful, laid back, content, amiable. But a closer, more discerning scrutiny betrayed something of the darkness, despair and insecurity under which they lived. There was on many faces a blank expression of futility and emptiness. Theirs was a fatalism, a passive resignation to the poor hand *karma* had dealt them. Like the all-night card games many idled away their lives gambling over, it was as if they had simply opted out of this particular round of the game of birth, death and rebirth, in the face of all the overwhelming poverty, corruption and selfishness in the seen world, and the evil and vindictiveness of the unseen world. Perhaps in the next incarnation fate would deal them more face-cards, a few more trumps. But clearly the deck was stacked against them and there were yet many more hands, many more games to be played, and many disappointments still to come before this cruel and repetitive game of living and dying was finally over, and oblivion attained. Most never really contemplated the end of the game. It was just too distant. And anyway in their despair, they had become tragically and ironically hooked on the very lusts and passions which kept them from Nirvana, and in the game, like gamblers who simply cannot leave the table even at the prospect of misery and bankruptcy, and the loss of everything, including their own souls. The only respite was to live in a world of fantasies and illusions rather than realities. Reality was too grim a fact and beyond their control, but image could be managed, and manipulated to be an end in itself. If they couldn't have authentic faces, then they would create masks, a smiling mask for every occasion.

Most of the men not working in the fields were lazily passing the time. Faces vacant, they sat or lay around, doing nothing except fumbling with a cigarette, a habit to which virtually every man was addicted. Many worked as little as possible, and even then wasted much of what they had on smoking, opium, or bottles of cheap whisky around which they sat in small groups flushed and red-eyed, noisily singing and shouting but rarely listening to themselves or others, far into the night. On special occasions such as a marriage or death or an annual festival at the local village temple, such activities intensified, along with gambling, cock fighting, or carousing in some cheap brothel. Emboldened by a little extra merit in hand – having attended the temple ritual or sat within earshot of the monks' chanting – they felt even freer to gratify their passions. Religious occasions invariably ended in drinking, gambling and illicit sex. All this was the accepted, even expected thing, of a Khmer man.

A Khmer woman, however, strictly forbidden any such frivolity, remained at home, with the endless round-the-clock toil of working in the fields, keeping the children, cleaning, cooking and hauling water. For many, with the passing years and growing family would come the moment when it would be her turn to hear through village gossip that her man had taken an additional wife, a younger woman, probably already expecting his child. And after the noisy all-night fairs run by the temple, usually at harvest time when the farmers had some money in their pockets, her husband might contaminate her with the widespread venereal disease, be forced into debt because he had wasted his money, marry off one of her young daughters to a drinking companion for the bride price he now badly needed, or disappear for months altogether. One by one her sons would fall into the same patterns, as soon after puberty they conformed to the drinking and sex habits of their fathers and peers. Few women had a husband who would be faithful all through life.

Not surprisingly, it was usually the women who provided what stability and backbone there was in the Cambodian family. But even then, used and abused, a virtual slave both to husband and sons until grandmotherhood, even if a wife could hold herself together, she had little time or energy for nurturing her children in the inner life once they reached school age. Most ethical and social training is the domain of the school and temple where, unlike at home, external discipline and conformity was ruthlessly applied. Faithful, hard-working and selfless women tended to make up the stable majority of the church, along with their numerous little ones.

By the time the bus had pulled into the busy depot in Phnom Penh and begun unloading, Put had made his decision. He would give up. He could no longer endure working like this. Leaving his bundles of remaining books in Phnom Penh and feeling angry and bitter inside, he set off again, this time for Kampong Cham. Now he went in search of work, real work which was paid for in good wages, not in abuse and futility.

After five months of moving around from this to that, he found that the 'real world' was no more kind to him now than it had been when he was an unwanted orphan roaming the countryside. There was nothing for it but to return to Stung Jas in Battambang where his family was waiting for him. His father-in-law was very angry with Put for withdrawing from serving the Lord, so Put, exasperated, moved his wife and family away to Battambang town. For two years he supported them by working as a *cyclor* driver transporting goods and people around this bustling market town. Finally, feeling constantly the restless desire to serve the Lord again, he struck out westward towards the Thai border to bandit-ridden and malaria-infested jungle hill country where uncleared land was cheap to buy.

The first thing Put did was to carefully mark off fifteen square metres of his land and dedicate it to the Lord. Here he would build a small chapel where the living God would be worshipped and his Word taught. The Lord blessed Put, and on his sixty *rai* of paddy and vegetable gardens, which had taken five years to clear, he raised enough rice to support his entire family. At the same time he had opportunity to teach the Bible in the four-by-ten metre chapel he had raised up on stilts, and to pastor a little group of about thirty people. In return the five families of Christians each gave him forty bushels of rice per year, and some tithe money.

Put and Lida raised several children here, including Chanty their first-born, a quiet and serious lad with a strong and enduring faith, and Samuel, a good-looking but headstrong and rebellious youth who would cause his parents considerable heartache. In a most amazing way, however, this prodigal son like his 'uncle' Chhorn would be the means by which the entire family would enter into a totally new life far away from Cambodia, free finally from the constant poverty and insecurity that Mr Put had known since he was abandoned as a small boy.

Chhorn, Ham and Put were typical of many who during these years were severely harrowed and pruned by the gardener's hand. Some, like Mr Put, soon regained their uprightness after being bruised by initial failures and discouragements, and went on to bear good fruit for the kingdom of God. But for others, like Chhorn, completely cast down by circumstances, it took many years and much prayer before they turned their faces back once more to the light of the Son.

During these years, several of the early Christians who had believed in the 1920s among the Khmer *Kraom* and in

Battambang died. The first missionary to Battambang, David Ellison, died in 1962, and was buried in the land he loved. The Cambodian Christians with deep mourning and thankfulness laid his body to rest with others already filling the little Christian graveyard in Phnom Penh.

In 1965 and for the next five years, the master gardener's pruning knife would be severely applied to prominent workers in the church, for he had in mind a rich harvest greater than they could ever have imagined. Back in 1955 King Sihanouk had abdicated, giving the throne over to his father Prince Suramarit, in order to become an absolute Head of State. In this position he could wield real political power and at the same time maintain and exploit the popular support he enjoyed as a semi-divine royal personage with all the attendant mystique of 'divine' protector, provider and even rainmaker.

With the war escalating in neighbouring Vietnam between the communist north and the American-backed south, Sihanouk was under pressure from the Vietcong communists to allow them increased access to sanctuaries in Cambodia along the South Vietnam border. From there they could infiltrate into South Vietnam their soldiers, weapons and supplies from China down the Ho Chi Minh trail from North Vietnam and Laos, in addition to using the Cambodian port at Sihanoukville. Taking the historical course of expediency and pragmatism, and thinking by placating the powerful north Vietnamese, he could maintain Cambodia as an 'island of peace and neutrality', Sihanouk allowed Cambodia's eastern border to be overrun and used by the North Vietnamese. He also began to adopt an increasingly hostile posture towards the United States. Following government-orchestrated demonstrations outside the American Embassy and a considerable propaganda campaign against the United States and the CIA, the Embassy was closed in 1965 and all American citizens expelled from the country. This included also virtually all the missionaries who had to leave as their visas expired and were not renewed.

Once again the Protestant church was identified with the latest national enemy, this time America, and denounced as an arm of the CIA. Almost immediately persecution broke out against the

Khmer Christians. In Phnom Penh, where opposition to the church was most severe, Pastor Sen Boun of Bethlehem Church was national church president, Pastor Hok of Bethany Church was vice president, Pastor Reach Yeah (Put's son Yeah) was treasurer and Elder Un was secretary. With the withdrawal of the missionaries, these men suddenly had thrust upon them the full weight of the financial and administrative affairs of the churches, publishing house, Bible School and other church property. At the same time they found themselves facing an increasingly antagonistic government, and a hostile people whose suspicion had been aroused through malicious propaganda against the church.

The trouble began one Friday afternoon during the weekly evangelistic meeting at Bethany Church. A mob gathered outside and began throwing stones and filth at the church. During the next few days windows were broken, anti-Christian slogans daubed on the walls and a brick was hurled through the glass display case containing Cambodian Bibles. Holding meetings in the church was becoming very dangerous and the believers were constantly being threatened and intimidated.

Finally, some government officials arrived at the church 'to survey the damage'. They declared that in order 'to protect the church and Christians from further damage', and to keep public order, the church would have to close. The Christian leaders were required to sign an official form agreeing not to hold any more Christian meetings without government approval. Not realising then that the entire chain of events had been cleverly set up, and that the government had no intention of ever giving the Christians permission to meet, the church central committee members signed the document agreeing to close the church, 'for its own protection' until 'the troubles' abated. However, whenever they went seeking permission from the Department of Religious Affairs to hold a church meeting, it was always refused. Although unable to obtain written permission Elders Un, Yos, Sonne and Cheong of Bethany Church were determined to continue their Christian activities, and were given oral consent by the officials to hold meetings in the church. Directly following the next meeting, however, police and government officials arrived at the church and arrested the four men for violating the original signed agreement and for holding an unlawful assembly. The Christians, it seemed, were being maliciously manipulated and abused.

At the prison, the four men were pushed into a single cell with a number of other people awaiting trial. Wasting no time they set themselves to pray for God's strength and wisdom, to sing hymns of praise and to bear witness to their faith in Jesus Christ to the other prisoners. During the several weeks they were detained, virtually all the twelve other prisoners in the cell came to believe in the Lord Jesus and joined them in prayer. When the guards threatened to put the Christians into solitary confinement if they would not cease their evangelistic activities, Elder Un replied that it would be of no avail, for he would continue to sing of God's grace and salvation at the top of his voice for all in the jail to hear.

While the four men waited in jail, a young Cambodian army officer, a fellow believer and member of Bethany Church, came to stand each day outside the prison gate. He waved no placards nor raised his voice in protest, but simply stood quietly for a time as a silent yet clearly visible testimony. All would know that here was a Christian unmoved in his faith, despite harassment from the government, standing in support of his brothers held behind these prison walls. This remarkable young man was Taing Chhirc, a Christian from Kampong Cham, whose energy and vision for the kingdom of God was already beginning to be felt in the church. Later he would emerge as one of the pillars of the Khmer Evangelical Church and ultimately one of its greatest martyrs. Those inside the jail, thus tested and tried, would also go on to bear much fruit in the subsequent years.

When finally the men were tried and sentenced, they were immediately set free because they had already served the required jail term while awaiting trial. The church was being pulled together in an unprecedented way as the Christians waited in prayer and were active in concern one for another. The persecution which had started in Phnom Penh gradually spread out into the provinces, and for the next five years until 1970, as the troubles and hardships continued, most of the dead wood and leafy foliage in the church was hewn away. Some believers, like

Un, quickly left the city and disappeared into the countryside where they continued to hold small house meetings, supporting themselves with their own hands and through the tithes and shared offerings of the whole church.

Young Pastor Hom and his wife persevered meanwhile in their work in and around Kampong Cham, urging the young Christians not to veer away from God's straight path or compromise with the world despite these difficult times of testing. Some found Hom's admonishing too hard to accept. Under the enormous weight of pressure to show themselves 'true patriotic Khmers' and to conform to the overwhelming majority, they slipped gradually back into their former pagan rituals and customs. The wide and unrestricting path of expediency and least resistance was irresistible to many. Hom and his wife were frequently short of money, for now there were no western funds to fall back on or missionaries to consult with when complex problems arose. Men of lesser faith would certainly have given up working in a situation like Kampong Cham, with only three Christian families in the town and a few others scattered in surrounding villages in an eighty kilometre radius. Most of these could only be reached on foot. But Hom did not allow the adversities of those years to undermine his faith. Rather he turned them into opportunities to prove his Lord's faithfulness and goodness.

This was a season in which the Lord seemed to be selecting and setting apart a number of especially chosen individuals.

The 1960s saw the emergence within the church of a growing group of well-educated urbanites, professionals with gifts of administration, leadership and Bible teaching. Foremost among these visionaries were Son Sonne and Taing Chhirc. And yet, in virtually every case, those with the patience, quiet humility, gentleness and love required for the pastoral ministry were the country people. Prominent among these were old Mr Put's son Reach Yeah. Like most of that first generation of Cambodian believers, Mr Put had died by 1965. Perhaps it was the rigour of life in rural Cambodia in those days that perfected these remarkable pastoral qualities in committed men like Pastor Hom and Pastor Reach Yeah.

Within just twelve years from 1953, following his one year of internship prior to graduation from the Bible School, until 1965, Reach Yeah had served in most of the main Christian centres in Cambodia. First, over in the border province of Prey Veng assisting Pastor Sok, then in Phnom Penh with Pastor Hok, and finally as a pastor himself in Kampot. This was followed by a time working to make taped teaching lessons for a Christian radio programme in Phnom Penh. Following his marriage in 1957 he worked among the villages of central Battambang with the ageing Pastor Haum.

In 1963 came a call to minister in the church at Kampong Thom. Here, like his colleague Hom in neighbouring Kampong Cham province, Reach Yeah learned what it meant to live truly by faith alone. From time to time they found themselves with no money left and the last of their rice supply used up, only to see the Lord provide for their needs in all kinds of unexpected ways. Here Reach Yeah personally experienced open persecution, being named by the local police as a traitor to the homeland and a betrayer of the Khmer people. In response he invited the police chief to come to the Christian meetings, in order to identify exactly where the treachery in his teaching lay. But the policeman who came could find no fault, and eventually the one who had been sent to spy on him for two months, himself found the Lord.

In 1965, when the missionaries were expelled and the official persecution against the national church began, Reach Yeah was called back to Phnom Penh to oversee the Bible School. He was also appointed treasurer of the central church committee. Amid strong government hatred, with churches being closed and padlocked one by one across the country, Reach Yeah learned the meaning and power of importunate prayer. He began to discern also the wisdom of providence in all the present troubles. The Christians were now meeting quietly in people's homes and experiencing a new oneness and fellowship in Christ. The genuine believers were clearly distinguishable from the others. Gifts and talents formerly hidden were discovered and used. Most of all, Reach Yeah recognised the tremendous value of learning obedience and endurance, and the considerable inner strength which the church was gaining with each new obstacle and attack.

The church was also being forced to organise itself properly under national leadership if it wanted any kind of official approval or recognition. They had to prove to the government that the Khmers were really in control of church affairs and capable of leading an efficiently ordered and administered church body. In the difficult war years of 1940-45, great strides had been made in this direction. But, sadly, the church had regressed when the missionaries returned and took over these responsibilities again. Reach Yeah recalled the decline in faith and commitment which had ensued then, and wanted it to be very different this time. Cambodian Christians had to learn to stand on their own feet with a clear vision of God before them.

The year 1965 marked a kind of coming of age. The Khmer church could never be the same again, and men like Pastor Yeah were determined that it should never be allowed to slip back into a state of lethargy and dependence. Surely after forty years they were ready to stand mature in Christ! If and when the missionaries returned, their relationship with the church and their responsibilities would have to be carefully negotiated. It would be necessary to emphasise the importance of the Khmer church managing its own affairs, fully supporting itself, and realising its obligation to take the gospel to all Cambodians, both within and around the country's borders.

In 1968 Reach Yeah became vice president of the national church committee, and with the situation stabilised in Phnom Penh he moved south to pastor a new church which was taking root in the strategic south coast seaport town of Sihanoukville.

Those vital years of thinning and pruning had effectively removed much that had been stunting and choking the church's spiritual growth. There had been fifty long years of breaking up the fallow ground, sowing the seed, tending the young plants, resisting the various pestilences, waiting for the early and late rains, enduring the painful process of thinning and pruning. But now 1970 was at hand, a great watershed year in the history of the Cambodian church, with the fields finally ripening for harvest. When that harvest season arrived there were numbered in the

whole of Cambodia only about three hundred Christians, the same
number as Gideon's army.

CHAPTER 7

THE FIELDS WHITE UNTO HARVEST

'The kingdom of God is as if a man should scatter
seed upon the ground, and should sleep and rise
night and day, and the seed should sprout and grow,
he knows not how. The earth produces of itself
first the blade, then the ear, then the full grain
in the ear. But when the grain is ripe, at once
he puts in the sickle, because the harvest has come.'

(Mark 4: 26-29)

The painful five-year period of pruning and thinning came to an abrupt end in 1970. The Cambodian church had been so harshly cut back during the preceding season of government suppression and virtual isolation from any outside help, that it was a small and hardy band of believers indeed which now remained loyal to Jesus Christ. In 1965, Cambodia had about seven hundred baptised believers with some two thousand adherents. In 1970 the total number stood at about three hundred souls, the size of Gideon's army after the Lord had finished sifting them out for the battle ahead. Before them lay yet another five-year-long season, not of pestilence and attack this time, but of unprecedented freedom for growth, fruitfulness and harvest, and all of this, amazingly, at a time of political upheaval, massive carpet bombing and cruel civil war.

In 1970, we begin to see a surreal aspect in the portrait of the

Cambodian church. Set against the familiar background of Cambodia's fields, sharply contrasting images emerge, images of war and peace, agony and ecstasy. No longer, outwardly at least, a hated and despised people, the Christians were to become a high profile, sought out people. After decades of ploughing and sowing with weeping, of tending and patient waiting, in the face of almost constant threat, the harvest season finally arrived.

Fellow workers with God had faithfully planted and watered for fifty long years, and now he made it all grow. Looking out over the vast Cambodian fields in 1970, disciples of Jesus saw fields white unto harvest. Before them lay the potential for a great ingathering. In a complete reversal of circumstances, all that had up until now loomed as an insurmountable obstacle to the church's breakthrough was now itself under attack and rapidly crumbling. The powerful and petulant Prince Sihanouk, ancestral head of Cambodia and divine head of the entire Buddhist hierarchy was toppled in a right wing military-led *coup d'etat* on March 18, 1970.

Despite the ebb and flow of great power rivalry in South East Asia, following World War II, Sihanouk had skilfully performed a kind of high wire balancing act of neutrality. But in the late 1960s he had leaned over rather dangerously to the left, allowing the North Vietnamese communists to use eastern Cambodia as a sanctuary for military bases and supply dumps in their war against the US backed regime in South Vietnam. The virtual Vietnamese occupation of eastern Cambodia which resulted, inflamed the Cambodians' deep and historical hatred of the Vietnamese, culminating in a right wing backlash against Sihanouk's growing pro-Vietnamese, anti-US position. Immediately following his downfall a massive outpouring of rage erupted against the Vietnamese community in Cambodia. Those who bore the immediate brunt of this pent-up anger were the nearly half-a-million Vietnamese people living in the cities. The slogan was 'Rid ourselves of the Vietnamese cholera'. In a bloody rampage in Phnom Penh on the night of April 13, 1970, seven thousand Vietnamese people were massacred. A thousand bodies were seen floating down the Mekong River past the city. Up to 200,000 others were then forcibly repatriated to South Vietnam This included much of the Roman Catholic Church. The small Vietnamese Evangelical Church building, now empty, was handed over to the Cambodian Christians. They named it Bethel, and along with Bethlehem and Bethany, it became part of that significant nucleus of churches in Phnom Penh, around which the subsequent people's movement would gravitate. This movement would expand outwards in ever widening circles across a capital soon to be swollen by refugees, bringing the population to somewhere approaching three million people.

Sihanouk fell from his high position, leftwards, into the outstretched arms of China. Here from his refuge in Peking, he became titular head of the Cambodian communist insurgents, dubbed by him 'the Khmer Rouge' years earlier when he was violently hunting them down in the late 1960s, ironically, though characteristically, just before he joined forces with them. Of course the Khmer Rouge never trusted Sihanouk then and still don't, though he is their most useful tool. They are simply of mutual benefit to each other as they doggedly pursue their own objectives regardless of the cost to the Cambodian 'little people' whom both purport to love and serve.

Now in unholy alliance they were openly at war with the new US-backed military government of General Lon Nol in Phnom Penh. Vietnamese communist forces now unashamedly swept westwards across Cambodia in support of their communist Khmer Rouge comrades. To the Cambodian military and intellectuals on the Lon Nol side it was as if war for national survival had been forced upon them. An extract from an open letter from the Congress of Cambodian Intellectuals (May 12, 1970) read: '…We ask you to remember that this is not a civil war. Cambodia has been invaded by foreign enemies, the Vietcong and the north Vietnamese…'

By 1972, however, with most of Cambodia overrun, the Vietnamese began to withdraw, replacing themselves with their Khmer protégés, the growing Khmer Rouge forces. Now the war became in fact a civil war with Cambodians killing Cambodians. One side was supported by the communist bloc and the other by the United States and her allies. The Khmer Rouge themselves at this time were a classic Leninist style popular front of all groups who opposed the enemy, Lon Nol regime. They included monarchists, liberals, Marxists, intellectuals and peasants. The cadres however were of two main varieties united for the present in their fight against the common enemy. There were the French educated intellectuals and their guerrilla bands who had long been fighting the Cambodian governments of Sihanouk. These were supported largely by China. And there were the cadres educated in North Vietnam and ideologically more akin to Ho Chi Minh. Now, together, with their growing peasant army and Spartan discipline, they, like Mao before them, set out to capture the countryside, encircle the cities reeling under the weight of refugees, and then slowly choke these towns to death. Prince Sihanouk, their new found ally and chief of staff served as an excellent bait, given the divine almost infallible status he enjoyed among the masses of peasantry. However, like all bait, when the fish is caught the bait is cast aside. But for the duration of the war, the Khmer Rouge leadership allowed the masses to believe that victory would mean the return of Sihanouk and all that he embodied of traditional Cambodian life and patriotic Buddhism. Secretly however, among the cadres he was no more than a puppet, a man never to be trusted. The Khmer Rouge were brilliant liars and by such means manipulated and deceived the Cambodian peasant masses who naively trusted them as fellow Khmers, and gave them the benefit of the doubt. This emotive appeal to Khmer nationalism and racism, continued to be used to great effect by the Khmer Rouge after their victory in 1975 and to the present day by all the Khmer political parties.

As the communists captured village after village and consolidated their control over the countryside, the people fled in terror to a handful of cities which dotted the landscape like beleaguered fortresses swollen with tens of thousands of hungry and sick refugees. Here the Lon Nol regime struggled to hold on to power, its energy being slowly but surely dissipated by the rampant corruption which massive aid handouts invariably brings, the dead weight of millions of needy refugees which the Khmer Rouge drove ahead of them, the need to protect large and unruly urban centres where infiltration was so easy, increasing apathy and war fatigue, and a lack of motivation to fight a war which involved killing fellow Cambodians. If the war began with a zeal for Cambodian nationalism and independence, on both sides it was increasingly becoming America's war.

The refugees brought with them terrifying reports of life in the 'liberated' zones under the Khmer Rouge. But since this did not suit the largely liberal and anti-American prejudice of the western media, it received little coverage or was arrogantly dismissed as exaggeration. It must be remembered that the modern liberal western media not only report what is news, but frequently decide, and even create what is news. (Under the beguiling creed of 'freedom of speech', they keep us captive to their own view of things, and unlike those they write about, remain largely immune from accountability or censure.) The fear and suffering in the countryside was compounded by the massive American bombing in what proved to be a futile effort to defeat Khmer Rouge guerrilla warfare. In fact it actually served to confirm Khmer Rouge propaganda that the Americans were the real enemy, destroying the countryside and the people by raining down their deadly cargoes of bombs and napalm on the people's villages and fields. At such times, the Khmer Rouge, often forewarned through their vast network of spies which had infiltrated the corrupt Cambodian military, withdrew to the safety of underground shelters or populated areas, returning when the raids were over and the farmland destroyed.

Thus the ranks of the Khmer Rouge swelled, as many of the peasant folk fought with the Khmer Rouge against what appeared to them to be a corrupt and exploitive military dictatorship backed by the terrifying B52 bombers of the USA. The peasants had known years of poverty and indebtedness to rich Chinese merchants, and the Khmer Rouge revolution promised them a new life of justice and equality for all, and the return of the highly romanticised and fatherly Prince Sihanouk. The entire country of Cambodia which up until now had been 'an island of tranquillity' midst the wars raging in neighbouring Vietnam and Laos, was overnight transformed into a vast battlefield of burned out villages, unburied dead, bomb craters, terror-stricken refugees, and a breakdown of all normal agriculture, education, trade and commerce.

The Khmer Rouge were fellow-Cambodians, yes, but they were burning down the Buddhist temples, smashing the sacred idols, and shedding much innocent blood – things which a Buddhist should never do. Aware that their lives were in danger, most people fled to the cities for reasons of sheer survival. Here protection, food, and medicine were said to be available. Caught up in this maelstrom of terror and death, all their old supports and securities in ruins, they found themselves not only physically endangered and displaced, but spiritually alienated also. Eternity stared them in the face; the old societal norms, the traditional ethics, the balance and counter-balance of Cambodian society was crumbling. They were in a spiritual vacuum, in a precarious and bewildering state of limbo. It was not possible even for the resilient and willowy Buddhist Khmers to bend with the wind this time, for the force was hurricane-like, levelling everything in its path. There was no middle way this time, no golden mean, no expedient path of least resistance. The choice was either to join them, stand and fight them, or be swept away. In such a state of confusion they found themselves in search of fresh spiritual bearings. Many had no heart to erect new idols when the old were destroyed. Had their *karma,* indeed the *karma* of the whole nation really been that bad? Had centuries of merit-making brought them to this? The ones who especially questioned and weighed up the old beliefs in the light of the harsh and compelling realities about them were the students, the intellectuals, the middle class; and it was these who made up a large proportion of the population which had fled to the cities in the face of the Khmer Rouge advance. It was they who had supported the overthrow of Sihanouk's tottering regime, and danced in the streets at the proclamation of the Khmer Republic on October 19, 1970. They had dared to overthrow the last Khmer god-king after centuries of Cambodian kings stretching back to the glorious days of Angkor. And it was they who now began seeking out the humble meeting places of a handful of Christians.

To the churches of Bethel, Bethlehem and Bethany they came, to home meetings and backyard assemblies, to packed home fellowships and to impromptu Bible studies in the shade of a nearby tree. They were found early in the mornings, waiting on the doorsteps of Christian homes; they purchased Bibles and hymn books and anxiously sought out those who would tell them about God, this living and creator God, and Jesus the Saviour. Some Buddhist monks recalled old prophecies. One in particular spoke of a coming time of terrible war when 'a great one, a god' would come to the 'place where four rivers meet' (Phnom Penh), 'with scars in his hands, his feet and side'.

The handful of pastors, just six in all, mostly of peasant stock, and the three church centres of Bethlehem, Bethany and Bethel were swamped with new believers and inquirers. Over the next five years these churches would bear fruit a hundredfold as daughter churches, spontaneous fellowships and cell groups sprang up all across the crowded city. They appeared as havens of sanity, or oases of peace and refreshment from the surrounding madness. They were like beacons shining out across a sea of darkness in which millions were drowning. Finally, their hour had come after so long, and at a time of indescribable suffering and anguish for Cambodia.

The popular myth in the West that Cambodians are a gentle and passive people has never been the experience of Cambodian Christians. Their fellow Cambodians were their merciless and vindictive persecutors. It is highly doubtful whether this myth even stands the test of history, for the Khmers have always been known by their neighbours as a cruel and feuding people who made good mercenaries. This civil war, the Khmer Rouge regime which followed it and the ongoing belligerence which continues makes it abundantly clear that gentleness and tolerance are but a thin veneer of religiosity, image and symbol. Reality is, and always has been, quite a different matter. Whether on the basic level of family life, or village and national affairs, violence, jealousy, deceit and revenge were a way of life. Keeping up the facade is just that, because facade is emotionally important to

Cambodians; and maintaining an external harmony is an integral part of social ethics imbibed from an early age.

The euphoric dancing in the streets, the rejoicing at the overthrow of the 'monarchy' in 1970, and the anticipation of the start of a new era of democracy and republicanism, the orchestrated demonstrations, (pro-American this time), all soon passed away as the truth that the pristine Khmer Republic was a government under siege, corrupt, and dependent entirely on the USA for its military and economic survival. And even that looked increasingly doubtful with the struggles of President Nixon drowning in Watergate.

The small Christian community in Phnom Penh beheld the cataclysmic events of March 1970 from afar. What would it all mean for the church? President Lon Nol and his increasingly dictatorial government was entirely dedicated to the Buddhist system. It was said he had a special room full of idols, and like Sihanouk before him, consulted spirit mediums and astrologers before making any major decision. The army and backbone of the regime was totally permeated by superstition. Soldiers' bodies were marked by tattoos, and fetishes were sewn into their garments or hung heavily in dangling clusters about their necks. These little carvings and images were all for divine protection against bullets and sickness, or to make them virile and macho in the booming underworld of brothels, bars and casinos. Even the war planes, guns and shells were blessed in religious rituals, sprinkled with holy water by chanting monks. Coloured cloths and other magical markings could be seen adhering here and there to military hardware. There would be little genuine sympathy for indigenous Khmer Christianity from this government and its powerful war machine, the entire focus of the Republic's attention.

If on the other hand the Khmer Rouge were victorious, the Christians knew they would lose all freedom to serve and worship God, and prominent ones among them would be slain. For the moment, however, the missionaries had returned after a five year absence (1965-70), and from among the desperate people there was suddenly this unprecedented interest and respect for the church.

A new generation of young intellectuals was also making its

presence felt in the church. Some of these were fluent in French and English, had been trained overseas, and were returning with new and innovative ideas. Some held high and prestigious positions in the government service, the military and various professions. This created some problems for the church's old guard who were unsophisticated rural people and not as at home in this new high powered and aggressive urban setting with an increasingly western feel about it. The familiar slow-moving committees made up of the few congenial elders and faithful old pastors were being overshadowed by this new wave of enthusiastic youngsters, and a vibrant urban laity now filling the churches. The centre of gravity was quickly moving away from the uniform establishment of a small inter-married rural Christian community, and the one denominational mission to whom all were unquestioningly loyal, into the hands of a dynamic new people movement centred in the crowded and besieged cities. Had all these things not come to such an abrupt end in 1975, there can be no doubt that the evangelical church would have divided into several groups following certain powerful and charismatic local leaders, as well as differing doctrinal emphases and worship forms. This would eventually come to pass fifteen years later in the 1990s.

While it was exciting to see such a massive response to the gospel, it nevertheless grieved men like Pastor Yeah, President of the National Evangelical Church, to see the growing disregard for the views of established leaders, as young Christians went for new ideas and novel, unknown ways.

Some of these men had found new financial sponsors, were loyal to other foreign teachers, or enjoyed lucrative and prestigious jobs with the new powerful and influential relief organisations. With such status, money, relief aid, and the English language, almost any door could be opened during the years of the Khmer Republic. While some used these new opportunities well, and to the glory of God, others abused them, creating divisions as they built their own personal empires. This problem too remains even more acute in the 1990s.

Despite the tensions and pitfalls the new realities brought, what was happening in Cambodia was undeniably a deep and profound movement of the Holy Spirit amongst its once ambivalent people. A spiritual restlessness now existed, a hunger for truth. There was a growing awareness of personal and societal sinfulness, and a sincere desire for the person of Jesus Christ accompanied by a zeal and urgency to tell others about him. The entire church it seemed was mobilised in making Christ known to half the nation now crowded like a captive audience into Phnom Penh and Battambang and the other cities. Ordinary young Christians rumoured the gospel to those around them, especially to family members, fellow students, and neighbours. The gospel of Jesus Christ was quite literally news, very good news, backed up by action, and it was sounding far and wide. The message that Jesus Christ was actually alive, a living Saviour who offered forgiveness, reconciliation, and eternal life now in the context of all the disintegration, alienation, and death, had the effect of a spark falling on dry tinder. It caught fire and burned brightly in hearts and souls once spiritually dead, and barren of all hope. Over the five year period from 1970 to 1975, the three leading churches in Phnom Penh exploded into thirty major centres of worship, as well as countless other cell groups and home fellowships. Towards the end, it became impossible, even irrelevant, to attempt to total the number of churches and house groups flourishing all across the beleaguered city and surrounding refugee shanty towns.

If you had been a Christian for a year or two in Cambodia in those days, why, you were an old Christian, and at least had your own house group, Bible study, or outreach programme. Ordinary young lay believers initiated ministry, for example, to the many crippled soldiers being dumped daily in the city centre. They were transported in on trucks from nearby battlefields around the city perimeter. These men were of no further use to the Republic. When the Khmer Rouge came, their injuries would condemn them to certain death. But for now they and their pathetic families lingered on in squalor and despair. Other Christians sought out the numerous orphans and ragged children who inhabited gutted buildings, forming their own pitiful communities across the city. Then there were the crowded hospitals and the schools which functioned intermittently. All were targeted for visitation. But above all were the teeming acres of shanties hastily thrown together, clinging desperately like so many orphaned children all about the fraying skirts of the once elegant capital; or again, like too many drowning men hanging on to an already swamped and sinking lifeboat. These refugees from the hinterland were all trying to eke out a living, ward off endemic sickness, and find some meaning or semblance of order to their distraught and shattered lives.

One graphic example of a church which sprang to life out of such circumstances was that of the old abandoned houseboat rotting high and dry on the banks of the Mekong River. Nothing but the river stood between it and the communists' front lines on the opposite shore. The owner was a believer, just six months in Christ, from Bethlehem Church. Along with some of the Bible school students who had started evangelising in the area, he had the boat patched up and turned into a Christian meeting place. 'Noah's Church' they called it. And with the sound of rockets whirring overhead, and the exploding of shells and bombs across the river, scores of people came here to seek out and worship the person of Jesus whose loving presence so filled this humble little ark of refuge. Though grounded in the middle of a field of vegetables, it 'floated' buoyantly above the rising tide of destruction which was surging all around it. The Bible School students who daily conducted services, prayer meetings, and Bible studies were typical of most Bible School students at that time. They were bearing responsibilities normally considered far beyond their years. Still other Christians flocked to lean-tos, old warehouses, or the shade of spreading trees. But in every place there was an unmistakable sense of single-minded urgency, a nationwide crisis of salvation, allied with a deep and sincere devotion to Christ. Theirs was a disciplined, innovative and rugged kind of piety, born out of the daily necessity to look to God alone for the wherewithal for life itself, and for strength and perseverance to endure one day at a time.

No one who witnessed these things could ever forget the compelling fragrance of the knowledge of Christ among those who in such self-forgetful ways ministered to those multitudes who for many reasons were being moved to seek God. The memory is of overworked, dedicated, mostly young men and women, tirelessly and patiently exhorting their alienated people to repent and believe the gospel. They seemed to be totally unmindful of themselves or of the foreboding and constant dull rumble of gunfire beyond the city which grew louder and louder with the passing months. There was something in their bearing which betrayed an allegiance elsewhere. Their minds were not set on earthly things. And there was about them the awesomeness of something which is indestructible. Each was possessed by a peace, and yet a pressing sense of vocation. Graceful and slender young women, poised and confident, dressed in traditional crisp white blouses and black floor-length sarongs, the red bound Scriptures clasped in their hands, hurried here and there in bands of fours and fives, busy with the business of the gospel of Christ crucified.

Youths in their prime, possessed by a seeming endless energy and purpose, the day's agenda set before them, travelled on foot, bicycles, *cyclor* and ubiquitous mopeds. Likewise scurrying from meeting to meeting all across the seething city; studying, visiting, teaching, preaching, praying, pleading, planning, proclaiming, exhorting – in constant motion. Here a group, heads bowed, Bibles held tightly to their breasts, sitting on the kerb at an isolated intersection. There a man, the perspiration shining on his animated face, arms extended, voice straining above the city's incessant noise and commotion, declaring the way of salvation to a rapt and attentive crowd: sitting, standing, peering in wide-eyed at all the windows, straddling the beams above his head; while outside, trying to get in, still others pressing in around the walls and openings, straining to pick up a few words, crouching to jot down some vital phrase caught as the speaker turned in their direction.

These young lay people and Bible School students not only gave out, but were eager to take in all the teaching they could. The best of them hung on every word which the few teachers they had spoke to them, transferring it from head to heart, reflecting on its meaning and immediate application both to self and others in this time of crisis. There was little place for accumulating knowledge as an end in itself. All teaching, especially at the Bible School, was now being discussed in terms of its practical application, since almost all the students were deeply involved in the service of Christ somewhere in the city, and came to classes with their minds overflowing with questions.

Most devoted their quieter waking moments to prayer. It was not uncommon at such times to come upon a group of them prostrate before the Lord, lying on their stomachs, bent over, heads to the ground, voicing out their adoration and supplications with great urgency and with tears. Spiritual friendships were forged among them as common burdens drew them together into tightly knit teams of twos and threes. One came to recognise and associate them in terms of these common bonds and visions which bound them together. Together they served, and so it appears, when the time came, together they grieved, and together they died. The sheer quality of their living and dying bore compelling testimony to Jesus Christ as Lord.

The discerning onlooker would have perceived in Phnom Penh during these days two kingdoms converging together and yet worlds apart. The kingdom of man and this world seen everywhere in the horror, the fear, armed soldiers, barbed wire, shattered bodies of innocent street vendors and other civilian passers-by, hit by flying red hot jagged shrapnel from the rockets which fell haphazard and unaimed all over the city; busy brothels, beggars, drunken loutish soldiers, noisy bands of ragged and unwanted orphans and street urchins; and the passing limousines of those who were doing very well out of it all. All these things the world's press, and TV cameras rushed to record. But there was another people, a people normally relegated to the margins of popular esteem. A people composed of those who were no longer unloved orphans out on the streets, but sons and daughters of the living God, members of the household of God and heirs to the kingdom of heaven. Into their lives the kingdom of God had come with its power, holiness and authority. Their God had not just looked down, he had rent the heavens and come down, down even into the suffering and filth of Cambodia. And they knew that even death and the grave would not separate them from him. For he had been there too, and beyond, to that uttermost point of distance from God. And now they need never have to cry in imminent death, 'My God, my God, why have you forsaken me?' Such was the ripeness of the harvest. Such was the quality and labour of the reapers. And such was the abundance of the ingathering. Under the relentless Cambodian sun, the fields were alive, white unto harvest.

By mid 1973, three years into the war, significant signs of new growth could clearly be discerned all over the Cambodian Evangelical churches. Certain critical events were now taking place which would further strengthen the resolve of the Christians, and expose the precarious state of the Cambodian government, the Khmer Republic. As time in Cambodia ticked away, the pace and intensity of the warfare, both spiritual and political, intensified.

Far away from the horrors of Cambodia in the tranquillity of the English Lake District, Taing Chhirc was holding the 1973 Keswick Convention spellbound as he addressed that large assembly of Christians regarding the spiritual plight of his people. 'May I ask you a very simple question,' he began. 'How many of you have ever prayed for Cambodia?' He might well have asked how many of them had ever even heard of Cambodia!

Typically it had taken a political crisis to awaken the church in the West, a church which has had the gospel for centuries, to heed the cry of a people still in a pre-Christian state of spiritual darkness and bondage. 'Do any of your churches and organisations have even one missionary in Cambodia?' he asked. Yet with no trace of anger or frustration, this soft spoken and gracious young man, a major in his nation's armed forces and general secretary of the Cambodian Evangelical Church, continued to press home his point. Echoing the zeal and agony in the soul of the Apostle Paul, he declared, 'How great is my sorrow and the pain in my heart for my people, my own flesh and blood.' He concluded by reminding them of their Keswick theme, emblazoned on the wall behind him, 'One in Christ...'

'Would you please pray for us, brothers and sisters in Christ.'

Wherever he went in Britain during that time while pursuing

degree studies in engineering, Chhirc's message was the same to both church groups and to individuals. None who met him could ever forget the urgency and the conviction with which he spoke, or the deep personal travail he was undergoing. Here was a man consumed by the love of God and the power of the gospel. Why had it taken so long for the good news of deliverance in Jesus Christ to reach the Cambodian fields? While Cambodians continued to slaughter each other and destroy their rich and fertile land with the assistance of the great powers' machinery of war, Chhirc saw hope in no other name than that of the Saviour God. 'I can only weep for Cambodia and for my people who have never known the true God.' He urged the Christians of Great Britain that, having contemplated the glory of Jesus Christ, not to tarry on the mountaintop 'making booths', but to hasten down to the plains where multitudes were waiting for deliverance and healing. 'I invite you to come down,' he concluded, 'I invite all of you to come down.' His impassioned voice cried out to those attending Keswick in the summer of 1973.

In all this, Chhirc was not relaying a mere emotional appeal, though he was not ashamed to give full vent to his powerful emotions. He was simply reiterating the call of God which was moving deep in his own soul. He had no peace of mind in Britain. The words of Christ to his disciples, 'If anyone would come after me, he must deny himself and take up his cross daily and follow me. For whoever wants to save his life will lose it, and whoever loses his life for me and for the gospel will save it,' echoed again and again in his heart. Just as vividly as when Jesus Christ had first met him some twelve years earlier in 1961 through two days and nights of weeping tears of repentance and joy, so now the Lord's hand was upon him. 'Send me back, send me back,' became his prayer in response to his Saviour's 'As the Father has sent me, so send I you.' And Chhirc knew without a doubt, that he was being sent back to Cambodia ultimately to suffer and die for the faith he loved and so coveted for his blind and groping people. He was put under considerable pressure to remain safely in England. It was another year before he was able to return to Cambodia. Just as he had kept solitary vigil outside the prison walls in Phnom Penh for his captive colleagues in the difficult days of 1965, once again he was being called to stand and bear witness. This time, however, he would not stand in silence, and neither would he stand alone. Within two years, and just days after the Khmer Rouge capture of Phnom Penh, he would be taken and executed, and so bear an even more compelling and eloquent witness as a martyr for Christ. Added to this burden of bearing the cross of Christ in Cambodia were other complex tensions and costly decisions involving his wife and child. They would remain behind in Scotland. As he left, his message to the Christians of Great Britain read:

Dear Brothers and Sisters in Christ Jesus,

Give us the right to believe in Jesus Christ the true God on whom you have believed for many, many centuries.

God has given you blessings upon blessings so that today you have many churches in which to worship him and learn from his living Word. You have plenty of books, booklets, tracts and films telling you about the true God; you have worship services on television every Sunday, and services on the radio every morning. God has given you wonderful things so that you can enjoy life on this earth in every aspect. You have a comfortable life, a high standard of living.

Please have a look at Cambodia. We still have many idols and temples up and down the country. These false gods have drained the life of our people by continual sacrifices and offerings, and we have become poor and weak, unable to defend our country properly against our enemies.

My grandmother spent most of her lifetime in a search for the true God. She sold her house and properties in order to get peace and salvation from many gods, and my parents have become very poor because of this. But God is faithful to his promise, 'seek and ye shall find'. I praise him for leading her to find Jesus Christ, and am thankful to God for providing me with a Christian home and family.

But now many of my fellow countrymen are fed up with the heavy yoke and horror of false gods and deceitful philosophies and doctrines. We are hungry for the truth, the One true God. We have been longing to believe in Jesus Christ the Lord and Saviour, but until 1923 had never heard his Name. Jesus Christ died 2000 years ago for our sins, but we have just heard this Good News.

Now please give us the right to believe in him, dear Christian brothers and sisters. Will you help us in any way the Lord may suggest you do? Most of all remember us in your prayers.

Yours in Christ's love,
Major Chhirc Taing

On his return journey to Cambodia in the autumn of 1973, he stopped briefly in Singapore. There he addressed the directors of the Overseas Missionary Fellowship (OMF)[1] at 2 Cluny Road, assembled in General Council, inviting this mission likewise to follow him into Cambodia where the harvest was great and the labourers all too few. To this pressing invitation to 'come over and help us' from a man of Cambodia, the mission directors concluded that God was indeed calling them 'to preach the gospel to them'. By early 1974 the first missionaries of an eventual band of five from OMF entered Cambodia, wading into a harvest for which they had not laboured but were now privileged to help reap. Joyfully they joined hands with men such as Pastor Reach Yeah, Son Sonne, Major Chhirc and the other godly leaders of the national Cambodian Evangelical Church, and also with the faithful and more experienced missionaries of the Christian and Missionary Alliance, the ones who had for over half a century laboured to plant the church of Jesus Christ in Cambodia.

As for Chhirc himself, he was very soon happily wading up to his neck in Cambodia's ripening fields. Shortly after his return to Cambodia, Chhirc wrote back to friends in Scotland: 'Hungry souls have poured into our fifteen churches in the capital each week. There has been a shortage of Bibles for many months, and we are running out of almost everything here. But not of the sweet love of Jesus, our dear Lord and Saviour who is manifesting himself mightily in our land.' From his base at Bethany Church right in the centre of that doomed city, Chhirc was providing renewed vision and leadership for the Cambodian church, and bearing bold testimony to great and small alike.

During that very same summer of 1973 when Chhirc was preparing to return to garrison the church, the Cambodian government was facing a major crisis in its war with the Khmer Rouge. After the signing of the so-called Paris Peace accords between the USA and United Nations on January 27, 1973, most of the Vietnamese army had left off direct fighting in Cambodia, handing over to the Khmer Rouge who by now were big enough, organised and equipped enough, to finish the job on their own. In February 1973 began two hundred days and nights of intensive carpet bombing by US B52s. This probably saved the city from falling in April 1973, but did nothing to weaken the resolve of the Khmer Rouge, and certainly exacerbated the hatred of many terrorised peasants for the US backed government in Phnom Penh.

On August 15, 1973 the US Congress halted once and for all the bombing of Cambodia. Some expected the morale of the Cambodian army to collapse, and an imminent fall. But they hung on. On all fronts that year, the wily Khmer Rouge advanced until they stood poised to deliver the *coup de grâce* to Cambodia's capital. They had rocketed the airport and cut all the roads in and out of the capital. Only a handful of missionaries remained, having sent their families out to Thailand ahead of them. But the church cried out to God for more time. They ringed the beleaguered city with their prayers and fasting, calling out from their churches and humble meeting places all around the city, that God might stay the hand of the encircling army of black-clad guerrillas.

In one of the great surprises of the war, the Cambodian army held firm, stood their ground, regrouped and beat back the communist forces allowing the city time to catch its breath once more. It would prove to be a remission of about two years. But for the church this brief period would be the most fruitful in its entire history. The growth was such that alarm was sounded in government circles, and at a Buddhist youth congress organised that year to fight 'outside atheists'. But sheer survival in the face of one battle lost after another against the Khmer Rouge, diminishing supplies of everything, rising inflation, rampant corruption, and a collapsed economy, kept the government's attentions diverted from fulfilling threats to stamp out this 'plague of Christians'. 'The immediate threat to this town is not its being overrun by communists but by Christians,' declared an army officer from a garrison south of the capital.

The year 1973 ended with about 1200 Christians in Phnom Penh celebrating the Saviour's birth in their various and sundry meeting places. This represented a near one hundred per cent annual increase from the 300 souls to be found four years earlier in 1970. On Christmas day large crowds including many young people and monks gathered at Bible and Christian literature displays. In all, 75,000 Bibles and other Christian books in either English, French or Cambodian were sold or given out. The obvious presence of Buddhist monks in their bright saffron coloured robes at Christian gatherings was clearly on the increase. These men, the principal transmitters of information, culture, and education at the grass roots level of Cambodian society, were now solitary or in little bands of threes and fours, seeking information about this personal God, the Lord Jesus Christ, and the Christian 'Holy Book'. There was always the possibility by this time of course that some of them, as well as keen and inquisitive students, were actually Khmer Rouge infiltrators sent in to spy on the church and identify her leaders and activities.

Indications were that 1974 was going to be an even more abundantly fruitful year than 1973. In contrast to the gloomy political outlook, the Cambodian church looked forward to the new year with anticipation, and with a confidence now thoroughly infused with that otherworldly spirit of joy and abandon, which always captivates reapers intoxicated by the quality and abundance of the harvest. Such indeed was the fullness of the season, that like the early church, their evangelism was by nature centripetal, drawing people into their communities by the transparency of their devotion to Christ. They had embraced his righteousness to their hearts, and feared his displeasure. And all this in a place darkening by the hour. In the first three months of 1974 alone, a further 400 were baptised. By mid-year the church in the capital had increased to upwards of 3,000. A growth rate in those six months alone outstripping the entire growth of the church throughout its fifty year history.

Out in the provinces, the government grimly held on to several major urban centres, but like Phnom Penh, all were surrounded and cut off, except by air, from their life support system in the surrounding villages and countryside, as well as from each other. The Khmer Rouge strategy of capturing the villages, and then surrounding the refugee-laden towns was very effective. From free towns such as Battambang, Siem Riep, Kampong Som, Kampong Thom, Kampong Cham, Pailin and Takeo, reports reached the capital of significant church growth. This growth usually followed crusades by various evangelists, or the arrival of Christian relief. The Khmer Rouge, however, would soon test the authenticity of these conversions. Inaccessibility, and the shortness of time, made an evaluation of many provincial churches impossible. In some of these towns there were pastors. Battambang enjoyed the ministry of the experienced and godly Pastor Hom, who sought to visit and nurture all these new believers and inquirers. He travelled far and wide across this war torn north-western province visiting villages as far afield as Poipet on the Thai border. All this would bear fruit in due season. But what disturbed his righteous soul most of all was the appalling decline in public morality since 1970 and the beginning of the war. Everywhere, undisciplined young soldiers strutted about brandishing their firearms, bullying and stealing by day, drunk and gambling by night. Brazen young girls hung around the many new bars and brothels. Students, their schooling disrupted by the war, were drawn increasingly into the evil about them. Parents neglected their responsibilities in the clamour for daily food and water. The rich and corrupt became more so, while the sick, beggars, leprous, and wounded, sat listless and unheeded about the raucous market places. Clearly the social and ethical fabric of Cambodia was coming apart, and Hom knew in his heart that all this, added to its long spiritual bankruptcy, would be Cambodia's death knell. Boldly he confronted these evils, calling upon his countrymen to repent and believe before it was too late.

After 1979, when a number of Christians from Battambang

escaped to the Thai border, it was clear that their faith was authentic and enduring despite their youth and lack of biblical knowledge. Hom's labours had not been in vain, and he was known and loved throughout the province. In other centres, lay Christians provided what leadership there was. Siem Riep had three young laymen. Though cut off from any help from the church leaders in the capital, they nevertheless worked single-mindedly to build up the thirty or so believers there. In still other places isolated from Phnom Penh, often discouraged and lonely, pastors or laymen clung to their posts. Some were forced to devote much of their time and energy to secular employment in order to earn enough to feed their own families.

The direct correlation between the level of Christian philanthropic aid and church growth cannot be allowed to escape our attention here. This was especially obvious in Phnom Penh. But with the desperate physical needs which existed, and no luxury of time to study the impact Christian relief might have on the church, negatively or positively, over the long term, it would be presumptuous to draw too many hard and fast conclusions. (It is interesting to note for example, that increased Christian relief in Laos at this time had no real spiritual impact or effect on church growth despite the similar context of war, an imminent communist take-over, and Buddhism. The church among the Lao continued as sluggish and weak as ever, right up until Laos fell to the communist Pathet Lao. Today, however, the Lao church is alive and encouragingly well.)

The political situation in the US and Cambodia in 1974 was confusing. Both spoke of a stalemate in the war, and the hope of negotiations with the Khmer Rouge and Prince Sihanouk. Perhaps the people of Phnom Penh had simply grown accustomed to the ever-present sound of artillery fire out there beyond their heavily fortified bastions. Though as the months went by, it was growing perceptibly more loud and persistent. In the United States the long agony of Watergate was drawing to a close, and President Nixon was removed from office in disgrace. President Ford found himself at the helm of a congress and nation thoroughly weary of political controversy, and the long costly Indo-Chinese war which many were now persuaded was unwinnable. The US seemed to be looking for a face-saving way out at almost any price, and the various communist forces in Indo-China were fully aware of it. The scent of victory was in the air in Peking and Hanoi. The western media, sensing victory too perhaps, continued to portray America in the worst possible light. Certainly few were exposing the atrocities of the communists. A mood of apathy was reflected also in Cambodia. Disillusionment had set in, especially among students, towards the aloof and blatantly corrupt government of Marshall Lon Nol. Ironically, by 1974 students had actually to be press-ganged into the hard-pressed army to help fill the badly depleted ranks. Officially, the figures were impressive, as corrupt Cambodian officers drew salaries for phantom armies and dead soldiers. Others even lined their pockets selling arms to the Khmer Rouge! Men such as these were already using helicopters meant to transport the wounded to hospital, to fly their families and substantial possessions to the border towns of Poipet and Pailin. There, a sizeable colony of Cambodia's wealthy and influential was massing in preparation for the final flight over into Thailand as soon as Phnom Penh fell, as they knew it soon would. The original purpose of the war, and the heady days of 1970 when hundreds of zealous youths had demonstrated in the streets, and enlisted in the new Republic's army to drive out the communist aggressors, confident of the steady arm of Uncle Sam around them, was fading from view. Somehow that arm had grown less steady, less certain nowadays. And anyway the enemy out there was no longer the hated Vietnamese, but made up of fellow Khmers, fellow Cambodian Buddhists with Prince Sihanouk at their head. Surely in victory the Khmer Rouge would be magnanimous, flexible, in the traditional Cambodian way. The indicators were, even to the most politically naive, that both Cambodia and their helpers, the US, were losing heart for this war. This all meant for the shrewd and patient Khmer Rouge that it was just a matter of time, of keeping up the pressure and propaganda, and Cambodia, like a rotten fruit, would fall from the US branch on which it now dangled, and disintegrate at their feet.

Meanwhile, as 1974 wore on, the noose around Phnom Penh

grew tighter and tighter, held by a reported 14,000 Khmer Rouge guerrillas who had the city virtually isolated. During March, the ominous news reached the city that the former royal capital of Oudong, twenty-four miles north west of Phnom Penh, had fallen. Hundreds were being killed as rockets rained down indiscriminately on the noisy and crowded capital by day, and a silent and hushed city under curfew by night. They fell into schools, crowded market places, busy intersections, spraying deadly metal shrapnel across a wide area. The suburbs, where hundreds of thousands of refugees clung to a precarious existence were under constant threat of bombardment. Heavily armoured convoys of supplies ran the gauntlet from the South China Sea up the Mekong River to Phnom Penh. The Khmer Rouge were now well in control of most of the river bank. There was a measure of relief after May when the annual monsoon rains began flooding the surrounding countryside, temporarily dampening the fighting. On July 9, Marshall Lon Nol made a desperate call for unconditional peace. It fell on deaf ears. A mere two vote majority at the UN was keeping his government from expulsion at the instigation of China and the communist world.

By August 1974 there were twenty major worshipping congregations in the city. Six of them had been established since the beginning of the year and were being led by capable laypeople. All were situated in the heavily populated refugee areas of the city. Right near the heart of the city, ministering to hundreds of high school and university students, a Christian Youth Centre had opened under the gentle and experienced leadership of Andrew Way. Later, Trieu Serey and his family, a Bible school student in his intern year, came to work with Andrew in this strategic outreach to enthusiastic and spiritually hungry young people. Just a few of these precious ones, now mature and middle-aged have survived to the present day. As students and intellectuals, they would have been prime targets for the Khmer Rouge pogroms. Now together with the twenty or so students at the Takmau Bible School, they discipled new believers at various city churches, increased the literature distribution, and ministered to hundreds of abandoned wounded soldiers and their despairing families clogging hospital compounds, abandoned schools, or wherever else they could find shelter. Plans were under way for a recording studio for the preparation of Cambodian Christian radio programmes to be aired on the current short wave facility, twice daily from the Philippines. Medium wave broadcasts which could more easily be picked up by the average radio receivers in Cambodia were also being planned. Christian radio was a lifeline to many believers isolated behind enemy lines, or in the provincial towns. Many of these listeners, especially students and soldiers, wrote requesting literature and correspondence courses. In June 1974, the Bible Society formed a committee in Cambodia to prepare a new translation of the Bible in Cambodian. At least one Cambodian ethnic minority, the Cham people, were having the Word of God put into their language by workers with Wycliffe Bible Translators and the Summer Institute of Linguistics. Others were labouring to master the languages of other tribal minorities all of whom were as yet totally unreached with the gospel. Sadly this work, and the Bible Society's new Cambodian Bible translation were lost with the fall of Cambodia the following year, the disappearance of qualified national Christian colleagues, and the flight of the missionaries.

Four Cambodians including Taing Chhirc were invited to be delegates at the historic Lausanne Congress of World Evangelisation convening that summer in Switzerland. Also outstanding among them was the zealous Son Sonne, a former Buddhist monk, but now apostle and servant of Jesus Christ. He had planted several new churches in Phnom Penh, and organised discipleship training programmes for the hundreds of new Christians under his capable shepherding. He used to speak affectionately of his four fine young sons as future pastors for the Cambodian church. The entire family perished within a year.

With the coming of December 1974, and the tapering off of the monsoon rains, powerful and persistent hands began to reach forward once more, to apply their stranglehold around the trembling throat of an already weak and gasping capital. The rising spectre of surging Khmer Rouge forces loomed large and threatening, casting a dark and sinister shadow over the city.

Everyone felt its chilling presence, and heard its restless movements, closing in on all sides. Daylight was fading fast, and the night when no man could work was at hand.

Now the night sky around Phnom Penh was alive, palpitating with the flashes and reverberations of exploding artillery shells. Beneath this glowing canopy the city waited, forlorn, and all but abandoned, for the end to come. Come it surely would, no one doubted that now. The question was, how soon?

Whether they cared to admit it, or were even consciously aware of it, I believe that the Cambodian Christians knew that Christmas 1974 would be their last opportunity to celebrate the advent of Christ. In retrospect, the unbridled energy of the church at that time could be likened to the final, wild, almost agonised leaps and flares of a candle flame, struggling to stay alive, refusing to be extinguished and die as its time melts away. The flame of life now ignited within them was living, moving, ever restless, a fire burning in their bones. Many waters could not quench it. It remained undaunted by the awesome power of the forces arrayed against it. Resolutely it refused to die. It was incapable of death.

Fully mobilised and straining forward to reach far beyond their human grasp, the Christmas festivities that year were like brilliant flares shooting up into the darkening sky, signalling hope to the distressed and sinking city. They plunged headlong into these celebrations with a zeal which was white hot. On each of the Sundays leading up to Christmas, the Christian community gathered at a different city church or centre of Christian activity, to join with the local congregation in worship, special events such as drama, singing, baptisms, literature distribution, and evangelism among the surrounding populace. The climactic moment came on December 24 and 25 when thousands of them filled the indoor arena of Phnom Penh's Olympic Stadium for a massive display of the message of Christmas through worship and praise, preaching, the distribution of gifts to hundreds of needy children, and a vivid illustration of the major events in salvation history from Genesis to the Second Advent. This was accomplished through a series of sixteen beautifully decorated tableaux arranged around the periphery of an indoor arena. Different city churches were responsible for each one. Many prominent men in the city, as well as large crowds of ordinary people, upwards of fifteen thousand (predominantly students) gathered to listen to the dynamic preaching of Son Sonne, receive literature, and engage in animated discussion with the scores of Christians intent on personally confronting them with the gospel of Jesus Christ on this special day.

Gone now were the platitudes, the social niceties, the easy banter of earlier days. Talk of eternal things was straightforward and undiluted. People living in the shadow of suffering and death have a unique capacity for isolating and focusing on the truly vital and essential issues of life. Not a few whose desires had been directed towards the beguiling pleasures of this world were now being awakened from their deathly slumber to the love of God. The growing fear in the stricken city was palpable.

While numbering the church was an impossible task, it had clearly grown in Phnom Penh in excess of 3000. During 1974 twelve new churches had been planted, all of them by lay people, bringing the total of main church centres up to twenty-six from the three or four a few years earlier. Over sixty per cent of the church was now under lay leadership. It was primarily the laity of God who were nurturing the new believers, and in the vanguard of this people movement.

Bethany Church now had a daily prayer meeting from 6-7 am, and in other places Christians were keeping all night vigils for prayer and waiting on the Lord. In all areas of church life there had been enormous growth. The visit of a team flown in from the ship *Logos* in September 1974 had provided new impetus for more effective use of literature, reading and distribution. With so many new churches, Cambodian hymn books were in great demand, along with the Scriptures. Over 200 people living in free areas across the country were enrolled in English Bible correspondence courses, and over 2000 more enrolled in courses in Cambodian. About 3000 children were attending Sunday schools, and several church primary schools had sprung up.

Significant among the emerging lay leadership were the twenty-five young Bible School students. Each had needed at least tenth grade to qualify for admission, and several were already married with families. All were active in planting churches before applying themselves to the Bible-centred programme. Consequently, at the Bible School still situated in a tranquil and picturesque spot, on the banks of the Bassac River at Takmau, just to the south of the city, the students were frequently engaged in lively discussion on how best to help new Christians grow and mature. Most memorable were their times of prayer, and the exciting reports about what they had witnessed of the hand of the Lord. With such a perfect integration of academic studies and its practical outworking, their teachers were spurred to redouble their efforts. Besides the Bible School staff, strategic resource people were brought in to highlight various areas of pressing concern. Foremost among these was the vital subject of pastoral ministry, for which they called upon the experience of a remarkable young lay pastor named Sin Soum. Only two years in Christ, he was presently shepherding hundreds of new Christians out at Horeb Church, situated in the midst of a huge refugee camp along the road to Pochentong airport.

When the Bible School students, and a few others enrolled in a TEE (Theological Education by Extension) course in Christian leadership at Bethlehem Church, completed their first semester, they fanned out over the country to assist in various church ministries. With the present crisis however, most remained in the capital. But others did manage to reach the provincial towns of Pailin, Siem Riep, Takeo, Kampong Cham, Kampot, Kampong Som and Kampong Thom. Here, they were an enormous encouragement to small and vulnerable churches, increasingly isolated from the leadership in the capital.

The gem mining town of Pailin right on the Thai border had a Khmer church pastored by Pastor Kong. It also had a population of 600 Brao tribespeople who had fled from their homes in the far Northeast province of Ratanakiri when the war engulfed their forest communities. Among these a Wycliffe missionary couple were working to translate the Scriptures into their language.

The leadership of the Cambodian Evangelical Church at this time was in the capable hands of Reach Yeah, pastor of Sarepta

Church, president; Sen Bun, pastor of Bethlehem Church, vice president; Lim Cheong, principal of the Bible School, vice president; Major Taing Chhirc, a leader at Bethany Church, executive secretary; Nou Thuok, one of Granny Rose's sons and a translator at the Bible School, recording secretary; Son Sonne, lay pastor and Director of the Cambodian Bible Society, treasurer.

Among the Phnom Penh leadership, inevitable tensions developed between the older and traditionally inclined pastors from a rural background, and the more sophisticated and cosmopolitan urban intellectuals. With the church growing so fast, and the laity taking an increasingly prominent role, questions were being raised about church administration and the limitations imposed on lay people. A backlog of believers running into thousands awaited baptism. And with people turning to Christ at the rate of almost one hundred per week by the end of 1974, was it right for them to have to wait until one of the hard-pressed half dozen or so recognised pastors got around to examining and baptising them? Could not the local lay leaders perform baptisms too? What about the Lord's table, church discipline, freedom to use other forms of worship, different ecclesiology, use of finances, means and levels of support, the involvement of various western mission and aid organisations, the charismatic gifts etc etc? Only the dire urgency of the time kept the lid on all these issues. But lurking not far beneath the relatively untroubled surface of unity lay deep and complex issues the church had yet to address. Only occasionally did these things emerge in those days. The Cambodian church, once small, homogeneous, and submissive under the benevolent and watchful eye of one denominational mission, was entering young adulthood. It desired to stretch its wings, exercise more authority, experiment with new ideas, court other friends, and at times be just plain rebellious against those who had brought it to birth. The more serious and noteworthy calls for change were coming from a handful of far-sighted men who could see that some of the old ways and forms were simply inadequate for the present situation in Cambodia. If the church was going to survive the approaching crucible of communism, complete suppression of all religious freedom, not to mention a world-wide dispersion which they could never have imagined, the church had to shift its centre of gravity away from a dependence on outside help, and a system in which full-time church leaders followed a fairly set pattern of doing things. Excellent as all this may have been in its season, there was now a need for the church in Cambodia to become more decentralised, and fully indigenous, nurtured by an imaginative, biblically literate, low profile, lay as well as 'ordained' leadership. A handful, either out of frustration with the present structure or through personal ambition, struck out on new and experimental paths anyway. Others, undaunted by the weight of tradition, though with no sense of malice, simply went ahead and did what they felt they had to do for the spiritual welfare of their people. Much of what was the authentic planting of the Lord, regardless of the motives and means, would become more clear with the passing of time. Ultimately, however, only eternity will vindicate the glory of God in all the events of those incredible days, when we witnessed the magnificent efflorescence of the Cambodian church just before the nation fell to the Khmer Rouge in April 1975.

The death-knell for the terminally ill Khmer Republic tolled loud and clear when it finally sounded. Shortly after midnight, at 1.20 am on the first day of 1975, the entire city was suddenly awakened from its fitful slumber by the pandemonium of an enormous bombardment of the city's defence perimeter from an encircling force of 80,000 Khmer Rouge troops. It was the long expected final offensive. Within four months it would all be over.

Daybreak found huge crowds hushed and grim-faced standing all along the banks of the Mekong where it flows majestically past the royal palace and splits off into two directions. They were pointing across to the further shore. Their eyes were scanning a spectacle of devastation, homes and villages lost behind the great wall of black smoke which was climbing slowly into the sky, broken only by the occasional glare of angry red flames raging along its base. Some, only hours before, had fled this carnage in small boats, paddling across the river to join the millions of others stranded in the shrinking city-wide refugee camp of Phnom Penh.

'What has your God to say about that over there?' they cried out in desperation to Christians who in groups of twos and threes were moving among the crowds testifying to the hope they had in Jesus Christ. Like angry bees diving in and out of the smoke, a few aged aeroplanes of the decimated Cambodian airforce were dropping bombs on an elusive enemy. They fell with sickeningly dull thuds which caused the ground to shudder, as if it too were trembling in the throes of a slow and agonising death. No, the Christians had no easy answers for what was 'happening over there', except that their eyes were not focused upon it, but on something, someone else, beyond the sky, beyond vanity.

Simultaneous to this tragic drama unfolding on the further shore, just a few miles to the south where the Mekong flows into the Bassac, at Takmau quite a different drama was in progress. Within sight of the falling bombs and plumes of acrid smoke, another large crowd of people was gathered at the water's edge. A gathering of Christians singing hymns to God, had come to witness scores of their brothers and sisters pass through the waters of baptism. Waist deep in the river, their faces calm and still, aglow with the flush of first love, a long line of Christians were standing with their hands clasped before them in an attitude of deep reverence. At either end of the line a Cambodian pastor was working his way slowly towards the middle, immersing them one by one as each confessed 'Jesus is Lord'. The pastors then repeated the ancient formula of the apostolic church, 'I baptise you in the Name of God the Father, God the Son, and God the Holy Spirit.' Each candidate disappeared momentarily beneath the rippling water to be raised up again by the pastor's arm across his or her back. Those gathered on the river bank were singing very gently, and their voices sounded like a thousand aeolian harps rising and falling with the breeze which drifted in off the water: *Amazing Grace*, *The Love of God* and other well-loved hymns of the Cambodian church. And their faces were full of joy.

At the time I remember recalling some words from Virgil's *Aeneid*, 'They were holding their arms outstretched in love, towards the further shore.' There juxtaposed together, like a bizarre surrealistic painting, were these two totally antithetical images. On the further shore were death, destruction, and the screams of war. While on the nearer side, reconciliation and eternal life echoed back in paeans of praise. And between the two, holding them momentarily poised in exquisite tension, the ancient river: faithful and long-suffering, ever silent, flowing on in its steady southward course towards the sea.

If any one of those ardent young people, the water of baptism still glistening on their faces, had glanced over his shoulder, he would have seen the long dark shadow which was moving towards them. Very soon it would envelop them all. Perhaps ninety per cent of those present on that unforgettable day, would shortly be transported to glory as their mortal bodies fell, victims in the ensuing slaughter. There can be no doubt that most had already considered the cost of being a Christian, and a Cambodian Christian at that, and found it eminently worthwhile. For indeed, as an earlier Christian martyr recorded, 'He is no fool who gives up what he cannot keep, in order to gain what he cannot lose' (from the journal of the missionary martyr Jim Elliot).

The sound of shelling and the terrifying rocket attacks were now a daily phenomenon. Nights were filled with the din of pounding mortars, crackling machine guns, vibrating helicopters, and trucks frantically ferrying soldiers back and forth from the battle zones. Most horrible of all were the terrifying sounds of exploding rockets, followed by a cacophony of shrill voices yelling in panic, barking dogs, and the roar of vehicles. From the roof tops by night one could watch the helicopter gunships strafing enemy positions right on the edge of the city. The night sky was illuminated by tracers and brilliant incendiary devices which hung suspended in the dark void like giant Chinese lanterns. Early in the year 1975 the last heavily armed convoy of fuel and supplies reached the port of Phnom Penh. Subsequent convoys were forced back or sunk. The Mekong River was now mined, and its banks controlled by the Khmer Rouge. This left just the airport at Pochentong, as the one tenuous but vital life-line between Phnom Penh and the outside world. An American airlift from Saigon struggled to keep the city supplied with rice and ammunition. But even these planes were in constant danger after February when the enemy moved its artillery and rocket launchers within range of the airport. And all the while the pitiful caravans of sick and malnourished refugees poured daily into the shrinking city from surrounding villages and sprawling refugee suburbs. Many had seen their entire livelihood vanish in flames, as they fled in terror carrying their pathetic bundles, and little children clinging around them.

Some of these found refuge in Christian communities seeking to share what they could with the new arrivals. Sin Soum together with his large and expanding flock was living very close to the edge of the city defence perimeter, and many refugees passing through spent the first night of their flight exhausted on the floor of a simple wooden church called Horeb. Sin Soum himself could be seen at such times moving among them, comforting, and praying with them. Always he directed them to the eternal refuge he had found in Jesus Christ, just two years earlier at one of the large crusades. He had baptised over 400 since the new year alone. Soon he too would perish on the 'killing fields'.

At the waterfront near the Royal Palace, nothing stood between Noah's Church and the Khmer Rouge on the further shore. From within, where some kind of meeting was continually in progress, rockets could clearly be heard whirring overhead. At Serepta Church, Pastor and church president, Reach Yeah, reported standing room only as preachers and teachers daily declared the good news of salvation in Jesus Christ. 'Our gods died and left us destitute,' the people said, 'but Jesus is alive!' Hundreds of students sought out Christian teaching from the Bible students at Takmau in those final days. Chom Chau Church had a rocket come through its roof but thankfully nobody was killed. The Warehouse Church at Tuol Kork was 'packed to the rafters', and hundreds more filled a nearby daughter church to hear the teaching of Son Sonne. Everywhere it seemed, people were quite literally spilling out of the doors and windows of the churches. There simply was no room to accommodate all the people who came seeking solace in the Lord Jesus Christ in those final precious hours of freedom. Chhirc's zealous younger brother was training scores of young people in personal evangelism. Others gladly took over the teaching of various Bible classes left by the evacuating missionaries.

A new ministry which began to take shape during those last days was outreach to the hundreds of wounded and amputee soldiers lying hopelessly around in hospital compounds, or begging on street corners. Over one hundred were being taught by the gentle and passionate En Keth, helped by Bunthol his colleague, also a soldier. Here were two men whom God especially burdened for these broken men who had been abandoned by the army and left to beg in order to live and support their families. Soon wheelchair evangelists could be seen on the city streets as these men, once so wretched, and constantly squabbling, found themselves transformed by the person of Jesus Christ who had gone in among them and touched their lives. These former soldiers would be bayoneted on their beds, or mowed down by the Khmer Rouge, as they tried pathetically to drag themselves out of the city on their stumps of legs during the terrible forced exodus immediately following the Khmer Rouge victory.

The multiplication of prayer cells, and reports of others preparing to organise small 'underground' churches was another development of the time. Literature was being dispersed throughout the church, and large stocks broken down. The Christians sensed the urgency of the hour. They were not unaware that suffering lay ahead. The cross they bore was a constant reminder. But they were filled noticeably with a great peace.

Reports of new opportunities, new churches, fresh initiatives, requests for teaching, testimonies, baptisms and so on were just too numerous to follow up. This report was representative of the time. A middle-aged widow happened to pick up a Christian tract which she saw blowing around in a crowded marketplace. On reading it over several times, she was immediately convicted in her heart of the truth and importance of the message she held in her hand. Not knowing where to turn for help, she set out early one Sunday to locate a church. She knew at least that this was the day when Christians gathered for worship. Finally, walking down Pologne Avenue, she happened to notice a sign which read: 'Good News Centre' hanging on the front fence of a house. Finding no one at home, for all were at church, she just sat herself down on the doorstep and waited. The first Cambodian Christian to return answered her questions and led her to repentance and faith in Christ. The following week she was back again at the door with a further request. Would someone come out to her home and tell all those waiting there the same message she had heard the week before. The young evangelist, on entering the little wooden house, found it packed by forty or so eager neighbours sitting cross-legged on the floor, waiting expectantly to hear his message. Thus began another church. And week by week the number of people sitting cross-legged on the widow's floor and all around the house grew and grew.

With the city all but written off, tension among its two and a half million trapped inhabitants was at breaking point. Food supplies were dwindling. Crime was rampant. The airport was at the point of being overrun. All escape routes were closing fast. Angry mobs began attacking food depots and shops.

Then the telegram came. All the missionaries of the Christian and Missionary Alliance and the Overseas Missionary Fellowship were to evacuate Cambodia at once. It was the end of February 1975. In six more weeks the Khmer Rouge would be marching victoriously into Phnom Penh. Agonising as this was for all of us, not to have left would have endangered the lives of others who might have had to rescue us from enemy hands. Our names and activities were certainly known by the Khmer Rouge's spy network, and we would have been a grave threat to the national Christians had we been with them when the communists arrived. Those we loved would have been condemned out of hand as 'lackeys of foreign spies, CIA agents, and enemies of the revolution'. Knowing all this, however, and the weight of missionary experience from China in 1951 after the communists seized power there, didn't make leaving any easier. It seemed somehow to be a betrayal of the very message we were there to proclaim.[2]

Our final Sunday evening service at Bethany Church on Monivong Avenue was painful beyond words yet unforgettably beautiful. Since we had only just heard minutes before that we were to be gone within forty-eight hours, the Cambodians around us as yet had no idea that we were leaving. Next to me in the packed church sat one of three enthusiastic young men, freshly arrived from the north of Cambodia. They were the lay leaders of a growing church in far off Siem Riep, and they had come all the way to Phnom Penh in pursuit of teaching, literature and help. About midway through the service, he touched my arm and with a winsome smile asked, 'Older brother, would you come back to Siem Riep with me and help us build up the church over there?' I looked into his eyes until mine misted over, but I could say nothing. Weeks earlier, I had been told by my OMF director for Cambodia that the Cambodian church had requested that I go to work with the church in Siem Riep when my language study in Phnom Penh was over. Was this what might have been? I thought. Suddenly I felt redundant, irrelevant. And he, still smiling, bursting with plans and strategies for Siem Riep, was blissfully unaware of the fact that at dawn I was to flee from Cambodia, and he and his companions would be heading back empty handed and soon to face death on the 'killing fields'.

At that moment our attention was diverted as one of the missionary families (the family of Norm Ens) also about to leave this land where they had devoted so many years of their lives, prepared to sing. The words they sang so beautifully, perfectly expressed my own heart:

By and by, when I look at his hands,
Beautiful hands, nail-riven hands,
By and by when I look at his hands
I'll wish I had given him more.
More, so much more,
More of my life than I e'er gave before,
By and by when I look at his hands,
I'll wish I had given him more.

And I thought of my own mortality, how soon it is all over. Our lives are like a vapour, here so briefly, then gone. It was as if I had twelve hours left to live, and I deeply regretted all the wasted time and personal shortcomings of my brief time in Cambodia. Now it was all over, the night when no man can work had come, and I was wanting to give so much more.

The Scripture reading which followed was from Psalm 34:1-7: 'I will praise the Lord no matter what happens.' The sung Scripture choruses included Isaiah 43:2,3: 'When thou passest through the waters, I'll be with thee…' and 'Would you be poured out like wine upon the altar for me?' The preacher's text was I Corinthians 1:3: 'Praise be to the God and Father of our Lord Jesus Christ, the Father of compassion, and the God of all comfort.' The service ended with the benediction: 'Behold, I am with you always. I will never leave you. I will never forsake you.' Jesus' own final parting words to his disciples.

The presence of God was so close, you could feel it everywhere, in all that was being said and done, and in the fellowship together, Cambodians and expatriates, while outside the Khmer Rouge rockets exploded across the city. Of course God is always there. The problem is we usually only really know it in such times of pain and crisis. Into our grief that night, Jesus came and wept with us and comforted us just as he had once done for Mary and Martha, at Bethany. Our brother 'Lazarus' would be allowed to die in order that the glory of God might be seen in his resurrection.

And so with bitter tears the missionaries left in two orderly groups, flying out in an old Dakota, just like the ones which fifty years earlier had limped over 'the hump' bringing our forebears out of China. Scrambling from a sand bunker at the edge of the runway, we boarded the little plane which lifted us quickly away from the beleaguered city. As the twin propellers spluttered and whirred, we circled high overhead. We strained at the small cabin windows to catch final glimpses of familiar places, cherished memories. As the plane banked sharply westward over sun-scorched fields, a landscape deserted of people, we turned our attention to a letter which was being passed around.

A short message had been handed to us by Major Taing Chhirc who had himself come right to the runway to see us safely away. This was the man whom God had so dramatically brought back from Britain to help direct the church in this crucial hour. The same man who had invited us in to help serve his people. Now our polite Asian host who had welcomed us months earlier had accompanied us again, bidding us a proper farewell. He had wept long and hard with some of us the evening before; tears of sorrow for his nation; tears of frustration that labourers for the vineyard whom he had personally 'hired' were being snatched away in the midst of the harvest; tears of horror and revulsion at the end which awaited him; and tears of loneliness for family and friends whom he would see no more. As he returned alone to face once more the clamour and panic of a city in the throes of death, one cannot comprehend the depths of his inner agony or understand how severe was the turmoil and pain within his great heart. Taing Chhirc, saint and martyr, was one of God's precious gifts to the Cambodian church. He loved not his own life even unto death. Thus, emotionally exhausted, and through a blur of tears, we read his parting words:

Phnom Penh,
February 26, 1975

To dear Missionary Friends,
'Where is the Lord God of Elijah?' he (Elisha) cried out. And the water parted and Elisha went across! (2 Kings 2:14). This verse tells us how hard it was for the young man Elisha to be left behind while the old and powerful prophet of the Lord, Elijah, was taken away.

'Where is the Lord God of Elijah?' This is also the cry of the young Khmer church leaders at this moment. Elijah had been sent by God to the Israeli nation during the dark reign of its evil King Ahab. Despite the mighty miracles Elijah had performed, the people had not changed their hearts from sin. Then the time came for Elijah to be taken to heaven and the young Elisha had to carry on the mission during those dark days in Israel. But Elisha's special request of God's power was granted. 'The spirit of Elijah rests upon Elisha.' And they went to meet him and greeted him respectfully (v 15).

Dear friends, do remember us in your prayers as we Khmer Christians are left behind to continue the task in the difficult days ahead. We do need God's greater power and wisdom as Elisha did. Please pray for us and ask God to give us the right words as we boldly tell our agonising people about the Lord, and as we explain to them that his salvation is for them now. May God add many more souls to his young church in the Khmer Republic, and let it grow stronger until the day of his return.

Your servant in the Lord,
Taing Chhirc

If Chhirc pictured us in his mind's eye taking off in that ancient Dakota as like unto Elijah soaring away in a fiery chariot, then clearly at this point his analogy had broken down rather badly. But I have no doubt that he received at least a double portion of the Spirit of Elijah as he returned to face the darkness.

Several more letters from Chhirc reached us in Bangkok, where we were listening anxiously to every radio newscast, poring over the newspapers, and praying passionately for those we had left behind in Cambodia. The next letter was brought by a fleeing Christian medical team. They arrived utterly worn out from a round-the-clock vigil at their clinics, caring for the many small children suffering from the ravages of malnutrition.

Phnom Penh
March 12, 1975

Beloved Friends,
Our land has become a desolate wasteland. Our streets and homes lie in silent darkness each night from 7.00pm At daytime there is fear of danger. Rockets fall right in the city centre, killing people and destroying shops and houses almost every day. Many people have deserted us.

This is the situation in Phnom Penh in March 1975. It reminds me of Jeremiah 9:1-2: 'Oh, that my eyes were a fountain of tears; I would weep forever; I would sob day and night for the slain of my people! Oh, that I could go away and forget them and live in some wayside shack in the desert, for they are all adulterous, treacherous men.'

However there is the only hope for our future as in Jeremiah 31:3-5, 'For long ago the Lord has said to Israel: I have loved you, O my people with an everlasting love; with loving kindness I have drawn you to me. I will rebuild your nation, O virgin of Israel. You will again be happy and dance merrily with the timbrels. Again you will plant your vineyards upon the mountains of Samaria and eat from your own garden there.'

We appreciate your prayer and intercession for us in these days of troubles and suffering in Phnom Penh.

Taing Chhirc

Finally, on Good Friday, crucifixion day, came another letter, brought out personally by a missionary who had managed to slip back in and out of the falling city to be with the Cambodian church as they celebrated Easter: the passion, death and resurrection of the Lord Jesus Christ. The letter was brief and poignant. His own passion, death and resurrection day was upon him:

Phnom Penh
April 4, 1975

My dear Friends,
'For me to live is Christ and to die is gain.' Please pray that this will be worked out in my life.

Your brother in Christ
Taing Chhirc

It was his final prayer request. Would we watch and pray with him in this moment of agony. He had underscored the word 'die' three times. The Lord answered his prayer. In life he was one who lived single-mindedly for Christ. And in dying a martyr's death, making the ultimate sacrifice, he bore compelling witness to his Lord; and so it was not waste, but gain for the Cambodian church, and for the beloved Chhirc, those tears all wiped away now, joy in the immediate presence of his Lord.

It was now April 1975, the hottest month in the Cambodian year, when the ground is baked hard, and a fine red dust adheres to everything, blown by hot dry withering blasts. In the countryside all vegetation is scorched and shrivelled. Streams and ponds lie parched in cracking dust bowls, forcing the people to sink their crude hand-dug wells ever deeper and deeper for a few cans of murky brown water. The Cambodian fields lie empty, dead and lifeless in the hazy glare of the relentless burning sun directly overhead.

The labourers are gone from the fields. The harvest is in and the silent fields contain only dry stubble, blowing chaff, dust and ashes. Even the last of the fish have been netted from the vanishing ponds. Now the people remain inside their homes rarely venturing forth into the blistering heat. Nothing will happen until the rains come.

On April 4, 1975, Good Friday morning, the church leaders met together in the home of Major Chhirc. He read to them from the Gospel of John, chapter thirteen, 'He poured water into a basin and began to wash his disciples' feet, drying them with the towel that was wrapped around him.' Then conscious of the hour, they stooped and began washing each other's feet. This would be the last time they would all be together on earth. Some had already received anonymous notes scrawled on banknotes from the Khmer Rouge warning of death. They knew they were marked men, but they were willing to die for Christ. Chhirc spoke for them all when, refusing an opportunity to flee, he said, 'The Christians need us. We must stay and help them. Who will take care of the sheep? If the communists are willing to die, how much more should Christians be willing.' And then he wrote his final letter, with the city falling about him, and his own death imminent,

The Lord is with us, isn't he? This is according to John 14:18, (I will not leave you orphans; I will come to you.) And we praise him because we are not on the losing side!...

Clearly Chhirc's final meditations had been on John's moving account of Jesus' last days on earth. In these circumstances, Jesus' promises to his followers must have sounded very personal to them in Cambodia, and very comforting – in particular Jesus' commitment to his abiding presence with his disciples.

A few miles downstream at Takmau, the Bible School students

stood and pledged: 'We will stand firm for Jesus Christ to the shedding of our blood.' They had taken up once and for always the cross of Jesus Christ. Their ambition had been redirected from laying hold of this world to laying hold of Jesus Christ. As with the pastors, all but a handful of these young people were about to die, adding to the martyrs of the Cambodian church, and the great cloud of witnesses which should encourage the Cambodian church today to faithful obedience to that gospel which like a brightly flaming torch has passed on to them.

On the first day of the week, Easter Sunday, April 6, 1975, over three thousand Christians were worshipping the risen Lord Jesus in the churches of Phnom Penh. At the suburb of Tuol Kork they gathered early in the morning in the open air at sunrise. At the newly formed Zion Church, scores unable to gain entry crowded around the outside. Under a lean-to about one hundred crippled soldiers worshipped from their wheelchairs. Bethany was packed with 250 worshippers. And such was the scene in the various and crowded churches and house groups all over the city.

The following Sunday, April 13, their last free Lord's Day, church attendance hovered at the 4000 mark, with a further 200 praying for salvation, and a reported 185 baptisms, bringing the total to over 400 baptisms for the first quarter of the year. The church was racing towards the finish line, straining, panting, reaching, pressing, lunging forward, hurling itself recklessly into the waiting arms of their Lord. When two Bible School students organised a Christian rally at a nearby high school, 850 students attended.

It appeared that people were turning to Christ for two reasons: they were attracted by the unique testimony of selfless love and practical concern displayed by the Christians, and they perceived in Christ himself a solid hope midst the surrounding flood of despair. Of their former gods they said, 'They gave us laws, but then they died.' The most frequently heard words on the lips of new believers were 'Jesus is alive'.

In his final sermon that day at Maranatha Church, Nou Thay, another of Rose's sons, made reference to the suffering and persecution of the early church, 'Though a thousand of us die, ten

thousand will be raised up!' Soon he and a faithful band of
followers would be martyred also. The Cambodian church was
standing in solidarity with the prophets and apostles of old:
'Blessed are those who are persecuted because of righteousness,
for theirs is the Kingdom of Heaven.' This final and climactic
beatitude was theirs too, for many were rejoicing in anticipation of
the great reward which awaited them in heaven.

At the same time as many in the church were fixing their gaze
heavenward and homeward, others were looking westward to
America for salvation. A semi-paralysed and weeping President
Lon Nol flew out on April 11. He had reportedly been encouraged
to leave with over a million dollars' worth of incentive. As he
went some wept, others cursed him. The newspapers were now
printing derogatory rhetoric against the US for its betrayal and
desertion of Cambodia in her darkest hour. A number of leading
ministers and military chiefs followed Lon Nol in quick
succession, and, likewise, with a good deal of accumulated wealth
in hand. They were heading for France, Australia and the United
States. The American ambassador at his fortress-like Embassy,
control centre for five years of much of the war effort, lowered
'the Stars and Stripes'. Clutching it carefully folded under his arm,
he walked out to a waiting helicopter and vanished in a cloud of
dust over the horizon, heading for an aircraft carrier cruising in the
South China Sea. Wealthy Cambodians in large numbers were
flocking like migrating swallows to the towns of Poipet and Pailin
on the Thailand border, preparing to fly across when the climate
changed. Others, more optimistic of the regime to come, or unable
to pay the enormous fees necessary to be flown out of the
besieged city, hoarded large quantities of rice, medicines, and
money. Rumours of this drove some of the masses, in desperation
and panic, to ransacking and looting. Chinatown, where wealthy
Chinese merchants were suspected of stockpiling large quantities
of rice, was a prime target. Each Cambodian in the only way he
knew how was preparing for the apocalypse to come.

With the fall of the strategic ferry crossing town of Neak
Luong, the Republic's last vital outpost, thirty-two miles southeast
of the capital on the Mekong River, everyone knew that militarily

the situation was hopeless. One of the great surprises at the end of the war was the incredible bravery with which ordinary Cambodian soldiers fought in those final desperate days. Even the new President Ford whose war-weary Congress had voted down any further military assistance for Cambodia, was deeply moved by the courage and commitment of the Cambodian army to keep on fighting. The battle of Neak Luong was hard fought and cost many lives. Those fleeing the ruined town brought horrendous reports of enemy howitzers blasting hundreds of rounds each day straight into the city from close range. Even after the town had been taken, a reported twenty thousand soldiers and civilians made a last desperate stand outside the city till they were forced to capitulate. Many now feared that a similar terrible and costly battle would take place for Phnom Penh itself. A few days later, news that the Seventh Army perimeter defence line at Pochentong airport had been breached was received with dismay and resignation. It was the beginning of the final countdown, and the beginning of 'Year Zero'. A new age was about to break in upon them, a nightmarish twilight zone of unmitigated pathos, an entire nation hovering in unreality somewhere between death and the sentence of death.

Following Easter celebrations, the church, with no hint of modifying its agenda, was assembled in annual conference. This was the time when for many years now, Cambodian Christians gathered for praise and thanksgiving to God, for evaluation of the year gone by, and to rededicate their lives in consecrated service to Christ. The church members would also select a new central committee to guide them through the coming year. While the church was thus gathered seeking the face of God for the future, the end came.

April 13, 1975 was New Year's Day in the Cambodian calendar and, running on a twelve-year cycle, it marked the end of the year of the tiger and the entrance of the year of the fleet-footed hare. But as the people tried valiantly to celebrate this ancient festival, fleet-footed Khmer Rouge guerrillas were already infiltrating the city suburbs. In a desperate attempt to maintain security and law and order, all meetings involving more than five persons were officially outlawed. On the following day, with the capture of the village of Po Sanh just one mile away, Takmau itself began filling with retreating government soldiers, falling back in the face of a massive and unyielding force of black-clad Khmer Rouge bearing down upon them. Then in the afternoon of April 15, Khmer Rouge forward positions began shelling Takmau itself, forcing the Christians to abandon the Bible School compound where they were meeting and adjourn to Bethlehem Church in the centre of the city.

The flight from Takmau that day, and the abandoning of the Bible School, marked the end of an era. This fifty year old seminary for the training of church leaders, begun in Battambang by the first pioneer missionary to Cambodia in the mid 1920s, then moved to its present site along the gently flowing Bassac at Takmau during the time of the *Issarak* uprising in 1949, was finished. Finally it too was overrun by the plague of destroying locusts. But the many seedlings lovingly nurtured in that seminary plot had now been transplanted, and were bearing fruit in fields all across Cambodia and beyond. (The old Bible School buildings remain to the present day, though the communists and subsequent regimes have cast many of the former furnishings into the river, and turned the place into a hospital.)

On Tuesday, April 15, the Christians, forced to leave Takmau, continued to meet in homes, and found a new centre around Pastor Reach Yeah, their newly elected national church president, and his Bethlehem Church community. Reach Yeah advised all the Christians not to go out into the streets but remain quietly in their homes praying. The pastors did their best to visit and comfort all the believers they could. But Bethlehem Church remained packed with Christians unwilling to leave, preferring to remain till the end, in the Church, praying and worshipping God.

PART II

CHAPTER 8

THE 17TH APRIL, 1975

'As long as it is day, we must do the work of him who sent me.
Night is coming, when no one can work.'

(John 9:4)

During the fearful night of April 16, the enemy hordes poised on all sides who had been laying siege to the city for the past four months made their final lunge at the city's trembling heart. The thrust was accompanied by a constant and terrifying barrage of rockets and shells fired at will into the defenceless city which now lay utterly helpless. First, Pochentong airport, and then the defence line to the north of the city collapsed. Thousands of weary and discouraged foot soldiers, along with hordes of terrified people from the outskirts, began streaming into the central streets of the shrinking enclave, wandering about, confused and aimless, looking for food and shelter. With the first blush of dawn in the eastern sky across the Mekong River, on the morning of April 17, there could be seen a deep red glow from fires burning to the north and south of the city. Huge clouds of dark smoke ascended from burning fuel depots and from the acres of crowded ramshackle refugee slum dwellings which clung pitifully all around the beleaguered capital.

As the merciless April sun crept higher into a cloudless sky on that never to be forgotten day, the sleepless and benumbed millions of Phnom Penh's people were greeted by the almost festive sight of hundreds of white flags and banners fluttering from every conceivable place: windows, roof-tops, vehicles, and from gunboats steaming up and down the river in front of the Palace. The Khmer Republic had surrendered. Phnom Penh had fallen. All that remained now was for it to be dismembered and thrown like refuse to the four winds.

By 8.00 am the atmosphere on the city streets was no longer one of doom but of euphoria. The war was finally over, and the enormous sense of relief that surrender brings was seen everywhere in the crowds of cheering, hand-clapping children, students and flower-throwing women. Many were out in the streets joining in the festivities, dancing and embracing, both civilians and former soldiers. All along the tree-lined boulevards through the centre of the city the revellers rejoiced that peace had finally come. Enthusiastically they greeted the squads and columns of bemused and sober-looking Khmer Rouge soldiers clad uniformly in their notorious black pyjama-like fatigues, walking, or riding in armoured vehicles all along the central Monivong Boulevard. Thousands of elated voices were crying, 'Peace, peace!' and leaping for joy, venting months of pent-up emotional anxiety in wild abandon. It was all over, five tumultuous years of cruel civil war, and over half a million Cambodians dead. Yes, the longed-for peace had come at last, they thought.

These tough, battle-hardened young zealots walking through their midst were not monsters after all, but fellow Cambodians, fellow Buddhists, the citizens of Phnom Penh assured themselves. Others, however, hiding behind closed doors, or fearfully peering down from upstairs windows, were more cautious. Theirs was an uncomfortable sense of foreboding. The older ones were perhaps recalling, somewhat cynically, a similar outbreak of ardour five years earlier in 1970, and the heady days immediately following the overthrow of Prince Sihanouk, the advent of the glorious Khmer Republic, Lon Nol, and the promise of massive American support. Five years earlier still, in 1965, crowds had again poured into the streets to join in anti-American demonstrations, and the new spirit of nationalism inspired by Prince Sihanouk, their 'father' prince. The masses are notoriously gullible and fickle, observed some that morning, harbouring distinct feelings of *déjà vu* and more than a little apprehension at the bizarre spectacle of this victory parade of communist Chinese-backed Khmer guerrillas, and talk of the return of Prince Sihanouk as their head.

Then, quite suddenly, it happened. At 9.30 am, as if according to some pre-arranged cue, the patriotic martial music which had been playing non-stop for several days over the radio was switched off. There followed a pregnant pause. And then a voice, harsh and strident: '...Long live the glorious powerful and ever victorious revolutionary forces of Cambodia; long live the great and valiant Cambodian people...We have not come to negotiate but are entering the capital by force!' At 10.00 am a classic Khmer Rouge sweetener was added, and the Buddhist Patriarch's voice was broadcast, calling for order: 'The war is over, we are among brothers... stay quietly in your homes,' he said reassuringly. (Within months the top Buddhist clergy would be murdered, temples desecrated and destroyed, and Buddhist idols and relics smashed. During this regime of 'Buddhist brothers', 40-60,000 monks would be killed.)

Having taken over the radio station and the Ministry of Information, the Khmer Rouge began requesting all former political leaders to meet at the Information Ministry 'to discuss ways of restoring order to the capital'. This was the first in a series of brilliantly orchestrated lies which the Khmer Rouge set in motion to secure their hold on a people psychologically ready to eat out of their hands. In the ensuing days, thousands of relieved and ambitious military officers and other high-ranking political figures from all over the country would be 'chauffeured' to their deaths, many proudly wearing their medals and military finery. Some even carrying expensive gifts for their beloved Sihanouk, the man they were told would receive them as heroes. The magnetic and backscratching names of Sihanouk and Buddhism were regularly invoked by the wily Khmer Rouge propagandists to cajole, manipulate, and dupe the war-weary masses of un-suspecting Cambodians. These were just the first to be entrapped and brutally slaughtered in cleverly spun invisible webs of deceit.

That morning about fifty former Republican leaders surrendered themselves at the Ministry of Information. They included the loyal Prime Minister Long Boret, looking nervous and totally exhausted from long torturous days and sleepless nights of struggling with unresolvable political problems, and untold personal agonies. Another fallen leader was Sihanouk's royal rival, the popular Prince Sirik Matak. He had been one of those behind the coup which overthrew his royal cousin in 1970. At the end he was heard saying 'I am not leaving my country. I was invited to run away, but I refused.' Then with his voice trembling, 'I really do not know what will happen to my family, but I must stay with my people.' A deeply sincere man, he had earnestly desired and worked hard for a better Cambodia. Now he realised with bitterness his one great mistake had been to put his entire trust in America, the nation which had now pulled the plug on its bewildered little ally. America had reneged on her original commitment made to Cambodia in 1970. It had proven too costly. The communist powers on the other hand: China, Russia, North Vietnam, unhindered by popular national opinion and stirred daily by increasingly negative media coverage, or by sensitivities to moral issues or human rights, never looked back until total victory was gained, regardless of the cost economically or in human lives. Their world-view, their agenda and mission was not negotiable but absolutely fixed. Utilitarian pragmatism in the West, usually based on profit and moral lassitude will inevitably falter in the face of such zeal and single-mindedness by those who are in no doubt at all about what they believe and what they want, and will go to any lengths to achieve it.

Long Boret, Prince Sirik Matak, and other prominent leaders, were all immediately executed by the Khmer Rouge at the Phnom Penh Sporting Club, near Wat Phnom, beheaded on the tennis courts. Some say the Khmer Rouge washed their feet in the blood.

In Peking meanwhile, at his headquarters, a jubilant Prince Sihanouk, puppet head of the Khmer Rouge, was fêting the victory at a cocktail party, declaring it 'the finest page in Cambodia's history!' A few days later, in exile in Peking, adding an appropriate note of irony, his mother, Queen Kossamak died. It was the end of an era.

As the sun blazed across the sky, the mood on the streets was rapidly turning sour. The hand-clapping and dancing gave way to the sound of gun shots and bull-horns. 'Everyone out! Out! Out!' the Khmer Rouge were screaming. The entire population was being compelled at gunpoint to leave the city immediately. Now hundreds of menacing, grim-faced Khmer Rouge, guns at the ready, were striding up and down the streets, moving systematically from door to door all over the city, ordering the numbed and terror-stricken occupants to get out at once. Any who reasoned, argued, procrastinated, or simply got in the way were summarily shot down in a burst of bullets, a sobering example to others.

Wholesale looting was also getting under way by the mostly teenage soldiers of the Khmer Rouge who had always boasted that they never stole so much as 'a grain of rice' from the people. They were now confiscating at gunpoint anything they desired, from watches to motor cycles. It was at this time that the people began hearing with increasing regularity sinister words on the lips of the Khmer Rouge: *Angka Loeu* (the Organisation on High). Whatever soul-less, faceless, Orwellian monster *Angka Loeu* was, clearly it was the ultimate authority, the new name in which all things were to be done.

By mid-afternoon on that apocalyptic day, the streets were filled with the awesome spectacle of a great forced exodus of between two and three million terrified people being herded like cattle out into the waterless and war-torn countryside in the searing heat of mid-April. The order to leave was absolute, and without exception: the old and frail, pregnant women, tiny children, malnourished little orphans, the sick and dying, and the hundreds of seriously wounded war victims still on their beds; thrown out like garbage into the gutter, and told to move out. An estimated 20,000 hospital patients, many gravely ill and barely able to crawl, were pushed out onto the streets that victory day. This was the most pitiful sight, as hundreds of them lay helpless where they had been tipped out into the city's hospital compounds. Sidney Schanberg, a reporter with the *New York Times*, who had stayed to witness the fall of the city, movingly described the scene unfold-

ing before his eyes: 'Two million people in stunned silence –
walking, cycling, pushing cars, covering the roads like a human
carpet – suddenly forced to abandon the capital... bent under
sacks of belongings hastily thrown together when the heavily
armed soldiers came and asked them to leave immediately
...hospital patients hovering between life and death dragged out of
the city in their beds, some with the saline drips still fixed in their
arms.'

This same wretched drama would be staged in every city and
town throughout the entire country. The script of the tragedy had
long been written, polished, and rehearsed deep in the dark and
inscrutable pre-meditations of 'The Organisation'. But it was here
in Phnom Penh, on April 17, 1975 that the heartless young zealots
of the People's Liberation Army, like a thousand busy and
uniformed stage hands, managed the opening matinee. It was a
flawless performance: 'US bombers are coming to raze the city...
no need to take many possessions... in a few days you can return
... it is for your own protection.... leave the city at once...!'

As the sun plunged westward, the bitter exodus was well under
way. Vast columns of humanity were inching their way along
hopelessly clogged arteries flowing out of the fallen city. The
oppressive evening air continued to echo with the noise of loudspeakers, raucous commands, the clatter of small arms fire, the
shrieks of lost and terrified little children, and the stunned silence
of a people suddenly enslaved. And encircling the woeful
pilgrimage 'to purification' and the great city, hung a vast canopy,
a giant funeral shroud of thick, black, foul-smelling smoke,
ascending higher and higher into the darkening sky.

That morning found between four and five thousand Christians
bowed in worship before the living God. The pastors and lay
leaders were all in their various churches and meeting places with
their people crowded about them. Most of the leaders had already
made their final farewells to one another. When the angry, gun-
waving Khmer Rouge soldiers entered their homes and churches
to drive them forth, they went out quietly, staying together in
small groups, and, as they had been ordered, carrying only enough
food and clothing for three days.

Major Chhirc, driven from his office along with his associate Minh Tien Vaun, made no attempt to hide his identity, as many were doing, or to leave the city. He went straight to the compound of the French Embassy which was now filling up with members of the foreign diplomatic corps and Red Cross officials (their vain attempt at establishing a neutral zone at the Phnom Hotel had been scuttled by the Khmer Rouge who recognised no laws or precedents except those of *Angka Loeu*), along with various foreign newspaper reporters, expat workers and other trouble-shooters who had decided to tough it out until the bitter end. All were rounded up by the Khmer Rouge and brought here. A number of high-ranking Cambodians and their families (some with French passports) also took refuge here. These men and women of social, political and military rank were hoping no doubt for Embassy protection, and eventually asylum with their former colonial master, France. This was a futile hope. The Khmer Rouge knew nothing of diplomatic immunities or such niceties, and very soon had the crowded Embassy compound under guard, turning it into a virtual prison. Chhirc had done all he could during those final days to proclaim the gospel to his people. He had even gained access to the local radio station and broadcast passionate appeals for national fasting, repentance, and faith in Jesus Christ. Now with the government surrender, it seems that he purposely went to where many of these fallen leaders were holed up, men who had long hated and opposed all Chhirc stood for, in order to make a final appeal to them in their hour of humiliation and imminent death. He would proclaim the gospel of Jesus Christ to them with tears and then die alongside them.

Chhirc was seen by a Christian lady who later escaped, being put aboard an open truck with other key men who had been separated out from ordinary civilians by the Khmer Rouge when they entered the Embassy a few days later. The latter group was simply sent packing along with other stragglers out of the city. But Chhirc, along with his country's leaders whom he so coveted for the kingdom of God, was led off to another destination. We can only assume that he was executed, along with the hundreds of other prominent Cambodians at that time. Chhirc was not only a

Christian leader, but an officer in the Lon Nol army.

There is however another possible scenario. Chhirc may perhaps have been released and sent off to join the crowds leaving the city. A young Christian, a few days after the fall of Phnom Penh, later in April, 1975, thought he recognised Chhirc, and Voan his colleague, from afar, in the middle of a great throng of people milling about on a roadside just beyond the city. According to this person, it was impossible for him to get very close to them because of the press of people, and he also feared attracting the attention of the Khmer Rouge who were constantly watching and scanning the masses for 'enemies of the people'. The two men were standing in the midst of the vast encampment. They appeared animated, proclaiming what our witness could only assume was the gospel, to all the people crowded about them. This was confirmed when he heard some people near him passing the familiar comments about the *Puok Yesu* teaching and giving out leaflets. Just then he saw a group of men approach them, tie up their hands, and lead them away with others they had already rounded up. Those who took them away were not uniformed Khmer Rouge soldiers, but quislings, men and women who under cover of being ordinary civilians, mingled with the crowds to spy and listen to their conversations. The 'old people' of the district, those who had lived in Khmer Rouge 'liberated' areas for some months, certainly had no illusions as to what was happening. One, just a child, beholding the scene, turned to her mother and said dispassionately, 'They'll be riding elephants down south.' On hearing this, the young Christian turned and inquired the meaning of the little aphorism. The explanation confirmed his worst fears. It was another of the Khmer Rouge's clever one-liners. The conventional Cambodian farm hoe, which in the hands of the Khmer Rouge was to become the standard instrument of execution by means of a blow to the back of the head, bears a well-known trademark. Each hoe has the mark of an elephant stamped on the blade. The word for the heel of the hoe, the part which was brought down against the back of the victim's head, is the same as the word used for 'south'. Hence, a person about to be bludgeoned to death with a common hoe was said to be going to 'ride an elephant to the south.' Our observer could only conclude that Chhirc and Vaun were summarily executed. Whichever of these two accounts we follow, or even a combination of both, and knowing Chhirc's great heart, as all of us who were there did, I think we can be fairly certain that following the Khmer Rouge takeover, Chhirc did not hide his identity but continued boldly to proclaim Christ to his countrymen whom he so dearly loved, and consequently was soon overtaken by a martyr's death. His faith, however, continues to speak, and those final words still ring in our ears, 'We praise him because we are not on the losing side. For me to live is Christ, and to die is gain. The Lord bless you all.'

Out on the packed streets, midst the stricken populace, Pastor Reach Yeah struggled to keep his family together. They marvelled at all the empty and abandoned shops, doors gaping open, contents strewn about. The air about them was languid and heavy, filled with the stench of death and burning. Along the road they passed bloated corpses, unburied and rotting in the hot sun. Others were visible floating in the river where Christians had once gathered for baptisms. Here and there abandoned along the wayside, among the flotsam and jetsam of shoes, bags, clothing, abandoned vehicles, and piles of discarded paper money now abolished and totally worthless, lay the injured and dying. Pathetic lost children sat looking out in stunned wide-eyed grief and incredulity at the pitiless terror which had enveloped them. Old people grimly awaited their fate. Some cried out in vain for pity, others were silent. Cringing, some struggled to their feet leaning heavily on sticks, or even crawled like animals painfully on all fours, when the gun-toting teenage bullies came and goaded them forward. If a former republican soldier foolish enough to be still wearing his army uniform was spotted, or a trendy teenager with long hair or flared trousers, or a painted prostitute or anyone else they took a dislike to, they were pulled out and led away.

By nightfall, Yeah and his party had moved only one mile. They had reached a point just beyond the edge of the city where the carnage and horror from the previous days of heavy fighting was all around them. They stopped for the night at a place called 'Bamboo Plain', cooked some rice, and then broke into smaller groups to pray. All around them as far as they could see, thousands of their stunned countrymen were squatting around glowing fires and cooking pots, or lying exhausted on their backs on the rough ground trying to sleep, and mothers trying to comfort wailing infants. The Bethlehem Christians including Auntie Song and her children kept watch on each other, and remained close together. After praying, they discussed the situation at some length. Plans were made to split into smaller more manageable groups, dividing their slim resources accordingly. The slower ones, the aged, those with small children, would separate from the youths and stronger ones who could go ahead and prepare the way, find a place to settle, or forage for food.

Sitting there that evening with his people, contemplating the last tinge of gold lingering on the western horizon, and the numerous camp fires flicking around him, Reach Yeah, newly elected President of the Cambodian Evangelical Church, could never have imagined what lay before him down that long and difficult road leading out from Bamboo Plain. He would be separated from all his flock who now sat comfortingly nearby, for four bitter years, and most of them would perish. Behind him, in the eerie city, Bethlehem Church stood empty in the gathering darkness. It was evening, and then darkness fell and for Reach Yeah and the thousands of other Christians in Cambodia, the beginning of a long and fearful night.

PART III 1975 – 1996

CHAPTER 9

THE SEED FALLS
INTO THE GROUND

'The dead bodies of men will lie
like refuse on the open field,
like cut grain behind the reaper,
with no one to gather them.'

(Jeremiah 9:22)

...Cambodia has achieved a distinction which has so far eluded
even those countries unfortunate enough to experience the full
weight of terror brought to bear by even the most monstrous
tyrants of our time; it is the first country to be transformed into a
concentration camp in its entirety...in Cambodia, ignored by the
outside world, the unburied dead cry for vengeance, and the living
dead for pity; and cry, both, in vain.

(Bernard Levin, *The Times* April 22, 1976)

The picture we have is one of a country whose past was made a
tabula rasa by a Draconian effort to pull the country forward from
its feudal past and restructure the social and political relations of
its citizens. What is to be questioned is the single-mindedness
with which the new vision crushes anyone and anything that lies
in its way or that does not fit into the new blue print.

(Père François Ponchaud, *Cambodia Year Zero*, Penguin 1978)

Having emptied and vandalised the cities, *Angka Loeu* (The
Organisation on High) proclaimed the birth of a new 'Democratic

175

Kampuchea' and proudly declared, 'More than 200 years of Cambodian history have been virtually stamped out'. It is difficult to dispute that claim. Within a few days, the Organisation on High had advanced faster and further than any other revolutionaries of modern times toward obliteration of an entire society.

(John Barron and Anthony Paul *Murder of a Gentle Land*,
Reader's Digest Press, 1977)

In the West today, there is a pervasive consent to the notion of moral relativism, a reluctance to admit that absolute evil can and does exist. This makes it especially difficult for some to accept the fact that the Cambodian experience is something far worse than a revolutionary aberration. Rather, it is the deadly logical consequence of an atheistic, man-centred system of values, enforced by fallible human beings with total power, who believe, with Marx, that morality is whatever the powerful define it to be and, with Mao, that power grows from gun barrels.

(David Aikman, *Time,* July 31, 1978)

Bright red blood which covers our fields and plains,
of Kampuchea, our motherland!
Sublime blood of workers and peasants,
Sublime blood of revolutionary men and women fighters!
The blood changing into unrelenting hatred
And resolute struggle,
On April 17th, under the flag of the Revolution,
Free from slavery!

(The Khmer Rouge National Anthem)

One of the most prominent Khmer Rouge officials murdered in Tuol Sleng was Hu Nim, who, like many of his peers, had become a Communist in Paris in the late fifties and early sixties. He had then spent eight years in the Khmer Rouge maquis, and he was Minister of Information in the Khmer Rouge government until his arrest in 1977.

In his 'confession', Hu Nim was compelled to declare that he too had been 'an officer of the CIA' since 1957, working toward

Cambodian women planting out the rice seedlings. Over 80% of Cambodians live in rural villages as subsistence rice farmers.

Gossip at the village well: cyclor drivers return to their villages and families with news of the gospel they have received in Phnom Penh. In this way village house fellowships spring up.

Busy Monivong Boulevard, Phnom Penh.

The gifted evangelist, pastor and Bible Society director, Son Sonne, in Phnom Penh, 1974. Nearly all such men would have been executed by the Khmer Rouge.

Pastor Hom in Khao I Dang Camp on the Thai/Cambodian border, 1979, with the Bible he had kept hidden from the Khmer Rouge since 1975.

The amazing Granny Rose in Khao I Dang Camp, 1980.

Sythan and his new wife outside one of the scores of house churches which sprang up in Khao I Dang Camp, 1980.

Major Chhirc. Photograph reproduced courtesy of Southeast Asian Outreach.

the construction of capitalism in Kampuchea… completely toeing the line of the American imperialists… On the surface it seemed that I was a 'total revolutionary,' as if I was 'standing on the people's side.' But, in fact, deep in my mind, the essence was service of the American imperialists. I wrote a thesis for my law doctorate which even took a progressive stand… These were the cheapest acts which hid my reactionary, traitorous, corrupted elements, representing the feudalist, capitalist, imperialist establishment and the CIA… I'm not a human being, I'm an animal.

Hu Nim was 'crushed to bits' in July 1977.
   (William Shawcross, *The Quality of Mercy*, Simon and Shuster, New York 1984, p43)

Cambodia is synonymous with utter disaster, a blood stained experiment in social engineering which left over two million dead… The Khmer Rouge had a paranoid hatred for anything to do with love and its expression: husband and wife, children, family, friends, culture and religion.
   (Elizabeth Becker, *When the War was Over,* Simon and Shuster, New York 1986)

The Khmer Rouge were Marxist fanatics. They laid waste the golden harvest fields transforming them into blood red killing fields.
   (Haing S Ngor,[1] *Surviving the Killing Fields*, Chatto and Windus, London 1988)

The fall of Cambodia, with the capture of the capital city of Phnom Penh on April 17, 1975 by the Khmer Rouge communists, finally ended the cruel five-year long civil war which had left over half a million Cambodians dead. But contrary to what the celebrating crowds on the streets of Phnom Penh that April morning had hoped, it was far from the end of Cambodia's suffering. What began forthwith on that catastrophic day was a revolution so horrific, so anti-human, and so radical, it defies description. A shadowy clique of neo-Marxist zealots, known only to the cowering starving masses as *Angka Loeu* (The Organisation on High), promptly activated its doctrinaire, text-book revolutionary metamorphosis upon a people already totally exhausted from five years of war and dislocation. Around an entire nation of seven million, *Angka* spun an impenetrable black cocoon within which, unhindered by the prying eyes of the world, they single-mindedly set about producing an instant communist utopia. The cost in sheer human lives is incalculable. Two to three million perished, hundreds of thousands fled the country, thousands more were left physically impaired, and millions were bereaved resulting in a devastated nation of mostly widows and orphans. The long-term physical, emotional and spiritual ravages which laid waste an entire generation will never be comprehended.

Reminiscent of the divine and unapproachable Brahmin priest-kings of Angkor who centuries before had ruled over a vast kingdom of enslaved peasants and labourers, these latter day enlightened Marxist priest-kings of *Angka* ruled from the empty and forbidden city of Phnom Penh over a nation of grovelling serfs toiling likewise to grow rice and dig irrigation canals, reservoirs and dams for the glory of their masters. Three years, nine months and twenty days later, Cambodia was a bone yard, a wasteland, a charnel house of total wretchedness and desolation; a place where torture and death had become a daily routine of life.

The great spiritual harvest of the previous five years, like so many freshly gathered sheaves joyfully heaped on the threshing floor, was about to be winnowed and cleared. What was mere chaff, dead wood, or dry stubble would be blown away, incinerated in the fiery crucible. The grain however would remain, hidden and stored away for later. Much of it, kernel by precious kernel, would fall into the ground and die, and by so doing ensure future harvests in this field, to glorify the Father's name again and again. Perhaps thirty per cent of the Cambodian people and ninety per cent of the Cambodian Church perished in the Khmer Rouge reign of terror from 1975-1979.

By the end of April 1975, the entire population from every town in 'liberated' Cambodia had been successfully evacuated like so much manure spread all over the war-torn and barren countryside and untamed wilderness areas. Here the people were to be 'purified', whittled down, and remade into new creations worthy of the new socialist utopian world of equality, freedom, and justice for all. This was the brave new world being ushered in by the 'Organisation on High,' whose army of gun-toting, mostly semi-literate teenage thugs was a kind of first fruits.

The highways and byways of Cambodia were quiet now, littered with the silent putrefying remains of thousands of unburied bodies, precious bones, uncared for, whitening in the sun; long since looted by passers by, picked over and gnawed by preying birds and wild dogs. The hulks of hundreds of abandoned cars and other wheeled conveyances were strewn every which way about hushed and echoing city streets and suburbs. And all along dusty roads, worthless and abandoned paper money blew in little drifts, and fluttered persistently about the corpses and cast off belongings of those who had once laboured and fought so hard to acquire it.

The last grim stragglers on this macabre pilgrimage had finally shuffled, limped and dragged themselves out into the fields and forests of Cambodia. Here they had a 'sacred' appointment with *Angka*. By the sovereign will of *Angka,* they were about to be cleansed of the past, and taught to become devotees of *Angka* – 'all powerful', 'supreme', 'infallible', 'very enlightened', the 'way', the 'truth', and the 'life'.

Re-clothed now in shapeless vestments of pure black, they must be transformed into *Angka*'s image, or incur his wrath and perish. 'We are reborn, thanks to *Angka*!' the nightingales of the revolution sang out over Radio Phnom Penh. There is no other god but *Angka*, and Pol Pot is his prophet, was to be the new statement of faith. The priests of *Angka* prophesied that when they had purged out all the reprobate, the 'sub people,' the urban filth, and had redeemed just one million chosen elect of pure revolutionary Khmer peasant stock, authentic sons and daughters of the earth, they would restore Cambodia to its former glory, the glory and prestige it had enjoyed during the golden age of Angkor, seven hundred years earlier.

Angka in its amoral brilliance made a virtual institution out of lying. Hereby it was able to bring quickly to the surface the first layer of dross, 'dandruff' they called it, to be wiped away from the new Cambodia. Apart from the well-worked line about 'going to be received as heroes by Prince Sihanouk', this heating and stirring process was kept up by persistent scrutiny of each person's personal history. The people were subjected to repeated interrogations and propaganda meetings. Self criticism and 'confession' were constantly called for. The bloodshot eyes of *Angka*, like the 'eyes of a pineapple' were all around, omnipresent, never lifting their penetrating gaze. Ever watchful for that tell-tale pair of glasses, for a hidden book, fine hands, refined features, educated mannerisms, a posture, gait, attitude, facial expression; *Angka*'s gaze was scrutinising everything and anything at all which might expose 'an enemy'.

Added to this was the fact that frayed nerves were kept constantly at breaking point by means of perpetual terror and intimidation. Physical health was broken by the daily grinding toil. And starvation rations and lack of medicine destroyed not only life but the will to resist. Not a few simply walked away and quietly hanged themselves. Others killed their own children and then themselves.

Initially, the Khmer Rouge liquidated intellectuals, military officers, professionals, religious leaders such as Buddhist abbots and teachers, civic and political leaders. All these were executed *en masse* – machine-gunned or, as bullets became scarce, bludgeoned to death in some desolate forest rendezvous with *Angka*. 'We do not kill you', the baby-faced Khmer Rouge lads would deride in reply to cries for mercy, '*Angka* kills you!' The killers often amused themselves by quoting little aphorisms to their victims: 'If you live there is no profit; if you die there is no loss'. 'Finally you are going to be of use to *Angka*, as manure for the fields.' And nothing pleased them more or massaged their depraved and insecure egos as acts of grovelling contrition from those they were tormenting. 'Those whom the gods wish to destroy, they first drive insane.'

The mass killings also included distraught wives quaking in line behind their husbands awaiting their turn. Finally the wailing infants of the condemned were rudely snatched up and torn to pieces with bare hands or held by the ankles and smashed against a nearby tree. The 'bad blood line' had to be completely purged. Although these killing places were generally away from the work camps, the heaps of stinking bodies and shallow mass graves were soon discovered by horrified workers who stumbled upon them when out foraging, gathering wood or herding cattle. The gruesome accounts of what they had seen were quickly whispered from person to person, commune to commune. Some Khmer Rouge brazenly swaggered back spattered with blood, carrying their dripping clubs and hatchets, laughing and bragging about the day's slaughter.

Systematically, and perfectly in accordance with *Angka*'s unfolding master plan, the nets were cast increasingly deeper and wider. Next they swept up the ranks of lesser officials, lower ranking officers, and on down to regular foot soldiers, and students with as little as four years education. *Angka* had a long memory. Those who had confessed to lesser crimes when they felt themselves to be safely below earlier sweeps of purgation, later found themselves being sought out, exposed on the surface.

Ultimately, the pogroms included anyone who by the whim or personal malice of a local cadre was identified as an 'enemy'. By 1977 all the 'new people', *ie* people from the cities, were being killed by deliberate execution or by equally deliberate slow starvation. A careless glance, an unguarded frown, a murmur, an attitude, any of these and you might find yourself, hands tied, being hustled off one evening, after work of course, into the nearby forest 'to meet *Angka*' and to 'enjoy a very long rest.'

Not a few people were tricked into betraying their identity simply by volunteering information on how best to build something, or by foolishly showing a measure of enthusiasm and know-how. This was noted, but when the project was over such helpful people disappeared. Others were turned in by the menacing and ubiquitous *chlop*, or spies, often just young children who everywhere were the ears and eyes of *Angka*. They even crept stealthily about at night listening beneath the stilted thatch dwellings to intimate and whispered conversations of the unsuspecting as they lay exhausted on the bare bamboo slats.

Removed from parents, these children now recognised *Angka* as their sole parent and provider. Many 'counter revolutionaries,' 'CIA agents' and various other forms of 'dandruff,' according to the wisdom and discernment of these precocious young quislings, were unearthed and dealt with.

The Khmer Rouge had many other informers who mingled with the people and reported all they had seen and heard, plus some, to *Angka*. As is tragically and frequently the case in such fascist situations, some wretched souls were forced by blackmail to turn informer in order to save, though usually in vain, some loved one, or in exchange for some desperately needed food or medicine which the Khmer Rouge had in abundance. Some Cambodians, especially in this context of survival of the fittest and shrewdest, where the law of the jungle is pre-eminent, used the situation to settle old scores, and take revenge. It was hardly surprising, given the long antipathy towards them, that Christians were especially vulnerable here, and a number were betrayed by fellow Cambodian sufferers.

There were few warnings, and prison usually meant hideous torture to exact more names, a confession, and then death. There was just one basic punishment for all mistakes great or small, and that was death. One by one thousands upon thousands of Cambodian people were beaten to death with hoes and clubs, bayoneted, shot, poisoned, roasted, slowly asphyxiated with plastic bags tied over their heads, buried alive up to their necks to be eaten by red ants, cast bound into rivers and wells, slowly and hideously tortured to death, their shrieks and wails filling the commune for days. Some were tied up to trees or shackled in rooms and left to starve, some fed to crocodiles; others slowly had their heads sawn off, were garrotted, burned alive, electrocuted, tied to stakes and disembowelled, nailed to doors, left with veins cut to slowly bleed to death. And there were innumerable other gruesome techniques too hideous to record.

One particularly sinister and self-ritualised method of execution was the cutting out of a living person's liver and eating it. The condemned were first stripped and tied to posts. A Khmer Rouge would approach from behind, and with a knife or hatchet, cut into the lower back of his screaming and hysterical victim, then reaching in wrench out the liver. And as the victim slumped, his body still quivering and jerking in its death throes, the Khmer Rouge would proceed to fry the liver before his eyes. These livers were eaten by the Khmer Rouge to give them strength. Sometimes they even forced them upon the distraught relatives who had been called to condemn their son or husband to death. These kinds of killings can only be understood in terms of the demonic, the black magic found in much of the popular animistic lore and crude ritual of ancient Khmer practice. Although officially frowned upon as 'reactionary religion', it was far more a part of the world-view of these ruthless semi-literate peasant soldiers of the Khmer Rouge than the scientific and materialistic rationalities of Marxist theory, which their middle class leaders had imbibed in the Universities of France.

Their obscene methods of torturing and executing women cannot be contemplated, but they serve to underline the low and despised place women had in their minds. Added to the death lists were all prostitutes, petty thieves, drug addicts and various in-curables such as lepers. All these were cleansed out. Their only use to *Angka* in the new Cambodia was to be 'fertiliser for the fields'.

In addition to the enormous numbers who were systematically massacred in this way, were hundreds of thousands more who perished from starvation and endemic diseases such as tuberculosis, cholera, malaria and dysentery. No modern or foreign medicine was permitted. All that existed in terms of health care for the people were a few ill-trained Khmer Rouge youths, usually the hard and sullen *mit neary*, the female Khmer Rouge. They manned filthy unkempt 'clinics' and administered herbal remedies, such as injections of coconut milk from dirty syringes, and dispensed an assortment of bizarre concoctions including coca-cola. Few were there with any profound desire to heal the sick or save lives anyway, let alone comfort the scores of dying who filled all the available space. These 'clinics' were little more than half-way houses on the way to the death pit, a feature of every commune, with its fill of gaunt and twisted corpses. Most people avoided the clinics like the plague even though desperately ill.

To end the first doleful year of 1975 under *Angka*, a further mass migration of the labour force was enacted. In October and November, tens of thousands of sick and weary human beings were again uprooted, herded across fields, crammed into railway box cars and trucks, and shipped like cattle to the north west of the country. They were relocated especially to Battambang, the nation's rice bowl, here to gather in the annual harvest at year's end. This first harvest under the Khmer Rouge was eagerly anticipated.

Harvest time in Cambodia was traditionally always a time for optimism, celebration, falling in love, and generosity. Now, psychologically as well as physically, it held out a glimmer of hope. But when it came and then passed, these hopes were cruelly dashed. *Angka*'s trucks arrived and carried it all away to unknown destinations. The people, their hopes shattered and bellies aching, tasted only bitterness and were filled with nothing but pain. They were finally learning that to survive you must let all ambition, hope, and emotion dry up, and concentrate your energy no further ahead than surviving each day at a time, just getting one foot in front of the other, remaining deaf and mute, and not glancing to the left or to the right. To hope in *Angka* was fatal, and to trust even your spouse or brother was potentially suicidal.

For untold thousands whose lives were already hovering on the brink of death after only a few months under *Angka*'s 'enlightened' leadership, this second exodus was the last straw. Many languished, and others were tragically separated from their loved ones during the chaos and turmoil of the mass upheaval, characteristically carried out with maximum brutal disregard for even the most basic of human needs. And so the mountains of dead grew higher and higher in the wake of the stinking human wreckage being herded at gunpoint northwards, to be dumped out into the fields of Battambang.

Meanwhile, inside *Angka*'s inscrutable brain located in the forbidden city of Phnom Penh, little grey cells were working feverishly to consolidate the revolution. With the initial dirty work of clearing out the refuse, *ie* two to three million people, and the threat of any counter-attack now past, shadowy figures of the Khmer Rouge politburo quietly took up residence in the ghost city.

On September 8, 1975, Sihanouk himself returned to Phnom

Penh, though most of his cabinet in exile chose wisely to go to France rather than face death in their liberated homeland. Ever since the communist victory, he had been performing exceptionally adroitly for the odious regime he now championed. At the United Nations General Assembly a month later, he had strenuously denied the numerous reports from Cambodian refugees fleeing to Thailand of slave labour conditions and mass killings. The refugees were obviously lying, as Ieng Sary the regime's foreign minister had also asserted. Furthermore, 'the capital had been emptied in an orderly manner, without bloodshed, and for humanitarian reasons.'

Much of the western media gave some credence to this line because at the time it was still politically correct to believe the worst of the US and the best of the Khmer Rouge. And in Thailand's crowded border camps trendy intellectuals openly scoffed as refugees poured out their woeful tales. Thus the true horrors of Cambodia under the Khmer Rouge were not yet widely known.

But Sihanouk, accompanied by his beautiful wife, Monique, caught up like puppets on a string, resigned themselves to their fate. He did at least have the personal satisfaction of having beaten the pro-American regime, and having humiliated the Lon Nol clique who had overthrown him. This was supremely important to him. Perhaps the sweetness of this revenge helped coat the bitter realities he knew only too well he must now swallow. A number of Sihanouk's immediate family, including some of his children, were taken away and killed by the Khmer Rouge. But the man himself, after being trotted around for a few months to serve the regime's sinister public relations and propaganda purposes, was shut safely away in mothballs, imprisoned in his own crumbling Royal Palace, ready to be dusted off again should the need arise. Before he 'retired completely and forever from the political scene' on April 4, 1976, with the honorific title 'The Great Patriot', and with a generous 'pension' of US$8,000 per year (just how he was to use this locked away in a country which had abolished money is not clear), he gave his blessing to the new constitution of 'Democratic Kampuchea' unveiled on January 5, 1976. It contained no provision for a Head of State.

The early months following 'liberation' also saw the return of hundreds of Cambodian intellectuals who had been studying in Paris, and those undergoing military training in the US. Encouraged partly by the return of Prince Sihanouk, and enticed by the Khmer Rouge's promise of a heroes' welcome, and the headiness of something new, revolutionary, nationalistic, they returned with joyful anticipation. Home-sickness also played its part. On arrival, the fortunate ones were summarily executed, the rest were tortured, despised, imprisoned and reduced to animals. A handful survived, and one or two intrepid ones even escaped to Thailand to give their account of this monstrous deception.

1976 was ushered in with great fanfare with the imposition of the new constitution on January 3. Article 20 stated: 'Every Cambodian has the right to worship according to any religion. Reactionary religion which is detrimental to Democratic Kampuchea (Cambodia) is absolutely forbidden.' This *Nineteen Eighty-Four*-like 'doublespeak' amounted to the abolition of all religious practice, even Buddhism. Clearly only the new state cult of the worship of *Angka* would be tolerated. A new and terrifying breed of gods was in power.

The event was marked by appropriate liturgical clichés backed up with a massive outpouring of song and dance, with definite Chinese Red Guard flavour, extolling the mighty works of *Angka*. For the Khmer Rouge cadre, the local priests in each commune, it was vital for survival to be found ideologically pure, to be 'holier than thou', to be fluent in the correct vocabulary and adept with the latest slogans. Practical know-how was secondary. And so again, like the vast temple complexes of Angkor built by conscripted labour centuries earlier to the glory of unapproachable priest kings (and to the economic collapse of the nation), the grandiose irrigation systems of canals and dams constructed at *Angka*'s behest destroyed tens of thousands of Cambodians, were ill-conceived, incomplete and never worked. At least the former god kings left behind monuments of beauty. The latter left only half-finished follies, costly holes and heaps of earth which served no practical purpose except as graves and burial mounds for those who slaved over them. Not only were Cambodians forced to lay down their lives for the insane architects of *Angka*, but were compelled daily at mass meetings to repeat their ridiculous slogans and applaud their blatant lies.

1976 would also see the abolition of the family, as *Angka*'s cold iron grip tightened. All individual, personal, religious, home and family life was totally abolished. People were simply state commodities to be used and disposed of. Indoctrination meetings intensified, the purgings of the 'impure' widened, and the spiritual darkness and despair deepened. In the fields it was now 'a time to work', 'a time to weep', 'a time to be silent', and 'a time to die'.

The hard labour in the rice paddies and irrigation projects was gruelling even for tough and hardened peasants, but for the millions of exiles from the cities, the 'new people', it was beyond endurance. They were forced to subsist on watery rice soup in order to make the one small condensed milk tin full of rice per person last the required two days. (Normally a Cambodian will eat at least the equivalent of one of these tins full of rice for each meal, three times a day. An adult worker requires about twenty kilos of uncooked rice per month.) They toiled in the sun from six in the morning until late in the evening, sometimes on moonlit nights well after dark. Even then they were required to attend the nightly commune political indoctrination sessions. There was never a day off.

The 'sub people' died like flies, as *Angka* intended. The living lingered on staggering around like walking skeletons, the weakest supporting themselves with broken off tree limbs, skins blackening through lack of salt. And hanging in tatters about their bones the regulation black garments, the death shroud in which they would soon be tossed into the mass burial pit. Now they were animals, beasts of burden, harnessed to ploughs, swaying under baskets of earth, clearing away the thorny bamboo and tangled underbrush with a few crude tools and torn bleeding hands. Already ground into the dirt under the heavy heel of *Angka*, the dark shadow of the grim reaper was ever near. The nauseating stench of death wafted everywhere. It was carried by the breezes in every direction. In their heads sounded a dull persistent pounding like the lid of a coffin being nailed down. They were being buried alive.

All around them if they dared to raise their sunken eyes were the youthful priests, and vestal virgins, (the *mit neary*) of *Angka*, armed, well fed, aloof, ever present, ever watchful. Overhead the blood red flag of 'Democratic Kampuchea' fluttered in the foul air. It waved mockingly to them from some far-off building, or nearby at the work site having been paraded out early that morning. Then, with sounding gongs 'the faithful revolutionary workers and peasants' had been awakened from their tormented sleep to arise and serve 'the Enlightened One', not the Buddha any more, but *Angka Loeu*, the 'Organisation on High'. But *Angka* was never placated, never satisfied. It goaded them on with incessant demands for harder work, more self-sacrifice, more self-criticism. Loud speakers hung from poles at every commune, blared out the commands and exhortations, and the paeans of self-adoration, the libretto of a revolution gone horribly wrong. 'The workers' pride gives them unspeakable joy, they are as happy as if they had just been new born.'

Cambodia, one year after its fall into the hands of the Khmer Rouge, resembled a dying wasteland dotted with fetid pools fouled by rotting carcasses and excrement, inhabited no longer by human beings, but by pathetic flocks of scrawny black crows, painfully cowering and cringing this way and that at the command of a fearful and hideous force. With their hollow eyes fixed on the ground before them, they scratched fitfully about in the filth, foraging for snails, crabs, and the occasional lizard, gnawing here on a coarse root, and over there shamelessly, secretly cannibalising the unburied carcass of one of its own.

Throughout the baleful weeks of late April and May 1975, immediately following the order to leave the cities, hundreds of Christians, many of them new believers, wearily trudged the crowded highways of Cambodia along with their bewildered countrymen. Like other extended families or tradesmen, they struggled to keep together in small family and church groups. But some inevitably found themselves suddenly separated and alone, swept aside or carried away down one of the currents of these turbulent rivers of humanity which flowed out of the cities, slopping its waste all along the road sides until finally draining out into numerous sluggish tributaries and creeping rivulets, to be absorbed into the parched and burning countryside.

Pastor Reach Yeah and some of the Christians from Bethlehem Church who were travelling with him, now realised along with all the others that they had been deceived. There would be no return. This was no three-day excursion for their own protection as they had been led to believe by the gun-brandishing Khmer Rouge. It was the beginning of a long, long march into a strange and hostile wilderness, to a place where each would need a goodly supply of spiritual resources if they were to be those well-watered gardens and oases throughout the long drought ahead.

The Khmer Rouge confiscated the Bible School van which the Bethlehem believers were using to carry their baggage, the little children and the weak. The others, the pace being so slow, had walked along beside it. As the days passed, groups began to split away and head out in various directions, perhaps to a familiar village, or to find lost family members. They had all spent an entire night praying together for guidance near an abandoned Buddhist temple along the way: 'Send us out in the direction of your choosing and direct our steps.'

Pastor Chau Uth headed for Siem Riep to the north. The great preacher, interpreter, and church leader, Son Sonne, and several other family groups headed for Battambang. Disaster soon over-took this latter group when crossing the River Mekong. One of the overcrowded boats in which they were travelling capsized, tragi-cally drowning a number of people including Son Sonne's young sons. The Christians retrieved the little bodies from the water and with great sadness they watched this great man of God bury his three boys for whom he had cherished such great dreams. It seems that the rest of them later also perished of starvation and disease.

Reach Yeah and his family, alone now, slept out under the trees by night and continued along the road by day. When it seemed that his wife could travel no further through sheer exhaustion and a high fever, they and a number of strangers travelling with them were separated out by the Khmer Rouge, put on motor boats and taken up river to Rogagong. This was the place where Auntie Song and her husband had had their short lived ministry years before. During the two-night stay here in these familiar surroundings, Yeah thought of those few Christian families who once lived in this now deserted town, and wondered what had become of them. Then they were off by boat again, rejoicing that they had been mercifully spared the long journey on foot. Northwards, through the port of Kampong Cham they sped, until finally they were unloaded at a place close to the border with Kratie Province.

Here they all lived in relative peace for about a year. It was an out-of-the-way place deep in the wilderness, and they were like pioneers cutting down the virgin forest, gardening, and growing rice. Yeah still had his Bible with him, and every day in some quiet and lonely spot he was able to take it out and read. Most often this was when he was sent to watch the grazing buffalo. Not only could Yeah read and meditate upon the word of God which he held in his hands, but he could also lift up his eyes and gaze upon the divine declaration in the Creator's handiwork which lay so rich and abundant all about him.

After the rains, when grazing for the buffalo was plentiful, Yeah had time to sit and soak it all afresh into his thirsty soul. The forest was bursting forth in an intense and dazzling choreography of light and life. Sunshine and shadow danced crazily across the rich green brocade of foliage. A rhapsody of birdsong filled the air. In the stillness of the early mornings, sparkling dewdrops trembled on filmy threads of gossamer like precious jewels set into the leafy ferns. Spinning balls of gnats ascended upward into the pale luminosity of the morning light. Above, in the leafy canopy, turtle doves tawny and speckled flopped clumsily from branch to branch growing plump on the berries which grew there. At the forest's edge a chequerboard of water-filled rice paddies reflected the immense sky out of which graceful swallows swooped and soared in search of insects. Along the embankments, sparrows quarrelled and tumbled among the scented grasses. The monotony of the paddies was broken by spiky sugar palms aureoled against the blue by their fan-shaped fronds. Sprays of feathery bamboo waved from atop little hillocks and termite mounds which everywhere dotted the landscape.

And when the sun had dropped in a blaze of colour behind the blue line of distant hills, Yeah rounded up the herd for the night. The steady pulsating of a vast chorus of tiny creatures chanting their melancholy plainsong accompanied him as he followed the slow steady pace of the buffaloes through the gathering dusk back to the village. And once again Yeah affirmed those first sublime words of Divine disclosure: 'In the beginning God created the heavens and the earth... and behold it was very good.' In this knowledge he continued to walk and not faint.

Paradoxically, but in harmony with their biblical antecedents, while many of Cambodia's mighty men and women of faith perished seemingly ignominiously during these four terrible years, some, in God's providence, were miraculously preserved. 'Hidden' would best describe it. Reach Yeah, the last elected national church president, was a perfect example of one of these. During 1976, as food became more and more scarce and many people around him began to die of starvation and sickness, Yeah and his family were moved to another place further over in Kratie province.

On arriving here, Yeah suddenly feared for his life. There, sitting among the Khmer Rouge cadres was a familiar face. The man's name was Pon. Pastor Yeah had known him well in Phnom Penh, but had no idea that he was a Khmer Rouge. Like many Khmer Rouge and their sympathisers, Pon lived an outwardly normal life in Phnom Penh, but he was actually a spy. Knowing how the communists hated Christianity, Yeah, a pastor, and indeed the President of the Cambodian Evangelical Church, felt very vulnerable. He never dreamed that he would meet someone way out here in the northern wilderness regions of Cambodia who would know so completely who he really was. Surely it was just a matter of time before he was accused and taken away to certain death.

Yeah began to pray earnestly for Comrade Pon that he might find favour and not hostility in his eyes. And to Yeah's great joy, the Lord caused Pon to become unusually friendly towards him, displaying genuine respect for Yeah's age and wisdom. Furthermore, Pon frequently took Yeah aside to question him about his faith in God, clearly not with any malicious motive, but with a deep inner thirst for spiritual truth. Yeah, with his long experience, shrewdness, and profound understanding of the ways of Cambodian Buddhist hearts, gently witnessed to this Khmer Rouge cadre of the Saviour Jesus Christ. It seemed to Yeah much of the time that he had his head 'in the lion's mouth', for who could tell what changing circumstance or whim of temper might at any moment turn this thoughtful comrade into his killer.

In time, Yeah felt confident and bold enough to show Pon his hidden Bible, a book strictly forbidden by *Angka*. Now more fully he could explain concerning the creator-redeemer God and his great design centred on Jesus Christ, the Son. On one occasion when they were discussing communist revolutionary philosophy, and the ideas propounded by the 'Organisation', Yeah handed his Bible to Pon opened at Acts 4:32-35. He explained how the first Christians were 'one in heart and mind', with no one claiming anything as exclusively his own, but rather as stewards, they held what they had themselves received from God with open hands, gladly and voluntarily sharing all things in common, with the result that there was not a needy person among them. The young cadre was amazed. 'You see,' said Yeah, smiling, 'I have been a radical too, for nearly thirty years, ever since I became a disciple of the Lord Jesus at the age of eighteen.' 'Truly,' beamed Pon, 'You, Grandfather, have trodden the revolutionary way far longer and deeper than any of us!'

Such were the opportunities granted to this wise old 'revolutionary', who with Bible in hand, shrewd as a serpent, innocent as a dove, bore witness to Pon and a good many more of *Angka*'s revolutionaries. But Yeah was always careful to speak only when asked. Otherwise he held his peace.

It must be said, that despite the atrocities committed by the Khmer Rouge, there were among their ranks a minority of principled people with high ideals. These were the purists, the idealists, left-leaning intellectuals, and genuine nationalists who abhorred the corruption and exploitation which had for too long been a way of life for Cambodia. These men sincerely believed that by a radical reshaping of the externals, a more just society would result. Such people quickly became disillusioned with the insane direction the revolution was taking. While remaining loyal largely from fear, they secretly warned people to flee imminent death, and in true revolutionary spirit sought to share what they could with the sick and hungry, and turned a blind eye as starving peasants reached for forbidden fruit.

Later when they defected to Thailand they denied any part in the mass killings and use of starvation as a means of social control. This of course is almost impossible to verify, for many were seeking to distance themselves from the excesses of this revolution gone horribly wrong. Most of them, however, were rounded up and liquidated in 1978 when *Angka* was frantically purging its own ranks of 'half-hearted reactionaries', 'CIA' and 'Vietnamese' agents. Of the thousands of dispirited and defeated Khmer Rouge who in late 1979 found themselves fleeing for respite to Thailand, not a few discovered the answer to their long and troubled search for truth and justice in the Christian gospel.

It is indeed one of the mysterious paradoxes in God's inscrutable ways, that while men like Chhirc and Son Sonne, indeed virtually all the choicest and best of the Cambodian church perished, betrayed in some cases by some precocious child spy, still others were afforded miraculous deliverance, angelic protection, and a spread table in the presence of their enemies.

As it is described in the Christian 'Hall of Fame' in Hebrews 11, so it appeared to be with the Cambodian church. While some 'shut the mouths of lions, quenched the fury of the flames, and escaped the edge of the sword; whose weakness was turned to strength', others were tortured. 'Some faced jeers and flogging, while still others were chained and put in prison. They were stoned; they were sawn in two; they were put to death by the sword. They went about in sheepskins and goatskins, destitute, persecuted and ill-treated – the world was not worthy of them.'

What a total falsehood is that fashionable but perverse teaching spreading out from the affluent West and gaining popularity among some churches in the developing world that Christians will and should be blessed with health and prosperity! The fact is that men and women in Cambodia, as in biblical times, whose lives burned with a holy zeal at times awesome in its ferocity, died of necessity in a world totally unworthy of them. They not only suffered, but died like dogs. Their discarded earthly tents lay strewn and unburied all across the land. These were people who stood in a direct line whether by life or by death with the prophets and apostles of old. They are the ones to whom the Lord speaks the final double beatitude.

All of us who would be transformed to Christ's righteousness must know that the cross is an offence, the very stench of death, to those who are perishing. Some form of personal suffering must result from authentic Christian living. The Word of God guarantees it. Suffering has been granted to us, and it will increase in direct proportion to the measure of our faith, obedience, and heavenly-mindedness. But as the Cambodian Christians discovered for themselves, none of these things is able to separate the child of God from the love of God which is declared in Christ Jesus.

For the remainder of the Khmer Rouge period, until early 1979, Reach Yeah and his family lived hedged around by God's restraining hand, provided for, and content. Thus while others laboured and died in the fields, he was given this responsibility of caring for God's more humble creatures, the cows and buffaloes. Each day he continued to lead them out to graze in some quiet place near the tranquil and majestic forest. And there too in the midst of God's creation, Yeah kept a divine appointment.

Like Hom, Yeah's Christian faith and love had long been affirmed and nurtured by the fact that God was the Creator. The tangible beauty and vast variety of his handiwork abundantly confirmed that all around them. I recall how soon after arriving in Cambodia in 1974, we were advised by Yeah, 'In your proclamation of the gospel here, you must begin by telling our people about God as Creator. Begin at Genesis 1:1, "In the beginning God created the heaven and the earth..."' Now Yeah himself was being sustained and renewed as he, an image-bearing creature of the Creator, dwelt there in the quiet pastoral solitude of the Lord's appointment, in the company of the grazing cattle.

It was here that it dawned on Yeah, as he ruminated over Scriptures he had memorised for years, that his testimony was exactly that of Psalm 23. He was being shepherded in these green pastures, and lacked nothing. His soul was basking in the warmth and peace of his Lord's immediate presence, even here in a land which had become a dismal valley of shadows where death stalked everywhere. The Khmer Rouge, his 'enemy', was kind to him, and his table was provided with sufficient food.

At night-time back in his little hut, where he lived with his wife, he would read his Bible and pray under his breath, slowly, deliberately. Sometimes he would murmur a hymn with a tune of deep melancholy, not from any sadness but characteristic of the Cambodian soul, one which pulsates with such ardour and passion that it evokes pain, a compunction that is cathartic.

> Nearer, my God to Thee, nearer to Thee!
> E'en though it be a cross that raiseth me;
> Still all my song shall be, nearer, my God to Thee,
> Nearer, my God, to Thee, nearer to Thee.
>
> Though like the wanderer, the sun gone down,
> Darkness be over me, my rest a stone;
> Yet in my dreams I'd be nearer, my God, to Thee.
>
> There let the way appear steps unto heaven;
> All that Thou sendest me in mercy given;
> Angels to beckon me nearer, my God to Thee.

From time to time, passers-by would surprise Pastor Yeah by inquiring, 'Who is that stranger who comes and goes and sits on the steps of your house?' At first Yeah was puzzled by this, for he was aware of no friend whom he had entertained or who might linger at the door of his house. But as the gossip persisted, Yeah came to understand who the stranger was, even though his own eyes were never opened to see him. Only the villagers and some Khmer Rouge saw him, and soon they too realised and feared. That simple thatch hut, on the edge of the commune, stood on sacred ground. It was visited with angelic protection, and no one dared to violate it.

Another member of the Bethlehem community driven out of Phnom Penh was Auntie Song. Progress had been so slow on that first day that she was able to slip back to her home again for the night of April 17, 1975. But by 9am the next morning she was back on the road. Auntie Song remembered vividly how the Christians had gathered together for the last time at Bamboo Plain with senior pastors Reach Yeah and Sen Boon, just a few days after the exodus began and before they broke up into smaller groups.

Travelling in her group of about six was the elderly but plucky Granny Naey, widow of Pastor Yan who had been killed nearly thirty years earlier by the *Issarak* Freedom Fighters. She was a leader of the Cambodian Christian women's movement, a Bible woman, and had lived and worked for years around the Bible School at Takmau where she was greatly loved by generations of students and staff alike. Well beyond three score years and ten, Naey was one of that first generation of believers, the same vintage as Granny Rose of Doentiey. Granny Naey was accompanied by her son, the former pastor Sarun, and his son Zachery, a young man in his twenties. Finally, there were three of Song's own children, Joseph and Nason, young men now, and her daughter Tieren.

Working their way steadily northwards, they trudged the hot roads sticky with blistering tar, and littered with the cast-off junk of the thousands who had preceded them. Hundreds of fellow sufferers travelled with them, sleeping here and there along the roadsides or sheltering in one of the many abandoned or burned out villages along the way. By now they were in territory which had long been occupied by the Khmer Rouge. Here, the rural folk, the approved 'old people', were unfriendly, eyeing this sorrowful exodus of townspeople, the 'new people', passing in droves past their villages, with contempt and scorn. This feeling was no doubt tinged with a measure of satisfaction at their fate. A resentment born out of years of pent-up hatred and jealousy towards perceived greedy rich city folk who always looked down on them. Well now it was their turn to suffer! Certainly few were willing to do anything to relieve the suffering of the sick and dying.

Song wept as she passed by those too weak to keep up. Some sat where they had been left, propped up under trees by relatives. All were patiently waiting for merciful death to find them. Any mourners who lingered tearfully beside such unfortunates were soon hurried on by the armed soldiers who constantly patrolled the long lines of people.

But nothing was more horrifying than the gruesome sight of the dead. Tiny babies, the flies hovering in swarms over their swollen bodies; the aged, sunken-eyed and faded away; ex-soldiers, with the same filthy blood soaked bandages which had bound the stumps of their recent amputations when the Khmer Rouge soldiers burst into the hospitals and drove them out onto the streets; bodies of every description, bloated, stinking, rotting, each one an untold tale of agony.

The utter tragedy and total indignity of what had befallen these unfortunate people tormented Song's sensitive and tender heart with a mixture of pity and terror. For many, the increasing familiarity with such ugly scenes produced a certain callousness, a determination to survive at all costs. But Song always suffered. For her, their twisted, staring, grotesque shapes were not those of dead creatures whose bad *karma* had finally caught up with them. They were human beings, men and women each unique in the image of God. Such a sight to her, and she would see many many more, was always unnatural and wrong. And as she walked along the road her tears flowed for them, the unburied dead.

Song sought to maintain a constant attitude of prayer. They were regularly threatened with disaster as fevers and dysentery struck this one and that one. At every checkpoint Khmer Rouge soldiers roughly questioned and searched each person. At the whim of some gun-wielding youth they might suddenly be split up and sent off in different directions to some appointed worksite. The most pressing concern however was food and water. Where would the next meal come from? Piece by piece they traded away all their extra clothing with the 'old people' for morsels of food and milk tins of precious rice. The next bowl of rice was about to become the all consuming obsession of the people, exceeding even that of personal pride or family relationships. Clearly, hunger and fear were to be the primary means of social control under *Angka*.

In wonderful ways Song's prayers were answered. A scrap of food provided here, a shared portion of rice there. When her son was too weak with dysentery to stand, an old man passing in his bullock cart gave them a lift. He had also warned her when she began talking about Jesus Christ to be careful. 'This is a new age, and such talk is dangerous.' Miraculously, even Granny Naey seemed to muster incredible energy, managing up to forty kilometres a day, a pace which exhausted even the younger ones.

Passing through the hushed and deserted town of Kampong Thom, they lowered their voices in awe at the sight of a once crowded and bustling city now standing in complete silence. Zachery went off to rummage around for food in the deserted houses and shops. Throwing open the door of one of the shop-houses, he suddenly caught his breath. He had stumbled into a house church. All around the walls were pictures of biblical scenes; Bibles and hymn books lay scattered about on the chairs. *Had the Khmer Rouge come and driven them out while they had been at worship?* thought Zachery. He paused to sit momentarily on one of the benches, a solitary worshipper, savouring the refreshment of this oasis he had found. He reached out a hand and laid it fondly on an abandoned Bible next to him, letting his thumb run across the edges of the pages which he knew were filled with the promises of God. He felt warmed and encouraged, no longer alone but with a sense of solidarity with these absent brothers and sisters. Why had God led him to discover this silent and holy place midst his scramble to find food? For a few sublime moments of contemplation, time stood still, and Zachery basked in the powerful peace of that hidden sanctuary, renewed by the presence of One who when resurrected from agony and death had promised, '…and surely I will be with you always, even to the very end of the world.' Quietly, Zachery crept from the empty yet inhabited room, leaving it undisturbed just as he had found it, waiting for the worshippers to return.

The weary party after weeks on the road settled finally at Phum Kor, about seventy-five kilometres from the town of Siem Riep in the northern province of that name. Here they lived in relative peace and safety for over three years until the Vietnamese army came and freed them from the cruel yoke of the Khmer Rouge. Like Reach Yeah, Song and the handful of Christians with her enjoyed a measure of freedom and favour in the eyes of their Khmer Rouge guards.

During those days they were able to lead twenty or thirty people to repentance and faith in Jesus Christ. Quietly, on certain evenings, around eight o'clock, people would come to them in twos and threes to hear about 'the Saviour of the world'. All would kneel on the earth floor to pray for one another's needs, and for the door of Cambodia to re-open. Uncle Sarun would lead the group in worship using the Bible and hymn book which he kept hidden under his house. Hymn singing was kept to a whisper. But when alone in the fields the Christians found themselves quietly singing and humming the hymns they loved.

There was one widow named Roeum who had a small child. She was one of those who when the gospel was carefully explained to her, quickly responded and gave her heart to the Lord. Later Roeum was moved to another commune close to the empty city of Siem Riep. Here she tirelessly proclaimed her new found faith in Christ, leading others in that place to believe on him also.

Another, a young man named Keo Dara, led to the Lord in those dark days by Auntie Song and her group at Phum Kor, escaped to Thailand in early 1978. At the refugee camp he gave us a firsthand report, confirming that our prayers were being answered for the Christians in Cambodia. Dara was able to tell us how they had just celebrated Christmas 1977 at Phum Kor, their third 'in captivity'.

By the end of 1976, the last of the Buddhist monks had been defrocked and sent to labour in the fields like everyone else. Many were executed. The Buddhist temples were turned now into warehouses, schools, clinics and prisons, and the idols smashed up and trodden under foot as landfill for road repairs. Some people, hungry spiritually, and bereft of their old religious moorings, gravitated to the Christians whose faith did not require any such trappings and props. Here in small and secret gatherings they found a new and infinitely more secure spiritual home.

What did persist however, unabated, was the real heart religion of the Cambodian people; namely, those crude and sinister practices of animism and spiritism. It puzzled villagers why the Christians were not harassed by all the restless and wandering spirits, especially since they paid them no respect or made no offerings to placate them. With so many people being killed, they were the more fearful of all these vengeful ghosts afoot.

Sarun at Phum Kor soon gained a reputation for his powers of exorcism, for many Cambodians were hopelessly bound by evil spirits. Even the Khmer Rouge secretly called on him when they were sick, demon-possessed, or in fear of some local malevolent spirit whom they had offended.

It is especially during times of sickness and death that the ancient animistic rituals of the 'Kru Khmer', the spirit mediums, are widely in demand. The young Khmer Rouge soldiers, themselves of superstitious rural peasant stock, ignored orders from 'on high' to abandon such foolish superstitions. On one occasion, Nason, Auntie Song's son, was bitten on the heel by a deadly poisonous viper. In excruciating pain, he was carried by excited neighbours from the harvest field back to his mother's shack. Messengers were immediately dispatched to call in the 'Kru Khmer', the local shaman, to perform the healing ritual of spitting the juice of chewed beetle-nut over the lad accompanied by various incantations. As is usual, a great crowd had gathered to enjoy the event, including, as Song knew well, Khmer Rouge quislings. Nevertheless, she cried out, 'No, away with all this. We are Christians. We believe in the living God!'

'Do you want your son to die then!' exclaimed the incredulous and offended villagers.

'If he dies, he goes to eternal life in heaven,' replied Song, 'and if he lives he does so by the grace and mercy of God.' Sending the spirit medium away, she fell on her knees before the doubled-over body of her son. He was already turning black and in considerable pain as the venom coursed its way through his bloodstream. All night she prayed, kneeling beside his trembling body. In the morning the people returned, standing before the house. One had already gone to the trouble of digging a shallow grave. They had come for the body, and to gloat. A smiling Song beckoned them up the ladder into the house. Before them sat young Nason, serene and well. He was able to walk about unaided, and with his exhausted but thankful mother testify to the power of the risen Christ, their Lord, their Saviour, and their ever present friend. There could no longer be any secret about the presence of Christians in this commune. And more and more people made their way on those appointed evenings to join others in Christian devotions, and to listen to the readings from the worn and tattered Holy Book.

On one such night while they were sitting listening to Sarun, the door swung open, and there stood the chief Khmer Rouge cadre. Sarun stopped in mid sentence as the dark figure standing in the doorway surveyed the scene. No one moved. Then without a word but a downward wave of his hand he beckoned Auntie Song outside. When they had walked a few paces beyond the house, he turned to her and said, 'Do you believe in Jesus Christ?'

'Yes,' she replied, 'I do.' Saying no more, he led Song quickly through the darkness to the forbidden area reserved for the servants of *Angka*, to his own house. As they kicked off their sandals and ascended the steps, Song was aware that she felt no fear but rather a sense that she was being borne along by strong arms which surrounded her. Once in the house she was no longer aware of a fearsome communist cadre but simply of a man at his mother's deathbed. He had hurried across the room ahead of her to a corner where he knelt beside a very old lady who Song could see was near to death. His mother was eighty-six and dying of dysentery. Her breathing was laboured and the light was fading from her eyes. Song was vaguely aware of others in the room watching but she took no notice. She knew why she was here. Song took the woman's frail and trembling hand in hers, and as two women, they spoke softly together of the things of Jesus Christ and the way of salvation. 'I have wanted you to come for so long,' she whispered, 'I believe, I do believe'. Song prayed and committed her to the Lord. The following morning the old lady died peacefully. While some of the Christians feared what might now happen, the Khmer Rouge chief never spoke of it again.

For Granny Naey, the rigours of life under the Khmer Rouge, but even more the separation from Christian family and friends, took its toll. Soon after their quiet celebration of Christmas 1976 in the midst of the harvest season, she died, 'of a broken heart', said Song. They had done all they could to make her comfortable, from searching for a piece of tender fruit she craved to weaving a rush mat to place beneath her, to alleviate the discomfort of her frail old body pressing against the bamboo slats of the sleeping platform. The lice which inhabited all the homes bit her mercilessly, but her spirit was strong right up until the end. Now, more than anything else, she longed for 'home', and 'home' she went. The Christians prepared a grave, and in it gently placed the well worn and cast off 'tent' of this godly pilgrim with great honour. Then together, standing around her grave, they joined together very quietly in a hymn:

Sing the wondrous love of Jesus,
Sing his mercy and his grace;
In the mansions bright and blessed,
He'll prepare for us a place.
When we all get to heaven,
What a day of rejoicing that will be.
When we all see Jesus,
We'll sing and shout the victory.

While we walk the pilgrim pathway
Clouds will overspread the sky;
But when travelling days are over,
Not a shadow, not a sigh.
When we all get to heaven.

Let us then be true and faithful,
Trusting, serving every day;
Just one glimpse of him in glory
Will the toils of life repay.
When we all get to heaven.

Here was surely one of the richest and best of those many precious seeds which fell that season into the blood-soaked ground of 'the killing fields'.

The young man with his wife and four children whom we mentioned earlier as the one who felt sure he had seen Major Chhirc and Minh Vaun, evangelising and handing out gospel tracts to the crowds along the roadside near Neak Luong, in late April 1975, was Rebina, grandson of Granny Naey and son of Sarun. Rebina had no idea where his relatives were, having been driven out of Phnom Penh in another direction.

Early in his flight from Phnom Penh at one of the frequent

checkpoints where the people were being 'liberated' of their valuables and vehicles, and 'enemies' were being sniffed out for execution, Rebina was spotted and called aside by one of the soldiers scanning the crowds as they passed by. The young Khmer Rouge cadre suddenly softened his voice, and looking straight at the Christian with eyes full of warmth and compassion said, 'I love you my brother, but from now on you must always say that you are a peasant labourer, otherwise you will in time be killed.' Rebina was so startled by this that he could say nothing, but only stand there transfixed, searching the eyes of this gentle stranger whose message and manner bore no resemblance to the uniform he wore or the gun he carried. The curious encounter was rudely interrupted when a tough and battle-hardened Khmer Rouge woman came over and demanded Rebina's motorcycle.

As he and his family walked away, draped in their pathetic bundles of belongings, he stole a glance backwards. Briefly he caught a glimpse of the upright figure of the young man in black looking intently after them, and then the crowds of people came between them. Rebina never forgot this advice. Shortly afterwards he saw many former teachers, doctors, civil servants, soldiers etc all volunteering 'to return to Phnom Penh and take up their former employment again and assist in the reconstruction of "Democratic Kampuchea"'. It was a brilliant ploy and many, hoping for respite from the present misery, unwittingly gave themselves up into the deadly embrace of the Khmer Rouge and were quickly disposed of. When these lies no longer worked due to bitter experience, the Khmer Rouge devised others. They had an uncanny knack for duplicity, for setting people up for the kill.

The family was eventually settled at Chamcar Ler, just west of the city of Kampong Cham. Rebina witnessed many terrible things, but it was in 1977 that the situation became critical. The orders coming down from *Angka* now were that all the 'new people' were enemies and must be totally purged. At Chamcar Ler, with the onset of rains in May of that year, the villagers were surprised by the sudden arrival of many thousands of these pitiful 'new people'. For days, men, women and children were trucked in from all directions.

The chilling news being whispered down from the local 'old people' was that all these arrivals had been rounded up and brought here to be killed during the slack season after the new rice crop had been planted. (The Khmer Rouge always killed people after they had first worked them almost to death.) Rebina could hardly believe that so many could be systematically liquidated. But on an appointed day it began. Each day large groups of the new arrivals were called up and taken away. None of them ever returned.

Months later, about November time, when the rains had ceased and villagers drove the buffaloes out into the forest countryside to graze, reports began filtering back of this one and that one having come upon mass shallow graves. Where the rains had washed away the sticky red clay, heads, arms and legs could be seen sticking out of the ground. Some of the gruesome remains were still bound and blindfolded, decomposing in the sodden earth. Still incredulous, Rebina was taken secretly by one of the villagers to see for himself. The sight was beyond description. Rebina had seen many terrible things but he was stunned by this spectre of massive wilful destruction of an entire class of people.

But what caught his attention as much as the gruesome killing fields and enormous grave sites, were the surrounding piles of abandoned possessions, strewn all over the area. Everywhere there were clothes, identification cards, photographs, suitcases bursting with garments, and every kind of personal belonging imaginable. While the villagers, to his deep disgust, foraged vulture-like amongst the carnage for gold, even to the point of ripping gold filled teeth out from skulls, Rebina wandered around picking up photograph after photograph. There they were, family portraits, photos of smiling wedding groups, graduations, religious cere-monies, girlfriends, new babies, a vivid kaleidoscope of Cam-bodia's pre-1975 upper classes passing before his eyes. A pictorial record of the elite of the land: professors, doctors, politicians, officers, wealthy entrepreneurs, socialites, strewn all over the dank forest floor at his feet, fading in the rain and sun. Some, like their owners, decayed forever beyond recognition.

There was an unreality about what he was seeing. The remnants of a once-secure, comfortable, glittering world was rotting out here unknown and forgotten in the forest, desecrated by rough hands, trodden under by broad muddy feet. He felt an urge to at least rescue the photos, pluck them from the mud, brush off the filth which soiled the beautiful confident faces and expensive clothing. But he could not. Their world no longer existed. They were ghosts of a past now fading away. Aloof as ever, it was as impossible for the likes of him to touch and hold them now as it had been when they lived. But he mourned for them nevertheless as they lay naked and exposed before him, their treasures spilled all about his feet. He felt even more keenly now than ever before the utter loneliness and poverty of his life as a Cambodian, yet he coveted nothing of theirs. Instead he turned away, deeply troubled, and walked back to the real world of torn and shapeless black clothes draped over expressionless skeletal bodies. But the pictures, the images of those beautiful, confident and happy faces danced before his eyes.

It was during this horrendous time in late 1977 that Rebina received the news that they had taken his wife and one remaining child and killed them. He was about ten kilometres away from the village at the time, out at a work site. There was no warning, no reason, just 'a call from *Angka*'.

'They've killed your wife and now they will kill you. You can't go back there,' a friend warned him.

Rebina fled into the forest weeping bitterly, wretched with grief and a depth of pain almost beyond endurance. He threw himself around a tree and cried uncontrollably, beating his fists hard against the rough bark above his head, crying out to God for strength. How long he stayed there with his head pressed against the wood, he couldn't recall. But when he turned aside he found himself surrounded by several doleful-looking oxen. Curious over the commotion, they had left off grazing and come to stand silently about him, looking on with their sad watery eyes and wet drooling noses. It was as if they understood. And Rebina's heart was arrested by this strange but nonetheless touching company of mourners, God's creatures who had come to stand silently by him in the forest in his moment of grief.

But now he had to flee. Somehow he had to reach another

commune in secret. To be caught travelling in open country without a permit would mean instant death. With nightfall Rebina started to work his way carefully through the forest towards a commune nearby where he had friends. He crawled on his belly across open stretches, floundered through muddy ditches, at one point even stumbling into some bloated corpses half submerged in a canal. But the most dangerous part was getting past the Khmer Rouge guardhouses at the edge of the commune. Crouching in the brush near one such outpost, just beyond the glare of the kerosene lamps which blazed within, he could hear very clearly in the stillness of the night their coarse and animated conversation. A handful of Khmer Rouge were enjoying a hearty meal of roast pork, fresh vegetables and generous helpings of rice. With their mouths full of food, they were discussing the day's work: 'We killed twenty-three from number four village… Did you hear the way that old woman squeaked like a pig when I stuck the bayonet into her guts? Yes, there's still at least another dozen before we're through here… How did it go in your area? Tomorrow we'll start with that bunch living down beyond the banana plantation… we can toss the bodies in that old well over there…' Rebina listened, dumbstruck, his heart racing. He shivered in a cold sweat, and his knees were trembling. As they noisily gnawed and belched and sucked at their food, they were planning an agenda of death for fellow human beings just as if they were farmers talking about livestock ready for the slaughterhouse. And here he was, one of those doomed beasts of burden, stampeding, half-insane with the stench of blood in his nostrils. The blood of his own kind. Rebina staggered away into the cover of darkness beyond. Mercifully by dawn he had reached the steps of his friend's house.

He managed to merge unnoticed into the new commune. One was much like another, and the Khmer Rouge by now had grown even more corrupt and inefficient. They knew that to survive meant primarily ideological correctness, telling *Angka* what it wanted to hear, faking the reports, exaggerating the yields, mouthing the ridiculous slogans. With the writing on the wall for them too, personal survival had become of paramount importance.

Though safe for the moment, Rebina was overwhelmed by his

loneliness, the loss of all his precious little children, and his lovely wife. For weeks he would imagine her stooping over the fire at some domestic task, or catch himself from crying out after a child whose voice reminded him of his own one-and-a-half-year old daughter. Some unexpected noise or scene would inexplicably rekindle a smouldering ember which still burned on in his memory. He drew comfort by reflecting at length on the past. He remembered Naey his godly grandmother who had raised him and loved him. Where was she now, alive or dead? And he remembered with fondness all the Christian friends he had known before in that other world. And the missionaries too who had patiently counselled him. How foolish and headstrong he had been. How he had hurt and disappointed them. But still they persisted, still they loved. Through the painful months of 1978, Rebina's mind was stayed by dwelling entirely in the past. To think on the present was intolerable. To think on the future, impossible. It became a time of journeying inwards, rethinking, re-evaluating, gaining new understandings of himself and God.

Typical of the thousands of Phnom Penh's new Christians now out in the countryside under the heel of *Angka* was a young man named Radha. He had been brought to faith in Christ in 1973, through the ministry of the Maranatha family of churches in Phnom Penh under the teaching of such men as Nou Thay, Granny Rose's youngest son. (The one who had almost died as a baby and whom she had lifted in her arms to God saying: 'Take him or spare him and make of him a man of God.') Although Radha was a relatively new Christian, like so many other young students during that season of harvest from 1970-1975, he had a keen mind, a discerning spirit, and a fresh faith in God.

When he saw again the empty city of Phnom Penh on being driven back through it shortly after the fall, he could only weep. He wept for her exiled people, most of whom had stubbornly refused the words of life which had been held out to them. He was convinced that centuries of idolatry and superstition, intrigue, oppression, and wholesale corruption were responsible for Cambodia's collapse. A nation notorious for its rejection of the gospel and persecution of the church, hopelessly bound by gods and spirits who sapped its strength, stunted its growth, and blinded its people to their real humanity and destiny; it could not but fall prey to such tyrants as the Khmer Rouge. There simply was no national integrity, moral courage or solidarity to resist the plague of evil.

Like all the single young men, Radha was put to work as part of a mobile work brigade. The rigours of constant movement from work site to work site, the endless hard labour and meagre rations, took a lethal toll on these men. Sometimes ten of them had to live on one condensed milk tin of rice per day. Most simply collapsed and died under the sheer weight of the burdens they were forced to carry, or yoked to ploughs dragging themselves through the heavy sodden earth in the ploughing season. In the cool season their frail disease-riddled bodies fell into the chilly waters where they slaved, bent over, digging out mud, often with their bare hands to make dams and irrigation channels. The heaviest labour fell on the shoulders of these mobile youth brigades.

Radha saw his parents and brothers and sisters for only a few days at a time between these long work assignments. At considerable risk, he kept his Bible with him at all times, hidden among a few scraps of clothing rolled up in his corner of the communal quarters for unmarried men. Sometimes at night, he would steal a glance at a few verses, and then lie down and meditate on them before the brief sleep he was allowed overcame him.

Each visit home while it brought the joy of reunion, for they were a close and happy family, also enabled Radha to see how much thinner and weaker everyone was becoming. Eventually this cousin and that brother began to die. By the end of 1976, over half the commune, about one thousand people had died. When news reached him of the death of a family member, he would go to the Khmer Rouge chief and plead for permission to return home for a day or two. But the icy reply was always the same, 'No, your return cannot bring them back to life again.'

He was deep in the forest cutting down trees and clearing the brush when he heard that his father had died. Although he pleaded desperately with the Khmer Rouge to allow him a day or so to return home, the same brutal answer was given, 'Why go, you can't make him live again!' Radha returned to his work hardly able to conceal the hot anger, the outrage, burning in his heart along with all the uncertainty and grief he was struggling to overcome.

Days later, the project finally over, he was permitted to return home. The first thing he noticed was the awesome silence and listlessness that pervaded the entire village. An air of death lingered everywhere. Reaching the little hut he thought belonged to his family, he turned away for he did not recognise the emaciated little girl squatting outside. Then the child called out, 'Bong' (older brother), and stretched out her bony little arms towards him. He recognised the voice. It was his own sister, but her body was now so gaunt and wasted, he hardly knew her. The child was too weak even to stand. Radha stooped over her and enfolded her shrivelled little form in his arms. They were both weeping uncontrollably, tears of joy, yet mingled with terrible anguish and despair. He held her tightly, desperately, trying to keep her too from being swept away by the powerful cold undercurrent towards the spinning vortex of this raging maelstrom which was dragging an entire nation to its death. Still no words passed between them. Their sorrow had passed far beyond what words could say. Their two hearts melted together in the rivers of tears which they poured one upon the other, she clinging to his ankles and he gently stroking the back of her tiny neck.

Then he saw his mother. She was positioned in the doorway, bent forward, holding on to a broken off tree limb which served as a crutch. In her other hand Radha noticed a few leafy twigs she had found and was about to boil for food. Her face was a death mask of grief. 'Your father is dead,' she said. At this Radha leapt forward to hold her as she swayed faintly and fresh tears began moistening the hollow bloodshot eyes. Now mother and son held one another in a long strengthening embrace. He felt her body so light and frail against him, heaving with great sobs. Her precious baby... it too had died... slowly starved, yet so patient, the way little ones are in death. Her milk had dried up and there was nothing to satisfy its pitiable wails for nourishment. It was beyond endurance! Choking and screaming with rage, Radha threw back his head and cried, 'Why have you done this to us, Lord... this is too much!'

After two days, Radha had to return to the work sites. Leaving his dear ones was wretched and full of pain, and his grief and anger were unresolved. As he trudged wearily back along the dirt trail he found himself weeping continuously for he was unable to wrench his mind from his great loss. Entering the dreary men's quarters with its stale obnoxious odour, he went over to his corner and reached into the bundle of clothes for the Bible. It was gone. Then he saw on the floor, discarded with all the other trash, the familiar red cardboard cover. He snatched it up, but it was only a shell. All the pages had been ripped away. In his absence the men had torn out the pages to roll their tobacco leaves in to make cigarettes, or to use at the latrine. A few days later news came that his little sister had died.

It was late in the spring of 1978 and the season for ploughing the flooded paddies and sowing the seed beds was again upon them. Radha's grief had turned to a deep hatred of communism and of the Khmer Rouge. In grim determination he set himself to prevail in prayer to God for the life of his mother and remaining brother. He knew in his heart that he had to abide far above this nether world or be destroyed by its malignant power. His desire was to possess God, even here, and to be held by him forever, in spite of all the suffering. He would mount up high over its blood-drenched plain in spiritual flight and there like an eagle with outstretched wings be held aloft on powerful wind currents. Hadn't God given him such a plumage, such pinions, such strength and desire? How he ached to throw off this earth binding mantle, this heaviness of heart, and soar heavenwards.

As a widow, his mother, though barely able to walk, had been put to work with the other women. His brother had gone off in a desperate bid to find food. Work hours were long, often until 11.00 pm followed by monotonous indoctrination meetings, and sleeping out in the fields against the paddy embankments covered only by a rough piece of sacking. For the young man in the mobile brigades, life was one long unrelenting drudgery.

Then with the anniversary of 'the glorious revolution', the local mouthpieces of *Angka* decreed that certain of the young men were to marry on an appointed day in a mass 'revolutionary' ceremony.

Angka needed more lives it appeared. In all nineteen couples were selected. For Radha who was one of the chosen ones it was yet another blow. How could he, a Christian, be mis-yoked with an unbeliever, and someone he didn't even know? Yes, he did long for a Christian wife and a family of his own, especially now, to love and cherish, but not this insane experiment in revolutionary social engineering. *Where on earth was God in all this?* he agonised. To *Angka* he was deemed good breeding stock to be used to produce children for the revolution, children which *Angka* would then take away and raise in its own grotesque image.

Mass pairing ceremonies such as this took place throughout the land, usually coinciding with the 'celebrations' surrounding the anniversary of 'the great day of liberation' on April 17, 1975. The couples, complete strangers to each other, would then be given a few days together to consummate the 'marriage', sometimes even under the leering eyes of *Angka*'s lackeys, especially if a couple were suspected of being less than enthusiastic about *Angka*'s revolutionary form of nuptial bliss. Following this the couples would be separated for months at a time as each returned to their male and female mobile work brigades and separate dormitories. As with religion, so marriage and the family were abolished in *Angka*'s 'brave new world'.

On the appointed day, Radha hardly dared raise his eyes to look at the mysterious young girl sitting opposite him in the line of women. She too had her head lowered. Neither did he pay any heed to the usual barrage of inane political propaganda, and exhortations to 'join together and build a glorious new Cambodia under the inspired leadership of *Angka*'. He could only see before his eyes and hear ringing in his ears the familiar words from II Corinthians 6: 14,15. 'Do not be yoked together with unbelievers...' He felt utterly trapped and helpless. Three times already, he had refused to marry *Angka*'s chosen partner. To refuse again would be his death.

The ceremony over, the nineteen couples in gloomy silence were led to their dismal quarters. They were to form the nucleus of a new model village, and were to live here together for one month. His new wife had with her a younger sister, and she was permitted to stay with them. On arriving at their appointed home, the sister baked a few cakes with some flour which the Khmer Rouge had graciously provided for the occasion, and laid them before the young couple who as yet had barely even spoken to each other. Radha, without thinking 'carelessly' bowed his head and whispered: 'Thank you Lord for this food.' At once the young woman in front of him stiffened and cried out, 'You are a Christian!' Radha's throat went dry and his heart raced. How foolish he had been! Was she a quisling? Would this be reported? Anxiously, he looked up at the woman, but her face was radiant, and for the first time he perceived in her a deep inner beauty, and a loveliness which even her regulation black clothing could not conceal. Leaning over towards him she confided, 'I too am a Christian just like you, husband!' Her face was glowing with joy. Excitedly they spoke of the past, their home churches in Phnom Penh, friends and mutual acquaintances in Christ. She was none other than the charming and winsome daughter of Pastor Choy, a member of Bethany Church, and a sister of Samon, the spirited youth leader at Bethany and former colleague of Taing Chhirc.

Both were overcome by the goodness and overruling hand of God, and the miracle of their being brought together in such a way and at such a time as this in a seemingly 'God-forsaken land'. Radha had found all he ever wanted, more than filling the void left in his life by the deaths of his father and six brothers and sisters. Now he had his own family, and his bereaved mother a new and devoted daughter. They lived quietly and happily together through those final chaotic months of *Angka*'s reign of terror. With the coming of the Vietnamese, they would be swept up in a great flood of refugees moving westward towards Thailand and beyond into all the world.

CHAPTER 10

THE SEED DIES

'I tell you the truth, unless a grain of wheat falls to the ground and dies, it remains only a single seed. But if it dies, it produces many seeds.'

(John 12:24)

Following the fruitful evangelistic crusade in Battambang City in June 1974, very little news filtered down to the main church in Phnom Penh concerning Pastor Hom and the Christians there. Battambang is Cambodia's second largest city, about 250 kilometres north west of the capital and only about fifty miles from the Thai border. This large northwestern province of the same name has a long forested border with Thailand and has, as we saw, in recent past been under Thai control. But most importantly, this rice rich province was also the seed bed of the Cambodian Evangelical Church back in the 1920s.

During the 1970-1975 war with the Khmer Rouge, the province of Battambang and its provincial capital remained largely free from the carnage of the war which raged over the rest of Cambodia. Having a road and rail link with Thailand at the Poipet-Aranyaprathet border crossing, the province never had its supply routes completely cut off, and enjoyed relative peace and prosperity compared with the rest of the country. Furthermore, Battambang was never really defeated militarily. The army simply surrendered when news of Phnom Penh's fall reached them. The

213

military here was in reasonably good shape and enjoying high morale under some popular commanders like In Tham. There was even a reluctance on the part of some officers to obey the order from the capital to surrender. Consequently, when the Khmer Rouge took over control of Battambang their rule was particularly ruthless for they knew that the province was full of potential resistance which could be fuelled from neighbouring free Thailand. Indeed along this border, rag tag bands of *Khmer Serey* or 'Free Khmers', were encamped, and occasionally they made hit-and-run raids into Cambodia. In Tham had been one of these early resistance leaders in 1975 till the Thai government put pressure on him to leave.

A significant mythology grew up around these liberation groups, some real, some phantom. Among a people desperate to throw off the heavy yoke of the Khmer Rouge, they became somewhat larger than life, embued with almost mystical powers and romantic names drawn from ancient Khmer folklore. From the perspective of the inmates of Pol Pot's national concentration camp, these unseen and righteous 'White Khmers' were poised like shining white angels who at a divinely-appointed moment would sweep down from their wooded mountain strongholds and vanquish the black-clad and bloodstained Khmer Rouge. This was the stuff of whispered exaggerated rumours and lingering hopes. But as the handful of young zealots who made it to their border sanctuaries between 1975 and 1978, and the hundreds of thousands who stampeded to the Thai border following the Vietnamese takeover in 1979, soon discovered, the *Khmer Serey* with a few notable exceptions were little more than bandits, smugglers, and opportunists, led by that familiar Cambodian breed of squabbling and corrupt politicians and military men, intent more on lining their own pockets and satisfying their own egos than serving Cambodia and her people. In this regard there has been nothing new under the Cambodian sun for many centuries. As soon as the Khmer Rouge machine was in place, the people of Battambang suffered a disproportionate share of *Angka*'s suspicion and fury.

For numerous would-be escapees, Battambang was also the last hurdle to overcome before reaching freedom in Thailand. Hundreds set their hearts and faces towards Battambang and refuge beyond. Very few however made it across the minefields, with their hideous booby traps, poison-tipped punji sticks, and wide-ranging Khmer Rouge foot patrols, or through the thick trackless bush with its numerous deadly hazards and pandemic malaria, to the handful of dusty refugee camps just over on the other side. These trails would soon be littered with the whitening bones of thousands, who in desperation attempted to run the gauntlet to Thailand preferring to risk death in the attempt than face almost certain death by remaining.

For these intrepid souls, their troubles were far from over when they set foot on Thai soil. For even here large numbers perished or disappeared, attacked by angry Thai villagers living in constant fear of butcherous cross border raids by the Khmer Rouge. The heads of a number of those unfortunate enough to fall into the hands of hostile Thai were impaled on stakes along the border. Some refugees were murdered by bandits, others were shot or turned back by Thai border patrol police, especially if they lacked the wherewithal to bribe their way into a camp. Many captured were used as slave labour, or in the case of some young girls, reportedly sent to brothels in Bangkok. Their fellow Buddhists in Thailand did not always receive them warmly, unless it became politically or economically expedient to do so. At times it seemed that a Cambodian refugee in Thailand had less rights than a dog. A dog, as a living animal, would not be killed by strict Buddhists for they fear slaying a reincarnated soul and the subsequent considerable loss of merit. But a decrepit refugee who had abandoned his country could be plundered, raped, or killed with impunity. His *karma* was already at a low ebb anyway.

Nevertheless, compared with others in the region who would not in those days allow refugees fleeing communist Indo-China even to land (and who towed crowded flimsy boat loads of Vietnamese refugees back out onto the stormy and pirate-infested waters of the South China Sea) Thailand was the more generous and humane. She allowed hundreds of thousands of potentially troublesome aliens into refugee camps on her soil, and mostly facilitated the efforts of various humanitarian agencies who helped to care for them.

Pastor Hom's church was called Jerusalem Church and strategically situated right by the central market in Battambang City. There were two services on Sundays, one for Khmer (Cambodian) speakers, and the other for the Chinese. The Chinese church both here and in nearby Pailin on the Thai border was pastored by Samuel Mok, helped by a Chinese missionary from Hong Kong based at the Chinese Church in Phnom Penh. During the 1974 crusade led by Ravi Zacharius, large numbers had attended, from aged Buddhist priests seeking for truth to the majority of students and thinking young people. All were disillusioned by the unsolvable crises of Cambodia and sceptical about the age-old teaching and folklore of popular Buddhism, clearly impotent against the powerful forces which surrounded them on all sides.

Throughout the final months of freedom, Pastor Hom worked very hard to encourage his little flock, following up new believers with teaching, and travelling out to the surrounding farming villages to visit the scattered pockets of rural Christians. The daily prayer gatherings were well attended, and as news coming from the beleaguered capital to the south worsened, the Christians drew visibly closer in fellowship and mutual support. Like Chhirc, Reach Yeah, Radha, and others, Hom despaired not so much at the gloomy military situation, but at the ruinous moral situation all around him. He could only compare this city to Sodom or Gomorrah. Cambodia could not but fall, as a result of its internal decay and corruption. In love only with materialism and the gratification of their own carnal lusts, the people of Battambang continually mocked and abused both the Lord and his servants by word and deed. Hom knew that soon Cambodia would self-destruct and that he and all his church would have to undergo a fiery crucible.

News of the capitulation of Phnom Penh reached the people of Battambang by radio in the early morning of April 17, 1975. Although there was not a Khmer Rouge in sight, the garrison defending the city dutifully laid down its arms in accord with the government's call to surrender. They were to receive the Khmer Rouge troops when they arrived, they were told, and the transition of power would be orderly and peaceful.

The Christians, however, did not share this general mood of optimism about the Khmer Rouge. They were stunned by the news and deeply concerned about how the communist victors would regard the church. Pastor Hom visited the Christians in their homes all through that memorable day advising them to stay in their houses and pray. That evening Jerusalem Church was packed to overflowing as the Christians of Battambang gathered to spend the night together watching and praying. A kind of hush, like the stillness before a violent storm, had fallen over the city. Hom stood up before his people and encouraged them from the Word of God, 'Whatever the future holds, God knows it already. He is still sovereign, and we know that whether we live or die we are always with him. Nothing whatsoever can separate us from the love of our God. Our trust is completely and absolutely in him.' But filled with foreboding and dread, many were weeping and crying out to God for strength and courage.

As the Christians continued praying throughout that tense and humid night, under cover of darkness, black-clad Khmer Rouge troops began entering the city from all sides. Peering through the cracks in the church door, Hom was astounded by the sheer number of *Angka*'s heavily-armed soldiers who continued to pour into the central market area right across from the church. Then what seemed to be smoke bombs, perhaps to drive people off the streets and into their homes, were set off. Several were exploded near the church, and it began to fill with foul smelling acrid smoke. The Christians covered their faces with wet clothes and cut open onions, an old soldier's device, to help dispel the toxic fumes.

Daybreak on April 18, 1975 was heralded by the sound of hundreds of rifles being fired as the Khmer Rouge began shooting into the air, filling the entire city with a terrifying and ear-splitting cacophony of noise. Then the soldiers, already in place, began moving through the streets, banging on every door and screaming the order, 'Out! Out! Out!' The entire city, every man, woman, child, old, young, sick or dying, was being ordered 'Out!' The same was happening in Phnom Penh and in every other newly 'liberated' city and town across Cambodia at this very moment.

Concerned that on breaking through the doors of the church the soldiers would discover this large suspicious gathering of Christians and perhaps turn against them, Hom, after final parting words of prayer, advised everyone to disperse into groups and return to their homes. He watched after them, deep in thought, as his beloved flock filed out through the doors of Jerusalem Church for the very last time. In the customary way with palms pressed together, each bade him farewell. Many he would never see again, and Jerusalem Church would be totally dismantled by the Khmer Rouge, brick by brick, leaving not a trace of where it had once stood.

Over in the market meanwhile, there was pandemonium. All buying and selling had been stopped, valuables were being confiscated, and piles of paper money cast into the street where it began to blow around like confetti in whirlwinds of dust, chased and flung about by excited street urchins. The tradespeople were all being forced at gunpoint to evacuate their shops and leave the city.

By noon, Hom and his family had joined the tens of thousands of bewildered and terrified citizens on the roads leading out of Battambang. Hom noticed their faces, filled with sorrow and fear, pale and drawn; many were weeping, crying aloud and beating their breasts. He could not help but compare the scene to what it had been a few days earlier: carefree, drinking, carousing, lusting, and grasping. It had all so suddenly come to an end.

During these few hours, Battambang was totally transformed from a lively bustling free-wheeling market town, to an echo chamber of deserted buildings and empty streets littered with drifting rubbish and bloated corpses. Here and there outside various well-known bars and brothels, the bodies of prostitutes and their patrons lay, tossed out on the street like garbage; their gaudy clothes still upon them, and their vacant upturned faces painted with rouge and mascara, cast aside like broken dolls. The sight of all this made Hom's gentle and sensitive heart stir and marvel within him. And as he slowly edged along with the great press of people, the pastor was pondering over many things, past, present and future.

He had been forced to leave behind vast supplies of Christian literature. With him he carried ten Bibles, a few hymn books, and some assorted Christian pamphlets. Hom carried all this along with some clothing and a little food in two baskets suspended from either end of a pole across his shoulder. The heat was intolerable and compounded by the slow and congested pace at which the grief-stricken throng shuffled down the roads now sticky with melting tar, and strewn with so much rubbish. One of his children was suffering with measles and the others tottered along bewildered, weeping quietly. They had to make frequent stops for the children's sake; to allow them to squat down on their haunches to rest, or lie on their backs exhausted.

Travelling with Hom were four other Christian families, all related to him in some way. His elderly mother Rin (the one who as a little girl long ago had wondered where the first corn seeds came from) was in considerable pain and could progress only very slowly. After two days and nights on the road they limped into the village of Kok Khmum, thirty kilometres to the north of Battambang. It was the familiar village where Hom had been born and raised. Here they turned left down the dirt road leading westward to where, just four kilometres further on, lay the village of Chkae Koun. Here he knew ten Christian families were living. It was one of those old Christian communities which pastors like Hom had been visiting for the past fifty years. In Chkae Koun he was among friends and family. But there were also a number of old and bitter enemies of these tenacious little plantings of the Lord, people who for decades were always looking for ways to hurt the followers of *Preah Yesu*.

No one however, including the 'old people' was being allowed to live even in these ancient rural villages. All former habitations had to be abandoned along with everything else 'pre-liberation'. New communes, organised by the Khmer Rouge according to *Angka*'s scientific and revolutionary specifications governing the administration of districts and zones, were to be built on nearby land which first had to be cleared.

In the confusion, Hom managed to slip back across country into Battambang to fetch more of his rice supply. It was becoming clear that this new arrangement was going to be permanent. The Khmer Rouge had by now blocked off all the roads, and Hom was forced to push his bicycle laden with the large sack of rice across the fields and over the paddy embankments. Coming upon a group of frightened people sheltering in the forest, he stopped and spent the night with them, telling them of the Saviour Jesus Christ. Before continuing his journey early the next morning he gave them one of his Bibles. Hom knew that very soon he would no longer be able to proclaim the gospel freely in this way.

Everyone was about to be categorised and split up into work brigades with their own living quarters and communal kitchen. No unauthorised communication or travel would be permitted between the various communes or labour zones.

The first thing everyone had to do was to build a crude shelter from grass and bamboo. No supplies were available. It was up to each family to find the wherewithal out in the forest. Even the aged and infirm were left to fend for themselves. Fortunately for Hom, unlike the many totally disorientated and helpless city people, he had been raised in the countryside, so he did know how to survive.

Next, they were all put to work making new paddies for growing rice and digging irrigation ditches and embankments. As was the case throughout the nation, this gruelling manual labour soon began to take its toll on the 'new people' from the cities, especially given the starvation rations, and total lack of western medicines which they were now used to. Malaria, dysentery, and cholera, compounded by severe malnutrition, killed vast numbers of them, adding to the growing mountains of corpses of those being rounded up and murdered in the continuous pogroms.

Occasionally, Hom would cross paths with another Christian, sometimes from another commune near by. Hom knew every Christian in Battambang. Though they scarcely dared acknowledge each other beyond a nod or a smile, they always sought to pray for one another, and share their own meagre rations with the less fortunate and the many among them who were sick.

Less than a mile away from Hom's brigade lived Auntie Siew, the elder sister of Song and Chhorn, but they were not permitted to meet or talk. The indomitable Auntie Siew, a hardy country woman of strong peasant stock, was now a privileged 'old person', appointed by the Khmer Rouge as a brigade leader in her village. Almost at once, jealous villagers betrayed her to the Khmer Rouge. 'She is a Christian, hands and feet of the Americans!' But to everyone's surprise, the leading Khmer Rouge cadre there, a man named Moeun, replied: 'Leave her alone! The Christians are among the best people I have. They despise all corruption, injustice, and immorality, neither do they worship your useless idols!' After that no one dared speak out against this particular Christian.

Apparently, Moeun's mother had been a Christian. (A few years later in a Thai refugee camp, free from fear of Khmer Rouge reprisal, this man opened his heart to Christ.) While Comrade Moeun was in control, at least, only those who seriously abused *Angka*'s laws were executed. Nevertheless, famine and disease took many lives here as elsewhere.

Auntie Siew's tough lean exterior, her lined and weathered face, and her loud rasping voice, concealed a heart of pure gold. She zealously upheld justice, worked hard to provide food for those in her charge, and never hesitated to speak of her commitment to the Lord Jesus.

On one occasion when rice stocks were critically low, she suggested to Moeun that he give her one of the commune bullock carts and let her go to Battambang to search for rice which might be stored in any of the abandoned houses. As with everything else she did, Siew sought the Lord's guidance. In Battambang she uncovered a good supply of hidden rice. With the cart fully laden she guided the bullocks back through the silent streets of the deserted city. The sounds of the wheels on the gravel road, and the steady creaking of the cart seemed unusually loud and intrusive. Coming to a familiar crossroads, she turned the animals in another direction and drove on till she came to a very old house. She had felt a sudden need to see it again.

There it stood, abandoned and completely overgrown. It was the house where David Ellison, one of the two pioneer missionaries to Cambodia had first lived back in the 1920s. This house and its

compound was rich with memories, and her tired eyes welled with
tears just at the sight of it. As a small girl before the Japanese
invasion and World War II she came here often with Prac, her
father. He used to accompany the missionary on his itinerant
evangelistic journeys into the surrounding villages. Although she
could not remember the time back in South Vietnam when she,
just a baby and near to death and her mother too with tetanus, had
first met this messenger of Jesus Christ, Yen, her mother, often
told her the story of how Christ had healed them. And then, how
they along with a number of other Kampuchea *Kraom*
(Cambodians from South Vietnam) families had travelled here to
Battambang, to farm this fertile land and be close to their spiritual
teacher and friend. By that time the old home had become the first
Bible school. Siew could still see in her mind's eye all those
students' faces, and remember all their names. And then there was
that terrible night soon after the war when the Christians had taken
refuge behind its stout walls as the *Issarak* rebels ransacked
Battambang market. Yes, how vividly it all came flooding back to
her. Somehow just the sight of it, the remembrance, was a comfort
and source of new strength. It reminded her of the goodness and
faithfulness of God over many years.

But her place of refuge and source of comfort, she reminded
herself, had to be more than a building, especially after what had
recently happened to their Jerusalem Church building. The
abiding presence of God and none else must be that refuge and
comfort from now on. With this truth fresh in her heart, she
brushed aside the tears with a corner of her *krama*, gazed once
more at the old home fixing it in her mind, then drawing a deep
breath, she gave the reins a shake and urged the bullock on back to
the present. Mr Ellison had died in the land he loved, and the
Christians had sorrowfully laid his remains to rest in the Christian
graveyard in Phnom Penh many years ago now.[1] All the way back
to Chkae Koun, Auntie Siew thought of him. She could hear him
speaking. What would her spiritual father want of her now she
thought. Surely, to do as he had consistently sought to do, portray
Jesus Christ before the Cambodian people.

During 1977 when everything had been strictly communalised

and famine stalked every commune and village in Cambodia, Auntie Siew fell very ill and was sent to one of the Khmer Rouge clinics in the former village Buddhist temple. All around her, people lay dying, most with no one to care for them. At night-time the place was filled with their agonised screams and groans. This was not so much because of the pain, but because of the terrible fear they had of the evil spirits which everywhere lurked about this place of death. Auntie Siew wanted the shutters and doors left open at night-time to allow cool fresh air into the stuffy and foul smelling ward. But for fear that the spirits would also fly in, the patients insisted on keeping every door and window firmly fastened. Her fellow sufferers were amazed at the peace and calmness which surrounded her at all times. She pitied their terrible spiritual plight, skeletal bodies draped with strings and fetishes, screaming and cringing before the dark shadows they saw coming towards them through the doors, then gasping as if being suffocated by some invisible hand. Theirs was a lonely, torturous and horrific death. The next day, stiffened and twisted, their bodies would be dragged off by the young Khmer orderlies who arrived each morning to toss them into the mass graves beyond, leaving a filthy vacancy for the next victim. These so-called clinics had little or no effective medicine to combat the malaria, dysentery, and parasites which plagued the wasted and yellowing bodies of these tormented souls. Auntie Siew prayed her way patiently through this ordeal until she recovered and was able to leave.

Young Kheang, a student converted at the June 1974 Battambang crusade along with his friend, Yusar, also had the terrifying experience of being left in such a place. As his body swelled and strength drained away, he wept and prayed for God's mercy and comfort. Then, through his tears he saw above him the supporting beams in the roof had formed a perfect cross above his head. He fixed his eyes upon it, and his mind upon the One who had been nailed in agony to a cross. He received the divine grace and mercy he sought. Eventually he recovered and later fled to safety in Thailand.

Pastor Hom kept his Bible secretly tucked away in the thatch roofing of his hut. At night-time, he would take it down and read a few verses before praying, and then wearily collapsing onto the bamboo floor for the few hours permitted for sleep. Often these hours were spent tossing and turning, wondering where the next meal would come from, or thinking about how to alleviate the suffering of his children who daily grew thinner and thinner.

The Khmer Rouge, at their regular indoctrination sessions following the day's work, declared, 'Cambodia no longer needs God! We can do everything with our own hands. We can even provide adequate water through our new irrigation systems.' In his dreams *Angka*'s slogans mocked and tormented Hom. The strident and repetitive revolutionary songs rang in his ears, and black clad dancers in straight lines danced their monotonous lock step revolutionary steps before his eyes. These soulless performances and their libretto of lies were bizarre choreographies of the gruelling labour in the fields. But what distracted and preoccupied him most of all was much more immediate. It was the ache in his stomach, the sharp hunger pangs which shot through his insides and caused his head to spin.

The question of food was everyone's all-consuming obsession. It was virtually all they ever spoke or thought of. After each harvest, *Angka*'s trucks would come and take all the freshly harvested rice away, and the people had to continue to live on the thin rice gruel. The anguished people crying out for just a bowl of rice, 'So hungry… so hungry…' wailed from their deathbeds. But *Angka* only extolled the revolutionary fervour of its forces: 'The People's Liberation Army do not steal so much as a grain of rice from the people.'

Even Hom, at times, became distraught, feeling he could endure it no longer. During the height of the famine he had prayed, 'Lord, O that you would just cut the slender thread of my miserable life here, and take me home to be with you in Paradise forever. Let us all now die together. I cannot endure this regime. It is beyond my strength.'

Hom was overwrought with worry for his family and his own deteriorating ability to work and provide. At times he barely had the energy to drag himself around the little shack in which they lived, to care for his wife, frequently racked with malaria and dysentery, and the listless ever-hungry children. But God did not choose to take Hom's life, rather he walked with him through the flames of the crucible.

The children had long since stopped their usual playing and singing. Their favourite haunts beneath nearby spreading trees or around dusty doorsteps had fallen silent. Now they just lay in dark corners of the home, doubled over, skin and bone. Occasionally, they would crawl outside to pass blood, or just squat blank-faced in the sunlight, heedless of the swarms of flies which crawled all over the sores on their sunken faces. The surrounding landscape was a wasteland, stripped bare of all edible roots and leaves. The banana tree trunks whose pithy insides could be chopped up and eaten were all gone. Even grubs, cockroaches, snails, crabs and lizards were hard to come by.

Hom could see that gradually they were all becoming like pigs. They ate the same filthy food and worse, stunk, squabbled and snapped at each other constantly, and thought only of filling their bellies. But even more hideous than life in a pigpen, some, half-demented by starvation, were driven to cannibalism. In his area alone, people had killed their own children for food. In another place, a woman cut her husband's throat while he lay sick with malaria and then sliced his flesh and roasted it. Freshly buried bodies were unearthed for their intestines. Those who disposed of the dead were envied, for at least they could hack off a limb or cut out a liver to boil with their watery rice gruel. Some people in desperation even carved hunks of flesh from living cattle, or lopped off tails to smuggle home and secretly cook.

Hom, mercifully, was kept from sinking to such depths as these. Using a skill he had learned as a boy, he managed to catch field rats which lived in burrows in the rice paddy embankments. There seemed to be during these years an incredible increase in the rat population. Rats came from nowhere and consumed enormous quantities of grain. The rats multiplied while the people died. And they died in such large numbers that in some villages there was no one left even to dispose of the bodies, and the village was simply abandoned. But a plague of rats, it seemed to Hom, had overrun the country.

Furthermore, despite all the hard work, crops were poor, and little else seemed to grow or produce much fruit. It was as if a great curse was hanging over the land permeating everything with blight and death. All through these years, Cambodia experienced fierce droughts in the dry season, and then devastating floods in the rainy season. These floods swept away the dams and canals which had been constructed at the cost of thousands of lives. Of course anyone with even a basic knowledge of these things could have predicted that, but *Angka* did not need engineers and textbooks. How could *Angka*, who had 'defeated the American imperialists', be defeated by mere elements? *Angka* was invincible.

So Hom acquired a little more food by catching rats. Some they gladly ate were tiny ones no bigger than a farmer's big toe. He dug them out of their holes, skinned them, and then roasted them on sticks over a fire. When at such times there was some extra food, he would rouse his children, gently stroking their emaciated little legs. Each would painfully lift itself up on one elbow and then without a word, eyes unfocused, as if food were the only stimulus they were capable of responding to, automatically reach out a trembling hand for a morsel.

The plight of the children was made even worse after everything was strictly collectivised, and each co-operative of about a hundred families had to share everything in common, eating what little food there was at a communal kitchen. The ones who prepared the food of course kept back the best for themselves and their friends. It was survival of the fittest, and everyone else would have done the same. If they were caught it would be death, but what was there to lose? By 1977, every item of personal property had been taken away, and this extended even to one's own children. Little ones above five years old were wrenched from their mothers and housed in separate quarters to be cared for by the elderly who were too infirm to work in the fields. Teenagers were assigned to the deadly male and female mobile work brigades, and frequently had to sleep out in the fields where they toiled each day. All were taught by the Khmer Rouge to mistrust, even to spy on their parents, and obey only *Angka* as the sole authority in their lives.

These changes brought the additional pain of emotional suffering to the already miserable lives of the children. Now they were denied not only adequate food, but the love and succour of their own parents and families. The little children separated from their mothers were often roughly treated by the tired and irritable grannies who now had to babysit them all day. Hom could hear the infants weeping and crying out for their mothers. He even went so far as to plead with the Khmer Rouge to show mercy. But his life was threatened and, as a Christian pastor, he knew that at any moment he could be led away and executed. Some of the children tried to jump out of the windows and escape, but such were caught and cruelly punished by being tied up to the wooden posts on which the building stood and left to stand there for hours in their own filth and misery. The distraught parents wept too, but secretly, for to show such distress could earn one 'a visit to *Angka*' – a visit from which no one returned. By 1978 the children had become independent and precocious. Now, they only played harsh war games, or spoke endlessly of revolution in blood-curdling terms. They were no longer little children but future killing machines, their impressionable minds filled with *Angka*'s poison.

Only one Christian was executed in the area. He was Chhorn's son Sokh. They said he was killed because he had 'bad blood'. His father had been a soldier for the former regime. Sadly, he was turned in by a fellow villager. Chhorn himself had been separated from the family since the day the Khmer Rouge took Battambang. They only knew that he had been stationed to the south of the city in Moung district, and assumed that since he was a soldier, he almost certainly would have been killed by now.

Another tragedy was the death of the young Bible School student, Seng. He had been sent to Battambang to assist Pastor Hom at Jerusalem Church for his intern year before graduation. Seng, a brother-in-law of Son Sonne, being a single young man had been conscripted by the Khmer Rouge into one of the 'noble youth brigades'. These ragged bands of young people were no more than fodder for *Angka*'s insatiable revolutionary machine, live offerings to this voracious new Molech consuming Cambodia's youth. He became very ill, and so weak that he was hardly able to stand without support. It seems that one day standing at a bathing spot on the river bank, he simply collapsed and rolled down into the water and drowned. Those who took his body from the river later reported the story to Pastor Hom.

Many people simply killed themselves, casting their children into deep wells, and then throwing themselves after them. Others were found hanging from tree branches, or lying dead from self-inflicted doses of poison made from plants of the forest. Not a few 'wanted' ones kept a length of cord about them in order to hang themselves quickly from the nearest tree should the Khmer Rouge come for them. Even in death, Cambodians preferred anything to the indignity of execution at the hands of some Khmer Rouge 'punk'.

The much-loved and charitable French Roman Catholic Benedictine priest from Mongul Borey, and the prefect apostolic of Battambang, Paul Tep Im Sotha, were both executed within days of the Khmer Rouge takeover. Refugees in Thailand reported seeing them together during the initial exodus doing all they could to alleviate the sufferings of the people. Refugees in Thailand some years later spoke of seeing a large skeleton they knew could not be a Cambodian, lying in a shallow grave with others. A crucifix still hung around the neck. Those who reportedly saw these remains had no doubt that they belonged to the kindly Battambang priest who refused to leave the people he loved.[2]

Catholicism in Cambodia was always closely linked in the popular mind to French and Vietnamese interests. For it was they who composed the vast majority of that church. Since both these communities were now bitter enemies of *Angka*, Catholicism was clearly one of those 'reactionary religions' which the new Cambodian constitution of 1976 would not allow, despite the smile of 'freedom of religion'. Just what religious observance *Angka* had in mind was never clear, for even historic Buddhism was dismantled and ruthlessly crushed. 'Pray to Buddha and see if he will give you food.' The argument was that Buddhism was not native to Cambodia but introduced from Sri Lanka and Siam. Like Christianity, it was the 'opiate of the people', deceiving them and lulling them into a stupor. It was all part of the *ancien regime*, the feudalism of the past which had to be totally wiped away. The magnificent Roman Catholic cathedral in Phnom Penh was completely destroyed by the Khmer Rouge.

A refugee report from a village in Siem Riep province told of the death of Haim, a Christian teacher, and his family. I have tried to reconstruct this moving story:

Unmistakably, through the tremulous glare of the early afternoon sun and his own light-headedness from the back-breaking labour, Haim knew that the youthful black-clad Khmer Rouge soldiers now heading across the field were coming this time for him. It was the hour when they always came, these brutish servants of *Angka Loeu* (The Organisation on High), dispatched to cull yet more of Cambodia's grovelling minions lingering in this particular twilight zone of the nationwide death camp.

Leaning weakly against his hoe for support – itself ironically the primary instrument of execution – Haim watched their easy, menacing, unhurried pace along the paddy embankment. His throat felt dry, an uncontrollable fluttering gripped his bowels, and his knees threatened to buckle beneath him. But he remained still. Haim was determined that when his turn came, he would die with dignity and without complaint. Since 'Liberation' on April 17, 1975, what Cambodian had not considered this day? Suddenly a bloodcurdling, naked scream shattered the unearthly stillness of the worksite. Haim swung round to see that another group of soldiers had seized their first prey: some pitiful wretch was being bound and dragged away blubbering uncontrollably.

Across the landscape, eerily, not a soul moved except for *Angka*'s black reapers. The scene resembled some bizarre party game of statues in which each hapless player strained every muscle to render himself immobile, invisible. Move even faintly out of line from *Angka*'s ruthlessly exacting standard of life and being, and you would be picked off, obliterated, 'fertiliser' for *Angka*'s crops.

Haim's entire family was rounded up that afternoon. They were 'the old dandruff!', 'bad blood!', 'enemies of the glorious revolution!', 'CIA agents!'. They were Christians.

The family spent a sleepless night comforting one another and praying for each other as they lay bound together in the dewy grass beneath a stand of friendly trees. Next morning the teenage soldiers returned and led them from their Gethsemane to their place of execution, to the nearby *viel somlap*, 'the killing fields'.

The place was grim indeed and bore many gruesome signs of a place of execution. A sickly smell of death hung in the air. Curious villagers foraging in the scrub nearby lingered, half hidden, watching the familiar routine as the family were ordered to dig a large grave for themselves. Then, consenting to Haim's request for a moment to prepare themselves for death, father, mother, and children, hands linked, knelt together around the gaping pit. With loud cries to God, Haim began exhorting both the Khmer Rouge and all those looking on from afar to repent and believe the gospel.

Then, in panic, one of Haim's young sons leapt to his feet, bolted into the surrounding bush and disappeared. Haim jumped up and with amazing coolness and authority prevailed upon the Khmer Rouge not to pursue the lad, but allow him to call the boy back. The knots of onlookers, peering around trees, the Khmer Rouge, and the stunned family still kneeling at the graveside, looked on in awe as Haim began calling his son, pleading with him to return and die together with his family.

'What comparison, my son,' he called out, 'stealing a few more days of life in the wilderness, a fugitive, wretched and alone, to joining your family here momentarily around this grave but soon around the throne of God, free forever in Paradise?' After a few tense minutes the bushes parted, and the lad, weeping, walked slowly back to his place with the kneeling family. 'Now we are ready to go,' Haim told the Khmer Rouge.

But by this time there was not a soldier standing there who had the heart to raise his hoe to deliver the death blow on the backs of these noble heads. Ultimately this had to be done by the Khmer Rouge commune chief, who had not witnessed these things. But few of those watching doubted that as each of these Christians' bodies toppled silently into the earthen pit which the victims themselves had prepared, their souls soared heavenward to a place prepared by their Lord.

The rapid spread of news such as this, of certain Christians boldly bearing witness to their Lord in death, was gossiped about the countryside. Eventually these reports were brought across to the refugee camps in Thailand; and not always by Christians, but by typical Cambodians who, until then, had despised the *Puok Yesu*.

The report of Pastor Prasaer's death in Kampong Cham by crucifixion because 'he refused to stop preaching Christ crucified', has yet to be fully substantiated. But the Khmer Rouge were certainly capable of such a thing, for even in the 'liberated' zones of Cambodia before 1975, villagers were found nailed to their door posts. The Khmers have long since perfected deceit, treachery, human torture, and butchery to a fine art; and all of it behind a broad beguiling smile.

During the entire Khmer Rouge period from April 1975 to January 1979, only a handful of Christians escaped alive to Thailand, and entered the refugee camps there. The largest of these early camps for Cambodians was at Aranyaprathet, about three miles from Cambodia, and just north of the Thai border town of that name. In May 1977 a young Khmer named Sy was injured by a Khmer Rouge bullet while escaping execution. From his hospital bed in Aranyaprathet where I met him, he spoke of a remarkable 'uncle' whom he had met in the prison at Kabinburi where he, along with a number of other recent escapees, was initially detained by the Thai authorities. The prison was so crowded that there was hardly room to lie down, but when this 'uncle' saw Sy's injury and the pain he was in, he gave up his own place so that Sy could be more comfortable. This was very unusual in the present ethical climate. But Sy soon came to realise that this man was no ordinary Cambodian. He was a Christian. Through the long hot days and nights of imprisonment, he would unashamedly sing hymns to God, pray aloud, and speak warmly to all those around him of Jesus Christ, the Saviour of the world. Sy himself, a good and single-minded young man, became a Christian at that time.

A few weeks later while speaking to a group of new arrivals from Kabinburi prison at the Aranyaprathet refugee camp, giving them sets of clean clothes, I noticed that one of them was named Pol. Looking at him, I said, 'Uncle, your name is that of a great Christian apostle'. (Paul is Pol in Khmer.) Immediately, he stood up and announced that he was indeed a Christian, born of Christians, from Kampuchea *Kraom*. It was none other than Pol Chhorn himself, son of Prac and Yen, brother of Siew and Song, and husband of Chamroeun who was at that time still in Cambodia at Ckae Koun with her widowed mother Granny Rose, Pastor Hom and other Battambang Christians. Pol Chhorn was the first of the old Battambang Christians to escape to Thailand. He crossed the border in April 1977, two years after the fall of Cambodia. What follows, translated from Cambodian, is his own account of his escape from Cambodia and *Angka*:

'I left from a village at 7 pm one night and arrived in Thailand twenty-four days later on April 13, 1977. The village was in Battambang, my home province in the north west of Cambodia. Before leaving I was very concerned about the many dangers involved, and I thought so much too of my beloved wife and children whom I hadn't seen for over two years since we were separated by the Khmer Rouge. Despite the terrible oppression and endless killings at the hands of the Khmer Rouge I was hesitant to leave. Finally, I knew that I could stay no longer. The fact that I had been a soldier for many years put my life in real danger as all the soldiers were being taken away, even those from the lowest ranks. I decided to make an escape.

'I walked for three nights towards the north-west (ie towards Thailand) and met no obstacle. Then, for a further four days I walked on through the afternoons. Suddenly, while hiding in a bush I saw fifteen Khmer Rouge soldiers coming out of the forest and walking straight towards me. What was I to do? My first thoughts were to make a run for it. But then all around was open flat country, so I remained quietly where I was. I did not know what to do. Rolling over on my face I prayed, pleading with the Lord to take pity on me. Then, opening my eyes, I saw that the soldiers were still moving towards me. A great fear gripped me. Certainly when they reached the bush behind which I was hiding, they would see me, and I would be killed. My eyes seemed to go blind, I couldn't see anything. Should I run or stay? 'O God,' I whispered, 'Didn't you hear my cry?' A thought then entered my mind that God never abandons his children. The Red Khmers came to within fifty metres of where I lay, then suddenly they turned to the south and went far away from me.

'Since it was nearly sunset I continued my journey. From now on, I would travel only by night. The danger of being spotted by the Khmer Rouge during the day was too great. After three nights of walking, I reached the river which we call the Bavel River, and I swam across. It was 1 am. Then as the sun was beginning to appear in the east I entered a rice field which had recently been harvested. There I rested until evening when I again continued on my journey. The forest was becoming thicker and thicker. The density of the bamboo thickets made travelling very difficult, and the thorns badly cut my legs and feet. However I continued through this difficult forest, because to take the easier paths would mean running into the Khmer Rouge or treading on one of their mines in the depths of the forest. Here they couldn't see me. But because groups of soldiers did sometimes enter and patrol the jungle, I pushed even deeper and deeper into the darkening forest.

'Looking at my canteen, I realised that my water was getting dangerously low. I continued through that forest for another three nights, and then the water ran out completely. This was a serious problem, and I was extremely thirsty. It was also the dry season when no rain fell. I had no idea how to solve this problem. The trees were large and tall, and the clumps of thickly entangled bamboos forced me to crawl close to the ground most of the time. It was also quite impossible to see in the total darkness of this forest by night. And so I crawled along, slowly fumbling and feeling my way forward.

'At last I prayed to God like this: 'O my God, Father of heaven and earth, where is the water? I am not able to find any water in this deep forest. I am sure you won't let me die of thirst as you have already saved my life several times on this terrible journey.' And so I continued on, little by little, with hope. Very soon I found myself on a piece of elevated ground covered in bushy bamboos. I stood up and forced my way through, not thinking about water, when suddenly, before my eyes lay a small pond. I stood and looked at it for a long time. It was really a pond I was looking at. I was so happy and said aloud, 'Thank you God for guiding me here.' Before touching the dark still water, I knelt down beside the small pond and sang this little song which I had learned as a boy to praise God:

> I know the Lord will make a way for me;
> I know the Lord will make a way for me;
> If I look to him and pray,
> Read the Bible every day,
> I know the Lord will make a way for me.

'At this quiet place many wild animals went down to drink. I drank lots of water, filled my canteen, and then I took a most refreshing bath. After bathing, I unwrapped my dried rice and ate it until I was quite full. I rested there for a while and felt my energy greatly renewed. Before leaving that special place and continuing my journey, I knelt again and prayed to God like this: 'All things, my God, you have already known. You know all our needs before we ask.'

'After a further two hours of walking the jungle changed to very thorny bamboos. Progress was now extremely difficult especially at night-time, and so I decided to walk occasionally in the day time in order to hasten my journey. Another day and night passed. Then I came upon a small abandoned jar which would hold about four litres. Picking it up I thought that it might have some water in it. But it was quite empty. However I was still happy, for this jar could be used to carry water in addition to my small canteen which only held one litre. I thought, 'Since God has given me this jar, he will soon give me some water to fill it.'

'That day I was not at all worried as I had been before. I somehow knew that God was going to help me and save me. Just before sunset I came upon another pond in the forest. This one did not have so much water as many wild animals had drunk there, and the water was very murky. After filling my canteen and the newly acquired jar, I enjoyed the rest of my rice. I was feeling so grateful to God for helping me in this most difficult time. Thus I continued on my journey praying, 'I believe dear God, that you already know all I need. You know that tonight I ate the last of my rice.' I travelled on from sunset until dawn, when I took a rest.

'As the sun began to shine, I continued walking. Almost immediately I came upon an animal with a thick scaly skin climbing up a tree.[3]

'When the creature saw me, it tucked its head under its belly and dropped from the tree. I picked it up, examined it, and asked myself, 'Is this a gift from God or not? If this is not for me, why have I met up with it? Certainly I could not have caught it if God had not previously prepared it for me.' After thinking, I killed it with an old soldier's knife I had. This was food from God, and I did not forget to thank him for providing for me yet again in these circumstances.

'The meat from that animal sustained me for the rest of my journey to Thailand, and ran out exactly on the last day. Along the way God saved me several other times which I cannot describe. I am only a witness, a voice, so that others may hear of the great power of God. He saved me, but not only me, for he will save others who believe in his Name.'

God did indeed save him on several other occasions during that amazing journey done almost entirely on his hands and knees. It was also a spiritual pilgrimage, for as Chhorn inched his way prayerfully through the dark protective forest canopy, beset by numerous perils, he crossed from a land of death into a place of refuge and hope. (Two years later in 1979, the surviving members of his family, his wife and four children and a new granddaughter, unaware that Chhorn was still alive, would also flee safely to Thailand. The entire family were finally reunited in France in 1981 after a six-year long separation.)

Chhorn was the only survivor of a group of six who set out for Thailand. The other five were all shot down when a Khmer Rouge patrol surprised them early on in the journey as they were crossing open rice fields. Thanks to his military training, Chhorn did not panic, but fell to the ground and continued to creep forward as the Khmer Rouge fanned out to the sides.

On another occasion, which he told me about later, he was hiding in a clump of bushes when a Khmer Rouge border patrol combing the area for would-be escapees, bayonets fixed, began probing the brush. One soldier, gun in hand, parted the branches and leaves just a few feet above him. Chhorn, cringing in terror, looked straight up into the man's face. But to his profound astonishment, no angry shout passed the soldier's lips, and the cold dark eyes continued to peer searchingly ahead. Chhorn could only conclude that an angel of God had reached out an invisible hand and placed it over the soldier's eyes. Certainly there were other incidents of angelic intervention in those dark days.

Along the way, biblical texts and stories learned long ago constantly came back to him. Forced to hide for a long period of time amongst some bullrushes, Chhorn smiled to himself and thought how much like baby Moses he was just now. He was a helpless child being hidden by God in the mud and bullrushes from the cruel edict of the new 'Pharaoh'. On reaching Thailand, he was most fortunate in meeting a very kind and friendly Thai farmer who immediately took him to his home and clothed and fed him.

During his escape he also recalled some advice he had once received from his mother-in-law, Granny Rose. They had been discussing what would become of the church in the event of a Khmer Rouge victory? What would they do when the missionaries left, the pastors were dispersed and silenced, and their churches and meeting places torn down? Replied Rose, 'It is for us not a question of *where* we worship, but *how*.' She was recalling the words of Jesus to the Samaritan woman: 'A time is coming and has now come when the true worshipper will worship the Father in spirit and truth, for these are the kind of worshippers the Father seeks.' (John 4:21-24). 'The Khmer Rouge may destroy our homes and our churches, but they cannot take his Holy Spirit from us, or plunder the vast reserves of his truth which we have stored in the treasure houses of our hearts.' Chhorn proved the wisdom of her words over and over again: 'God is spirit, and his worshippers must worship him in spirit and in truth.' Even traversing that vast open graveyard of western Battambang, or crawling like an insect through the densely forested approaches to the Thailand border, the presence of God could be sought and found.

One could fill a book with such escape accounts alone. Christians were miraculously led by lights which suddenly appeared before them, crossed minefields arm-in-arm, discovered groves of fruit trees in the forest, had dreams in which they were given strengthening liquids to drink, or saw visions revealing the way to take. Even Buddhists and animists, recently out of Cambodia in Thai jails, confessed to me how they had cried out to God during their perilous flight to freedom. 'You mean the Lord Buddha; or the spirits of the forest?' I queried.

'No, not them,' they replied. 'We prayed to the God who is above all gods, to the living God who surely hears when we cry out to him.' This was the testimony of some even though they didn't know his name.

Another Christian who turned up in Aranyaprathet refugee camp just a few months after Pol Chhorn in 1977, bringing more welcome news of Christians in Cambodia, was young Samuel, the troublesome and often wayward son of Sou Put. Samuel, who had also been a soldier for the Lon Nol Republican government knew he had to flee or die. Like a cat which amuses itself goading and tormenting the little mouse it has caught before killing it, or abandoning it to die of its wounds, was the way Samuel described *Angka*'s cynical policy of purposely driving their reeling and dying captives from place to place.

Before fleeing to Thailand, he had first slipped back to Chkae Koun village where his parents, Chhorn's family, Pastor Hom, and other Christian friends and relatives were living. Hom wept when he saw Samuel and pleaded with the young man to remain faithful to the Lord. So too Samuel's older brother, Chan, a man in his twenties but with a piety far beyond his years. Daily, Chan carried with him to the fields a cloth bag in which he kept his Bible and hymn book. He would seek every opportunity to slip off alone into the quiet of the surrounding bush for a time of fellowship with his Lord through prayer, and meditation in the tattered pages of the Scriptures.

Samuel told us of secret Christian gatherings, and a memorable prayer meeting he attended in an abandoned hut. Here six young men, led by a devout young Chinese Christian named Peter, earnestly cried out to the Lord for his mind and will for their future. Shortly after this, Samuel bade his tearful mother and anxious father, and all the rest of the family, farewell. Then at nightfall he slipped away into the forest with some others. They were headed for the Thai border in search of the 'Khmae Saa' (The White Khmers), an underground resistance movement about which they had heard reports. These ex-soldiers desperately wanted to take up arms and return to kill as many Khmer Rouge as they could.

The rumours which circulated among Cambodia's oppressed masses that such groups, led by well-known, almost legendary military figures, were forming in jungle and mountain strongholds were like a magnet to young men like Samuel. They dreamed of driving out these godless 'blacks' (the Khmer Rouge always wore black) and setting up a new and just government. Most of these reports were highly exaggerated, and figments of the desperate imaginations of a people longing for a pure white 'messiah', a deliverer, a saviour, to come sweeping down out of the hills to rescue them. At best the resistance groups were small, ill-equipped, and confined to the margins of Cambodia where they sniped at the occasional Khmer Rouge patrol. At worst, however, they were no more than self-serving gangs of roving bandits and cut-throats, squabbling among themselves, and financed by smuggling valuable teak wood and various cultural artefacts out of the country to sell to corrupt Thai border officials. For a very high price they would serve as couriers and guides to wealthy Cambodians, notably Chinese, seeking freedom in Thailand and the good life in America – the 'Golden Mountain'. Some joked that there were almost as many organisations for the liberation of Cambodia, as there were Cambodians planning their strategies from the bars of Paris and Los Angeles.

Samuel found the men he was looking for, but like others before him, soon became disillusioned with the resistance groups, as well as the rigours and dangers of life in the jungle. During one foray against the Khmer Rouge he narrowly escaped death. Badly injured, and weak with chronic malaria, he began to come to his senses. All his life he had been irresponsible, impetuous and undisciplined. Despite his Christian upbringing, Samuel had never really made a personal commitment of faith in Christ, though he had always admired his family's devotion. Somehow other things always came along and distracted him. And he knew that radical changes would need to take place in his life, changes he just wasn't prepared to make just yet. Now, however, lying there in that spartan jungle hideout, in complete misery and loneliness, he reflected on his life so far. He grieved at what he saw. His life was a winding trail, littered with failures and broken promises. He recounted the many times his mother had wept over him, her endless patience with him, and how they always took him back, even that time when he ran away and got involved with evil men. How it would break her tender heart to see him now here with this lot, he thought. He had foolishly let them cover his chest with tattoos to ward off evil spirits and give him prowess and protection in battle. How weak-willed he had been to consent to that, he who had heard the message of the gospel so many times. Finally, Samuel experienced a personal awakening like the prodigal in the pig pen. He had a dream in which his mother appeared to him saying: 'Pray to the living God, and trust in your

Saviour.' This he did, and recovered from his sickness.

Samuel left the jungle and entered the Cambodian refugee camp at Aranyaprathet. Here, though shy and hesitant at first, he entered into the life of the growing church, was baptised, and continued to grow in faith until his resettlement in the United States in 1978. (For him too was eventually the joy of reunion with his family when Sou Put led them to the border following the Vietnamese takeover of Cambodia in 1979. By 1981 they would all be together again starting a new life in 'the New World'.)

Finally, in our portrayal of the Christians during the Khmer Rouge years, we return to the life of Granny Rose. Rose, along with her husband Koeum, both over seventy years of age, had retired in 1973 and returned to their ancestral village of Doentiey. Doentiey had not changed very much over the years. It was like most other villages, a cluster of wooden thatched houses on stilts, a few shops, a stream, and a temple. Around its approaches were vegetable gardens, banana trees, tall coconut palms, and beyond that the vast and fertile rice growing plain of central Battambang.

It was in this humble place fifty years earlier, on that memorable night in 1923, that her father, Uncle Has, and the others, had lingered around the lantern, deeply engrossed in the chapters of God's Word which they had received that afternoon from the missionary David Ellison in Battambang market.

The fall of Cambodia and the forced evacuation of all the townspeople in April 1975, found Rose and Koeum already settled back in the countryside with the privileged status of 'old people'. Like Auntie Siew, they were clearly of acceptable peasant stock, and hardly a target of suspicion, except of course for their devout Christian faith. Rose had many relatives in this village, and it was some of her nephews who had built a small bamboo and thatch hut for them. Her one great passion in this world was her five sons. All of them had been serving the Lord in one ministry or another. But now she had no news of what had become of any of them.

While it was widely known that Rose and her husband were Christians, for they certainly made no secret of it, and they did have old enemies in the village, the Khmer Rouge didn't seem to bother them. Furthermore, one of Rose's relatives by marriage was the chief Khmer Rouge cadre in the district, and he kept something of a benevolent eye on her. (The old custom of respecting the elderly was still maintained by some.) Knowing that Rose had friends in high places, Koeum often said that he hoped the Lord would take him first, for he knew Rose would be taken care of. Such banter always provoked the ire of this feisty old saint, and she would scold him for his 'selfishness'. 'If you want to die, well, go ahead and die then.' But most of the time it was Rose herself who was weak and poorly.

Like all the old folks too frail to work in the fields, she was assigned to care for the small children who had been removed from their families. This was very exacting work requiring her to be always on her feet, lifting and bending. Rose's back finally gave out one day and she collapsed. They carried her home to Koeum who was devoted to her and always so lovingly tended to all her needs. He nursed her and prayed over her, but still insisted that the Lord would take him first.

About mid-way through 1977, soon after the rains began to fall, when all the village was subsisting on one small tin of rice each day for six people, Koeum fell seriously ill. Rose watched him grow weaker and weaker. Both knew he would not recover this time. The Khmer Rouge wanted to take him to their clinic. But Rose would not hear of it. She knew that when he died they would just take and sling his body out onto the heap of grotesque corpses in the pits which were a feature of every commune in those days. No, Rose insisted, she had taken care of him for over fifty years, and she alone would care for him now. For two more days Rose busily foraged about for food, begging a few morsels from neighbours and preparing a thin soup from grains of rice and some vegetable leaves. She sat beside him through the long night hours, coaxing him to drink a little from a spoon, moistening his lips, and soothing his brow.

One night he opened his eyes and said, 'I've been with you my darling for a long time, but now I'm going home to God.' He asked her for a drink of water, and then to come close to him. She could see in his steady gaze a deep peace, and there was no pain. At the last, unable to speak, he raised his hand in a faint wave, as if to say 'Goodbye'. The Lord was calling him home, and as she bent to kiss his lips, she saw that they formed a gentle smile. Then, looking down at him lying in death, she whispered, 'He was indeed your child and now he sees you face to face.' Beside his hand lay the open Bible which he had struggled to read right up to the end. That same Word of God, first received all those years ago when as a young man in her father's house he had pored over it in the lamp light, had been a lamp to his feet and a light to his path these fifty years of pilgrimage.

The powerful sense of the Lord's presence with them during those final precious moments together remained with Rose, comforting her, and relieving the loneliness. There were of course no coffins or funeral preparations in those inhuman days. Rose prepared his body as best she could, and by morning had him wrapped up in their mosquito net ready for burial. She had never been a woman to despair or capitulate in the face of opposition, and especially now. Stepping outside she tore away some old boards and tin from an abandoned house and persuaded a neighbour to fashion it into a crude coffin. Then, she went herself and began to dig a grave. Soon, other villagers moved by her determined spirit, came and helped her. They even shaped a simple cross out of two boards and with it marked the place of his burial.

Oblivious to the orders from 'The Organisation on High' against such things, Rose was moving to the sounds of other orders from 'on high'. No one raised a hand against this indomitable old woman standing out at the edge of the village all alone under the blazing sun, bent over the grave of her husband, rocking slowly back and forth. She committed his body to the ground to await the final resurrection. The sound of her loud praying, her weeping, and spirited singing rose and fell on the ears of the villagers all afternoon.

Her vigil done, she returned to the empty house. There she sat down and began to think and pray about her present situation. She had no real friends here, and now no Christian fellowship either. None of her many relatives in that place had ever believed the gospel, but only bitterly opposed her. And anyway, who would want to be burdened with a worn out old woman, another useless mouth to feed? She thought of her own death which surely could not be far away. If she died here, godless hands would carry her remains away, and sacrifices offered to appease the spirits that would surround her grave. She couldn't bear the thought of it. She had to go to a place where there were Christians. And that could only be Chkae Koun in the district of Tmar Koul. This was thirty kilometres away across difficult fields. But she had heard that her daughter Chamroeun (Chhorn's wife), her grandchildren, Pastor Hom, and other members of the old Battambang Church were living there. She decided there and then that she would set off for Chkae Koun.

'No! *Angka* will take care of you, Granny,' the Khmer Rouge leader insisted when she asked for the necessary permission to travel outside her own commune. Rose returned home and prayed to God to open the way for her to leave. Already she was weak, exhausted from her mourning, and her old legs were badly swollen. 'You'll have to strengthen these old legs of mine too Lord,' she prayed.

In the end, Rose simply up and went. 'You can shoot at my grey head if you want to,' she called out to the boyish Khmer Rouge soldiers guarding the road blocks beyond the village, 'But I'm walking along here by the grace of the living God.' She must have looked a most unlikely sight, 'an old woman staggering along like a drunkard,' she described herself later with a chuckle! Almost immediately on that first day she met a friendly young woman who was also heading for the Tmar Koul district. 'It will take us three days and nights,' she told Rose, 'But don't worry, I'll get you there.'

The going was very difficult and painful for Rose. The small paddies were full of ruts and holes, and each was surrounded by a rough earthen embankment. Because the rains had started, the fields were a quagmire of sticky, slippery mud. At one point, she sank down in the sod shaking her head towards the sky and saying, 'Lord, I don't think we're going to make it.' But, reassuringly, the reply came back, 'I have already prepared the way for you, what do you mean by saying you won't make it?'

'Then harden and strengthen these old knees,' she called back, giving the side of her leg a slap, and, taking the woman's arm, she pulled herself up again and on they stumbled.

They passed many ugly and disturbing sights. The peaceful and evocative atmosphere of this green pastoral landscape, the warm russet of the forest canopy just beyond the ever changing fields, the waving thickets of feathery bamboo, and numerous tall spiky sugar palms high against the sky – it had all been violated. Children in smart school uniforms no longer came running laughing along the embankments, or stopped to hook catfish in the flooded paddies. Women no longer gathered to gossip, and bicker over the prices at the market, as they beat their laundry against the rocks beside the stream. Young lads no longer reclined lazily on the backs of the water buffalo, or played sad songs of unrequited love on their bamboo flutes as they drove the herds out to find fresh grazing. Wandering pedlars no longer shuffled along the dusty roads, hips swaying jauntily from side to side beneath the weight of their wares hanging in two flat baskets which bobbed up and down from either end of a willowy pole balanced over one shoulder, crying out or ringing a bell as they went. Old women could no longer be seen squatting in the shade to replenish their red beetle nut chew on a fresh piece of leaf, deftly tucking it away with an air of sublime satisfaction behind a row of broken and blackened teeth. Men were no longer seen whiling away the hours seated in the shadow of small thatched shelters fanning themselves with straw hats and puffing easily on their homemade cheroots. No dogs barked, no temple gong tolled reassuringly from the nearby village, no rooster crowed. All was deathly silent. Even the egrets which normally fed in the watery paddies, white against the lush emerald green of the young rice, were gone. All nature seemed to hold within it some dark intrigue. The passing breezes whispered fearful secrets. A pervasive stench of death wafted from stands of distant trees which leaned and nodded together, wearily swaying back and forth in the prevailing wind, recounting the evil deeds performed in their midst. Here, whitening in the sun, a half dozen or so gruesome skeletons lay strewn in the undergrowth, their skulls blindfolded and arms still bound with cord, lest they too should up and leave this terrible place. And over there two tattered scarecrows, or are they women, stagger and weave under the weight of a plough they are pulling. All across the landscape knots of gaunt and ragged creatures draped in black, bent over, toiling, faces down, expressionless.

Rose shuddered and felt that she was traversing the valley of the shadow of death. The two women spoke little but thought much, pressed on, avoiding the roads and work gangs, moving in a north-westward direction towards Tmar Koul.

The first evening they saw smoke rising from fires. The Khmer Rouge were cooking their full pots of rice. From the roadside a group of them called out, 'Where are you going, old Granny? What are you doing crossing from district four to district three?'

'I'm going to see my daughter in Chkae Koun,' she called back, as matter of factly as she could, pointing with her chin towards the horizon ahead.

'That's impossible!' came the reply.

'What's this!' Rose protested, 'an old lady not permitted to visit her daughter?' Then, turning to face them, Rose recognised the speaker, an arrogant, swaggering youngster toting a Chinese-made AK 47 assault rife. Calling him by the unflattering nickname he had had as a small boy, she shot back, 'Hey, I remember you when you used to romp and play stark naked in the dust behind my house with the other village urchins at Doentiey. Are you now going to shoot me?' At this the Khmer Rouge soldiers burst into loud guffaws and began teasing their mortified comrade. Rose waved, smiled, and continued walking.

A little further on they came upon some *Mit Niery* (Khmer Rouge women comrades). Their black hair was uniformly cropped short and held back with a plain steel clip on each side of the head. They were squatting around the carcass of a cow, hacking it apart. 'Hey Granny, it's late, come and join us for a meal.' With an audible prayer of thanks, Rose and her companion smiling broadly, turned aside, and joined the wiry and notoriously heartless Khmer Rouge women in the first meal with meat they had eaten for a very long time. As they began eating, they asked Rose who it was she kept talking to like that. 'To my Lord,' she told them. They smiled sympathetically and refilled her bowl. In fact they feasted the two travellers so royally that evening, and with such a rich variety of food, that Rose was quite overwhelmed. But she couldn't help thinking of the people back in her village who right at that moment were sitting gloomily in threes and fours around a single ladle full of watery rice.

The following morning, they pressed her to stay, for they enjoyed her winsome spontaneity and warmth. But she agreed to delay only long enough to explain to them the way of salvation in Jesus Christ, and then she told them she must be on her way. It was just as well she had eaten so well because on this day they had to wade across swollen streams, and traverse fields deep with mud. That night, exhausted and aching from head to toe, they slept out under the stars in the shelter of an embankment.

A boy with a raft kindly paddled them over a wide and fast flowing river the next day. But hardly had they set off again when Khmer soldiers from a village close by rushed out, seized them both, and threw them into a cage-like prison. The prison was full of other unfortunates suspected of trying to escape. Every day a number of them were taken out and executed. The prisoners were in a pitiful condition. Some had obviously been there a long time, lying in their filth, starving, covered in lice-infested rags and barely conscious. For these, death came as a merciful release. This district, they told Rose, was a notoriously cruel and harsh one where the Khmer Rouge zealously killed many people, and constantly combed the surrounding fields for would-be refugees fleeing by this popular route towards Thailand. Sometimes the Khmer Rouge returned from their sorties simply with a sackful of heads, and a bundle of stinking clothes to be recycled.

Rose did not fear for her own life, but prayed desperately for her companion who had tried to help her. She reminded the Lord of his love for those who gave one of his children even a glass of water in such a time as this. 'And she has done far more than that for me,' Rose prayed on fervently from where she crouched in a corner of the fetid jail.

Early the next morning, someone came, opened the cage door and beckoned her out. This stranger handed her some rice in a tin and told to continue on her way. She did hear later that her companion was also released and permitted to stay with relatives in that village. Alone now in the fields, she thanked God for his miraculous deliverance, wondering if the one in black and of few words who had set her free was one of God's angels sent at his command.

With no one to help her, and much weakened by her stay in the jail, Rose took courage from the fact that God was at her side and she was nearing her goal. She was suffering from severe stomach cramps, her legs were like jelly, and at times she was reduced to crawling forward on her hands and knees, drinking muddy water out of holes made by the buffalo's feet. Sometimes she was tormented by the thought that perhaps her daughter whom she hadn't seen for three years was dead, or had been moved elsewhere. In her darkest moments she did wonder if she would after all die out here in the fields like many others, a lost and wandering fugitive. But the Lord encouraged her heart, telling her that she was not alone but walking with him beside her. She would not die. Thankfully, she passed through the remaining districts without any hindrance from Khmer Rouge patrols.

As she drew near to the outlying houses of Chkae Koun, excited people came running and calling out across the fields to meet this muddy and delirious stranger they had seen staggering about and falling in the sodden paddies beyond the village. Barely able to talk from exhaustion and emotion, she whispered, 'Chamroeun, my daughter, is she here?' Instantly they recognised the name, and hurried back shouting for her daughter to come. When Chamrouen arrived, breathless and alarmed, fearing some new tragedy had taken place, mother and daughter stood staring at one another in complete incredulity. Neither had any recognition of the other, so totally had these three terrible years changed them. Then as their eyes penetrated behind the death masks *Angka*'s foot had stamped on their faces, they fell upon each other, weeping and crying aloud.

They rarely saw Pastor Hom who was out working in the fields all day. But every night the Christians prayed, kneeling on the frayed grass mats on which they slept; and in whispers sang their hymns from memory.

Life was especially difficult for widows without menfolk in the household. There was no one to go the long distances for water, or catch rats in the fields and forage in the forest for crabs, grubs, and edible roots. But God took care of Chamrouen and Rose for the remainder of *Angka*'s 'Reign of Terror'.

Following the Vietnamese takeover of Cambodia in 1979, Chamrouen's sons returned to her safely from the now disbanded mobile work brigades. Only Sokh, the one who was betrayed, was lost. But poor Rose received no news of any of her sons, though she never ceased to inquire after them.

In November 1979, Granny Rose was among the hundreds of thousands of Cambodians massing on the dangerous Thai border in search of relief. With her daughter's family, Pastor Hom, and twenty other Christian families from Battambang, she moved to the safety of the new Khao I Dang refugee camp just a few kilometres inside Thailand.

What a dynamic and irresistible witness she proved to be in this refugee camp. Granny Rose was single-minded and tireless in her zeal for the kingdom of God. Her life blazed brightly with confidence in the God whom she had proved through almost sixty years of the vicissitudes of life in Cambodia. In Khao I Dang camp she was vigorous in the sharing of her faith, going from straw hut to straw hut speaking to all who would hear. Never had she known such opportunities and overwhelming interest. Young Christians stood in awe of her. When Granny Rose preached, a hush fell and people listened. But when she prayed, you knew you were standing on holy ground. And God answered her prayers in amazing ways as she knew he would.

Eventually, it seemed as though she and her daughter and family would be re-settled in France with her daughter's husband, Chhorn. We were concerned. It couldn't be right for Granny Rose to be dropped into some gloomy highrise apartment block in France. She might as well be placed on the surface of the moon, so alien would the environment be to her. The culture shock would kill her, we feared; she would never be able to learn the language; she would hate the cold weather; she would miss the moving fields, golden with the ripening harvest.

But God knew all that too. When in February 1981 they were finally moved to the transit centre in Bangkok, it was discovered that Granny Rose had cancer of the liver. For several weeks we visited her, talked and read to her and sang her favourite hymns, for we loved her as our own grandmother. Then one night after several days in a coma, she died; and while we missed her, we rejoiced. During those last memorable days spent together with her, she dreamed and spoke much of being reunited with her mother and father, and of course with Koeum who had insisted on preceding her 'home'. And in heaven she was at last reunited with her missing sons. We could just imagine Rose stepping into heaven and feeling perfectly at home; no trauma, no culture shock, no language barrier. She was a nobody here, a simple rice farmer and water carrier. But what a radiant princess she must now be in the kingdom of heaven! Precious Rose, fragrant with the knowledge of Christ.

Throughout these four years, into the silence and deep darkness of Cambodia, thousands of God's people had been praying. They were encouraged by groups such as 'Cambodia for Christ' (which became Southeast Asian Outreach), founded for this purpose in the United Kingdom by Taing Chhirc shortly before he returned to Cambodia to witness powerfully for Christ in life, and then again through a martyr's death. He had implored us to 'pray for Cambodia and pray that the powers of darkness would be removed'. By mid-1978, three years after this ruthless regime seized power, the writing was clearly on the wall. Deliverance for the Cambodian people was at hand. But from a singularly unexpected, even 'inappropriate' quarter. And though it still lingered momentarily, come it most certainly would.

'Watchman, what remains of the night?
Watchman, what remains of the night?'

And the watchman replied:
'Dawn will soon be here,
but it is still night.'

(Isaiah 21:11b,12)

CHAPTER 11

THE SCENT OF WATER

'At least there is hope for a tree: if it is cut down, it
will sprout again, and its new shoots will not fail.
Its roots may grow old in the ground and its stump
die in the soil, yet at the scent of water it will bud
and put forth shoots like a plant.'

(Job 14: 7-9)

Almost immediately following the communist victories in Indo-China (Cambodia, Vietnam and Laos) in 1975, the solidarity they had enjoyed in the face of a common foe, the USA, began to disintegrate, and the historic racial and nationalist tensions between them, far older than Marxism, began to reassert themselves. This was exacerbated further by the rivalry between the two great communist powers, the USSR and China who had also become deeply involved in the Indo-China conflict. The Vietnamese communists, with their now massive and well-oiled military machine, fell into line with the Soviets against their historical enemy but erstwhile comrade-in-arms, China. Since Cambodia's Khmer Rouge identified ideologically with Mao Tse-tung, his Red Guard Movement, and the Cultural Revolution of the late 1960s, and since Peking had been the base of the exiled Prince Sihanouk and the Khmer Rouge movement he headed from 1970-1975, there arose increasing antipathy and distrust between those two small client communist nations. Moscow backed

Vietnam and Peking backed Cambodia in the vacuum left by the retreating USA.

Ironically, the same thorny issues which had provoked Lon Nol's regime, and Sihanouk's before it, now began to irritate *Angka*. The Vietnamese were entrenched in disputed areas along their common border and were occupying islands claimed by Cambodia. This was made worse by *Angka*'s arrogant rhetoric and grandiose expansionist ambitions to recover the territory and the glory of the ancient Khmer Kingdom of Angkor. They claimed that the southern part of Vietnam belonged to them in its entirety. They even declared in January 1977 after numerous unprovoked raids into Thailand, murdering women and children, looting and kidnapping in border villages with their customary savagery, that they were settling an 'internal affair'. The territory was theirs!

The Khmer Rouge became increasingly paranoid with the passing years. Victims of their own terror and propaganda, they began to suspect even one another in the highest echelons of power, and cast suspicious eyes over entire sections of cadre and ranks of armed forces. The first to be liquidated in a classic Leninist united front scenario, were the assorted Sihanoukists, monarchists, socialists and liberals who had followed Sihanouk their 'father king', or joined the Khmer Rouge rebel front, not as communists, but out of disgust with the corruption and incompetence of Lon Nol's Khmer Republic. Skirmishes between Sihanoukist soldiers and the Khmer Rouge were already taking place in 'liberated territory' before the fall of Phnom Penh in 1975.

As we have already noted, within months of his 'triumphant return' in 1975, Sihanouk himself was placed under house detention, in his old palace in Phnom Penh, and no one was permitted to go near him.

In 1977 it became clear to *Angka* that the economic miracle based on rice production in the fertile north west region (primarily fertile Battambang) which the second forced migrations of late 1975 were to facilitate, had not materialised. *Angka* did not blame its own social and economic ineptitude, and neglect of the transportation and communications infrastructure, nor its labour camps, engineering naivety, lack of tools, nor the fact that its people were dying like flies of disease and starvation. No, *Angka* was beyond reproach. How could a revolution which bragged endlessly that it had single-handedly beaten the USA, the most powerful nation in the world, not also wage a successful war against nature, the earth, the rain, even God himself?! Its enlightened plans had clearly been sabotaged by reactionaries, conspirators, enemy agents, CIA spies, and pro-Vietnamese elements! The answer was to purge out these 'enemies of the revolution' from top to bottom. As top economic ministry officials fell, zealous pro-Pol Pot soldiers, the *puok nieredey* (south westerners), were dispatched to the north-western zone to ruthlessly slaughter fellow Khmer Rouge cadre whose loyalty was suspect. The south west zone commander was the notorious hard-liner, Ta Mok, a close henchman of Pol Pot. At first the suffering villagers rejoiced to see their cruel taskmasters bound and led away to torture and death. The new masters had come cleverly disguised as reformers invoking the magic name of Sihanouk, and encouraging the people openly to criticise, even participate in 'people's courts' and the execution of these 'class enemies'. But it was all just another brilliant double-edged sword. When the old Khmer Rouge had been dealt with, the *puok nieredey* removed their benevolent masks to reveal a new cadre even more ruthless than the former. Furthermore, they quickly rounded up and killed all those enthusiastic reform-minded people who had spoken out.

Auntie Song and the people at Phum Kor remembered these bizarre and tragic events very well. In mid 1977 the *puok nieredey* arrived in force. Mass meetings were held in the former temple. The air was rife with rumour and gossip. The name of the popular freedom fighter In Tham was heard. There was talk of Sihanouk being restored to power and the end of 'the Khmer Rouge genocidal clique'. Their former Khmer Rouge masters were taken to 'a place of peace', or beaten to death by angry mobs as the *puok nieredey* looked on. But Auntie Song wisely kept away from it all, and advised her family to stay clear of these angry meetings and debates. Ten days later at the height of the euphoria, when the village temple was packed with excited people expecting In Tham to appear in person, a fleet of trucks pulled up outside. The crowded temple was encircled by soldiers, turning the noisy meeting into an instant prison of condemned men. All were killed by grenades tossed in among them. The aftermath was indescribably horrible.

Tragically, about this time, young Zachery, grandson of old Granny Naey and Pastor Yan martyred by the *Issaraks* years earlier, was also taken away and killed, as a member of 'the uprising of the seven hundred'. His father, former pastor Sarun, saved his life by feigning madness, and was sent off to work in the communal vegetable gardens. The garden was beside a river, and here Sarun kept himself alive on the fish he caught there in secret.

With the fanatically pro-Pol Pot *puok nieredey* in charge, the pogroms against the 'new people' grew even more intense and the net of suspicion was cast wider and deeper. Facing certain death if they remained, Auntie Song's two sons, Nason and Joseph, decided to flee. They were never heard of again. And as the Khmer Rouge regularly dragged back the mutilated remains and sacks of heads of those caught escaping towards Thailand, Auntie Song secretly wept and feared the worst. Now she was alone with no one to help with the heavy work. *How much longer will this nightmare last?* she prayed.

Yet unseen to the prayerful Auntie Song, deep within the grey cells of its evil brain, housed inside the empty shell that was Phnom Penh, right down to its bloodstained fingertips, the monster *Angka,* the 'Organisation', was self-destructing, stricken with a deadly malignancy. *Angka* was out of control, savagely tearing at its own body, consuming its own flesh in a frenzied orgy of bloodletting. These latter day revolutionary sons and daughters of French radical politics, like their late 18th century forebears, were drowning in the blood of their own 'reign of terror', insatiable in their feverish paranoia to destroy all 'the hidden enemies'. It was their neighbours the Vietnamese who finally, for self-protection, strode in and put the rabid animal, wildly running in circles tearing at itself, out of its misery.

In a five-hour long speech on September 27, 1977, Pol Pot told the nation that *Angka* was the Communist party of Cambodia and he, long known by his *nom de guerre* Saloth Sar, was its leader.

The nation was now being ruled by a shadowy triumvirate of inter-married colleagues united since student days in Paris in the 1950s. This unholy trinity comprised Pol Pot, Ieng Sary and Khieu Samphan. Pol Pot and Ieng Sary were brothers-in-law having married two sisters – French-educated radical students, the brilliant Khieu Ponnary, who reportedly went insane, and Khieu Thirith. Khieu Samphan, like Robespierre, was a dedicated and single-minded purist. He had been hunted and humiliated by Sihanouk till he also fled to the forests to join the rebels in the late 1960s. Most were advantaged intellectuals of mixed Khmer-Chinese blood.

By 1977 this clique had liquidated a number of their fellow ministers and life-long revolutionary comrades such as Hou Youn, Hu Nim, and Nhim Ros, former leader of the discredited north-west sector. Now the genocide was extended beyond former soldiers, intellectuals, lepers, 'new people' etc, to minority ethnic groups such as the ancient Chams and Chinese, and then to vast numbers of Khmer Rouge with the wrong political pedigree, especially those with a Vietnamese connection. And it was for this final and ultimate requirement of self-purgation that the now infamous extermination camp of Tuol Sleng in Phnom Penh was used. Under the command of the sinister Comrade Duch, Tuol Sleng was established by *Angka* primarily for the torture and liquidation of members of its own cadre who had 'betrayed *Angka*'. Tuol Sleng would become the pinnacle of *Angka*'s entire complex structure of terror and death.

About 20,000 men, women and even children were betrayed with a smile, a kiss and a warm embrace, before the cold steel closed around their wrists and they were hauled off to their appointment with Comrade Duch, the regime's Grand Inquisitor. Virtually all who entered its doors were executed, after making the correct detailed confession. Today, along with the mountains of skulls and bones, there are detailed records running into hundreds of thousands of pages of 'confessions', macabre photos systematically taken of each victim, and all the crude instruments of torture, lying on display at this 'modern day Auschwitz', called Tuol Sleng, or 'Hill of the Poison Tree'. And there is no doubt that

Tuol Sleng was just one of many such centres of systematic torture and execution all across the nation. Mass graves continue to be discovered even to the present day. There could be up to 20,000 of them.

The absurd confession and fate of Paris-educated Hu Nim, the Minister of Information till his disappearance in 1977, is a classic example. After three months at Tuol Sleng, he admitted that he had been

...an officer in the CIA ...completely toeing the line of the American imperialists.
On the surface it seemed that I was a 'total revolutionary', as if I was 'standing on the people's side'... But, in fact, deep in my mind, the essence was service to the American imperialists. I wrote a thesis for my law doctorate which even took a progressive stand... These were the cheapest acts which hid my reactionary, traitorous, corrupted elements, representing the feudalist, capitalist, imperialist establishment and the CIA... I'm not a human being, I'm an animal.

(William Shawcross, in *The Quality of Mercy*, Simon and Shuster, New York 1984 p43)

Hu Nim was 'crushed to bits' in July 1977.

Concentrated in this former high school compound, Tuol Sleng was essentially a microcosm of Cambodia under the Khmer Rouge. Tuol Sleng encapsulated all that such Stalinist regimes are and must be. *Angka* was now executing more of its own revolutionary sons and daughters than Sihanouk or Lon Nol had ever succeeded in doing. The thirst for endless scapegoats to carry away the guilt for the mistakes, lies, and murders of those determined to hold on to power at all costs, was, of course, unquenchable.

Out in the strategic Eastern Zone bordering on Vietnam, comrade So Phim a vice-chairman of the state presidium was in command. Because of his failure to stop the Vietnamese counter-attacks and incursions, and the heavy defeat of wild and reckless Khmer raids into South Vietnam with its far superior and better armed troops, So Phim himself was suspected of 'collusion with the enemy'. In May 1978, there was a revolt against Pol Pot from this region led by So Phim. Phnom Penh was now locked in a bitter conflict with its own right arm. Pol Pot ordered the shelling of So Phim's headquarters in Prey Veng. Hundreds of eastern zone cadres were rounded up, even those who spoke with the accent of the Khmer *Kraom* of South Vietnam. New lists of traitors were drawn up and dossiers opened. In one month, four hundred east zone cadres were 'called to meetings', trapped and brought to Tuol Sleng. Many, in vain, were still convinced that *Angka* would treat them justly. Each, after long interrogations, whippings, burnings, electric shock treatment, water tortures, and the gruesome snake pit, ultimately 'confessed his crime', signed an eloquent and detailed confession acknowledging it, was slaughtered. At the end it seems that a desperate and incredulous So Phim appealed to Pol Pot himself for talks. Under the guise of 'negotiations' Pol Pot devised a clever trap for his east zone commander. At the end, betrayed, bewildered, a cornered animal, his family and friends being mown down around him, he shot himself.

Out of conviction that the Pol Pot – Ieng Sary clique was evil, and consumed only with the lust for power, So Phim's top aides, including his deputy Chea Sim, and Heng Samrin, a member of the executive committee of the Party's eastern zone and commander of its fourth division, together with thousands of troops, fled into the open arms of Vietnam.

Pol Pot, in revenge, unleashed his fury against the east, slaughtering in excess of 100,000 people. Most were bludgeoned to death in the fields. Others were uprooted and moved away in a total cleansing of this 'evil region'. By late 1977 Vietnam had already built up a sizeable fighting force from among the tens of thousands of Cambodian refugees who had fled there, and with the formal breaking of diplomatic relations between Cambodia and Vietnam on December 31, 1977, the new year opened with full-scale warfare along their common border. History was repeating itself yet again as Vietnam capitalised on Cambodia's incorrigible penchant for corruption, internal feuding, and self-destruction. The Kampuchean United Front for National Salvation was formed for the liberation of Cambodia. It was a force of about 15,000-20,000 Cambodians with the massive support of Vietnamese troops and weapons. Vietnam was about to help overthrow the very regime it had helped install in a similar popular front invasion back in 1970. That struggle had taken five long years. This one lasted just a few months, for *Angka* was already terminally ill, bleeding from a thousand self-inflicted wounds. The great tree all eaten away on the inside by termites was about to come crashing down. But still the government in Phnom Penh continued to deny vigorously the reports of mass murders, and in a diplomatic offensive invited in Western journalists to see for themselves. Most were stunned by even what they were permitted to see of the empty city of Phnom Penh, and unimpressed by the showpiece work sites they were taken to. The spectacle of Ieng Sary, *Angka*'s plump and avuncular foreign minister at the UN and other international forums, indignantly denying the accumulated evidence of over three years of mass terror and genocide, was yet another window into the heart of the Khmer Rouge. The tragedy is that the Khmer Rouge have yet to be held accountable by the world community for these lies and the massive crimes they have committed against their own people.

Compounding these problems, the country was beset by devastating floods which overnight washed away the ill-conceived irrigation projects which had cost so many lives to build. What rice remained was taken away to feed the troops battling in the east, and, some suspect, to be hoarded away in jungle strongholds along the western border for the days soon to come when the Khmer Rouge would once again be a guerrilla army. The Cambodian people, groaning under the dead weight of slave labour and this final frenzy of killing, had to subsist on the few spoonfuls of thin rice gruel dished out from the communal kitchens day by weary day.

But as 1978 wore on, bent backs straightened from their toil. The labourers listened and gazed eastwards from where the unmistakable sounds of heavy arms fire grew louder and louder. It was a sound they were not unaccustomed to, and one which now filled their troubled hearts with an anxiety alloyed with excitement. Around them they observed the mood of the Khmer Rouge growing evermore vitriolic against the *puok yuon*, 'the savages', their pejorative name for the Vietnamese. Then they saw the carts loaded with wounded Khmer Rouge fighters rumble through. Long columns of dispirited black-clad soldiers moved steadily westward towards Thailand, and whispered reports spoke of hospitals filled with the injured. Rumours and gossip were rife, and here and there trembling hands pressed hidden radios to their ears. Something cataclysmic was taking place. Surely the hour of their deliverance had come.

The 'saviour' of the remaining Cambodian people who were still staggering around in their communal boneyards, 'living in the land of the shadow of death,' appeared on Christmas Day 1978 in the unlikely and traditionally despised form of the 'Samaritan' Vietnamese. On that day the major offensive to take Phnom Penh began. Out of the east they came, driving across the landscape like a great juggernaut, a *blitzkrieg*, gathering weight and momentum as it rolled westward all across Cambodia till it stopped at the Thai border. Ahead of them in confusion and disarray fled the Khmer Rouge and their thousands of Chinese advisers, burning and destroying everything as they ran in a ruthless scorched earth policy. They burned homes and fields of ripening grain, smashed utensils, dug up the roads, poisoned the wells, and seeded the country with yet more of their hideous punji sticks, booby traps and mines.

The dazed Cambodian people everywhere warmly welcomed the Vietnamese in their green fatigues as true liberators, with a rapture bordering on euphoria. The fortunate ones were quickly enveloped behind the advancing lines. But others were caught in the cross fire or suffered terrible reprisals in Khmer Rouge counter attacks as battles, especially in the far west, ebbed and flowed. Most pitiful of all were the tens of thousands of starving and deathly-ill civilians who were driven like cattle by the Khmer Rouge into the malaria-infested forests along the Thai border, there to serve them, as the Khmer Rouge war machine, aided by the Thai military, was rebuilt in safe border enclaves. They were also helped by China of course, and others who feared Vietnamese expansionism. Now began a protracted guerrilla war against the new Vietnamese-backed regime and the Cambodian people, a bitter civil war which would continue all through the decade of the 1980s and on into the 1990s.

The successful Vietnam offensive was masterminded by General Van Tien Duay who had in April 1975 planned the final attack on Saigon. With fourteen divisions (about 130,000 men) backed by air cover, the Vietnamese adopted an 'open lotus' strategy, racing up the major roads splitting the Khmer Rouge apart, isolating and then surrounding them. While the Khmer Rouge fought like tigers, they were out-manoeuvred and out-gunned. Furthermore, they could count on no support whatsoever from the people. Indeed, isolated stragglers met a gruesome end when they were caught by the angry masses.

After just thirteen days, on Sunday January 7, 1979 at high noon, Cambodian troops backed by Vietnamese forces marched victoriously into Phnom Penh. At last, forty-three months of mindless savagery were ended. They found the capital deserted and deathlike. The 'rats' had already fled the sinking ship.

Just days before the Vietnamese arrived, Pol Pot had gone literally on bended knee to talk to Sihanouk still detained in his palace. He hadn't visited the Prince all this time, but now, clearly, the moment had come to use him again, to cover the obscene regime once more with this withering fig leaf of respectability. Would he go forthwith to the United Nations in New York and plead Cambodia's case before the world body against Vietnam and her allies? That Cambodian sovereignty had been violated by a blatant act of Vietnamese imperialist aggression was the line he was to take.

After the Chinese had flown them safely to Peking, Sihanouk, closely shadowed by his Khmer Rouge masters, slipped deftly back into his old role once again. At the United Nations he did as he had been told, angrily lambasting the 'Vietnamese imperialists' without whom he would have still been sitting captive in Phnom Penh. Chubby and buoyant as ever, up he had popped like a piece of colourful flotsam from a sinking ship, chattering, weeping, giggling, gesticulating, leaving everyone completely confused about where he *really* stood, what he *really* believed and what his plans were. Nothing had changed.

Meanwhile, far away from the spotlights, the terrorised Cambodian masses at that moment were entirely in one mind about recent events. They had been rescued from death. Drowning men do not fuss over the national, cultural, political and historical pedigree of the one who has just thrown them a lifeline.

The scattered remnant of the Cambodian church saw in these tumultuous events the hand of God, a decisive answer to their cries for deliverance. Sure enough the Lord had answered their 'complaint' just as mysteriously as he had answered Habakkuk's in raising up 'Babylonians... ruthless and impetuous people, who sweep across the whole earth to seize dwelling places not their own... a feared and dreaded people... a law to themselves promoting their own honour... guilty men whose own strength is their god.' (Habakkuk 1:6-11) Surely it is one of the profound mysteries of divine providence that our holy God uses wicked and heathen 'Babylonians' as swift and terrible instruments of his judgement against evil nations while still holding them accountable for their own godlessness, arrogance and guilt. But the unchanging message to God's people, be they Jew or Cambodian, is as unchanging as it is uncomplicated: 'the righteous shall live by faith'.

Only a few hundred Christians remained of the thousands who had joyfully thronged Phnom Penh's numerous meeting places in the revival days of 1973-75. And only three pastors had survived.

In the commune at Chamcar Ler, albeit falteringly, Rebina, despite the loss of his wife and children, clung to the Lord with whispered prayers and tearful pleadings. Just how long he might have maintained his emotional equilibrium, or escaped the scrutiny of the Khmer Rouge (for he was a fugitive listed for extermination) is impossible to say. Neither is it important, for into the twilight zone he inhabited came the Vietnamese army, snatching him and his nation from annihilation.

In late December 1978, distant rumblings in the south east heralded their approach. Daily, Rebina noticed the Khmer Rouge cadres growing increasingly restless and irritable. Then one day they started disappearing, following the black columns moving westward. To Rebina and his countrymen, whatever it was that loomed over the eastern horizon could never be worse than the present nightmare. Just the prospect of change filled their hearts with fresh hope that perhaps there was life after *Angka*.

There was a brief and eerie hiatus between the silent departure of the last Khmer Rouge and the noisy arrival of the Vietnamese. Momentarily, they hung suspended in time, yawing uneasily between two worlds, the one utterly despised, setting in the west; the other nervously anticipated, rising out of the east. And over on the Thai border, Cambodian refugees in camps observed in the sky for a number of days, 'V'-shaped formations of large birds winging their way back into Cambodia. *It's a good omen*, the exiles nodded one to another.

From his hiding place in the forest one afternoon, Rebina observed truck loads of uniformed troops driving up to the village. Abandoning his cover, he raced down to meet them and join in the excitement. A truckload of young Vietnamese soldiers had pulled up. They were unloading some sacks of rice for the people. One of them was waving a portable radio. Rebina pleaded with the soldier to let him have it for just a few moments.

Excitedly, fiddling with the knobs, Rebina scanned the airwaves for something, for anything: some news, a voice from the outside, a word from beyond this land of the shadow of death. And then he heard it... rising above the crackle and the static... the sound of voices singing...

> Silent Night! Holy Night! All is calm, All is bright
> Round yon virgin mother and Child,
> Holy Infant, so tender and mild...
> Christ the Saviour is born! Christ the Saviour is born!

Rebina looked up through the tears streaming down his face at the smiling young soldier. 'Christmas?' he inquired. 'Is it really Christmas?'

'Yea, yea, Christmas!' called back the youth, seizing his radio as the truck sped off.

A voice had indeed come to him. From outside his sad and quarrelsome world, a clear and precious Word had been spoken through the static and interference. It was the Word of the Eternal and Creator God, made flesh, suffering along with Rebina, full of grace and truth. It was Christmas in Cambodia again.

Up in Kratie province near the Mekong River, Pastor and Church President Reach Yeah and his family also watched the Khmer Rouge flee westward across the river, leaving them in glorious freedom. It was an opportunity for several in the village to openly join with Yeah professing their new found faith in Christ.

And so it began to happen all across the Cambodian fields, the unnoticed stump of the church, hewn so low, seemingly dead in the dry ground, was 'at the scent of water' budding and putting forth tender new shoots.

In January 1979 Pastor Reach Yeah and his companions constructed a large bamboo raft, and on that 'ark' for twenty blissful days, they were carried effortlessly back down on the currents of the mighty Mekong River, safely back once more to Phnom Penh, the city of their bitter exodus nearly four years earlier.

The Vietnamese would not allow returnees to land at the waterfront or enter the city centre for some months yet, so they passed on down and came ashore at the south eastern edge of the city in February 1979, near to the old Takmau Bible School. Here they built homes, caught fish, foraged for fruit, roots and wild vegetables, and worshipped God with renewed and thankful hearts. On Christmas Day 1979, they were celebrating with other returnees back at the site of the old Sarepta Church in the suburb of Tumnup Tik.

Just south of Takmau, Pastor Yeah discovered old Pastor Siang, the Khmer Evangelical Church's missionary to the Khmer *Kraom* in South Vietnam. He had returned from a fruitful and relatively unhindered ministry in South Vietnam in 1979 after the Vietnamese had driven out the Khmer Rouge. Now he was living quietly at a banana plantation. Here in a shady open-sided thatch shelter surrounded by the broad green banana leaves, a church was beginning. It was a small flock, gathered from local believers, some new, some old, and others who had loyally followed this gentle, grandfatherly pastor all the way from South Vietnam.

In the seclusion of this plantation another planting was emerging. And it was all happening in secret, virtually within the shadow of the former Bible School where over the decades hundreds, including Pastor Siang himself, had been baptised and discipled; and where year by year the nationwide church had met joyfully in conference. The martyred Taing Chhirc had been the last to preach there just two days before Cambodia fell to the Khmer Rouge. But now those seeds which had been scattered and had fallen into the earth were, at the scent of water, germinating underground and pushing their way up between the hard clods of earth. New fragile green shoots were unfolding and stretching themselves upwards: a recognisable 'planting of the Lord'.

Everything in Phnom Penh had been ravaged and ransacked by the Khmer Rouge. Heaps of litter and abandoned rusting vehicles cluttered the approaches to the city. Grass and brush grew in the roads, and small trees had taken root in some of the buildings. The smell of decay and desolation was everywhere. But slowly, life was returning to the neglected and derelict capital, and as more and more people slipped past the official road barriers the city began to take on the appearance of a great squatter camp.

One of the number of Cambodian Christians who had made their way back to Phnom Penh in 1979 was former Bible School student Sokun. He was dismayed when he saw how everything in the once beautiful city had been pillaged and ruined by the Khmer Rouge in their house-to-house 'purges'. There was ample evidence that the Khmer Rouge had carefully stockpiled western medicines and other consumer goods for their own exclusive use. As in all communist systems, 'some are more equal than others'.

All the familiar 'Christian places' he loved had been taken over or boarded up. The Bible School at Takmau, stripped of all Christian symbols, had been used by the Khmer Rouge as a hospital; Bethany Church had been gutted and surrounded by barbed wire; Bethel Church was a filthy warehouse; Bethlehem Church had been absorbed into the hideous death camp prison complex of Tuol Sleng.

Finding himself wandering down Pologne Avenue beside the Olympic Stadium, he spied the old Christian Youth Centre building where he used to come for Bible classes with OMF missionaries and Cambodian church leaders right up till the time when we in OMF were forced to flee, just prior to the fall of Phnom Penh in April 1975, after which Serey and other Khmer Christians kept the programme going. The place appeared to be empty, so Sokun out of nostalgia climbed over the fence, waded across the knee deep grass of the front lawn and pushed open an unlocked side door. He expected to be greeted by the usual sight of upturned furniture and ransacked rooms, but not here. To his utter amazement, underneath four years of accumulated dirt and cobwebs, nothing had been touched since the Christians had abandoned the place all that time ago. The house appeared somehow to have been passed by, a tiny enclave, unsoiled by the filthy hands of *Angka*.

In his mind's eye, Sokun could see the faces and hear the voices of those who had once poured in and out of the Bible classes here. He allowed himself to be transported back. Was it only five years? It seemed a lifetime, another age, so far away now. And all those echoes, the merry laughter and banter of youthful voices, the ardent preachers, the classes of trainee evangelists, those who came daily eager for Bibles. Bibles! Shaking himself from his reverie, he hurried across the room to a large floor-to-ceiling cupboard where stocks of Christian literature had been stored. Throwing open the doors, there they were before him. This was no dream. He ran his hands over the cases of Gideon Cambodian Bibles left behind after our frantic bid to distribute all the Christian literature before the communists came.

In 1975 as we prepared to leave, we had despaired over these Bibles. There was just too much literature to absorb. Sadly, some would have to be left behind to fall into the hands of the Khmer Rouge. But now to Sokun and the other Bible-less Christians who carried this precious cache away, it was clear that the Lord had kept his Word safe, right there under the noses of the Khmer Rouge, specially for them, the remnant of his people, when they returned to Phnom Penh. They had had all their Scriptures confiscated by the Khmer Rouge, or lost in the chaos.

It seems that that house consecrated to God on Pologne Avenue was used by God in at least one other remarkable way after we had abandoned it. It was in late 1979, when thousands of demoralised Khmer Rouge and the multitudes of dying wretches they had driven into the forests with them under Vietnamese shelling, were spilling over into Thailand. I was helping as an interpreter for two Christian paramedics among those tens of thousands of diseased and malnourished refugees, collapsed all over the forest floor along the Thai-Cambodian border, south of Aranyaprathet. Most were dying of malnutrition, dysentery and cerebral malaria. Midst all the crises and pressures, and with scores of nameless victims being carried away each day to mass graves and an uncertain eternity, it was difficult to feel any sense of the sovereignty of God in their lives or indeed mine. It was then as I scurried from one emergency to another that my attention was strangely drawn to a young Khmer Rouge soldier lying in the leaves, close to death. Not that there was anything unusual in that, but from his wide questioning eyes which seemed to follow me everywhere as I moved to and fro in front of him, I knew I had to stop and talk with him.

There was nothing else I could do for him in the circumstances except to hold his head, and soothe his burning temples with a damp cloth. Bending close to his ear, I began to talk to him saying that I had some very important 'good news' to tell him. But as I uttered the Cambodian words for 'good news', it struck a chord of recognition within him and he struggled to tell me in a voice full of urgency of a time during the revolutionary war against the Lon Nol regime when he lay wounded under a tree. A stranger from the nearby village had appeared and told him of the living Creator God and Saviour Jesus Christ. Though he secretly tried to discover more of this 'good news' he never met anyone who could help him. Then in April 1975, following the fall of Phnom Penh and the forced exodus of all the people into the countryside, he found himself a member of the Khmer Rouge garrison guarding the empty capital. On one of his regular patrols he passed a house which had an unusual signboard fading in the sun on its front fence which again spoke of 'good news'. Day by day as he passed the empty house it fascinated him, and he wondered who had lived there, and what was this 'good news' they had. He felt so close to finding the answer to his quest, but the house, like all the buildings in Phnom Penh, lay empty and silent. Hardly able to restrain my excitement, I asked exactly where in the city the house with the signboard was situated. It was undoubtedly our Good News Centre, at 10 Pologne Avenue! The place where I had lived prior to my flight from the falling city in 1975. Then I told him that it was I who had lived in that house, and now I would gladly tell him the same 'good news' we had once proclaimed there, and so I did, as he listened intently. That the sovereign hand of God had been upon us both bringing us together in this far away, seemingly 'godforsaken' no man's land, a place of war and death and at such a moment, was awesome beyond comprehension.

I know he found peace with God that hot afternoon because the last audible word which passed his lips was 'Jesus', and then he slipped into a deep coma. The next morning when we arrived early at the camp, it was just in time to see the orderlies carrying his stiff and lifeless body away towards the mass burial pits. I went and sat down quietly for a few moments under the trees beside the place still marked by the crushed leaves where a brother whose name I never discovered had lived briefly and then, without moving, died in Christ. Though it was a grim and terrible place, surely, I thought this is holy ground, for here the sovereign God had appeared to a seeker of the kingdom and taken him quickly home. And to me, God had given the reassurance that despite everything, he was still in control. Furthermore, it dawned on me at that moment that the Lord's everlasting arms would reach and enfold even the Khmer Rouge. And so they did over the months and years which followed.

* * *

It would be a hard thing for many of the Cambodian Christians to forgive from the heart these former Khmer Rouge, even the ones who turned to Christ, and sought to join them in the fellowships springing up in the refugee camps in Thailand.

Rebina, by the grace of God, was enabled to deal with this issue at once. 'Here are guns,' the Vietnamese soldiers told the men of his village. 'Go and kill the Khmer Rouge and all their quislings who have killed your families.' There were indeed a number of ex Khmer Rouge and their sympathisers who had filtered back into the civilian population and were trying to be very inconspicuous.

Rebina could never forget their faces. However he refused the guns anyway, saying, 'No, I won't seek revenge, for then I would have a hand in their sins.' And he remembered the words, 'Vengeance is mine saith the Lord, I will repay' and 'When your enemy is thirsty give him something to drink'. How glad he was that he had these reminders hidden in his heart especially when he saw the grisly murders done by others, hacking and torturing to death suspected Khmer Rouge.

Meanwhile at Phum Kor where Auntie Song was still grieving over the loss of her sons, the Khmer Rouge were running off into the western forests. The people fearing they might return and kill them all because they had come under the influence of the Vietnamese began to drift away from the commune in a movement which would soon swell to a mass movement of people rivalling that of the forced marches of 1975. Only this time everyone was going back, retracing footsteps, criss-crossing the nation in a massive search for the past and their lost ones.

Virtually without exception all were searching, searching for lost family members. 'A voice is heard in Ramah, weeping and great mourning, Rachel weeping for her children and refusing to be comforted because they are no more.' (Jeremiah 31:15) They crowded onto the broken and pot-holed highways and byways, moving mostly on foot in every direction. Like a sudden blizzard, notices appeared covering telegraph poles, walls and tree trunks, listing names and dates, birthplaces and ages of families, giving accounts of who had survived the terror and where they could be found. Some even offered a 'reward'. Around these *ad hoc* notice boards anxious crowds gathered to scan the names in the hope of finding a lost loved one. The air was filled with an outpouring of years of pent-up tension, excitement, happiness and despair. All the communes were breaking up and disintegrating. The Vietnamese were encouraging the people to 'return home'. Fortunately it was January, cooler, and what rice there was, ripe for harvest. The people strode in and harvested what they needed willy nilly, before moving on. Free at last to forage and fish and glean what they could, most could survive for the time being. Few were concerned about the ravaging of the 1978 harvest or planting for harvest in 1979. Urgent personal and family recovery was the first priority. But when food stocks were exhausted, the famine crisis of late 1979 would be catastrophic.

Before the little band of believers at Phum Kor set off in various directions they prayed, together rejoicing in God's merciful deliverance and seeking his blessing and guidance. Sarun decided to return to Phnom Penh. But Auntie Song said she would head westwards to Battambang where she had her roots, family and many Christian friends. With her was her daughter Tieren. They walked, and they hitched rides on the crowded Vietnamese army trucks which raced back and forth over the crumbling highways. Travelling through Siem Riep and on westwards towards Sisophon, she recognised no one. The old familiar towns and villages through which she passed were overgrown, looted and falling apart. Abandoned four years ago, they were inhospitable places, littered with the occasional gruesome skeleton and heaps of debris. At last, full of emotion, she came near to Battambang and the villages of Tmar Koul and Chkae Koun. There she found her older sister Auntie Siew, her brother Chhorn's wife Chamrouen, Pastor Hom and Christian friends she had known since childhood. There was so much to share, so much to ask, but mostly too much to weep over. What heart-rending experiences they had all endured since last they were together.

But the further west she travelled the more precarious was the Vietnamese control. At Chkae Koun they lived in constant fear of Khmer Rouge night raids and bloody reprisals. She observed how out of humanitarian concern the Vietnamese sought to avoid firing into villages full of civilians, but the Khmer Rouge with no respect for human life fired at will whenever they desired.

1979 was a cataclysmic year full of danger and uncertainty on every front as the pro-Vietnamese regime sought to consolidate its hold on power and mop up the pockets of Khmer Rouge resistance inside Cambodia which still terrorised areas of the countryside.

The question of rice was a secondary concern to the new government also, and would not be addressed till late in the year when with virtually no crops planted, the country was deep in the grip of famine. A famine on a population already weakened by four years of slave labour and starvation rations. With the Thai border so near, and reports of food and medicines being distributed there by international humanitarian organisations, hundreds of thousands of Cambodians began running the gauntlet of Vietnamese troops, minefields, bandits and Khmer Rouge guerrillas to get there.

In April 1979, Auntie Song joined them on the dangerous trek to Nong Chan, a vast sprawling encampment of tens of thousands of refugees situated in the volatile no man's land on the Thai/Cambodian border.

Such camps were increasingly being controlled by one of the three anti-Vietnamese resistance factions who skimmed off much of the humanitarian aid for themselves: Communist Khmer Rouge, Royalist Sihanoukist, or Republican Khmer Serey; the oldest of the groups (led by former Prime Minister Sonne Son) had been there ever since 1975 sniping at the Khmer Rouge. Now these groups, all of whom had fought each other at one time or another over the past ten years, were coming together in an uneasy alliance of convenience to form a tripartite guerrilla army to harass the pro-Vietnamese Heng Samrin puppet government in Phnom Penh. By 1982 this anti Vietnam tripartite coalition based on the Thai border was a fighting reality in a civil war with the 'Vietnamese puppets' in Phnom Penh.

Despite the usual window dressing of Prince Sihanouk as leader, militarily and politically the movement was dominated by the Khmer Rouge who had the only viable, experienced and rigidly disciplined fighting force of several thousand fanatical troops.

Thailand would give them safe havens inside their border, and be a conduit for Chinese armaments. Clearly, Cambodians were going to be continuing to kill Cambodians for a long time yet.

Nong Chan, fortunately, was not a Khmer Rouge led camp, so the atmosphere was casual, freedom fighters lounged around in makeshift coffee shops, and here the black market between Thailand and Cambodia, with all the attendant corruption and vice, did a roaring business. Auntie Song, like most, was shocked and disillusioned by the selfishness, greed and wholesale corruption which characterised life at Nong Chan. Her heart was deeply moved at the low physical and moral condition of her people. Even the veneer of ethics afforded by Buddhism seemed to have gone, destroyed by four years of Khmer Rouge brutality. All that remained was the law of the jungle, the survival of the fittest.

By May 1979 the situation along the border was critical. All the official camps and detention centres were bursting with masses of refugees. The borders were crowded with tens of thousands of squatters and feuding guerrilla armies who could only live by means of the hundreds of trucks and tankers loaded with the food and water which had to be hauled in every day. The massive threat of Vietnamese infiltration into Thailand loomed large, and Thailand's own local border villages were in constant danger. It was for the Thai government a security nightmare. And despite massive foreign humanitarian aid, and some resettlement overseas, who would take all these new 'illegal immigrants' off Thailand's hands? Clearly they were not going to return to Cambodia in the present climate of political uncertainty, guerrilla warfare, and famine. It wouldn't be till 1993, fourteen years later, that the last Cambodian refugees were either resettled in the west or repatriated to Cambodia. Furthermore, from north to south, Thailand's eastern border was already dotted with refugee camps filled with Hmong tribespeople from Laos, Lao, Vietnamese 'boat people' and Cambodians, many of whom had been waiting for resettlement overseas since the refugee crisis began in 1975 with the fall of Indo-China to communism.

Thailand was awash with refugees, and as the Vietnamese army pressed westward in 1979 so the flood tide of 'illegal entrants' heightened. In an effort to keep these post-January 7, 1979 arrivals under control and less accessible to foreigners, some Thai military border commands resorted to secretly and violently pushing them back, shooting at them, and handing them over to Cambodian guerrilla groups inside Cambodia.

Although Thailand forced back tens of thousands, and many to their deaths, they did permit hundreds of thousands of refugees into their country from 1975-1993, as explained earlier. The Philippines and Indonesia, both poor nations, also set up camps. Islamic Malaysia agreed to receive for settlement only Muslim Cambodians, or those who converted to Islam, and reluctantly allowed refugees in till they could be resettled in the 'West' or later repatriated. For those nations, the flood of refugees pouring out of Indo-China was a nightmare. Malaysia warned that she might be forced to shoot at the mostly ethnic Chinese boat people trying to land on her shores. And Hong Kong agonised over the many restive Vietnamese refugees encamped there. 'The quality of mercy' had become very 'strained' indeed.

It is my belief that had there not been since 1975 the wide open resettlement programme for Indo-Chinese refugees to go to the West, many would never have abandoned their homes and crossed international borders. Once started there was no end to it, for indeed most of them would have seized the chance to live in the affluent West if they could. The expectation of resettlement in the West was like a great magnet which attracted hundreds of thousands to the refugee camps. Apart from those whose lives were in real danger were they ever to return home, the refugee camps might better have been kept consistently as places of short or long term temporary refuge till the people could return home, just as they tend to be in the rest of the world. Many of these people possessed the very skills and qualifications their country so badly needed. But of course few of the neighbouring countries into which these refugees poured were prepared to put up with them for an indefinite period of time. Thus Thailand's decision to call them 'illegal immigrants' and not refugees was understandable. Not enough accountability, it seems, is required of those nations who create these refugee problems and use them as pawns in their own sinister political and military strategies.

The United Nations High Commission for Refugees (UNHCR)[1] in 1979 found itself in an impossible diplomatic situation. To protest against Thai violations meant they incurred the anger and indignation of the Thai for 'meddling in their internal affairs'. Not to protest was demoralising, and earned them even more disrespect politically, as well as the anger of refugees, and the justifiable accusation all round that the organisation was a toothless tiger. Individuals who did valiantly stick their necks out and made their feelings known in Thailand soon found themselves *persona non grata*. Besides, Thailand along with a number of other nations in the region had never been a signatory to any United Nations convention on protocol or on the status of refugees anyway. Much that the great international organisations like the UNHCR or the International Red Cross sought to do was frequently scuttled by immediate political pragmatics in Thailand, Cambodia and Vietnam.

It is the height of credulity to believe that the political agendas of individual nations in times of such regional crises will have any serious reference to the humanitarian niceties of organisations like the UNHCR. If and when a nation does acquiesce to such external constraints, it is only because for the moment it is politically or economically expedient to do so. No country will compromise its own perceived national self-interest, sovereignty or integrity for the sake of refugees and their 'rights'. This is to be expected.

In this instance, while the UNHCR was primarily concerned about political correctness and protecting the 'rights of refugees', Vietnam and Cambodia were concerned primarily about winning their war with the Khmer Rouge, and the Thai along with their allies in ASEAN[2] with halting Vietnamese expansion. Suddenly, here were the Thai giving welcome refuge and strategic military assistance to the Khmer Rouge communists who, only two years earlier, were massacring their people and violating their territory. Fellow Buddhist Cambodian civilians were not always so welcome.

Why should they, a developing nation, have to suffer the fall-out from something others had ignited, the Thai reasoned. And why should they facilitate what they saw as vast numbers of opportunistic, largely economic migrants who were simply wanting to get to 'the good life' in the West? Certainly the 'resettlement in the West' factor clouded the issue and confused the motives. It was an added incentive which encouraged many people to stampede out of Cambodia who really need not have done so, at least not on a permanent basis. Thus the not always so innocent 'refugees' became expendable pawns in a prolonged political and economic chess game:

'If you want to help the needy Cambodians inside Cambodia then you must recognise the legitimacy of our government,' said the diplomatically isolated and newly-installed pro-Vietnam regime in Phnom Penh facing a trade embargo from the West all through the 1980s.

'If you want to help the needy Cambodians inside Thailand, then you must buy all the wherewithal to do so here, and hand over supervision to us,' said a corrupt Thai army.

As for China, ASEAN and the West, particularly the United States in the 1980s, they were content to see Vietnam as isolated as possible and getting nicely bogged down in its own 'Vietnam' (ie Cambodia). China, in its desire to 'bleed Vietnam white', also 'punished' Vietnam by an invasion in March 1979 though they came out of it rather badly mauled. But what was most remarkable of all in 1979 was how quickly the nations of the world were prepared to overlook the genocide of the Khmer Rouge and embrace them in international forums such as the United Nations.

The international villains were now not the Khmer Rouge but the Vietnamese, except that is initially at least to the overwhelming majority of Cambodian people. Clearly, despite the rhetoric, few governments were genuinely concerned about the plight of the beleaguered Cambodian masses inside Cambodia. Anti-Vietnamese sentiment was still very strong and they were going to be punished for invading Cambodia no matter what.

In June of 1979, the situation in Thailand came to a head. Auntie Song at the crowded Nong Chan site on the border was beginning to realise that she had jumped out of the frying pan into the fire. There was the threat of Vietnamese bombardment, danger from rival Cambodian guerrilla groups, bandits and Thai soldiers. Daily the blackmarketeers poured in with their wares. These were mostly Thai and Chinese operating out of Aranya Prathet which now began to take on the appearance of a gold rush town. But there were also a fair number of fellow Cambodians, some of whom had bribed their way out of the old refugee camps inland to come and join in robbing, exploiting and cheating their own people. The Cambodians paid for everything with their hidden treasures of gold and jewellery kept concealed in all manner of ingenious places during the Khmer Rouge years. The trade was given an unexpected fillip with gold prices soaring that year on international markets. For refugees with little or no gold, life was hard indeed. With all this treasure about, murders, rapes, frauds, and robbery were a daily occurrence in and around the camps where the law of the jungle held sway. Fortunes were made and lost. Scores lost their lives in road accidents as these fatalistic dare devils raced their Japanese pick-up trucks up and down the once sleepy rural roads along the Thai/Cambodian border.

Thus when a fleet of over one hundred buses arrived at Nong Chan camp on June 8 1979 with the Thai army assuring the people that they were going to be transported 'to another safe camp' it seemed entirely reasonable to Auntie Song, though she might have been forgiven some scepticism when the less enthusiastic were violently herded onto the buses at gunpoint. The buses were crowded and airless, but smiling Thai soldiers encouraged them that in less than an hour they would arrive at a newly prepared site.

Like the others, Auntie Song was full of anticipation as the convoy of buses sped westwards away from the Cambodian border, and she was enjoying her first bus ride in years. Some even thought they were going to Bangkok. But strangely, the buses were now heading northwards and still they hadn't arrived. The light-hearted banter began to give way to a worried silence, and when it became clear that they were being driven back in an eastward direction a panic began to grip them. It was 10 pm and Auntie Song was staring fixedly out of the window as the bus raced through an unpopulated and forested countryside. Suddenly, along with others, she caught sight of a road sign momentarily illuminated by the bus's headlights – Sisaket! They were in the trackless jungle region of the Dangrek mountain range bordering north-eastern Cambodia, heading for Preah Vihear.

Now the bus was labouring and bumping up a steep incline. It had started to pour with rain. Their worst fears were realised when the buses came to a halt, and the strident voices of gun-toting Thai soldiers with bullhorns began shouting, 'Get out! Get out!' Out they stumbled, hungry, weary, and now soaking wet. There were old people, mothers clinging to tiny children and young men in their new designer jeans acquired on the black market. At 5 am, Song feeling very hungry and wretched found herself being herded along with hundreds of others of her tearful wailing countrymen. She could hear a helicopter circling overhead, and all around with loud hailers Thai solders with guns and whips were driving them on into the deep forest. A grey mist shrouded the treetops. They were high on a mountainous plateau. Occasionally shots rang out over their heads as they neared a steep ravine. In horror, Auntie Song realised that they were all about to be pushed over the edge and into the steep-sided valley below. On the other side was Cambodia. 'Look, there is your country, now go!' Song heard the Thai soldiers shouting from behind her as she gripped her daughter's arm.

Into the 'Valley of Hell', they tumbled, wave after screaming wave. Thousands followed thousands, over the several days of the sordid operation. Unable to keep their footing on the steep slippery and root-entangled mountainside they fell headlong with their screaming little ones, losing what precious supplies the Thai had not already relieved them of. Like heaps of rubbish tipped over a cliff, they tumbled forward and slid, battered, bruised and unwanted into the valley below. It was impossible for all but the fittest and boldest to attempt to scale back up the steep space to the Thai side again. Some who did, despite their bribes and entreaties, were shot.

But the worst was yet to come. Resigned to their fate, the Cambodians struggled forward across the wooded valley floor. It was then that the pandemonium broke loose.

The quiet valley suddenly became an echo chamber of explosions and screams as one after another in quick succession mines were triggered. The whole valley was one vast minefield. For hours the air was filled with their screams, and then the moaning of the wounded and dying. Auntie Song's daughter beside her was struck by shrapnel, and a woman in front of her was blown to pieces. Auntie Song found herself surrounded by chaos, horribly disfigured corpses, blood, and complete hysteria. Petrified, the survivors stood frozen in their tracks. Then they began inching forward again, but now to avoid more mines, stepping on the bodies of that unfortunate first wave who had set off the mines.

Those driven across here in following days met with fewer mines, but had to endure the sickly stench and gruesome spectacle of the bloated and mutilated corpses lying rotting and infested with insects on the forest floor. Here and there was the pathetic sight of a dying soul lying twisted among the leaves, horribly injured, abandoned, arms outstretched in supplication. Many of the dead were Chinese Cambodians, aggressive entrepreneurs, hoping for a better life in Thailand and beyond in California.

'So what do you think of the Thai now?' asked the cynical young Vietnamese occupying soldiers who met the gaunt and bedraggled survivors several kilometres inside Cambodia, 'Filthy eh?' At a village about fifteen weary kilometres further on, the Vietnamese put the reluctant returnees into trucks and drove them further inland towards the provincial capital of Kampong Thom. The Vietnamese soldiers gave them basic supplies and allowed them to disperse.

Auntie Song rarely missed an opportunity to speak of Jesus Christ to whoever would listen. She discovered, as did Pastor Hom, who was also finding opportunities to chat with this one and that one, that the young Vietnamese soldiers far from home always gave her a listening ear. When confronted by her bright smile and kindly voice enquiring, 'Do you love the Lord Jesus?' even the most 'macho' became pensive and serious. Some smiled and nodded approvingly. Others coveted her prayers for their safety and families, or engaged her in further conversation. Many Vietnamese have a Roman Catholic background, and the persecuted evangelical church in Vietnam had grown and strengthened considerably through all the long years of war and hardship.

It was still June and the onset of the rainy season. Song was almost permanently soaked as footsore she trudged on, sleeping alongside the road and trading for rice with the few fragments of gold she still possessed. She was still surrounded by the thousands of other returnees who were likewise heading west along the main road from Kampong Thom towards Siem Riep.

The sad procession often fell prey to local bandits who robbed and beat them, even stripping the clothes off their backs. In isolated places they were afraid of tigers by night, marauding tribespeople, and as always, the merciless Khmer Rouge guerrilla units.

Then one day in July 1979, she found herself right back where she had started in the district of Kampong Kdey at Phum Kor. She had come full circle. How excited the villagers were to see their old spiritual grandmother again, and they marvelled as she related all that had befallen her since they had parted six months earlier. Finally, she passed through Siem Riep and the ancient ruins of Angkor, on to Sisaphon, and then once more having trudged hundreds of kilometres, back in Battambang.

For the time being she shunned any suggestion of another flight to the Thai border. But by year's end with a relaxation of Thai restrictions and the setting up by the UNHCR of the vast new 'holding centre' at Khao I Dang over in Thailand, the intrepid Auntie Song was on the move again, dodging the bullets and the bandits along the Thai border. On one occasion as she fled through the bush under a hail of bullets with a group of fellow Christians, she called out with the suggestion that perhaps they should stop and pray about the situation.

'Pray as you run!' the others yelled back.

Altogether an estimated 45,000 Cambodians seeking refuge at the Thai border were rounded up from various sites and driven back across that 'Valley of Hell' as it became known, in June 1979. Ironically, some of them only days earlier had been personally greeted by Kurt Waldheim, the Secretary General of the United Nations during a visit he made to the border camps.

Another of these crowded makeshift camps in Thailand for the detention of 'illegal immigrants' in early 1979 was in a small field in the village of Taphraya, about thirty kilometres north of Aranyaprathet. Here in April 1979 arrived a band of twenty-six Cambodian Christians headed by Taing Vek Huong, brother of the martyred church leader Taing Chhirc. Because of his former links with 'Campus Crusade' in the USA, influential people in both Thailand and America saw to it that Huong's family were, within two weeks, whisked away to the United States. This was an incredible feat. The rest of their party arrived a few weeks later.

Before these Christians left Taphraya camp however, they had begun zealously witnessing through personal evangelism all over the crowded camp. Furthermore, they targeted ten of the most promising men, gave them intensive instruction, and appointed them as teaching elders. By the time these ten were also taken away a few weeks later, three other men, all new Christians now, were ready to take up the responsibility of evangelising, organising the fifty or so Christians, and distributing Christian books. Small cell groups multiplied as more and more expressed their desire to join in studying the Bible, to worship and pray with the Christians, and seek forgiveness of sin and reconciliation with God through Jesus Christ. Although that original group of mature believers were only in the camp such a short time, it was sufficient to ignite an incredible interest and responsiveness to the gospel. Once started, the movement towards Christ spread like wildfire. The same thing happened twelve months later among the tens of thousands at Khao I Dang following its opening in November 1979. I still have in my possession on little scraps of paper, lists of names in Cambodia script of some of these cell group members. Their eager faces have faded from my memory. But the earnestness and spontaneity with which they searched the Scriptures, huddled in groups all over that filthy and overcrowded camp, will always be remembered. How precious are such moments of fellowship, and how painful their passing. Most were in their teens and twenties. But some were older, including one who had formerly been a monk for eleven years, and even a few ex Khmer Rouge, one seventeen-year-old I recall, with a wounded arm. These were tense yet such busy and exciting days.

In early June 1979, I had to leave my home in Aranyaprathet at the border to go to Bangkok and then on to Malaysia for my wedding. On June 9, one of the leading Christians in Taphraya managed to send a telegram to me in Bangkok. Though carefully worded, he was clearly hinting at some great danger. A few days later, postmarked June 10, 1979, a brief letter arrived. It had obviously been handed to a sympathetic local Thai to mail just as they were being forced onto those fateful buses. Without being specific, it spoke of a fearful catastrophe which had befallen them, of some dreadful news they had just received:

'With prayers to Jesus Christ – He is Lord of all, to the Father, and to the Holy Spirit.

Dear Elder Brother and Pastor in Christ,
Please be informed that due to recent news reaching us here, we are oppressed and surrounded on all sides by deep fear and worry. That is to say, a great catastrophe has come down upon us, and we are all in imminent danger of losing our lives.

We have taken courage and strengthened our hearts in this terrible situation by reading in God's Word:
                'I will never leave you,
                I will never forsake you.'
                Therefore with boldness we can all say,
                'I will not be afraid because the Lord is my Helper.
                What can man do to me?'

In conclusion, we all pray to the Father, to the Lord Jesus Christ and the Holy Spirit, that you, Elder Brother, might have joy, happiness and victory in all things, and that you may continue to help save those lost lambs who, because of sin, still wander afar, and that through the name of the Lord Jesus Christ, they might be set free from the pit of death.

The Christians in Taphraya

By the time the letter reached me, these fifty or so saints along with 45,000 other Cambodians had already been herded into the notorious 'Valley of Hell'. But one of these Christians, a young man named Khiev Tan, miraculously managed to crawl out of the carnage and back into Thailand. In his pocket he had my card with the OMF's Bangkok address on it.

In an incredible journey which he later related in the *New York Times*[3] under the pseudonym Chey Rith, he not only escaped death, but managed to travel incognito hundreds of miles across Thailand first to the OMF mission home in Bangkok then to the UNHCR and the American Embassy, and thence to a new home in the USA.

Later that year when Thailand permitted the opening of the vast Khao I Dang 'Holding Centre', only a few kilometres south of Taphraya, I met a number of refugees who had survived this brutal forced repatriation. One, not a Christian, told me how at one point along the painful trek back across Cambodia's northern wilderness he saw: 'a remarkable group of people sitting together beside the road. They had books open before them and were talking to their God.' Another, a Christian, who eventually made it back to Thailand in October 1979 reported that three of the Taphraya Christians perished immediately on the mines, and two or three others had languished on the long journey with little food or water, back into the interior. The rest he assumed had returned to their homes all across Cambodia.

Some, like Auntie Song, however, waited for the political climate in Thailand to change, and then slipped out again. These also told yet again the terrible story of their betrayal by the Thai, and the forced repatriation across the minefields and dense forests with no food or water.

But most of these tender young seedlings raised up in the intense climate of those uncertain days at Taphraya, are today, presumably, somewhere in Cambodia, struggling no doubt to mature as Christian men and women in that desolate spiritual wilderness. And as for Khiev Tan, like many others, he too has disappeared into another spiritual wilderness, no less threatening to his spiritual survival, the USA.

It was the cheapness, the low value placed on individual human lives which was the scandal of 1979. I realised it when I went looking for a frail young mother sent from a jungle border camp to a nearby hospital because she was bleeding to death after a premature delivery in the forest. After some days of waiting, the husband asked me to try to locate her. When I presented her name at the hospital, the nurses roared with laughter: 'You don't think we bother with their names do you! If you don't see her here, then she's out there somewhere in that big hole.'

My wife, Margaret[4] realised it when Moeung a young Christian man at the Aranya Prathet camp, locked up in one of the long houses with hundreds of others to be driven back over the border the next day, pressed into her hand through the window bars a grubby scratched negative of himself. 'You won't forget me, will you, sister?' he pleaded. With all his family already dead at the hands of the Khmer Rouge, he too was about to die. He desperately needed to know that at least someone possessed an image of him, some proof that he had lived, and might perhaps be missed.

Cambodians died in our arms on hospital steps while disinterested Thai medics joked that they 'couldn't raise the dead'. Others who were admitted were never heard of again. Once I advised a young man to flee from the hospital when we suspected the doctors were going to secretly remove his kidney for transplant rather than remove a kidney stone. And many others were simply left to perish in the forests where they had collapsed.

Multitudes more Cambodians stormed the gates of death that year as in previous years, unknown, unidentified and unnoticed, except by those who searched their pockets for money or cigarettes, or stripped off a still useable garment before they were abandoned, to be recycled, as the Buddhists believed, by *karma* into another life form.

In Thailand as in Cambodia, strict Buddhists will not even lift their hand to kill a mangy dog, even a rabid dog, as it is sinful, bad *karma*, to kill any living creatures, for all are reincarnated lives. But many Cambodian refugees didn't even enjoy the rights of a dog. The 'open season' on Cambodian people declared by the Khmer Rouge in 1975 was still plainly in effect throughout the region. Certainly, few saw them as beautiful and unique creations of the Creator, to behold with awe.

Through all these troubles Pastor Hom remained quietly with his family in Chkae Koun where he had been living since forced from Jerusalem Church in Battambang by the Khmer Rouge in April 1975. Sometimes the Khmer Rouge chose not to execute an individual, but rather to keep him alive in daily suspense, and work him slowly and agonisingly to death, or till his mind snapped.

Hom, a well-known and much-loved Christian pastor, was the perfect candidate for this latter sentence. He survived the ordeal only by God's grace, and restraining hand upon the Khmer Rouge. They were also confronting a man trained in the discipline of devout prayer. Every night whatever the circumstances, he set aside precious time and energy to pray together with his wife. Sometimes he found himself keeping company with God all through the night. In late 1977 just as the Khmer Rouge crucible was being stoked up to its most ferocious intensity, Hom experienced a number of unusual dreams. In one he saw a great golden key in the sky. Then a person walked across the earth, reached out his hand and took up the key. He awoke so shaken and excited by this vision that he related it to his wife. He felt sure that some great deliverance was close at hand. On subsequent nights he experienced more such powerful dreams. As he shared secretly with other Christians concerning these dreams, he discovered that some of them too had been experiencing the same things. They became convinced that God was preparing to intervene in their circumstances. Some new thing was about to happen and they were to watch and wait for it. So while their outward circumstances continued to deteriorate, inwardly, Hom and his little circle of Christian relatives were buoyed up with a profound sense of great expectation.

Then, in 1978, everyone was abuzz with rumours of the Vietnamese invasion. And they could hardly restrain their excitement when suddenly it was being whispered about that Phnom Penh had fallen to them, and the Khmer Rouge leadership was in flight. Still the signs continued with regular testimony from this one and that one, from near and far, a Christian experiencing a miracle, a sudden intervention by the hand of God – perhaps a healing, an escape from death, provision of food, or an unexpected reunion with a lost family member. God who had heard their cries had come down to move among them, awakening them from that deadening and anaesthetising soul slumber which prolonged pain and hunger can induce.

It was late one night in January 1979 when Pastor Hom, wide awake, heard the sound of heavy guns coming from the direction of Battambang city. Listening to the sound of the steady booming of the guns as it was carried northwards on the night air, Hom felt new hope stirring within him. Morning light found the villagers of Chkae Koun excitedly watching the circling flight of an airplane over on the horizon dropping bombs on Battambang.

Later that day two very exhausted and dishevelled strangers appeared in the village. They were Khmer Rouge soldiers who had fled all the way from Phnom Penh. They told of the massive Vietnamese onslaught. Pastor Hom knew not only from the state of their torn and filthy black clothes, but by the passion in their voices, that what he was hearing was all true. The capital had fallen. A new regime was in power. *Angka* ruled no more. To those who listened in awe-struck silence to the account of the sheer speed and totality of the invasion it seemed apocalyptic, almost beyond belief.

Then they saw hundreds of Khmer Rouge coming towards them, struggling down the dirt road which ran through Chkae Koun from Tmar Koul on the main Battambang to Sisophon highway. They were moving westwards towards the Bavel River and beyond into the thick forested regions on the Thai border. They were a sorrowful sight. Between them they were carrying their wounded slung in hammocks suspended from poles, hobbling along on sticks in a state of shock, disorganised, some horribly wounded. In their wake, all along the roadside, lumps of black strewn among the green grass showed the places where others had fallen or been abandoned. They had obviously been caught by surprise and fled in great haste for they carried no supplies. As 'the black ones' limped through the village, the people according to their acquired habit with the Khmer Rouge, shrank back, averting their eyes, as if somehow trying to make themselves invisible.

But Pastor Hom could see that the Khmer Rouge were too pre-occupied with their own escape, like hunted animals limping into the forest for cover, to be bothered any more with the likes of them. Their eyes were dark and cold, betraying no hint of fear, just hatred. Now, finally, had come the day of their 'long march'. The hunter, hunted. The victor, vanquished. Yes, they had torn down his church stone by stone. They had slaughtered virtually all his fellow pastors and numerous other Christian brothers and sisters. And they had sought to destroy him too. But as he watched them that memorable afternoon stumbling painfully and wearily into history, Pastor Hom was rejoicing in the knowledge that the future belonged not to *Angka* but to him and to the people of God.

Later, he heard how the Khmer Rouge in Sisophon and Mongkul Borey were quickly overrun, caught in a pincer move-ment between the heavily armoured Vietnamese divisions moving rapidly westwards from Siem Riep and northwards from Battambang. Here also, the Vietnamese gladly allowed the people to finish off captured soldiers of *Angka*, the Khmer Rouge, who had been their cruel taskmasters for almost four years, releasing a savage outpouring of blind fury and revenge.

When, in a few days, the war enveloped Chkae Koun, Pastor Hom gathered up his family and a few possessions and went out to hide among the giant anthills in the scrubland round about. With the Khmer Rouge either driving people into the malaria-infested western forests ahead of them, or simply slaughtering them, it was vital to get quickly behind the Vietnamese lines or hide away from the village and main roads. For two weeks they lived in the bush, sleeping in the dewy grass up against the rice embankments while the fighting raged about them. Safe now under Vietnamese control, they moved back to Chkae Koun camping under a tree on the eastern approaches rather than in the west facing the Khmer Rouge guerrillas.

Wonderfully, all the Christians had survived the fighting. But they sensed that Chkae Koun was too vulnerable to Khmer Rouge counter attacks, so they decided to move several kilometres further east to Tmar Koul on the main highway. Desperate for food, Pastor Hom slipped back into Chkae Koun alone, first to collect their precious axes, knives and cooking pots which he had buried in the ground or hidden underwater; but mainly to gather in some sheaves of the unharvested rice in the surrounding fields and sweep up some kernels from the threshing floor. But the sound of firing close by sent him quickly scurrying back to his family.

To add to the difficulties were the thousands of Cambodians pouring through the area. All Cambodia it seemed was on the move. Days were occupied with foraging for rice in the fields. But as the multitudes were all doing the same, they were forced to go deeper into the countryside where a number were killed by lurking Khmer Rouge, gangs of thieves, or from stepping on land mines.

Nights were even more fearful. At the height of the fighting around Tmar Koul, the Christians, unable to sleep, prayed in groups out in the fields where they camped from two in the morning until five.

Although they were free, all the basic means of life now had to be fought for along with multitudes of others. It was survival of the fittest. Water was a major problem. The Khmer Rouge had purposely polluted wells and pools by throwing dead bodies into them. And then there were the crowds escaping and crowding around and polluting it further with their filth. But there was little choice other than boiling it if you could and drinking it anyway. Seeing that the food situation was deteriorating rapidly and the fighting around Tmar Koul was still going on, Pastor Hom decided to move them all to Battambang city. It was every man for himself. By the time they reached the city pulling their makeshift cart, so had tens of thousands of others.

Battambang had already been derelict for nearly four years. But now the masses crowded in, chopping down the trees, pillaging, and turning everything upside down, all reduced to foraging around like pigs in a great filthy pigsty. Every day, like all the others, he grimly searched for food, 'like an old buffalo', he mused, hauling his cart behind him. The Khmer Rouge had killed most of the livestock, pigs, chickens, ducks, cattle etc and meat was almost impossible to find. But he had good reason to be thankful for his deft skill, learned in boyhood, of catching rats. And for rice, he was forced to search for kernels under people's houses or compete with the rats for it in former granaries.

His wife walked for miles every day to find clean water and haul it back. One by one they all became ill. The children had chronic diarrhoea and scabies and then they caught measles. An epidemic was sweeping the slum city of squatters. Running sores infected their eyes and worms crawled from their festering noses and mouths. His youngest child was at the point of death. The little thing was wasting away. His mouth was a mass of sores, gums receding, unable to take any sustenance.

One night at about nine o'clock, Pastor Hom watched him raise a tiny shrivelled fist and with one finger extended point to his tongue. He hadn't been able to speak for days. Hom took an orange which he had earlier traded for some of his precious rice. He squeezed one or two drops into the child's mouth. His wife, weeping silently, coaxed a few drops of milk from her breast onto a curled leaf and eased them into the child's open mouth. Then, having given all they had, they bowed their heads and Hom committed the little boy into the Lord's keeping, concluding '...though you have granted me this great suffering, my heart has not grown small towards you. I still love you with all my heart. But it is a heart filled with tears.'

At one in the morning, Hom reached out his hand and felt the child's little body. It was stone cold. In the morning they wrapped him up and laid his remains to rest in a little grave they had dug among the trees. But the father could not forget his baby son. He felt sapped of all energy. He cried out to God to please relieve his grief and give him peace, for his heart was deeply shaken.

It was the recovery of the Christian fellowship in Battambang as more and more of the Christians returned and discovered one another that really saved Hom and his wife from despair and destruction. Working together in mutual interdependence, sharing what they had, pooling their resources, helping one another with the children and the sick, provided them all with the security and daily means of life they needed. Hom the pastor now had more time to teach the Bible, conduct worship, visit around and pray with the many troubled and needy people.

Returning to Chkae Koun, his birthplace, now firmly under

Vietnamese control, he even had opportunities to speak of the Lord to Vietnamese soldiers, sitting together out under a tree in the quiet fields. After years of suppression under the Khmer Rouge, he was now rediscovering the joy of his pastoral calling all over again, and his faithful heart was full of thanksgiving. Yes, this was indeed his great love, to be out and about with the gospel, praying for the sick, bringing deliverance to those tormented by evil spirits, witnessing unashamedly to all who would listen, leading the assembly of brothers and sisters in worship and praise. He reflected on his calling to pastoral ministry all those years ago, and how God had confirmed it and brought him back to it again and again. But the question remained. Could he endure as a pastor in this new post-revolutionary, post-missionary, brutalised Cambodia where all innocence was gone and men's hearts remained torpid and indifferent?

With the onset of the rains in May and June, he set about planting his garden with pumpkins, peanuts, beans, corn, potatoes and taro. And as he had done in those familiar fields since boyhood, he prepared three *rai*[5] of land for rice.

But by October 1979 the news that food supplies, medicines and humanitarian aid were freely available at the Thai border was spreading like wildfire. People were returning with carts loaded with sacks of rice, tools and supplementary food for their children. They spoke of clinics staffed by westerners, feeding stations for young mothers and children, and, of course, the attraction of colourful clothes and consumer goods available for a price on the black market. There was even the possibility of following thousands of other Cambodians who had been resettled in the West if you had the bribes to get into one of the inland refugee camps.

With village life returning to pre-Khmer Rouge normality, Pastor Hom was beginning to feel the old familiar icy blasts of anti-Christian resentment once more. The constant need to walk the forty kilometres to Battambang in search of medicines for the children who were frequently ill was a strain. As the months passed he became wearied and discouraged by the rapid increase in corruption and greed all around him. It all seemed to grow in direct proportion to the people's recovery of their health and strength. Nothing it seems had changed in their hearts as a result of *Angka*'s reign of terror. If anything, the people were even more selfish and godless than ever.

Hom was clearly a physically, emotionally and spiritually exhausted man. The demands on him as a pastor to a very troubled and sometimes wayward and divisive flock, and also as the father of a young family, were legion. With the mid-season rice crop ripening, he had to watch over it day and night. The rats which were so numerous had to be killed or driven off as they consumed the ripening grain. He managed to harvest only about half of what he had planted.

But something else was gnawing at him. He was restless, depressed. He could see no real hope for himself as a pastor in this evil place, or for his family. He watched the many people heading out daily for the Thai border. He listened to the reports of rice and medicines in areas free from the control of this pro-Vietnamese communist government. Here it was a struggle. There were so many dangers and uncertainties. There was a haunting fear that the Khmer Rouge might return. The border beckoned. It seemed to offer hope, a change, freedom, respite. So Pastor Hom took his remaining half sack of rice and traded it for gold. The going rate was one *hun*[6] of gold for fifteen condensed milk cans full of husked rice. The gold was needed to pay the 'fees' for the journey. Some were legitimate like the *ramot*[7] ride at one *hun* per person from Kok Kmum to Mongul Borey. Others were more questionable like the 'fees' to Vietnamese soldiers and other armed Cambodian 'security patrols' which constantly halted the groups of people struggling across country to the Thai border. Each stop cost three to five *huns* of gold, around seventy-five tins full of rice.

The closer the travellers came to the vast border settlements the more dangerous life became. The area was infested with bandits, cut-throats, so called 'couriers' who were mostly charlatans charging exorbitant prices to guide wealthy Cambodians safely into the Thai camps. At best they simply robbed the desperate travellers of their valuables, and then abandoned them in the bush to fend for themselves. At worst they raped and killed. Mines and booby traps were an ever present menace. Then there were the assorted resistance groups including the Khmer Rouge who usually killed the people, but sometimes brought them captive to their border strongholds as recruits or support personnel in their avowed struggle to drive the Vietnamese out of Cambodia.

Only the hardened and experienced Cambodian border-wise black marketeers knew how to avoid these obstacles. The border relief operation was in fact radically transforming daily life in north west Cambodia by attracting hundreds of thousands to it and away from their legitimate labour of rice production to become dependent refugees, black marketeers and immigrants. This upheaval in Cambodia's rice bowl province only deepened the food and security crises which in turn, like a vicious circle, created even more refugees, all hopelessly vulnerable, politically compromised and stranded. Much rice was taken back into Cambodia especially by those who were strong, had bullock carts, and the financial wherewithal to get to the border and transport the free rice back home. Not infrequently this was then sold for profit to the less fortunate inside.

Cutting north westwards across country, Pastor Hom's family and the other Christians spent the nights camping out in the fields beside the now well beaten trails leading the hordes of economic pilgrims to meccas with names like Nong Samet, Kok Soon and Mak Moon. The children shivered in the heavy night dew, and all were too fearful to sleep. Hom struggled along pushing an old bicycle from which hung all their worldly goods; a very holey mosquito net, some clattering tin plates, a bundle of clothes wrapped up in a *sarong*, some soiled blankets, a blackened rice pot, a water dipper, their diminishing rice supply; and seated on top, one at a time, a very unhappy and footsore child.

When, several days later, they struggled into the vast and sprawling outskirts of Non Samet, just inside Thai territory, it was under a hail of shells from Vietnamese batteries firing on the resistance groups who had established their bases right inside these lucrative camps. Such groups were also constantly feuding among themselves, mostly for control over the black market and

Young men being led away to execution. A painting by a survivor of the Tuol Sleng extermination camp on display in the genocide museum in Phnom Penh.

Don Cormack baptising near Phnom Penh, 1994.

Don and Margaret Cormack with their daughters Elizabeth, Margaret-Grace and Katherine, at Chefoo School, Cameron Highlands, Malaysia, 1993.

Sunday School nativity play, Phnom Penh, 1994.

Mass grave.

Skulls from the killing fields.

A young Christian with his cyclor outside a church in Phnom Penh, 1995.

New recruits for the Boys' Brigade, on parade 1995.

the patronage of the Thai army bosses. Their leaders were little more than corrupt war lords who, if they were not first murdered, set out for the 'West' just as soon as their pockets were suitably lined. Once there, maintaining their social status and military rank, they could organise 'the liberation of Cambodia', and continue to fleece the Cambodian *émigrés* supporting the 'liberation' groups.

Rice had to be obtained from the daily distribution points for which (for a fee of course to the local indigenous administration) it was necessary to register your name. Everything else, from dusty withered vegetables to great battery-driven stereo tape recorders, could be bought at outrageously inflated prices from the Thai and Cambodian black marketeers. The pastor was amazed at how quickly the people lusted after the trinkets of luxury and the status which came with them. He was also struck by how incredibly hard the foreign relief workers drove themselves to provide food and medical help to the refugees despite the heat, the filth and the quagmire of corruption and greed in which they struggled with such optimism and obvious concern.

After a week of moving around to find the safest and most advantageous spot, their little supply of gold was exhausted. Now they were forced to beg for rice, and even to send the children off to wheel and deal on the black market. There might have been at least some clean water supply at the camps, but what pools and streams existed were used for bathing, laundry and latrines. These fetid pools, drying and cracking in the hot sun, were full of parasites and disease. So even water had to be purchased. Fleets of tankers brought it in every day as the volatile situation permitted. Just one kerosene can full of water cost twenty Thai *baht*.[8] With no money, feverish and weak, Hom's family followed the hordes of desperate Cambodians now foraging in the trampled and very dangerous surrounding forest for edible leaves, roots and wild potatoes.

The situation was becoming critical. After a brief meeting to discuss and pray it through, a number of the Christians decided to call it quits and head back home. If indeed there was a home left to go back to. Discouraged, Pastor Hom went outside and stood by the flimsy, half-finished shelter he had been making for his family out of bamboo and grass. In his hands he had his old Bible. It was very battered and stained now and a few pages were missing. All through the Khmer Rouge years he had managed to hang on to it, hiding it under the thatch, in amongst heaps of bedding, or buried out in the bush. Now he thumbed through its familiar pages, and opened it to Psalm 91. Not far away shells were falling again on one of the camps. He paused and looked wearily in the direction of the bombardment. Was it the Vietnamese again, the Khmer Rouge, or perhaps the Thai army settling an internal dispute with one of the camp warlords? Certainly more tragic reports, some true, some exaggerated, of Cambodian families being blown out of their huts, bodies ripped open, forever maimed and scarred with hot jagged shrapnel, would soon be running rife. What was he to do? To focus his concentration, he read aloud the words: 'Because he loves me,' says the Lord, 'I will rescue him; I will protect him for he acknowledges my name. He will call upon me, and I will answer him; I will be with him in trouble, I will be with him and honour him…' Yes, he would not turn back now. He would stay and await the Lord's deliverance.

It was the ceaseless search for a water supply which brought him wandering one day into a corner of this vast shanty city where I happened to be working. He chanced to hear some people gossiping about a foreign Christian teacher nearby. Surrounded by other Christians who were walking with him, he hurried over. I was just leaving one of the hot and crowded little huts where I had been teaching, and was walking away surrounded by families seeing me off, and the usual throng of curious onlookers and excited children all eager to help carry any bags or books. As we rounded a clump of bamboo atop a dusty knoll at the head of a muddy water hole, we heard them calling out behind us and excitedly waving their arms. I shall never forget turning round in my tracks and seeing the little procession hurrying towards us in single file along the narrow path on the steep bank surrounding the pool. One face, definitely older, haggard and sunburned, shone out above the others. Full of character, it glowed with an unmistakable light and warmth. I said to myself, 'This can only be the beloved Pastor Hom of Battambang.'

In no time at all, we were surrounded by Christians from across the camp including those who had come with him. After all the embracing and tears, we sat down in the shade of the tall bamboo and Pastor Hom with broad smiles began introducing me to the Christians from Battambang. Sitting on the ground nearby, her grey head covered with her *krama*, was Granny Rin, his old mother, traumatised, overcome with emotion, very frail, and almost blind. She had been uprooted from the village where she had lived all her life. In this chaotic place she didn't belong.

The Christians had so much to tell, but they were also eager for news from the outside, especially of missionary friends they had known and loved for years. Then as they sat trembling in absolute silence, I brought them up to date with all the news I could remember. I told Chamrouen and her children all about Chhorn – her husband, their father – whom they hadn't seen for five years and were certain had been killed as a former soldier. I told of his escape, his coming to Aranya Prathet refugee camp in 1977, the mature Christian leadership and powerful witness he gave to the church there, and how a year later he had been resettled, and was now living safely in France. And then it was So Put's turn to hear that his headstrong son Samuel had also escaped later in 1977, I had baptised him, and now he was alive and well in the USA. And so it went on. They were so hungry for news from the outside.

Samuel's mother quietly dabbed her eyes with the corner of her *sarong* as she heard how her importunate prayers for Samuel had been so wonderfully answered when he had seen her in his dream in the forest, imploring him to turn back to Jesus his Lord. I promised to dispatch urgent telegrams to them as soon as I could.

There was no shortage of helpers as we hauled supplies of desperately needed sleeping mats, plastic sheeting, blankets, mosquito nets, high protein food, and medicines from my red Toyota pickup to the growing assembly of saints and their new found 'friends'.

All agreed to let Pastor Hom be responsible for the distribution of these things to those whose need was most urgent. I wished the many friends 'back home' who were praying or who had sent us specially designated funds for refugee relief could have seen the happiness and thankfulness on the faces of these people that afternoon. But the best was yet to come.

All the Christians with their families and friends around them seated themselves on the ground beside the tall bamboo. They wasted no time in discarding their black Khmer Rouge garments, and soon looked again like typical Cambodian country folk, only much thinner.

Facing them, sitting cross-legged behind a cardboard box full of Cambodian Bibles and hymnbooks, was Pastor Hom. These precious books he began to distribute among his people, most of whom had lost all their Christian literature. It was now time to worship and thank God for all these blessings. Using the cardboard box as his lectern upon which he had placed his own tattered old Bible, he began exhorting his listeners, taking the opportunity clearly and simply to explain the facts of the gospel to all the curious onlookers.

I was walking back to the truck for more literature when the singing began. It was so unusual to hear a chorus of voices singing together in unison in such a place as this that I stopped to watch.

The golden colours of evening washed the sky, and the camp was relatively still. As the growing awareness dawned upon them that, yes, they could sing here without fear of death, their voices grew in volume and ardour. Before long I was unable to see the Christians for the vast crowd which was gathering around them to behold the amazing spectacle. Hearing only the sound of their voices from within the midst of the crowd, I began to concentrate on the words they were now singing with a quality of rapture and conviction I had never heard before, or indeed since. It was an old much-loved hymn translated from the English. The last time I heard it sung was in 1975 at Noah's church on the waterfront of besieged Phnom Penh. That was just before they entered the fiery crucible. And now here among the exiles it sounded again:

The love of God,
How rich and pure
How measureless and strong;
It shall for evermore endure
The saints' and angels' song.

And the Lord whispered to me in that moment: 'They came forth from the furnace with no smell of the burning upon them.' No trace of bitterness, no anger, no 'why this?' or 'why that?' But there they were kneeling in the dust, ragged and hungry, all had lost at least one family member to the Khmer Rouge, extolling the love of God. They were rich with the fragrance of the knowledge of him. A fragrance acquired no doubt from walking close to the Son of God through the flames. And I was convinced that they would have extolled the strong love of God as indeed others had, even to the grave, for with suffering Job they could repeat, 'Though he slay me, yet will I hope in him.' Little wonder the crowds were drawn irresistibly to them that day. They were being attracted not to religion, not to a band of defiant survivors, but to the aroma of Christ, lingering naturally about these very plain earthen vessels there in the shade of the bamboo along that war ravaged border.

Pastor Hom had come to this area of the camp that day because he had heard that it was a good place for digging wells. Yet there within them was the wellspring of pure thirst-quenching water which many others in the camp were searching for. The scent of it, as it welled up from within these Christians, and as it became later a spring in the waterless depths of the Khao I Dang Holding Centre of over 120,000 refugees, would produce a great and spreading tree. A new tree but growing out of an old stump, whose branches would reach into all the world.

Again he said, 'What shall we say the kingdom of God is like, or what parable shall we use to describe it? It is like a mustard seed, which is the smallest seed you plant in the ground. Yet when planted, it grows and becomes the largest of all garden plants, with such big branches that the birds of the air can perch in its shade.' (Mark 4:30-32)

CHAPTER 12

THE SEED PRODUCES MANY SEEDS

'Still other seed fell on good soil. It came up, grew and produced
a crop, multiplying thirty, sixty, or even a hundred times.'

(Mark 4: 8)

In the weeks leading up to the final collapse of Phnom Penh on
April 17, 1975, thousands of Cambodians could see that the writing
was clearly on the wall for Lon Nol's Khmer Republic, and moved
their families and goods westwards towards the Thai border. Most
were crowding into the notorious gem mining border town of
Pailin opposite south east Thailand's Chantaburi province, and to
Poipet, a dusty and rather seedy little town right up against the
Thai border, facing the Thai market town of Aranyaprathet, five
kilometres inland. A narrow meandering stream called Klong
Luek, with steep banks covered in dense vegetation, clearly defines
the border here. Over it ran a railway bridge and a road bridge
where most overland trade between the two countries passed.

In other places the border is not so clearly marked, and forest
trails link the few small and scattered hamlets on either side of this
almost entirely forested border region from north to south. Along
Cambodia's northern border with Thailand runs a chain of rugged,
uninhabited jungled highlands known as the Dangrek mountains.
To the south the precipitous and densely-forested Cardamom
mountain range forms a natural though ill-defined demarcation.
These areas were the domain of charcoal burners, hunters, teak

wood smugglers, fugitives, subsistence rice farmers and market gardeners. In the deadly drug resistant malaria-infested region of Pailin, only the toughest risked life and limb mining for sapphires and rubies. The four hundred and fifty miles of border were largely inhospitable, infertile and remote; the haunt of wild boar, shy mouse deer, wild dogs, monkeys, poisonous snakes, and even the occasional tiger.

But within five tumultuous years, from 1975 to 1980, this largely forgotten and undisturbed no man's land became the focus of world attention, a vast arena where countless thousands of Cambodians wrestled in a life-death struggle. With the triumph of the Khmer Rouge, these virgin forests were seeded with the paraphernalia of death. Minefields, booby traps of concealed holes with sharpened bamboo spikes at the bottom ready to impale any would-be refugee, trip wires attached to grenades, lethal arrows, or heavy logs intended to crush the victim, all marred this wild and pristine country.

The bustling and free-wheeling border towns of Poipet and Pailin, untouched by the war, became deserted echo chambers, ransacked and left to decay, as the people were herded away to labour camps inland, inhabited only by their ghosts and the shadowy figures of black-clothed Khmer Rouge soldiers quartered there. These roving killer squads patrolled the entire border, menacing and killing anyone caught heading towards Thailand. The green forest glades became boneyards, stinking from piles of rotting human flesh, and the leafy trails littered with the bones of the thousands who tried desperately but in vain to get out.

On the Thai side, villagers were killed by day on exploding mines as they went about their work in the fields, and by night as raiding Khmer Rouge gangs descended on them, rustling cattle, kidnapping, burning and, always as gruesomely as possible, murdering. This led to more border patrol and Thai army posts. Several refugee camps were established, financed by the UNHCR and under the control of the Thai Ministry of the Interior to house the few thousand Cambodians who did make it out between 1975 and the end of 1978 when the Khmer Rouge themselves began fleeing here.

But the border really came alive in 1979-1980 when hundreds of thousands of refugees, many under Khmer Rouge control and at the point of death, poured into the area. At the same time the 'landbridge' organised by international relief agencies to send rice over into famine stricken Cambodia serviced long convoys of hundreds of bullock carts and bicycles which came in search of aid. A number of enclaves were formed for the squabbling Thai-backed anti-Vietnamese guerrilla factions, including the notorious Khmer Rouge. These ensured that war was also sent back into Cambodia along with the rice. Thailand by then had vast numbers of troops and equipment pressed up against this eastern border, as also did the scores of relief agencies, flush with funds, which poured in from all over the world. All this transformed the sleepy town of Aranyaprathet almost overnight into a kind of wild-west gold rush town, bursting with all manner of goods and people: aggressive, florid-faced foreigners, sporting the latest border chic, and their insatiable appetite for a 'good time', the *nouveau riche* blackmarketeers, Thai soldiers, prostitutes and other parasites, journalists, and assorted experts and observers of all stripes.

Rents soared as the mostly Chinese landlords cashed in on the bonanza. Some relief agencies even competed with each other for choice properties. Our stifling little two-room shop house went up from US$15 per month to US$150 per month overnight and, along with one or two other expatriates who had been resident there for some years, we were soon as good as out on the street.

From the upstairs window of our next home with a brothel on one side and a den of smugglers on the other, we could watch Thai men living opposite, cleaning their pistols for another day. Break-ins were commonplace, armed men appeared at windows, and by night scuttled over the roof. Relationships carefully nurtured with local officials, market people and neighbours soured rapidly as the townsfolk saw in a white face merely an easy going, dollar laden 'do gooder', ripe for picking. Without the help of the local Thai Christian community who sought to keep their integrity, and the mutual support of fellow Christian workers, life in the new glitzy Aranyaprathet would have been very difficult.

The quiet border roads along which groups of buffalo once

lazily ambled, chickens scratched, and villagers pedalled their bicycles with no need of any highway sense, now became daredevil race tracks roaring with the ceaseless rush of noisy motorcycles, speeding army vehicles, racing pickups, overloaded and rickety buses, great red water tankers, and convoys of smoke-belching heavy trucks loaded with rice; all leaning on their deafening air horns as they hurtled back and forth, relying only on their Buddhist amulets for safety. By night, highwaymen lay in wait for unwary stragglers. There were some horrendous pile-ups and many deaths. Cremations were a regular attraction out in the field next to the local Buddhist temple.

In the week prior to the fateful April 17, 1975, a number of Cambodians ready at the border jumped the gun. The Thai simply sent them back across. But when at 8 am on the notorious 17th, the people in north west Cambodia heard over their radios that Phnom Penh had surrendered, over they poured *en masse* into Thailand. Many were well-to-do businessmen, military and government officials, who had planned this for months. Others were villagers familiar with the forest trails. Then as the Lon Nol troops in Battambang surrendered and the Khmer Rouge bore down on Pailin, a long convoy of military vehicles and private cars drove into Thailand.

Among these first refugees was Pastor Kong who had been planting a church in Pailin. He had with him twenty Christians. This group very soon began witnessing in the Chantaburi refugee camp, and it wasn't long before many baptisms were taking place and a Christian ministry was expanding throughout the camp, with meetings every evening. This group enjoyed the help of some hardworking Southern Baptist people, church planting among the Thai in that south-eastern province. Pastor Mok of the Chinese Church in Battambang also fled to Thailand in those first days.

As in Phnom Penh two days earlier, the Khmer Rouge were welcomed with great fanfare by the local residents of Poipet on April 19, 1975. 'Peace has returned to Cambodia,' the citizens called out joyfully. The Lon Nol soldiers dutifully surrendered their weapons. The new Khmer Rouge authorities slashed food prices in the market and everyone was very happy indeed. A number of Cambodians who had recently fled to the Thai side even crossed back over, concluding that their fears were unfounded. The fact that a few thieves were summarily executed, and one or two very wealthy businessmen were liberated of their possessions did not unduly spoil the party. But the Khmer Rouge (reminiscent of *tuansay*, the crafty little rabbit of popular Cambodian folklore, who gambolled about the countryside duping the gullible peasantry), brilliant in deception and pantomime, having won the trust of the townsfolk, disarmed potential opposition and secured the border. Then they brought the week-long honeymoon to a very abrupt end.

Following *Angka*'s masterplan now being imposed all across the nation, they turned their guns and bullhorns on the people, emptying Poipet and all the other border communities of their citizens forthwith, driving them towards the new labour camps, the human abattoirs in the interior. An eerie silence fell over the border towns, and along litter-strewn roads, wild dogs gnawed and gorged themselves on human flesh. Subsequent visits to the ramshackle bridge from which the busy border town of Poipet could once be seen, revealed only an eerie silence. No one lived there any more, save a handful of elusive Khmer Rouge soldiers with guns. Poipet was a silent ghost town. Not even the sound of a barking dog or a crowing rooster broke the uncanny stillness. But in the mind's eye it was just possible to imagine, beyond the empty town, out in sunbaked fields, the groping brutalised remnants of its people.

It was on this bridge that I had my first sight of the Khmer Rouge. On Saturday April 19, 1975, the day the people of Poipet first met them, I was standing on the Thai side of the coils of rusting barbed wire strung across the Klong Luek bridge. On the other side of the wire a number of Khmer Rouge, dripping with AK 47 assault rifles, grenade launchers, pistols and rockets, engaged with us in 'a frank exchange of views'. Crowded behind the Khmer Rouge, staring back over at us, with an expression so strangely wistful and pensive that I am unable to forget it or describe it, stood the Poipet citizenry. As yet they were blissfully unaware of the magnitude of the misery which awaited them. But it seemed to me that they sensed they were looking across at freedom for the last time.

The first Cambodian refugees were to be found in groups of hundreds encamped in the forests near streams and pools, sheltering under branches and the blankets they had brought with them. Fortunately, the rains had not yet begun. Eventually they were rounded up by the Thai army and contained in small camps, or in the environs of isolated Buddhist temples.

From the very beginning, Christian missionaries were in the vanguard of those providing food, clothing and shelter. But we were also to provide far more. Speaking both Cambodian and Thai, we could also offer friendship, comfort, counsel and spiritual succour. From single copies of Cambodian Christian books and tracts snatched from Phnom Penh as we fled, large quantities of Christian literature were printed in Bangkok for distribution. There was also in Thailand a good stock of Gideon Cambodian New Testaments which the Gideons kindly allowed us to distribute.

The more prestigious of those first refugees, such as ranking military and government families, were soon on their way to transit centres for resettlement in the USA. The best known were on Guam Island, and Camp Pendleton in California where another former OMF Cambodia hand Rose-Ellen Chancey had a very extensive and fruitful ministry among these disorientated and searching exiles. She was able to link many of them up with caring American families and churches.

By 1976, the UNHCR was financing several Cambodian refugee camps in Thailand. They numbered about five and were spread around the border between Surin in the north and Trat in the south. These were guarded by the Thai who on the whole were very relaxed and helpful. Life in these camps was good, considering what they had just left behind them. Basic needs were met by the UNHCR, the Thai Red Cross, and supplemented by an array of local and expatriate workers concerned to improve quality of life, especially for the children. Up until late 1978, the numbers flooding in were manageable and non-threatening to Thailand's security, tolerance and limited resources. This steady influx of

Cambodian refugees, after the initial rush in mid-1975, had a persistently horrifying tale to tell.

Only a small minority of all these who sought to run the gauntlet made it alive to Thailand. Regular visits to local border police station lock-ups usually uncovered a huddle of stunned and bedraggled new arrivals crouching nervously in a corner. Questioning would reveal that these were but the tattered remnants of scores of daring Cambodians, mostly young men, who had set their faces towards Thailand and liberty. The rural folk were aware of the dangers and odds against them. But they preferred to die escaping, than to be led off like dogs on the end of a rope into the forest to be knocked over the head by some teenage Khmer Rouge killer. Others, city folk, students, professionals, unaware that the beckoning western forests, silent and green, bristled with punji sticks and minefields, ran headlong into the bayonets of the ever vigilant Khmer Rouge patrols, or tripped easily into the beckoning booby-trapped forest trails. Many simply lost their way in the trackless jungle, died of thirst, snake bites, or fell exhausted from malaria and dysentery.

The spectacle of these arrivals, especially as the months of privation wore into years, was atrocious. That fellow human beings should be wilfully reduced to such a pitiful, grovelling physical and emotional state by other men and women especially of their own race and religion was beyond comprehension. Here was a genocide perhaps even more culpable than that perpetrated by the Nazis against the Jews.

The worst cases sat sullen and emotionless, the filthy black designer rags of *Angka* hanging loosely from their wasted frames. Their eyes were watery and unseeing, sunk back into hollow sockets in gaunt yellowed faces. Psychologically they were tormented still by fear, by the fate of those they had left behind, the nightmare of the Khmer Rouge regime, the recent nerve-wracking flight, and their present uncertainty in the hands of the Thai. Some were struggling with guilt having abandoned wives and children. 'Am I dead or alive?' whispered one through the bars, recovering from severe malaria fever. Occasionally rope burns on the upper arms indicated a frantic escape from the death sentence. One or two, victims of a mass execution, were only stunned by the crack on the back of the head with a hoe by some flagging young servant of the revolution. These revived to find themselves lying amidst a heap of bodies and the buzz of flies. Under cover of darkness they dragged themselves away in the forest. One, the lone survivor of sixty men, was pulled from the bushes on the Thai side having had his throat slit open by the rusty knife of a Khmer Rouge. He recovered from the resulting tetanus, but was left severely brain damaged having lost so much blood.

Their bare feet were caked in dirt, calloused and lacerated by the thorny bamboo. Gunshot wounds had to be treated, cuts sutured, thorns removed, and lice and parasites treated. Nearly all of them shivered and sweated intermittently from bouts of malaria, a disease now pandemic in Cambodia. From time to time an apparently well person would create a big fuss over some minor thing like a small cut, a mouth ulcer, or a broken nail. This puzzled me till I realised that behind this little wound a far more serious wound was festering, unseen and uncared for. These were the hardest of all to heal.

How vastly different was the testimony of the Cambodian revolution here on the border from the lofty rhetoric of *Angka*'s leaders being politely applauded in international forums around the world, or the endless litany of praise for the revolution which daily spewed forth from Radio Phnom Penh: 'Smiling happy people laughing and joking together', 'a festive atmosphere constantly prevailing', 'the people's utter delight with the collectives', 'enough food for everyone', 'health and sanitation measures have expanded rapidly'.

But what an immeasurable joy it was indeed to watch these exiles, over succeeding weeks and months, gradually come back to life. *Angka*'s stinking black weeds of mourning were consigned to the flames, months of ground-in filth were scrubbed away, and on went clean fresh and colourful clothes. I still possess the dog-eared notebook which I used to take with me to the Aranya Prathet prison. In it along with lists of names, places, dates, sundry needs and reminders, are the waist and leg measurements of men eagerly anticipating their first new pair of trousers in a long time. The excitement and banter which accompanied those 'fitting' sessions in dismal and crowded cells also helped break their sadness and introspection. It wasn't long before teasing, chuckling and clowning brightened the gloomy surroundings. Sometimes even the Thai guards joined in the fun. But nothing lifted their spirits more than good food, especially the treats they had been denied for so long. After subsisting on grubs, leaves, roots and tree bark how they rejoiced at the sight of eggs, fruits, bread, tins of condensed milk, sugar and sweet cakes. For the former urbanites, downing that first ice-cold Pepsi was sheer bliss.

But there were many serious moments too, and tears, as their woeful tales poured forth, often late into the night. When each man spoke, the others listened in respectful silence. They talked for so long some nights that I found myself unable to get out as the night guard with the keys had fallen asleep outside! Despite the bars these days were very precious and memorable. Fresh from Cambodia but not yet released into the world of the border refugee camps, here in the prisons, minds were focused, hearts sensitive, and words perceptive. And deep bonds were woven between us.

The Thai guards for the most part were wonderfully indulgent once you had established a good rapport, if somewhat bemused by all the care being lavished on such lowly scraps of humanity as these. 'You are accumulating so much merit that in your next life, you will at least be a prince,' was the verdict of one Buddhist police chief when he was finally convinced that I wasn't there 'for money or women'. Sadly, after 1979 and the onslaught of hundreds of thousands of refugees, and when literally hundreds more highly visible foreign experts poured into the area, these friendships with Thai officials forged over the months and years were lost, drowned in the rising tide of greed and anger. While the Thai were solidly Buddhist, they had a definite respect and sensitivity towards all seriously 'religious' people, and spiritual things. This was hardly the case among many of the secular westerners who treated Christian missionaries with utter contempt; and Buddhism with a kind of disingenuous patronage which their desultory lifestyles exposed as superficial and dilettante.

In some cases, the new arrivals were detained in prisons for months before being cleared for release into a refugee camp. Those who were seriously ill or injured also spent long periods of time in hospitals. Lonely, and with no friends or relatives to sit by and look after them as is the custom in this part of the world, daily visits to care for their practical needs forged strong and enduring relationships. Frequently, during times of crisis, we stayed with them through the night.

As the missionaries ministered to their physical and emotional needs, which were legion, they were able to speak naturally to them in their own language of a loving Creator and Father God. During the long stays in prisons and hospitals, Cambodians frequently read thoughtfully through the Scriptures. This was especially true of the educated ones, who longed for something stimulating to read after being starved of it for so long. (Most older Cambodians are literate due to extensive education programmes instituted in Prince Sihanouk's time. But many since had their formative years disrupted by two decades of war and chaos.)

Frequently, it transpired that they had seen or spoken to Christians in Cambodia. Few were totally ignorant of the Christian gospel, revealing how faithful and zealous the Cambodian church had been in making Christ known, especially from 1970-1975. For some it was the culmination of a long spiritual pilgrimage, and they were anxious to submit their lives to Jesus Christ as Saviour and Lord.

Soman (meaning: 'please read') was one of a group of twenty-three young men packed into an iron cage on a rough concrete floor at the old Aranyaprathet police station (now demolished). Over sixty had originally set off on the escape. During the long and exhausting trek through the dense forest towards Thailand, they became so desperate that they were driven to eat leaves and drink one another's urine. When all hope seemed lost, Soman cried out to the living God for food and water. Shortly afterwards they found themselves walking through a grove of beautiful fruit trees. He and his companions feasted on the delicious fruit, rested, and then much strengthened pressed on and crossed safely into Thailand.

Late one night, after all the others – lying pressed together like tinned sardines – and the prison guards, had dropped off to sleep, Soman and I sat in a tight corner reading John's gospel together in whispered tones by the pale flickering light of a home-made oil lamp. Quite suddenly, as if a beam of pure light had penetrated his heart, he called out: 'This is the truth – a most wonderful truth.' He knelt forward, leaning on his elbows, and supporting his head between his hands began poring intently over the passage lying open on the floor before him. He was still in this position when I slipped unnoticed out of the prison a little later. During the three months that he was locked in this cage, he studied John's gospel many times over, as well as *Pilgrim's Progress* and a number of Bible study courses. He always greeted me with a host of questions from his well-thumbed booklets. Like others in the prison, his body soon became covered in scabies, caught from the germ-laden floor which was never disinfected. But this did not hinder his constant meditations on the Word of God.

Then a group of new refugees from his former commune brought the terrible news that the wives and children of those who had fled earlier had been taken away and clubbed to death. They couldn't be sure if Soman's family was among them so he was left with the torment of nagging uncertainty. But Soman did not move from his new found sanctuary in Christ, or waver in his faith in God, though he wept and prayed at great length. And despite all Soman's efforts and all that they had seen and heard, none of his fellow prisoners believed as he had. He was the only one who turned and acknowledged that God had been their Saviour.

The seed of faith which was now bearing fruit had been sown in Soman's heart many years earlier. As a schoolboy he had been handed a gospel of Matthew at the school gate one afternoon while on his way home. He read it and valued it, keeping it in a high place of honour on a top shelf. And although he never met a Christian again in his village in far off Kratie province, until our encounter in the prison at Aranyaprathet, he treasured in his heart a desire to know more of this Jesus of Nazareth. The booklet was destroyed later when the Khmer Rouge burned down the family home. But silently a little seed of faith was germinating beneath the surface. His father who had also regularly taken the gospel booklet down and read it thoughtfully and aloud to himself, died calling on the 'God of the book of Matthew.'

Later, on being released into the camp, Soman organised a number of cell groups for Bible study and discussion. He also built for himself a little study loft on a bamboo platform up in the roof of the crowded refugee longhouse. When he needed to be alone to think and pray, to grieve over his suffering motherland and his lost wife and two small sons, he climbed up the wooden ladder and pulled it up behind him. It was also Soman who began to play a delightful two-stringed Cambodian violin to accompany the worship times. With the help of Salieng, one of his escape group, for they were all now very closely bonded, Soman made a beautifully painted sign and nailed it high on the front of the building which the Christians were using as a church for all the camp to read:

> If my people,
> who are called by my name,
> will humble themselves and pray
> and seek my face,
> and turn from their wicked ways,
> Then I will hear from heaven
> and forgive their sin
> and will heal their land (2 Chronicles 7:14)

Other seeds of faith which had been sown earlier were bearing fruit too. A teenage boy, Vichet, the only one of his large family to believe, had first received a tract in the Phnom Penh market. A young girl, Somaly, had always secretly admired the dogged yet gentle determination of an evangelist from Battambang whom she noticed regularly visiting the outlying villages. On another occasion, as I was reading John's Gospel aloud to a group of prisoners, a young man interrupted to say how he had heard these same words before over a hidden radio which he used secretly to tune into, even at the risk of losing his life if discovered by the Khmer Rouge. Some refugees had seen the living testimony of little hidden groups of Christians under the Khmer Rouge, like the one at Phum Kor led by Auntie Song and Sarun, though they were too fearful to join. They could see that these people, without temples or idols or priests, could still worship and serve their God. But especially they could talk with him in any place and circumstance. Not a few knew of the power of the Name of Jesus on the lips of his people over the various evil spirits which tormented many villagers.

Though frequently ridiculed and despised, there was no denying that Christians had a reputation for being generally more moral and honest, people of integrity. And wherever there was a humanitarian need, invariably there were Christians, Cambodian or foreign, on the spot with medicines and food. It appeared too that much of their suffering, and a good deal of the corruption and exploitation they were seeing around them, was the work of those claiming to be Buddhists. These things provided the discerning refugee with much food for thought.

Most exciting of all were the accounts of those who had experienced divine intervention as they cried out to God for help during the hazardous flight to freedom. One family who had been wandering lost in the forest, spoke of a guiding light which appeared ahead of them and led them safely to the Thai border. Another, desperately hungry, but unsure whether certain berries were poisonous or not, was suddenly surprised by a monkey which dropped down from a branch and began happily eating the fruit, thus assuring them that it was safe. Some groups, like Pol Chhorn, actually found themselves led to food and water in the heart of the forest. There were also accounts of healings, restored energy, helpful dreams and visions, even 'Khmer Rouge' who tipped them off, or secretly guided them to safety. When questioned about whom they had prayed to, they could not recall a name. No it wasn't to the Buddha, for he was a wise teacher but dead for 2,500 years now. And anyway, he never claimed to be God or Saviour. The object of their prayers was a personal and living presence who they were convinced transcended all created life, and yet was present right there in the forest with them, both watching and hearing. For a number of those who experienced such things, the biblical accounts were a confirmation, as well as further illumination into unseen truths and divine mysteries. But, even more than these tangible benefits, it was the comforting fact of unconditional forgiveness of sin, of peace with God, and the removal of the sting of death, which attracted a considerable number of these homeless refugees to a reconciliation with their heavenly Father.

It was encouraging when people like Dara and Lian escaped in 1977 with news of an underground church in Cambodia. Dara had fellowshipped with Auntie Song's people at Phum Kor, and Lian had exchanged a smile of recognition with Pastor Hom when they passed in the fields. And a few Christians like young Samuel and Chhorn had escaped to the camp at Aranyaprathet with moving accounts of divine protection.

From Surin Camp on Cambodia's northern border with Thailand, where John Ellison (son of David Ellison, the pioneer missionary to Cambodia) and his wife were working with the Christian and Missionary Alliance, came more thrilling news of Christians miraculously saved from death, and of others who realised on hearing the gospel that it was the Lord God who had heard their cries and delivered them. Here is one of these accounts:

'Jang Beung had been a soldier in Cambodia for four years. When Phnom Penh fell, he and his family were living in Samrong, fifty miles from the Thai border. Surrendering his arms, he felt in no immediate danger since he had not been a high officer. Then a cattle herder told of the fate of a group of soldiers who had been cruelly deceived into believing that they were being taken to the famous ruins of Angkor Wat for a special merit-making Buddhist festival. They were driven just a few miles into the country and then ordered out to dig their own graves before being brutally struck down with hoes. The man himself had been a witness.

'Upon hearing this report, Jang Beung and others were so alarmed that they made immediate preparations to escape. More than fifty left that night. After walking through the forest for a day, half of the group was suddenly attacked by Khmer Rouge soldiers. The only fatality was a small baby whose head struck a stump when he stumbled and fell. In the confusion the whole group scattered and Jang Beung and his wife could locate only two of their children. The older son was missing. Their food was gone, but they continued on their journey for another day.

'By nightfall the wife, Cheun Teng, came down with a violent fever and such dizziness that she could not walk further. They knew Thailand was not too far away, so the father decided to take the two children to safety and food and then return for his wife. He left the hammock and a small bundle of clothing for her. Cheun Teng slept fitfully that first night in the forest by herself and awoke very thirsty. She managed to find water nearby, but after quenching her thirst she could not find her way back to her hammock. For the next eight days her only bed was the ground. She had no food, but somehow she received strength to travel a short distance each day. She told us. 'I had no fear as I walked along because I felt the presence of several people walking just ahead of me, leading the way.'

'After four days of walking, her feet were so badly swollen that she could hardly hobble. One night, when her strength was exhausted, she dreamed that someone gave her lemon juice to drink. When she woke up she found she had strength to go on. After eight days of this painful travel, Cheun Teng came to a small shelter in a potato patch and stopped to rest. By this time she was so emaciated from hunger and her legs were so swollen and lacerated by thorns that she literally could not go a step further. Four days later the owner of the shelter and his wife came to work in their garden and found her lying there – more dead than alive. They carried her to their home and cared for her. She was very relieved to learn from them that she was now in Thailand and only five miles away from the camp where her husband and children had gone.

'After seven days of care she was able to resume her journey in the luxury of an oxcart and was met halfway by a tearfully joyful husband who had just that day been informed of her safety by the village chief. He told her how he had trekked back into Cambodia to get her but had lost all hope when he found only their few possessions. He assumed that the Khmer Rouge had carried her off.

'There was amazement and rejoicing in the camp that day when her story was told. All agreed that in her weakened, starved condition and with no guide to show her the way, the journey would have been humanly impossible. They recognised that only the Lord and his guiding angels had brought her out safely. What a reunion she had with all three of her children! The older son had come to the camp earlier with another group.

'Ten days later both Jang Beung and Cheun Teng accepted the Lord into their hearts and are rejoicing now over their new-found faith as well as their miraculous deliverance.'

By Jean and John Ellison in *Alliance Witness*

By 1977, two years into the terror, sizeable camps of Cambodian refugees were well established around the Thai/Cambodian border. Prasert Camp in Surin province was a sprawling complex of corrugated iron longhouses and neatly thatched huts holding about 5,000 refugees including a few hundred Khmer Rouge defectors held separately. Three hundred kilometres due east of Bangkok was Aranyaprathet where a camp was built consisting of twenty large wooden buildings each housing thirty 'families', and a mass of thatched shelters on stilts sprawling over the entire back half of the camp. This was the largest, holding 7,000 at that time. Other camps were opened along the border in Chantaburi and Trat provinces to the south for several thousand more. In the rainy season they were a quagmire of yellow mud and floodwater, and in the dry season became fetid dustbowls swarming with flies. Cambodian refugees continued to trickle into these camps at an average rate of about fifty a week.

Thailand also had at this time tens of thousands of Lao and Hmong refugees in camps along their far north eastern border with Laos. And along the south coast more camps were filling up with Vietnamese boat people.

From the time Indo-China fell to the communists in 1975, missionaries were actively helping all Indo-Chinese refugees fleeing to Thailand. Most of them had worked in either Vietnam, Laos or Cambodia before, and had knowledge of the language and culture, as well as a relationship with the national church. Now redeployed in Thailand, each refugee camp was covered, at least on a part-time basis. In Chantaburi and Surin, missionaries to the Thai already working in the areas where camps were established, simply extended their ministry. Regular meetings were held in Bangkok to co-ordinate the outreach in the camps. These were very helpful and strategic times when workers from various missions came together to share, discuss papers, brainstorm, plan, allocate responsibility for things like literature production, relief supplies and discipleship training, as well as to worship and pray together in a common calling to proclaim the gospel among the refugees.

In each of the Cambodian camps churches were taking root. Nothing very high-profile at first; in Aranyaprathet for example, just a handful of refugees sitting cross-legged in a circle on a wooden platform, heads bowed around a piece of bread and a cup of red 'Fanta', celebrating the Lord's Supper. These small cells would grow into sizeable gatherings crowded into some available shelter, their Bibles open on the floor in front of them, straining to hear the teaching above all the raucous noises of a hot and crowded camp.

Week by week more friends and neighbours, or newcomers, joined the Sunday morning worship times. They sang their Cambodian hymns to the accompaniment of a guitar, a traditional violin, or perhaps just a small hand-held gong chiming out the tempo. It wasn't always easy for the leaders to instil a sense of reverence in the church meetings as newcomers chattered, laughed and behaved casually as they were accustomed to doing on Buddhist feast days at the temples where it is not necessary to seriously engage one's mind or really participate in the worship and instruction. The desired 'merit' is gained simply by virtue of being present, they believe.

At the Aranyaprathet camp gathering, before a special meeting or festival, the Christians would carry the stone water jar which stood at the foot of the steps leading up into the meeting place, and stand it in the midst of the seated worshippers. Rather than the people pouring water over their own dusty feet as they entered, each Christian now poured a dipper of water over the feet of the one next to him or her and on others as they entered, washing them as Jesus had done to his disciples. Given the cultural distaste for feet as a lowly and rude part of the body to be kept out of the way, and certainly never allowed to touch another person, this act of humility was a very powerful symbol reflecting the way of Christ.

Special prayers and anointings were regularly conducted for the sick. Those with artistic gifts painted dramatic murals depicting biblical stories, employing their own beautiful Cambodian spiritual motifs and styles, to cover the bare plywood walls. At Aranya Prathet it became a tradition to enjoy a 'love-feast' of fruits on festival days. Long denied those bounties, the Cambodians could scarcely contain their joy at the sight of the boxes of durian, mangoes, oranges, grapes, mangosteens, rambutans and pineapples we would bring in from the town market. The Cambodians for their part would have already decorated the whole meeting place with leafy foliage, palm fronds, and flowers. In all the camps the Christian communities were sources of joy, hope and comfort. They stood apart as happy caring people, bright lights in the surrounding gloom.

Reminiscent of Phnom Penh days, bright and energetic young men led these church groups, visited, distributed literature, conducted Bible courses, and liaised with missionaries who came in regularly from nearby towns to disciple them. The missionary's role was largely teaching the leadership, preparing new believers for baptism, bringing in literature and Christian cassette tapes, praying with the sick, helping conduct funerals, weddings, and baby dedications, answering the numerous questions, liaising with camp authorities and generally trying to help resolve the many moral and social problems which were endemic in these crowded, emotion-charged places.

These churches among the exiles were an integral part of the camps. The believers shared the same horrendous background and present uncertainties and tensions as everyone else in the camps. They were therefore not immune from the many physical dangers and moral pitfalls of life in such places. A major problem was the fact of so many young men looking for wives. A young woman whose family had sponsorship papers fetched a particularly high bride price. Such marriages of convenience rarely survived for long the exigencies of life in the west. Some men made hasty and bad choices. Tensions and jealousies erupted. The incessant idle gossip sapped spiritual strength. The boredom and claustrophobia of camp life was a severe test of moral integrity. A number who started well, later found being yoked to Christ a great hindrance and fell away. When the chips were down, being an authentic Cambodian Christian was still a very costly commitment.

But some very remarkable Cambodian Christian leaders were raised up in these early camps. A number of them continued to initiate new outreach and carry forward Christian ministry among their people even after the unsettling move to a 'third country'. They came from all walks of life, and all classes of Cambodian society. There was Chhorn Da Yut, an ex-boxer and Saroeun an ex-resistance fighter, his legs still full of shrapnel from an exploding land mine. Tiem had been a truck driver, and Nareth an army officer. Sun Tek had fled Cambodia with his pregnant wife Kim Hoeung. On the way, right there in the forest, she gave birth prematurely, very shortly after their first child had died. Then, when a Khmer Rouge patrol surprised them they became separated, and a very weak Kim Hoeung was lost for days in the forest with her newborn baby. When they finally tumbled into Thailand, they were rushed to hospital where Christians surrounded her with love and constant prayer. The frail little baby died, and so nearly did the mother, of malaria and shock. Later, when Sun Tek found her again she had already become a Christian.

The refugee churches were also like churches in railway stations. It was difficult to build stability and continuity. One was always starting from scratch, and this was discouraging. No sooner had leaders been trained when they were invariably selected for resettlement overseas, and eagerly climbing aboard the buses which arrived monthly to take them away to Bangkok and a new life in France, Canada, the USA or Australia. For these Christians, their young faith was about to be severely tested.

Some, as they left the camps behind, also abandoned their Bibles. Christianity had simply been a useful social and psychological prop during the dreary days of camp life. Now they were assured of a secure new life in the West, they had no more need of a new life in Christ. This discernible falling away which began as they moved to the transit centres in Bangkok, would become a stampede out of the church and into the glittering 'new world' soon after they touched down on foreign soil.

This second Cambodian harvest in the Thai refugee camps from

1975-1980 was a harvest of tares as well as wheat, as the winnowing would quickly reveal. In the context of the dull and uninspiring refugee camps, Christianity was very attractive. In the context of Los Angeles, Paris, Montreal and Sydney, it was far less so.

Selection for resettlement overseas was the overwhelming obsession of most people in the camps. The morale of the camp was never higher than just before some western embassy immigration officials arrived to conduct selection interviews. And it was never lower than just after the lists of the chosen had been posted. For some the waiting was intolerable. Boredom, confinement, overcrowding and emotional insecurity exacerbated the social and moral turbulence in the camps. Drinking, gambling, infidelity, delinquency etc all took their toll.

But not all the refugees idly frittered away those years of hiatus between the deadly oppression of Cambodia and the deadly liberty of the West. They turned those colourless and crowded settlements surrounded by high barbed wire and armed guards into pleasant friendly communities. The more resourceful among them set up little stalls selling cakes, noodles and soft drinks. Barbers, tailors, and watchmakers did a steady business, and anyone who could teach French or English soon had himself a school of eager students of all ages. On empty patches of ground the men planted fruit trees and vegetables to supplement the very basic food rations. In the centre of these gardens where it was relatively private and shaded, a thatch roof on stilts might be found. Here, slung easily in hammocks or seated cross-legged on split bamboo benches, the men could smoke their hand-rolled cigarettes and while away the time forever discussing Cambodian politics, the resistance, and the pros and cons of resettlement in this or that country.

Thai officials sometimes allowed the refugees day passes to travel to nearby towns. Here, if they had some cash, they could buy supplies to furnish their little businesses in the camps. The UNHCR, Red Cross and others ensured that food and health were sufficiently cared for. Indeed, a good many local Thai villagers outside the camps eyed rather enviously the easy 'pampered' existence these 'aliens' enjoyed, and a future in America!

The irrepressible creativity and buoyancy of the camp children in devising all kinds of games despite the conditions was incredible. They amused themselves with home-made tops, kites, marbles, stilts, carts, and their merry voices helped make the camps happier places. Some of the men painted in oils famous scenes from the great temple ruins of Angkor. Others made exquisite carvings of animals and mystical dancing maidens out of soapstone, using only simple hand made tools. Workshops produced indigenous musical instruments for the older men who could still remember how to play them, to entertain at weddings and festivals. The women knitted, crocheted, made cloth on hand-made wooden looms, styled and blackened each other's hair, baked the much loved French bread in crude ovens made from oil drums buried in the earth, and cultivated spices in kitchen gardens to flavour their traditional Cambodian soups and dishes. When water was at a premium, as it always was in the hot season, all the family took their 'bath' squatting out in the middle of the garden, pouring the precious dipper of water over their heads and letting it run off between the rows of vegetables.

Sadly, however, with nightfall, some of these hands turned to gambling, drinking, immorality, brawling, robbery, rape and even murder. Too many Cambodian refugees, once they had recovered their strength, began to display a penchant for indolence, corruption and treachery.

In each camp, a core of Christians stood out as a loving, caring people who eschewed evil. The church did of course have its own internal tensions and discipline problems. Most were only babes in Christ. But the Christians were clearly not what they had once been. It was interesting too that, invariably, Christians were found in positions of responsibility in the camps: hospital orderlies, interpreters, handling relief aid etc.

Christmas and Easter were times when the church went all out to proclaim the Christian message. Several days of meetings for worship were planned culminating in public baptisms and testimonies. When there was sufficient water and permission was granted, a large crowd gathered at a river or pool in the rice fields near the camp. With their faces uplifted towards the clouds which drifted over their homeland only a few miles to the east, they sang out the familiar hymns: *O Happy Day, A Shelter in the Time of the Storm, Nearer my God to Thee, Fairest Lord Jesus, The Love of God.* Whether the winds wafted their voices, to whisper words of comfort in the ears of their brothers and sisters still groaning under the heel of *Angka*, I do not know. But it was for them that the newly baptised Christians among Cambodia's exiled children sang. Services at Aranyaprathet camp always ended with everyone standing as one person led in prayer for Cambodia before the final historic Benediction:

> 'May the grace of our Lord Jesus Christ,
> The love of God, and the fellowship of the Holy Spirit,
> Be with us all, evermore. Amen.'

Christmas always culminated in a magnificent song and drama presentation of the nativity story. Heavily made up in the Cambodian theatrical style, and draped in all the bed covers we could muster, they re-told the familiar story of Christmas. In Cambodian theatre, it seems, there must always be one character to provide some comic relief. This was invariably one of the shepherds in the likeness of a simple but lovable Cambodian village buffoon. But nothing was allowed to distract from the simple poignancy of the birth of the baby Jesus in Bethlehem. In 1976, as I recall, the Cambodians at Aranyaprathet camp, unfamiliar with the traditional ending in which everyone is gathered triumphantly about the manger in Bethlehem, continued the story on to its tragic and moving sequel. We saw dramatically portrayed Mary and Joseph and the baby fleeing through a forest from a cruel ruler. We saw heartless soldiers dashing out the brains of little children (they used dolls!). And then the entire drama was brought forcefully home in a climactic ending set in a dusty refugee camp in a neighbouring country with Mary, Joseph and the baby Jesus sheltering as refugees.

The impact on the camp was enormous. Right after the Christmas Day celebrations of 1977, a tall middle-aged Cambodian man came over and handed me a sealed envelope. Inside, a very serious letter in formal Cambodian written style had been drafted. Attached to it was an ID sized photograph of the gentleman, and beneath the final greeting was his thumbprint:

Aranyaprathet Refugee Camp
Dec 25, 1977

'...Kindly allow me to enter and embrace the Christian faith from Jan 1, 1978 onwards. I can see without a shadow of doubt that the way of Jesus Christ is the way of salvation, the means of rescuing all mankind...

With my highest respect I hereby affirm this with the thumbprint of my right hand.'

Mr Van Rean became a devoted disciple of Christ, and a much loved 'uncle' to many in the church. He was baptised on May 11, 1978, with twenty-five others in the camp. A few months earlier we had heard through the resistance grapevine in the camp that they had helped Mr Van Rean, a prime target of the Khmer Rouge pogroms, to escape from his commune at a place called 'The Eyes of God'. He was kept hidden somewhere deep in the forest, and was very weak and in rags. The Christians immediately sent in food, clothing, medicines and a mosquito net with one of the resistance couriers, and his life was saved. Shortly afterwards he entered the camp and saw the Christmas play. Thus, as with Soman and others, the seed which was now bearing fruit was the Word of God sown many years before. Van Rean recalled how twenty-five years earlier in 1953, he had been given the Book of Proverbs. The wisdom of that book had thrilled his soul and left him forever thirsty for more.

Eventually he was resettled in the USA. Unlike many, he resisted the temptation to re-marry in the camp and prayed patiently for his wife and family still in Cambodia. Much later, following the 1979 upheaval, I heard that all the family had escaped and are now reconciled with this dear brother in America. For Van Rean, his unique thumbprint was the only appropriate way to seal the written covenant he made with his Redeemer that Christmas Day in 1977.

There were many other memorable conversions to Christ during these years. Most who readily responded to the gospel, it must be said, were former students, young intellectuals, and those keen to learn English or French and get as far away from Cambodia as possible. Several seemed to be so ashamed and disgusted with what Cambodia had become that they no longer really wanted to be identified with things Cambodian. This included Buddhism which is virtually synonymous with being Cambodian. One very cultured lady once remarked, reflecting her Buddhist world-view, 'In my next life, I want to be anything but a Cambodian.' And yet others who responded were of real hard core Khmer peasant stock, steeped in all the ancient lore and traditions of Cambodia. One such man was Mr Mon.

Mr Mon, a former village school teacher, was also a powerful spirit medium. He could perform rituals for various illnesses, tell fortunes and, some claimed, even make it rain. One night in one of his trances, and an apparent fit of jealousy, he stabbed and killed another man and then turned the knife on himself. But his own life was saved by prompt medical action, and he ended up in a Thai prison. With him he had a Bible, for Christian literature had been distributed widely in the camp. For the first time he began seriously reading it over, slowly and aloud the way Cambodians do. By the time he was released he was more than ready to openly profess his faith in Christ. Once back at the camp, he gathered up all his old books, fetishes, and demonic paraphernalia and publicly burned the lot. The people in the camp all knew what he had once been, and marvelled that even he had joined the Christians.

Sopat was yet another beautiful trophy of God's amazing grace in those uncertain days in the Thai border camps. Many times I had passed through the little wooden camp clinic yet somehow failed to notice him lying there. Perhaps it was because he lay so still, or because of the absence of people around his bed which was pushed into a back corner. There was a long scar from a recent operation running down the middle of his swollen stomach. The rest of him was haggard and emaciated. It was clear from his long, dirty nails, and feet caked in mud, that he had not been washed for days; a filthy tattered cloth was all that covered him. I bent down brushing the thick matted black hair from his forehead, and said a few words in Cambodian. His glazed eyes remained fixed on the ceiling, his thin pale lips drawn tight and motionless. Again there was the familiar distant stare I had seen so many times before on the faces of Cambodian refugees crowded into these stifling border camps and prisons.

My efforts to communicate with him were in vain, and he finally turned over very slowly onto his side, his skeleton-like back towards me. A medical record beside him was virtually blank: Sopat, male, thirty-one. The next few hours were spent equally in vain trying to locate a friend or relative somewhere in the camp. No one knew him, or wanted to know him. All referred me elsewhere with the same short response followed by an awkward stony silence. Finally, I approached the busy camp doctor: 'Hopeless... full of cancer... no, no one knows... just pain-killers... help? Sure, do what you like.'

There were times when the heavy clouds of despair and hopelessness which hung over these places threatened to crush one's spirit. And this was such a time. Now, with a dull ache in the back of my head, I went back into the clinic. Sopat had not moved from the position on his side facing the wall, so I sat down on the edge of the bed, rested my hand on his shoulder, and waited. After a long while, he turned and looked at me for the first time. I said nothing but proceeded to remove the dirty cloth wrapped around him and replace it with a clean one I had brought with me. Glancing back at his face, I saw that his eyes were moistening, then tears came, but no sound. 'I have come to help you,' I said. 'Tell me if there is anything you would like.' Then I gave him a drink, washed his face, and promised to return tomorrow.

I had seen Cambodians die before, alone, tragically, needlessly: yet with Sopat it was somehow different. I just could not accept that he was to lie there and slowly die, forgotten and unwanted like a dog on the roadside. He was a man in the image of God and I loved him. Back home that evening, I poured it all out before the Lord: the deep sorrow at his human plight, the bitterness, the utter misery of it all. God surely must have seen him too. On into the night I had to keep on praying, weeping, asking. I could give God no peace on this one. My entire faith it seemed, frail enough as that was, was being concentrated on this man, Sopat.

Next morning I went straight in to see him. I had his *sarong*, now washed and clean, along with some sheets, cloths, soap and things. He seemed pleased to see me, and so as I began the long job of cleaning him we chatted about his family in Cambodia, and the long and dangerous escape through the jungle. It was when I had almost finished that he suddenly asked, 'How can I know what will happen to me after I die?' I looked back at him speechless, hardly able to believe what I had just heard. Thinking I had not understood his Cambodian, he re-worded the question. I sat down and very simply told him of the living God and Jesus, the Saviour. He listened, concentrating, as if I were confirming something he had already suspected. 'Yes, I believe, I believe it,' he said quite excitedly. I talked on further, but he seemed to know now. It all made such complete sense. His face was relaxed and he smiled, 'I believe in Jesus. He is the truth.'

Breathing great prayers of thanksgiving, I hurried over to fetch Chhorn. He could explain and confirm all that I had begun to say far more clearly. Precious Chhorn, lone survivor of a long testing escape from Cambodia, always so incredibly patient and kind and possessing such a strong faith in his Father God who had so wonderfully brought him to us.

'Has he come to explain more about Jesus?' Sopat turned and whispered to me as I brought Chhorn to the bedside. It was that moving story of the dying thief on the cross next to Jesus that Chhorn chose to speak on...

'With me in Paradise,' Sopat repeated the words slowly to himself, feeling their soothing balm penetrating deep, driving out the fear, the uncertainty, the loneliness, conscious now of deep peace, warmth and comfort flooding in. We prayed together, and then Chhorn went over to speak to the astonished old lady sitting up in the next bed. I enjoyed these exciting moments of new life with Sopat, and words could never express the joy we knew as we spontaneously embraced each other as brothers in Christ.

The Christians were equally thrilled when I told them the good news. From then on they visited him every day, keeping him clean and comfortable, bringing the best of what little spare food they had. In this way they continued to encourage him in his faith by their testimony and fellowship.

With the passing days, his stricken body grew thinner and weaker till he could scarcely move. His spirit however soared free and victorious. At the end, we were all with him, including young Lot who had daily washed and cared for him so tenderly.

It was the final triumph. At 9 o'clock that Friday morning, his breathing became shallower and shallower. He seemed to be communing with the Lord under his breath. His face, radiant and serene, was full of peace, and bore no trace of anguish or pain. For a moment he seemed suspended between two worlds, as we with bated breath witnessed the passing over of one of his precious saints. We were drawn very close to the presence of God as Sopat lingered on the brink of eternity. Then, very suddenly, he was quiet; two beautiful smiles flickered across his face and he was gone. And we were left watching his poor earthly shell, as the world of the refugee camp came crashing in around our ears once again. But Sopat was gone; gone to be with Jesus, in paradise – as promised.

Soman, Salieng, and Lot all helped to wash and dress his body for burial. The Thais who brought the rough wooden coffin kindly allowed the Christians to do everything. Sopat's body, dressed now in the best clothes to be found, and with a piece of hand-embroidered cloth over his face, was carefully placed in the coffin. The Christians painstakingly attended to every detail.

Six of the Christians, including Chhorn, were permitted to go to the graveyard, a place on the edge of town, set aside especially for vagrants and the very poor. Here, barely a mile from their beloved Cambodia, the Christians prepared a grave for one of her exiled sons. 'Victory is complete! Where, death, is your victory?' Chhorn's clear and steady voice was all that broke the sultry midday stillness.

Then, after Sopat's body had been committed to the earth, the Christians filled in the grave. This proved to be a long hot task as it was midday, and the earth had become so hard. They took turns, making sure to pack the earth carefully around the sides of the coffin first. As we left the graveyard, there was a warmth of assurance among us that all had been done according to God's will, and the knowledge that there was great rejoicing in heaven as Sopat, free at least, no longer an unwanted and homeless refugee, entered in.

A few days later I was teaching in one of the refugee longhouses when I noticed two men who had been associates of Sopat, though they had always remained hovering in the background through his sickness and death. I went over and shared with them what had happened. Moved to tears at what they had seen and now heard, one declared, 'It is truly amazing! He was such a feared and wicked thief in Cambodia.'

Chhorn, who in his own Christian pilgrimage had had a plentiful share of struggles and setbacks, had been instrumental in transforming several people's lives. Men like Sopat particularly appealed to Chhorn. He had a heart full of compassion, especially for the sick, the poor, the unlovely. Having been a soldier for many years, he was very interested in the anti-communist resistance movements. He had an immediate rapport with these groups, each of which had their own concentration of men in the refugee camps. Good, bad and ugly, they trusted him with their money, their secrets and their fears.

There was always a certain air of secrecy surrounding these groups of freedom fighters and their comings and goings. Tales of their exploits, true or exaggerated, had a definite romantic appeal. I suppose it gave some small sense of satisfaction that at least someone was fighting back against *Angka* even if that amounted to little more than sniping around the periphery of what seemed like an absolutely immovable, undefeatable black monster sprawled all over Cambodia. If some of them were rogues, then they were romantic rogues; as colourful and daring as they were irresponsible and unpredictable. With a few notable exceptions, they were lone rangers, scarlet pimpernels, swashbucklers, mavericks, hopelessly addicted to 'the good life' they had been accustomed to as soldiers and officers of Sihanouk and Lon Nol. They certainly shared none of the rugged and spartan discipline of the Khmer Rouge. They seemed incapable of working cohesively together. But they did provide another of those badly needed dreams or illusions for the Cambodian people, cushioning them from the harsh realities in Cambodia and the refugee camps. For many Cambodians, not surprisingly, illusions are far more significant than reality. And they were able to keep illusion and reality in two watertight compartments of their minds.

Nevertheless, most of the young idealists who joined the resistance groups shared a deep passion to free Cambodia from the bondage of radical communism, and one day to return and rebuild. This appeared in stark contrast, it must be said, to the majority of Christians who couldn't get to the 'West' fast enough. This tended to confirm the already widespread belief that Christianity was a 'western' religion, and those who converted to it were abandoning their essential Cambodian-ness. In the early 1980s some resistance groups operating along the border actively discouraged Christianity because, they said, as soon as a person becomes a Christian his only desire is to go to America. Devout Buddhist resistance soldiers were prepared to die for Cambodia, and so most definitely were communist-inspired Khmer Rouge, but few Christians. Their support for Cambodia, it seemed, would be from a safe distance, and sometimes with a view to bringing out all the other Christians brothers and sisters. I believe this attitude has lost the Cambodian church a great deal of credibility in Cambodia. For such actions declare that it is better to save one's life, than to risk losing one's life, or endure hardship, for the sake of the gospel in Cambodia. As missionaries, are we introducing Asians to Western dreams, priorities and values or to Christ crucified?

Just before the fall of Phnom Penh and his own martyrdom, Taing Chhirc had told a missionary friend: 'Communists are willing to die for what they believe. Is not Jesus worth more than all these things?'

Occasionally, however, one would come across some inconspicuous saint manfully swimming against the strong current flowing from the refugee camps to the West. One such man was Khuy Sy. On April 17, 1977, as the Khmer Rouge were celebrating the second anniversary of their victory in Cambodia, and about the time also when Pol Chhorn was crossing the border into free

Thailand after his gruelling twenty-four-day escape, Khuy Sy, recognised as a former Republican soldier, had been arrested and tied to a tree to await execution. The Khmer Rouge always enjoyed prolonging their victim's agony, like a cat playing with a mouse. In this case, however, the delay enabled this little mouse to spring from the trap.

The afternoon sun beat mercilessly down upon him, and he was growing weak from hunger and thirst. Around his upper arms the ropes which held him to the tree trunk cut cruelly into his flesh. In desperation he found himself crying out to the living God of heaven and earth whom he had once heard about at a church in Phnom Penh a few years earlier when he was a student. As he prayed, he also struggled with the bonds which held him.

Fortunately, there was no one around since all the commune were required to attend the mandatory April 17 revolutionary 'celebrations'. From the commune's central meeting place he could hear the strident tones of the Khmer Rouge cadres shrieking their customary exhortations for greater effort, punctuated at the given cue by mechanical shouts of *Cheyo!* (Victory!) from the ranks of impassive and weary listeners. Khuy Sy had heard it all so many times before that he could have given a convincing rendition of the entire performance. Ultimately, it was just a matter of memorising set lines, and then delivering them in as earnest and convincing a way as possible. The Khmer Rouge sought to outdo each other in zeal and ardour for the revolution. Their lives depended on it!

But right now, Khuy Sy's life depended on freeing himself from these ropes before the meeting was over. As he struggled and strained against the cords, he felt them becoming looser. His eyes skyward, straining every fibre of muscle he could, and breathing prayers for deliverance, he finally broke himself free from the tree, though his wrists were still tied in front of him.

So intent had he been on freeing himself that he had failed to notice that the meeting had ended. As he scurried across an open rice field with his bound hands raised up high so as not to impede his running, he heard the excited voices of the Khmer Rouge behind him, screaming *'Chap! Chap!'* (Catch him! Catch him!)

His heart was pounding, his knees felt as if they might buckle at any moment, and his throat was as parched as the sharp dry stubble which tore at his feet. Panting, he struggled towards the cover of the forest beyond. Then he heard shots, felt a searing pain in his left hand, and the warm sensation of blood running down his arm. The bullet had missed his head by inches, but completely shattered his left thumb. But he did not stop to look. Having reached the line of trees he ran on through the forest, into the thickest undergrowth deep in the bush, till finally he stumbled and collapsed headlong in sheer agony. His lungs were burning and he felt nauseous and delirious. But he lay there gasping for breath like a hunted animal run to ground, straining his ears for the sound of his pursuers.

Getting the ropes off his wrists was a long and excruciating ordeal. The pain in his left hand was throbbing right up his arm, and he could see now the shattered bone and flesh, the dark blood forming a pool on the leaves in front of him. He shook off his tattered black shirt and wrapped it as tightly as he could around the injured hand. Then he grasped it tight to his chest with his good hand.

Surely, he was a dead man, he thought, virtually naked and unprotected from the swarms of mosquitoes and the thorny bush. He had no food or water, he was badly injured, and the Khmer Rouge would be out in force hunting for him. But he had God, he thought. That he knew now for certain. Hadn't he escaped from the Khmer Rouge just minutes before his execution? Surely the same God who had done that would watch over him, strengthen him and guide him through this hostile forest to Thailand.

Khuy Sy had been a good soldier and he knew something about survival. He could read nature's signposts in the forest, such as on which side of the trees the moss grew, and the path of the sun across the sky. He knew he was about thirty-five miles east of the Thai border.

For seven days this tenacious and prayerful young soldier struggled on, clutching the aching blood-soaked bundle to his chest, picking his way through the deep forest, carefully avoiding any open spaces or human trails. All he had for sustenance was the heavy morning dew which he licked gratefully from the broad leaves. On day seven, he was discovered by a patrol of Thai border police, and taken straight to one of the prisons for refugees at Kabinburi. As yet no attention was paid to his hand, but at least there was food and rest, and the assurance that he was free from the Khmer Rouge.

He was pushed into the crowded cell where all available space had been staked out by others who had preceded him. It was then that he met Pol Chhorn who had arrived only ten days ahead of him. After what he had just come through, Khuy Sy's heart was already fully alive to God. Now, here was a man twice his age who without any hesitation when he saw Khuy Sy's weak and feverish condition gave up his place to allow him to lie down. Every morning and evening he watched the old Christian unashamedly kneel and call out to God in prayer. He too was thankful for a safe escape, and he had a wife and children somewhere over in that 'hell' with the Khmer Rouge. But of all the Cambodians pressed in that cell, only Chhorn showed any real concern for the young man. As far as Khuy Sy was concerned, Chhorn had been heaven sent, confirming that God's hand was upon him for good.

It was to be four days before Sy was finally sent to the hospital at Aranyaprathet. And it was here, three days later, while visiting another refugee struggling in a violent malaria induced delirium, that I noticed him a few beds away. It was obvious that he was a refugee, just skin and bone, his skin dry and black bearing the fresh wounds inflicted by the forest. The rope burns still clearly discernible on his upper arms confirmed his story. His hand had already been operated on once.

In countries like Thailand, hospital patients are entirely dependent on a friend or relative who comes in and stays around the clock with him, caring for all the patient's needs: food, washing, clothing, even making sure the person gets the needed attention. These people are to be found all over the wards, sleeping beside or under the patient's bed, squatting in corners together passing the time of day, carrying containers of food, emptying slops, making their charge comfortable. A patient who has no one to perform all these functions is in a very miserable situation. He is left to his own devices unless some sympathetic medic, or more likely a hospital visitor takes some interest. If the patient is bedridden, or seriously ill, then of course his predicament is very bad. Thus for new escapees like Sy who landed up in such places it was very lonely, frightening, and humiliating. Added to this, the Cambodians could not speak Thai, and many of the locals despised them as 'useless refugees' or even 'Khmer Rouge'.

Happily, I adopted Sy and we fast became friends. The fact that a strange white man speaking his language should appear out of nowhere on this isolated border when he was again in need, and a Christian missionary at that, did not completely surprise him. He had already experienced so many tokens of God's love in the past two weeks since he had struggled and prayed his way out of those bonds, that he simply smiled a radiant smile when I went over and greeted him.

His craving was for fried duck eggs on rice washed down with ice cold Pepsi! When I was there the hospital staff were very helpful, and as he gained strength and began to walk around, they let him spend time at my little shop-front house near the market. Here we could talk freely and he could spend long days reading and sleeping and recovering himself while I was away at the camp. His faith in God was strong and he made a firm commitment to consecrate his life to him.

But Khuy Sy was unique, quite unlike all the other Cambodians I had known. He was a very private and thoughtful person, and felt uncomfortable when other Cambodians peppered him with questions, as they invariably did to all new escapees. When he was eventually released into the camp, he stayed barely long enough to complete the outpatient treatment on his left hand which had had skin grafts and was now minus a thumb. His few real friends included Chhorn of course, who by now had also been sent to the camp, and Sarin, a Christian leader and ex-resistance fighter till a mine exploded near him badly injuring his legs. As soon as Khuy Sy had ascertained the whereabouts of the anti Khmer Rouge resistance in the forest he was gone. He never returned to the camp again.

Occasionally he would show up at my door in Aranyaprathet alone, or with a colleague. Sometimes he wanted Christian books, sometimes mosquito nets and clothes, or sometimes just to spend a few hours in solitude. When I pressed him, he told me that small groups of them were penetrating back into Cambodia surveying the situation, rescuing ex-soldiers, taking in medicines, and sometimes ambushing Khmer Rouge patrols. Khuy Sy had seen much evidence of the mass killings and was more convinced than ever that the Khmer Rouge had to be stopped. It left him utterly dumbfounded that no effectual moves had been taken by any western democratic government to isolate and condemn this genocidal regime, but quite the contrary. The biggest danger they faced, he said, was from the hidden mines and booby traps as they moved stealthily under cover of darkness, through the forests.

Six months later, a Thai man dropped a note at my door. It was written in Cambodian by Khuy Sy. He was in a nearby Thai military hospital seriously wounded along with a number of others. They had come off badly in a surprise encounter with the Khmer Rouge as they were advancing through a rice paddy. A number of the resistance had been killed. Everyone had scattered, and Sy had had to make a second solo trek badly injured back out to Thailand. Nothing would persuade him to tarry or rest awhile at the camp. As soon as he was well again, he was away; a modern-day Christian zealot, doing what he felt he had to do for his family and for his country.

I never saw him again for fifteen more years, though one or two letters were exchanged by means of resistance couriers who passed in and out of the camps. In 1979, Aranyaprathet camp began filling up with hundreds of 'illegals', sneaking in under the wire by night from the border, where hundreds of thousands were now encamped, following the Vietnamese backed revolution which overthrew the Khmer Rouge. At that time I received one more piece of welcome news of Khuy Sy.

There was an ex-student from Battambang named Savoeurn whose brother and handicapped sister had also been Christians. He loved this sister and secretly admired her lonely stand for Christ. Under the Khmer Rouge, Savouern found himself assigned to a commune near Mongkul Borey. Here he met a most remarkable man known only as 'the mad hunchback'. He certainly acted strangely, sitting out in the fields or prancing around with his arms lifted heavenwards apparently ranting and raving. To add to the effect, for he was actually feigning madness, he was short and somewhat deformed, possibly from polio. How it all began we don't know, but by the time Savoeurn saw him, he had already been dubbed *chkuet* (insane) by the Khmer Rouge. This was not an unusual malady in those insane times. Since he was apparently mad and subhuman, he was assigned one of the most dreaded and foulest tasks of all, that of gathering up the commune's human excrement and mixing it into fertiliser. Nevertheless, he continued to laugh and cavort around, to talk to the air and wave his arms. He was, they all observed, quite mad.

Secretly however, 'the mad hunchback' was contacting young intellectuals like Savoeurn and speaking to them of Jesus Christ. Concealed in the stuffing of a pillow, he had a Bible hidden. Formerly, he had been a professor and could speak a number of languages. What sounded like unintelligible ravings to the illiterate Khmer Rouge, were in fact prayers and praises to God in a variety of foreign tongues, spiced no doubt with creative renditions from this man's fertile imagination and dramatic ingenuity. Savoeurn and a few others were led to Christ by 'the mad hunchback'.

In the camp, Savouern was a profoundly changed young man. Whereas he had formerly been rather irresponsible, now he was more serious, hardworking, and concerned for others. Early in 1979, a number of seriously wounded Khmer Rouge soldiers were brought to the local hospital for treatment. Savoeurn volunteered to go in and look after them. He was given permission to stay at my house nearby. This was a grim and thankless job which no one else wanted to do, especially for Khmer Rouge! He washed those he found lying helpless in their own filth. He helped clean their old and infected wounds which were full of foul-smelling pus. He was never more content than when serving the helpless: dripping water between the clenched teeth of one seriously ill with tetanus, nursing a poor thin boy dying of a burst appendix and a tiny baby dying in agony with a bowel blockage, or comforting a forgotten old lady dying of a huge brain tumour.

Every day, he risked contracting all kinds of diseases in order to show practically to 'friend' or 'enemy' alike the deep love and compassion of God. It was at this time that Savoeurn received the sad news that his father had starved to death under the Khmer Rouge. I recall how bitterly he wept for his father. But when it was time to go on duty at the hospital, he washed his face and went back to care for the men whose regime of terror had been responsible for his father's death. A few Khmer Rouge teenagers whom he did lead to Christ were sent back later into Cambodia at the time of June '79 repatriations. I often wonder where such ones are today.

Later in the year, when a number of daring souls, including several Christians, began venturing back to their villages and families in Cambodia from the camps with medicines and clothing, Savouern, along with a few others headed back also towards Mongkul Borey with supplies for their families. Savoeurn and I spent many hours packaging and painstakingly writing Cambodian instructions on the various medicines. They were mostly for worms, malaria, dysentery, as well as many vitamins. But buried deep in his pack, Savouern also carried a new Bible, and a hymnbook, to give to 'the mad hunchback', who had first shown him the way to sanity.

These daring groups had some amazing adventures during their exploits in and out of Cambodia. Two Christians knowing they were approaching an area where there were booby traps and mines decided to walk side by side with their arms around each other so that if they stepped on a mine they would die together. As they inched forward they watched and prayed. Suddenly, the ground gave way under them and they found themselves falling into one of the Khmer Rouge's gory pits. But because they were locked together as one, they lodged on the sides of the hole and were able to scramble out. A little further on they startled a wild boar which ran down the trail ahead of them and tripped a wire which triggered off a concealed explosive. This was cause for a double thanksgiving. Firstly, the grenades were exploded, and secondly they had fresh pork!

When Savoeurn arrived back on Thai soil, he took refuge briefly in a Cambodian resistance jungle camp. Here he met Khuy Sy, who, when he discovered Savoeurn was a believer and a friend of mine, took him to his own hut and showed him his collection of Christian literature. Even out there in this jungle hideout for Cambodian anti-Communist freedom fighters, fanatically Buddhist and superstitious people, the Lord was not without a witness. We also heard later that Khuy Sy had managed to rescue his wife and children and that they were with him in the resistance. It seemed Jesus Christ still had at least one known zealot among his Cambodian disciples.

There were a number of other Cambodian Christians who, mostly because they had family still in Cambodia, did not join the stampede to the West, but returned home. One willing returnee, however, stood out beyond all the others. He was a young lad named Chen. Chen was fourteen years old and had been brought from the border to the Khao I Dang camp hospital because he was terminally ill with stomach cancer. With him was his elder brother Chem who was sixteen. Both were country lads and came from a small village about forty kilometres inside Cambodia. They had become Christians, and most days I used to sit with Chen in the hospital. We would read Bible stories together and discuss their meaning.

One day he took me completely off guard when he said, 'Uncle, in my village, back in Cambodia, no one has ever heard the gospel of Jesus Christ. I want you to go and tell them.' Not very convincingly, I tried to explain that the country was closed to foreigners, it was illegal, and the mission I worked with would never allow it. He was puzzled that these human constraints should stand in the way of proclaiming the message of salvation to those who desperately needed it. I suggested we pray that God would send a Cambodian Christian to his village.

There were in Khao I Dang at that time several thousand Christians. But I knew from experience that they tended to become very upset at the suggestion that God might have brought so many of them to a place where they could hear the gospel, believe, and become disciples of Christ, in order that they might proclaim him back in Cambodia rather than all go off to California. A good number were gifted evangelists and teachers, but none of these returned. Chen however was determined that his home village should hear the gospel.

A few days later, he greeted me with his usual sunny smile and proceeded to explain that since I wouldn't go, and no one else was able to go, he would go himself. 'But you are so weak and thin,' I reminded him. 'You need to remain here where you can be cared for properly'. Nothing however would alter his mind. 'Chem has agreed to come with me and help me,' he said. His mind was made up.

The doctors had operated on Chen some weeks earlier, but it was too late. They had given him about three months to live. Armed with tracts and gospel portions, he returned with Chem to the border, and then set off back to his village. Not only did Chen have advanced cancer, but the way was fraught with dangers: mines, bandits, Khmer Rouge guerrillas, and all the privations of war-torn post 'Killing Fields' Cambodia. He was probably about the 'weakest', most 'foolish', 'lowly' and 'despised' Christian to be found anywhere in the border refugee settlements at that time. But he was the one who gladly trusted and obeyed when the Lord beckoned.

'Behold your God, he comes to you humble.' One can hardly imagine the amazement of those Cambodian villagers when this pathetic looking little lad, leaning on two crutches, stood before them holding out his gospel tracts. Most of them would have given all they had to have been in the place he had just left, a secure refugee camp complete with food and medicines and a possible sponsorship to America. What important message was this that had compelled him to return so willingly to them. Chem explained later how some in the village received him gladly, while others were disdainful. But only eternity will disclose the consequences of Chen's unique mission to that village.

He died soon afterwards, on the Cambodian border. His ashes are interred at Christ Church in Bangkok. Now he is free from his pain, though he never complained. He is safe 'at home with the Lord'. But I have one unforgettable memory of Chen. It is the appearance of his feet. His little feet were skin and bone, caked with grime, battered and bruised. Yet in all my life will I ever see a more beautiful pair of feet than those? They were so swift to go with the glad tidings of salvation. Chen, in the sheer beauty and simplicity of his faith, saw an urgent spiritual need, realised that he was the one being called to fulfil it, and went straightaway and did it. And I still have the little cross which he wove for me from the plastic tubing of his saline drip. Chen had a way of making something beautiful out of something painful.

This insignificant little seed fell into the ground and died. And in so doing produced many seeds in the Cambodian fields.

CHAPTER 13

THE HARVEST OF WHEAT
AND TARES

'Another parable he put before them, saying, "The kingdom of heaven may be compared to a man who sowed good seed in his field; but while men were sleeping, his enemy came and sowed weeds among the wheat, and went away. So when the plants came up and bore grain, then the weeds appeared also."'

(Matthew 13: 24-26)

With the opening of the massive 'holding centre' at Khao I Dang in November 1979, the old Aranyaprathet camp and others like it were somewhat upstaged. Soon they would be phased out completely. With no more Cambodians legally permitted into them, and bus loads being taken out monthly to transit centres in Bangkok for emigration, numbers began falling fast. In late 1981, the last refugees were shipped out and the old place closed down. It will be remembered by many for its crowded, noisy, airless longhouses, its confining barbed wire fences, and the toilets and water pipes which never did function. But others will recall it as the place where they met Jesus Christ. Even this dusty old camp for refugees was 'beautiful in its time' for here in its grim surroundings, hundreds of Cambodians came face to face with eternal truths, repentance and faith.

Thousands more heard the gospel in other such camps all around that border. Hundreds who believed, were baptised and discipled, are now dispersed all across the world, beginning a new

333

dimension to the history of this church, the church of the Cambodian diaspora. These were the exported grain. Just what will be the impact on the motherland of this far-flung and fragmented church among the Cambodian dispersion, remains to be seen.

But before leaving this era of the refugee camps in Thailand (1975-1993) there is that final and massive influx of refugees into Thailand to consider, and the lively churches which flourished in their midst.

This people movement of Cambodians towards Thailand began in late 1979 with a second build-up of refugees undeterred by the expulsions earlier in the year at the 'Valley of Hell'.

The pressure of refugees to the north of the Thai border town of Aranyaprathet led to the setting up of Khao I Dang camp, containing at its peak about 130,000 Cambodians. Because many of them were from the middle classes, former town dwellers, it was referred to by some as 'the last stand of the Cambodian bourgeoisie'. Khao I Dang was the largest refugee camp in the world at that time. Pressure to the south of Aranyaprathet led to the setting up of the controversial Sra Kaew camp, holding about 30,000 Cambodians. Many of them were dying, for these were the ones who had been herded into the forests by the Khmer Rouge. Thousands of these Khmer Rouge were granted asylum at Sra Kaew also, including some notorious murderers. These two massive camps were very different, but in both, the gospel made a profound and enduring impact.

The Khmer Rouge hold on power collapsed rapidly all across Cambodia throughout 1979 following the Vietnamese lightning invasion and establishment of a pro-Vietnamese regime in Phnom Penh on January 7, 1979. Supported by China, Thailand and the other nations of ASEAN (Singapore, Malaysia, Philippines, and Indonesia), and with the diplomatic support of the United Nations, the Khmer Rouge, with their command structure still intact, began to re-group for another protracted civil war, against the puppet Heng Samrin government in Phnom Penh. This would be by means of hit-and-run guerrilla tactics, striking at isolated communities from secret bases just inside Cambodia and from sanctuaries provided by the Thai government along the common border.

It appears that a decision was made by the Khmer Rouge leaders to split their forces into two. One group would remain inside the country, and the other head for the border. This latter contingent of several thousand Khmer Rouge had with it tens of thousands of virtual prisoners, Cambodians who had been corralled by the fleeing cowboys of *Angka* and herded westwards to help maintain the war effort against the hated *Yuon* (the Vietnamese).

For some months these pitiful columns of captives were driven up and down the border through its rugged terrain, growing increasingly frail and hungry with the passing weeks. Finally, in October 1979, their Khmer Rouge drovers dumped them like great heaps of stinking refuse on Thailand's doorstep. There was little else Thailand could do but accommodate them.

It was these heart-rending scenes which the media swooped on in late 1979 and flashed around the world under headings like 'Holocaust in Cambodia'. The popular interpretation was that these horrendous pictures were a window on the whole of Cambodia. A visit to the border north of Aranyaprathet where even larger concentrations of hundreds of thousands of Cambodians not under Khmer Rouge control were massing, would discover aggressive, blackmarketeering, ambitious people in reasonably healthy condition, and put the lie to such emotive and exaggerated claims.

A more accurate understanding would have been that these thousands of nameless skeletons stumbling around and sprawled listlessly all over the border scrubland south of Aranyaprathet waiting in silent agony for merciful death, were a graphic illustration of life under the Khmer Rouge, the plague from which Cambodia had so recently been liberated.

The Thais' major concern in all this was to help bring about a Khmer Rouge recovery to serve as a trip-wire against a perceived threat from Vietnam. Despite all the misery the Khmer Rouge had inflicted on their own people and on Thai border villages, they could now do little wrong. The villains, according to the five nations of ASEAN, were the Vietnamese, the ones who had rid Cambodia of the Stalinist Khmer Rouge. This pro-Khmer Rouge and anti-Vietnamese posture also suited the United States, still smarting from its ignominious defeat by North Vietnam only four years earlier. They called it 'holding your nose' diplomacy.

It was easy to pick out the Khmer Rouge from the civilians in these deathly places. Almost without exception they were strong and well fed, in stark contrast to those at their feet, starving, malaria-racked scraps of humanity lying in their own diarrhoea in the leaves all over the jungle floor. And still the Khmer Rouge watched them like hawks. A project to dose them all with the antimalarial drug 'Fansidar' was called off when it was discovered that their overlords simply came in and confiscated the pills for themselves. I personally saw a large Khmer Rouge cache of syringes, blankets, rice and medicines stolen from the people and relief teams.

The abject misery of these unfortunate people, who after four years of struggling to survive under the Khmer Rouge, should end up perishing in such a place and in such a way as this was beyond comprehension. The sheer inhumanity of it all defied reason. If it had been as a result of famine or some natural disaster it might have been more tolerable. But it was all so needless. And to make matters worse, in order to continue to help them, we had to tiptoe obsequiously around the same sullen Khmer Rouge cadre and corrupt calculating Thai army officers who were responsible for it in the first place.

Most were dying of a lethal strain of cerebral or falciparum malaria compounded by amoebic dysentery, tuberculosis, and starvation. The humid air was heavy with the stench of disease and death. An eerie silence pervaded the place as no one spoke, no one moved unless compelled, and no one cared or even noticed the needs of a neighbour. Their hearts and minds seemed frozen hard, held in the icy grip of an interminable winter. They simply squatted, alone, huddled in groups, smoking rolled leaves to alleviate their aching bellies, or lay prostrate, groaning, coughing painfully, twisting this way and that. Some had several layers of dirty grey-black rags wrapped tightly around them to keep in the body heat. They feared coldness as a harbinger of death.

Very occasionally, one would catch a glimpse of some poignant indication of the human spirit, a reminder that all these filthy ragged bundles of bones were in fact human beings after all. I recall a distraught middle-aged Chinese woman stumbling towards me cradling in her arms the long emaciated body of her totally wasted teenage son. He must have been taller than she was, but he was now very light, just skin and bones. The lad was all that remained of her family. She must have been dragging him around from place to place like this for days. But despite those steady loving arms around him, his life was fast ebbing away, running through her fingers like sand. She knew she could hold him no longer. As the woman dropped wearily on one knee, her son's limp body fell back over the other. The scene perfectly resembled a medieval portrait of the weeping Mary holding the crucified Jesus in her arms.

Unaware that she was being watched, she laid her son carefully on the ground. Then, with a piece of bark, she painstakingly scraped away at a place under a tree until it was clear of leaves and sticks, a smooth levelled area on the black earth. She then unrolled a new straw mat she had acquired and lifted him tenderly onto it. For some time the mother busied herself making him as comfortable as she could, even scooping out a hole beside him in the earth where she could roll him over to relieve himself. Finally, she sat beside him wiping his cavernous face with the corner of her faded *sarong*. The youth was a picture of despair. His huge panic stricken eyes were wide and pleading. They seemed to shout at me, 'For God's sake do something!' But in that forest, there was nothing we could do for him medically. He was in the final stages of starvation. His distended bowel hung out of him ulcerated and bleeding from chronic dysentery.

The next day he was gone. Almost certainly he died during the night, and the mother, for the last time, lifted her remaining son in those strong arms and bore him away to bury him. She would never have permitted the team of rough orderlies who hauled away the dead every morning, to toss her son into the common grave. The secret grave site would have been painstakingly dug out and prepared by the aching, loving hands of that mother. I never saw her again; that awesome, dignified lady. But for several days, till falling leaves obliterated it, the neat little clearing under the kapok tree, made by a devoted mother as a deathbed for her son remained, a still life portrait of love.

In a sense that young man had been fortunate, for he at least had someone with him, someone who selflessly loved him, who would bury him and remember him. Hundreds of others hadn't. The 'hospital' area we had set up in one of these deathly places comprising a couple of tents surrounded by rows of straw mats crowded together under a stand of trees from which saline drips were hanging, was filled with scores of little orphans. Each of them needed intensive care. Yet they were so incredibly long-suffering and calm. Long past crying and screaming, they sat patiently, soundlessly on their mats, watching stoically as this one and that one died and was carried off. Their parents had either died, or they had become separated from them in all the forced marching back and forth, sometimes under fire, as the Vietnamese forces drove the Khmer Rouge and their captives westward. Sometimes, one would come across a child sitting silently beside the dead body of its mother, reluctant to leave. Where else was there to go? Others, their worn and haggard faces belying their tender years, grimly hanging on to a younger sibling.

As they came in, each child was bathed and dressed in clean clothes. Sometimes as you peeled the coarse rancid garments from their scrawny little bodies, clothes patched, repaired and repatched, close inspection would reveal another world gone forever. Here, an ancient tear painstakingly and resourcefully sewn with such a neat row of little stitches that could only have been done by the caring hands of a mother. A mother desperately trying to prolong the life of the only shirt her little one possessed. And as you fingered those tiny stitches and looked again into the dark, melancholy eyes of the child, it was just possible to recover a fleeting glimpse of that lost world. A mother had born, loved and protected this child. A Cambodian mother had fought valiantly right here to repair some measure of dignity, some vestige of normal family life, some covering against all the powerful forces arrayed against her and her child. But evil hands had torn and ripped her world to shreds. And all that remained for us to do was drop the filthy rags into the fire.

One day, as I stood interpreting for one of the only two doctors at a place called Klong Wah where thousands needed their immediate attention, a little lad of about eight came up to me calling, 'Uncle, uncle, please come and help me carry my older brother over here where he can be given medicine.' The boy explained that the brother, about twelve, was lying a good two kilometres away in the bush, unconscious in a malaria coma. But I couldn't just walk away from my responsibilities as interpreter and the enormous task I already had on my hands helping to care for hundreds of dying people right there. Only a few yards into the forest there were more. How could I justify going so far and using up so much valuable time for just one? I told the boy I couldn't go with him, but to get one or two to help carry his brother in. Of course I knew even as I spoke that it was unlikely anyone was going to expend their own limited energy on a dying boy. His bad *karma*, his fate, had brought him to this sorry state, they would be reckoning subconsciously. Who can or should alter that? Certainly the fit and healthy young Khmer Rouge men and women who lounged around in their own exclusive shelters, cooking their pots of rice and remaining aloof from these 'slaves' and 'class enemies' wouldn't lift a finger to help. When once we did try to harness their energies to assist in the washing of the sick, they absconded as soon as our backs were turned, unwilling to get their hands dirty or risk infection. They even abandoned their own when it looked like a hopeless case.

The boy however would not be put off. He persisted in crying out after me, till I finally steeled myself and ignored him. After about an hour of whimpering and pleading, he fell silent, deep in thought. He knew that I was the only lifeline there was to save his brother's life. Next thing, I felt a pair of sinewy arms grip me round the legs, and a pair of ankles lock around mine. And there he clung like a leech. Now it was my turn to protest. But his lips were sealed. He clearly wasn't going to let go his vice-like grip on my legs till they followed him to that place where his brother lay dying. I was thus compelled to go with him in order to get rid of him! His dogged importunity had gained him the victory. And I reflected as I pursued him through the trees that this was surely what serious believing Christian prayer was all about. It entailed a crucial element of 'violence'. It involved patiently holding on to the knees of God, even in the face of apparent silence and lack of movement. The older brother's life was saved.

But that was not the end of the story. Watching all these things was a French-educated Khmer Rouge cadre who was rather grudgingly helping us take care of the orphans. He was quite bemused by it all and my 'weakness' in caving in to the will of a mere boy. However, later, the incident paved the way for us to talk about the essence of love. What it is, and where it comes from. As a result of the importunate orphan boy this cadre's heart was opened, and in time he also came to follow Jesus Christ. What became of the boy and the elder brother he saved, I do not know. God knows.

As yet, the massive relief effort gathering momentum around the world in response to the highly emotive media cries of 'holocaust' had not arrived. The UNHCR and International Committee of the Red Cross appeared to be bogged down in the unenviable red tape and diplomatic wrangling which is sadly such a major part of large-scale international relief. Low-key Christian mission groups and others already operational on the Thai border, were able to respond immediately, launching effective and flexible 'guerrilla attacks' on the problem with medical staff and relief supplies: foodstuffs, blankets, mats, plastic sheeting, shelters, water tanks, and latrines. These workers had on the spot practical experience in tropical medicine and refugee relief, and a knowledge of the local situation and language.

Later when the 'experts' from the large international secular agencies arrived with lots of money and political clout, they tended to view the low-key Christian groups with suspicion and contempt. Even some large Christian relief organisations trimmed their sails to the prevailing wind and were far less 'up front' about their Christian motives and convictions on the field than they appeared to the home support constituency. In the clamour to land a strategic 'ministry' in the camps, pragmatism took precedence over an uncompromising identification with Christ and his people.

Three years later, when I was on furlough in Canada, old

footage of the border crisis, just described, was still being aired on some TV appeals long after the emergency had passed. I suppose it was good fund-raising material. And with the use of subtle exaggeration and half truth, the impression is tacitly given that this particular agency is the only one doing anything, and if you don't give your money to them then nothing will happen. But as long as people only want to respond with money to emotive appeals, such agencies will never be accountable for their methods.

Within a few months the crisis was over. The weakest had died and the others had responded rapidly to western medicine, rest, and nutritious food. This included the Khmer Rouge of course, for whom this timely sojourn in Thailand was a morale-building rest and recreation period before returning across the border to terrorise Cambodian villagers once more. By mid-1980 at Sra Kaew and Khao I Dang, there were already too many relief organisations, and it was no easy task getting some of them to pull out. The relief agencies were of all kinds from the sublime to the ridiculous, scrambling over one another to plant their flag in a Cambodian refugee camp. As a result, millions of dollars were wasted or carelessly used, with some of it even falling into the ready pockets of unscrupulous local officials.

But back in October 1979, the situation for tens of thousands of Khmer Rouge victims languishing along the mountainous and forested south-western Cambodian border was critical. Even more importantly, for Thailand's strategic interests, the rump of the Khmer Rouge army was at its most desperate. There was a real danger that if the Vietnamese didn't finish them off, then starvation and disease in the malaria-infested forests would. Consequently, at the end of the month, the decision was made in Bangkok to open a camp for 30,000 Cambodians at a place called Sra Kaew ('Lake of Diamonds'). These dying ones who had stumbled out of the jungles and mountain passes into Thailand along with several thousand Khmer Rouge were to be trucked into this new refugee camp about forty miles inside Thailand, just off the main road to Bangkok.

No doubt there were many more Cambodians like these in

scattered pockets all through that forested region. They were just too weak, or lost, or prevented by their Khmer Rouge captors, to make it to the main collection points south of Aranyaprathet, such as Klong Wah, Klong Kai Toeun, or Ban Laem.

Brief forays into the bush revealed gruesome sights and smells of those cut off and left behind. Among some bushes I saw an old man struggling with an enamel plate to dig out a shallow grave in which to bury the body of his wife which lay beside him rolled in a mosquito net. He could only stagger about with the aid of a stick himself. Many were left by the wayside because they couldn't keep up. Neither do I know what became of others discovered and treated by roving medical teams, but who then had to be left along the forest trails because there hadn't been the time or manpower to move them, or because the next day Thai soldiers barred further entry to that area.

Late one evening, as we were about to pack up and go home exhausted, two excited journalists rushed over to tell us of a terrible discovery they had made. Further down the border was a makeshift hospital under a thatch roof on four poles set up some days earlier by another medical team but then cut off by the Thai army. Inside we discovered bloated dead bodies, the saline drips still in their arms. Others, in an appalling state, moaning intermittently, were hanging on to life by a mere thread. All around in the fading light were the ghostly shadows of hundreds more dying people. The only sound, the steady pulsating cry of the crickets. It was a nightmare.

The Sra Kaew camp was a low lying piece of hastily levelled scrubland which had been scraped bare by bulldozers, leaving a muddy rutted field full of stubborn roots. It was the height of the rainy season.

The UNHCR had been given only about forty-eight hours' notice to get the place ready to receive thousands of starving and critically-ill people. It is an eternal credit to them that they accomplished as much as they did in such a short time and in such appalling conditions.

On October 24, 1979, the first batch of about 8,000 were dumped in this quagmire. Fleets of buses and trucks from the border descended on rain-soaked Sra Kaew camp, packed tight with these weak and terror-stricken creatures. Not a few perished on the way, still propped up in the crush. The madness continued for five more days. None of us who were there that first sleepless forty-eight hours will ever forget it.

I remained at Sra Kaew late into the night, as did others all working flat out to get the sickest ones under cover and cared for. Those who were well enough were given some basic supplies and plastic sheeting and left to fend for themselves. That night the rain poured down sending torrents of water gushing down the canvas roofing onto the dying beneath. There they lay on their damp soiled mats on the muddy root-infested ground, huddled together in rows of hundreds, a great writhing black carpet of humanity. In the morning, tragically, a number of them were discovered drowned right where they lay. They were simply too weak to move themselves out of the muddy puddles which had formed around them.

More mass graves began to fill with nameless old people, youngsters and mothers, all pressed in side by side, covered in lime, and then earthed in with the red mud. One poor soul was almost buried alive, but at the last minute someone just happened to see her move. Hundreds perished in those early weeks.

The latrines flooded, drainage was virtually non existent, and the doctors and nurses arriving now in increasing numbers scrambled about in the sea of mud trying to create some semblance of order in their crowded and chaotic hospital tents. A few yards from a low tent where babies were being born, rows of dead were being laid out, rolled up in straw mats for burial. But within a few weeks the situation was transformed. The several thousand patients were in wooden beds, up off the ground. Pebbles were poured in for flooring, drainage channels were dug, and the camp gradually rebuilt.

The Khmer Rouge maintained a sinister authority in the camp. They threatened UNHCR officials who challenged their control, biting the very hands which fed them. They cruelly intimidated and tortured camp inmates who disobeyed or displeased them, in their own inimitable way. And all the time, the Thai army stood by and did nothing. Their solidarity appeared to be more with the Khmer Rouge than with the suffering Cambodian people. *Realpolitik* had triumphed over mercy.

In June 1980, about 7,000 hardcore Khmer Rouge and their supporters returned to the border to continue 'the struggle' in Cambodia. They were all fit and well, fully equipped and rebuilt, thanks directly to the Thai, and indirectly to the UNHCR and various relief organisations. The Khmer Rouge and their Thai army backers wanted many more to return, and certainly would have forcibly repatriated thousands, but this time the UNHCR were ready. After what those unfortunate people had already endured in the jungles with their Khmer Rouge bosses, the poor response to exhortations for them to return to free the motherland was hardly surprising. The Khmer Rouge, characteristically, had one of their nasty little ditties ready for the occasion:

'Those who go back first will sleep on cots,
Those who go back second will sleep on mats.
Those who go back third will sleep in the mud,
And those who go back last will sleep under the ground.'

With the departure of the Khmer Rouge, the dark shadow and tension which had hung over the camp at Sra Kaew was gone.

All this time, a quiet yet determined Christian witness had been going on in this most difficult of camps. A number of the relief organisations which did such sterling work there in those difficult early days were Christian. Literature was distributed and groups of believers and seekers after truth began meeting quietly in huts and Christian medical wards. The best Christian medical teams not only worshipped and prayed together after duty hours at home, but also began each day praying with their Cambodian helpers in the camp. The difference in the deportment and lifestyle, the priorities and outlook between these Christian medical and relief teams and the increasing volume of others crowding the notorious foreign quarters at 'tent city' near Sra Kaew was very stark indeed. Even easy going Thai soldiers expressed shock at some of the westerners' blatant immorality and godlessness.

Two overseas Cambodian Christians came to work for a short term assignment at Sra Kaew. One was a young woman, Thavy Ngeth, and the other a mature seminary trained pastor from the United States, Dararith Pen. (Before going to the States in 1965, Dara and Taing Chhirc had worked closely together as deacons at Bethany Church in Phnom Penh.) These two had a considerable impact at Sra Kaew from late 1979 to 1981 because both were Christians of the humbler kind who delighted in sacrificially serving others, not in building a kingdom or reputation for themselves.

Help also came from a number of old Cambodia hands of the Christian and Missionary Alliance who came to help in the medical work. But with their vast background in Cambodian language and culture, they were also able to witness and disciple. Within a year, about six hundred Cambodians at Sra Kaew were regularly attending Christian meetings and being taught the way of Christ. Many more came regularly, requesting Bibles and Christian counselling. Later in 1980, Pastor Hom and a number of seasoned Christians from the vast Khao I Dang camp were transferred to Sra Kaew, which now had two camps. With a godly pastor like Hom, a systematic and disciplined theologian and teacher like Dara Pen, and the help and encouragement of missionary friends, the church at Sra Kaew prospered and was built up.

Not surprisingly, there was opposition. It arose from three main quarters. The Khmer Rouge, when they were there in force, forbade their own members any contact with the Christians and threatened individuals who did become Christians with torture and even death. This intimidation took the form of calling people away from meetings, threats, and sometimes direct torture such as being shut up in an empty water tank out in the tropical sun during the hottest hours of the day. Despite their crude attempts to thwart the Christian ministry, not a few young people abandoned the Khmer Rouge and joined the church fellowships. Later, they refused to return with them to make war in Cambodia. And some who did return to Cambodia, went back rather different people from what they had once been, as a result of their contact with the gospel. It would be interesting to discover one day what became of them.

Secondly, there was the usual opposition in the form of ridicule and abuse from the hard core Buddhist community. Only this time it was given added weight by the support of some foreigners who took it upon themselves to champion the Cambodian Buddhist cultural cause. 'Christians are not true Khmers' was the line of argument. 'Alien Christianity is a dangerous threat to our ancient indigenous culture' was a popular slogan. Pastor Hom was quick to point out that what threatened the Cambodian nation was not Christianity, but the greed, corruption and belligerence which they were continuing to perpetuate.

The third point of hostility, linked to the second, came from some of the secular and cynical foreign relief workers. Though, no doubt, brilliant and dedicated people in their vocations, many were offended by the cross of Christ. Even more of a stumbling block to the church were those of the liberal and accommodating school who went by the name of 'Christian' but denied all its fundamental tenets in a blur of popular syncretism. One scholar and priest was commended by the press in a religious article for trying 'to discourage potential converts' and urging Cambodians 'to begin again from Cambodia's once powerful Buddhist roots'.

By 1981, the hostility towards Christians in Sra Kaew became such that Dara Pen's 'Emmaus Bible School' discipling programme had to reorganise and meet secretly, and the Sunday gathering for worship was suspended. Christians were advised by their leaders to keep a low profile by meeting in small house groups. None of all this was new to Cambodian Christianity, but bottled up in a crowded fenced-in refugee camp, the intensity of the pressure and immediacy of physical danger were made worse. Towards the end of 1981, these pressures did ease somewhat, helped perhaps by a thinning out of the camp population as key leaders on all sides began to leave for overseas resettlement.

Powerful secular and pseudo-religious relief giants allied to established anti-Christian and reactionary Buddhist religio-political groups, and the Thai Army High Command, could wield considerable pressure against Cambodian Christians in the emotion-charged camps. These things, however, only stiffened the Christians' resolve, and the churches were ultimately the stronger for it. It was certainly a good orientation on what to expect as they dispersed and resettled all over the strongly secular western world.

But nowhere was antagonism to the church more absolute than at the huge Khao I Dang Holding Centre for Cambodians which opened one month after Sra Kaew, in November 1979.

Having opened this so-called 'holding centre' which cost the UNHCR millions of dollars to construct and maintain, for as usual there was no water supply and it was out in the middle of nowhere, the Thai, three months later, tried to encourage all these refugees to return to the border again. But by then of course virtually all faces were set like flint towards Long Beach, California and other imagined western 'Shangri-La's'. And as soon as western embassies began sending in their people to conduct selection interviews, Khao I Dang was transformed into a powerful magnet attracting those still at the border willing to run the gauntlet of bandits and trigger-happy soldiers through the barbed wire into the sanctuary of this UNHCR camp. The pull extended even further, reaching all across Cambodia as news spread that resettlement overseas was possible from Khao I Dang. Many abandoned everything to get out. Many sacrificed all they possessed, including their self-respect, in order to pay the many bribes needed to get to the border staging areas for the final dash to Khao I Dang. Those with contacts and gold, of course, had a definite advantage. Many perished in the attempt. Others, hopelessly uprooted, found themselves compromised and stranded in these lawless, rebel-controlled border settlements, unable to return home lest they be arrested as spies for the other side. Thousands now remained stuck, helplessly trapped in this border no-man's-land for many more years. Their dreams of emigration to America had given way to the nightmare of surviving one day at a time on handouts and the black-market.

Along with tens of thousands of his countrymen moving into the Khao I Dang camp went Pastor Hom and many of the Battam-bang Christians, about twenty families in all. These included Samuel's people, Auntie Song, Auntie Siew, Granny Rose, and

Chhorn's wife and children. Later in June 1980, Pastor Reach Yeah and his family fled there too from Phnom Penh. These and other Christians entered either when it first opened, brought there on Thai trucks, or they smuggled themselves in from the border by whatever means they could.

As soon as Khao I Dang opened, a dusty twenty-five acre expanse of scrubland surrounded by barbed wire at the foot of a high headland, the Christians quickly formed house churches and became very active in evangelism all across the camp. Despite the confusion, wastage and social problems, the vast Khao I Dang camp brought over 120,000 Cambodian people together in one place where they came under the sound of the gospel. Most would probably never have heard it otherwise. Perhaps, in God's providence, what seemed from a finite, human perspective as so unwise and short-sighted, will from the perspective of eternity have been a vital chapter in the planting of the Cambodian church. Ultimately, there are no second causes.

By Christmas Day 1979, only one month after Khao I Dang opened, it was obvious that Christianity was going to be a major force in this place. As December 25 dawned brightly over the bustling, dusty, semi-built camp, over a thousand Cambodians spontaneously came together in the open air to celebrate the birth of Jesus. They were seated all over a vacant area at the back of the camp, right at the foot of the wooded mountain slope after which the camp was named. It was on this very spot, soon after, that the Christians erected a large open-sided bamboo and thatch church which could seat about a thousand people. The mountain, the Christians renamed Sinai. Throughout that Christmas Day, from a hastily erected wooden platform, the 'old Christians' from Cambodia filled the air with sounds of Christmas carols and the proclamation of Advent. Their singing echoed up the mountain side and across the vast campsite. Thousands came to ask questions, listen carefully, and take away Cambodian Christian literature. The largest Cambodian local church in this people's entire history was coming together.

For those of us who had been with the Cambodians the last time they had gathered in their thousands like this to celebrate

Christmas Day, in Phnom Penh in 1974, it was a deeply moving experience. After five terrible years, only a small remnant remained of those who had rejoiced in the birth of Jesus on that last unforgettable Christmas Day before the darkness fell. All the others were now rejoicing 'upon another shore, and in a greater light'. And although there were tears of sadness for so many missing ones, they were mixed with tears of joy as we beheld all around us the fields white unto harvest.

Early in 1980, a committee of Christians including Pastor Hom and Sokun, a former Bible School student from Takmau, a fiery preacher and brilliant organiser who had been one of the founders of Noah's Church in Phnom Penh, went to the UNHCR office in the camp to ask for permission to build a church. They were told they could. But the UNHCR officials, concerned that they might be seen to be favouring Christianity, took the initiative to put up a Buddhist temple nearby as well.

Without the considerable help and encouragement from Western aid officials, it is questionable whether a temple could ever have got under way so fast, if at all. In the old Aranyaprathet camp for example, despite frequent collections from the people for the building of a Buddhist temple, in its five-year history no temple ever materialised. But that camp had no Westerners zealous for the preservation of Buddhism to make sure it was done. Since merit for the next life can be gained through the actual act of building a Buddhist temple, which accounts for the many partly-built temples in Thailand, Laos and Cambodia, we must assume that it was the UNHCR who acquired the lion's share of this merit!

Once building supplies were delivered, the Christians set about planning and constructing as large a church as they could. But it would not be big enough. At both the two Sunday morning services a thousand or so crowded inside, and twice that many could be seen seated all around outside in the hot sun. Huge numbers also gathered early every morning for prayers. There was always some activity, some teaching programme, children's meetings, Bible memorisation or singing practice, taking place in the church seven days a week. Yet although this large and prominent building was the spiritual and administrative centre of the church at Khao I Dang, the real day-to-day grass-roots movement was taking place in up to fifty dynamic little 'house churches' which sprang up all over the camp, and a number of larger 'section churches'.

Following the pattern they had always followed in Cambodia, the Christians elected a Central Church Committee of about twenty-five men and women to oversee all the ministry of the church throughout the camp. The committee was made up of two pastors who took it in turns to chair the meetings, a president, vice president, secretary, as well as the elders, deacons, deaconesses, a representative from the growing Chinese language section of the church, and youth representatives. This larger group met weekly. But an inner core of about a dozen met early every morning to plan and pray through the day's work. The older Christians and mature teachers focused on teaching the Bible and basic Christian doctrine to the various house church leaders. The idea was for these leaders then to teach this material in their own smaller house fellowships back in their own sections and subsections of this camp metropolis.

Daily, following the large morning prayer and worship times, enthusiastic groups fanned out with literature, cassettes and posters, to systematically evangelise all through the camp. Others visited the hospital area to pray with the sick and dying. Needy widows and orphans were also cared for and warmly adopted into the church family. Prayers were said every evening in all the house churches, and each night prayer vigils were held at the main church as groups took it in turn to keep this perpetual attitude of intercession a reality. From time to time the entire church met in their thousands, seated in circles in and around the main church for entire days, even in the hot sun, devoted to prayer and fasting, especially for Cambodia. There were also marriages to prepare for, baby dedications, baptisms, counselling and exorcisms for a number of demon-possessed people who were brought by family members for deliverance. Those who had been recently delivered from demonic oppression usually lived day and night in the main church or with a pastor's family for a few weeks. Here they felt secure and could devote all their time to reading the Scriptures, prayer and receiving instruction. There were always people in the church to give counsel to anyone who came by seeking help. This bamboo thatch church, dedicated to the living God, became the real place of authentic refuge and peace in the claustrophobic and stressful refugee camp at Khao I Dang, a 'refugee camp' in the refugee camp.

Christmas and Easter were seasons of great celebration, drama and evangelism. But all through the year, the amazingly resourceful and creative young people staged tremendous dramatic and choral extravaganzas on a platform put up behind the church. Tens of thousands packed round even hanging from branches of the few surviving trees, to watch long epic stories on the life of Moses, and Daniel, or to see short but very moving dramatisations of parables such as 'The Wise and Foolish Virgins'. The church was wonderfully gifted in the areas of teaching, evangelism and administration, with a host of willing helpers. Foremost among those who worked hard behind the scenes to co-ordinate all these things was the young man Radha. He too had ended up in Khao I Dang with his wife whom the Lord had so miraculously given him, and their first child, born at the border.

The UNHCR was in no mood to aid the growth of this Christian movement by providing any more building materials. In fact they looked upon the Christians and their evangelising zeal with ambivalence at best and cynicism at worst. Faced with a virtual embargo on more visible churches, a large group of several hundred Christians in the central sector of the camp, under the leadership of one of the camp's most promising young leaders at the time, named Seth, all contributed one or two pieces of thatch or a bamboo pole from their own huts to a common pool till there was enough to erect a sizeable centre for teaching and worship. Though there were threats from Cambodian section leaders to have it torn down, the UNHCR office allowed it to remain. It proved to be a strategic centre of teaching and fellowship. Teaching sessions here often followed one after the other, with people pouring in and out of classes till late in the evening when they met around oil lamps and candles. And when Cambodian camp leaders, hoping to get rid of it, declared it illegally situated, the young men together literally lifted it up and marched with it to another site.

Another resourceful group led by an outstanding young man named Sythan built a church entirely of old rice sacks stretched over a bamboo frame. We called it affectionately 'The Sackcloth Church'. For what a joy-filled place that was as eager young disciples poured onto the mats which covered the earth floor to learn of heart repentance and faith in the Saviour. These humble house churches had a very special warmth and family-community spirit about them. Sythan and his colleagues were typical of scores of other devoted young men and women who in the radiance of first love, packed all their time and energy into wholehearted service of the one who had granted them forgiveness and everlasting life. Only a year or so before, Sythan had been one of those forced to grope around collecting human excrement for fertiliser for *Angka*'s fields. After he had mixed up a canful, they made him taste it first.

What happened at Khao I Dang was clearly a great people-movement into the church, a glorious continuation, despite the horrendous Khmer Rouge disruption and decapitation, of what had started in Phnom Penh in the early 1970s among these same middle classes of Khmer society. It was an abundant harvest. But, inevitably, as is generally the way with mass movements, it produced a plentiful crop of both wheat and tares. What the ensuing persecution at Khao I Dang did not winnow out, the choking briars and smothering thornbushes of life in the materialistic West did. It is impossible to say how much has survived, for we can only survey what is visible, and God is still working. But as tens of thousands of Cambodians from Khao I Dang and other such camps were dispersed out across the world to nations like Canada, USA, UK, France, Germany, Switzerland, Australia and New Zealand, mixed in among them was a significant minority who would continue to be salt and light in the Cambodian communities of the Diaspora.

Characteristically, opposition and persecution were not long in coming. Unlike the believers at Sra Kaew camp, they did not have to contend with the crude persecution of the Khmer Rouge, but they did have to cope with considerable hostility and abuse from fellow Cambodians supported by the secularists and pro-Buddhists from the large contingent of foreign aid workers.

By April 1980, there was a rising and increasingly vocal tide of hostility to the church in Khao I Dang. Outright slander and persecution broke out following particular events which highlighted the uniqueness of the body of Christ. With the world's media in tow and armed with telegrams of support from big names on the international Christian scene, a liberal-minded American priest arrived at Khao I Dang with the popular idea of organising a massive display of Cambodian solidarity and prayer for peace in the Motherland. The idea was to get all the religions in the camp to join hands and hearts in a massive display of ecumenical inter-religious unity under the populist banner of 'Peace'.

The Christians who hardly needed anyone to organise them into praying for Cambodia did not care to perform for this media event, let alone join hands with Buddhists and Muslims in some kind of superficial show of spiritual oneness. The Cambodian Christian leaders could find no biblical grounds for such a thing but rather warnings against it. The foreign event organisers dismissed offers to show them from the Bible why they could not participate as fundamentalist obscurantism. The organisers then tried to strike a bargain by asking the Christians to at least be willing to be filmed at their church 'on the day'. Or could they not at least let their children join in an apparently innocuous little dance with flowers and streamers. The church committee however stood its ground explaining that regularly they prayed and fasted for Cambodia, and were working hard through the gospel which transformed men's hearts, for real peace in Cambodia. The organisers were not pleased. It was very embarrassing for them that this large and most visibly active religious community in the camp would have nothing to do with their politically correct multi-religious event. Neither was it an easy thing nor indeed a natural thing for these Cambodian refugees, beholden as they were on foreigners for the very means of life, to have to refuse this request. But the church was completely united on the issue. To join in this event would be for them like 'praying with the prophets of Baal'. They stuck uncompromisingly to their unpopular but biblical position.

When the big day dawned, the other religious groups obediently went along to the meeting. They were refugees used to being pushed around, and they owed an enormous debt of gratitude to the world-wide community. Refusal didn't cross their minds. External conformity was a way of life. But for the thousands of Christians, it was a day of fear and intimidation. Some were physically bullied and dragged there by camp section leaders zealous to impress. Local Cambodian vigilantes noted their names and issued grave threats. They even warned that they would lose their regular rice ration if they didn't participate. And a number of others had threats and abuse hurled at them. Some of the Christians, especially young women, fled to the church for refuge or went into hiding till the terrible 'day of peace' was over. It is amazing how easy it has always been for outsiders to divide Khmers and get them to attack each other. Why does Khmer society lack this essential cohesiveness and national loyalty in a practical, positive, ongoing way?

But the damage was done. 'What kind of Christians were these who didn't even obey their own western Christian leaders?' grumbled the Buddhist leaders. 'They obviously have no love for Cambodia if they won't even join in a day of peace for the nation,' the people murmured. 'They have deserted and shamed their people and their nation.'

'They are no longer true Khmers.'

'They should be expelled from the camp.'

'They have offended our Buddhist-Thai hosts and should be punished.'

'They just want to go overseas.'

'They are despicable apostates adrift from the historical traditions of our people.'

Thus the outcry against the church spread all across the camp. The Christians felt reasonably safe during the daytime when UNHCR and Red Cross officials were in the camp, but in the evening after all the foreigners had left, the camp returned to 'the law of the jungle' with armed thieves, vandals and rapists breaking in from the outside, and disreputable elements among the Cambodians making trouble on the inside.

The Christians, after much heart-searching, called a halt to all their evening meetings and night-time prayer meetings in order to protect innocent people from harm. The big church was permanently occupied by some of the young men to protect it from those who threatened to come and burn it down. The house groups went 'underground', crosses were removed from atop Christian homes, and the church leaders moved quietly from place to place, sometimes even sleeping in different homes at night. It was weeks before the furore abated. Sadly, things were never quite the same again. The old fires of suspicion and hatred towards Christianity had been stoked up. The 'Day of Peace' may have massaged the egos of its foreign innovators, but for the Cambodians it had only fuelled unhappiness, division, misunderstanding and conflict. Sadly, this kind of ill-conceived and heavy handed interference in the Cambodian church by western religious groups from left to right with their own particular agendas and love of media extravaganzas, would continue to plague and distract the Cambodian church.

One day in the midst of these troubles, I recall sitting listening to Granny Rose. She was propped up in a cloth hammock in Pastor Hom's little thatch chapel, looking wearily across the camp. A withering wind was blowing up yellow dust clouds all across the now treeless site. Occasionally, she wiped her smarting eyes with the faded *krama* she had wrapped around her head. 'They will all have to learn sooner or later that to be a genuine Cambodian Christian is to suffer persecution from your own people.' And then, with a wry smile and a note of urgency entering her voice, she continued, 'I've known it for these past sixty years now, and as the day of Jesus' return draws nearer, these evil forces will grow stronger. But he has never deserted us yet. The Lord himself showed us how to persevere against the Devil during his forty days in the wilderness. Yes, when all seems to be going well, and God's children grow complacent, sitting around twittering and chattering, then trouble is at hand. Even now among the wheat, though we are unaware of it, the Evil One is sowing his tares!' Her words were prophetic.

Quick to catch the drift of things, and aware of the anti-evangelical sentiments of most of their foreign bosses, some Cambodians working in the hospital wards screening patients and interpreting for the doctors, drove away Christians who came to pray with the sick and dying or give out literature.

The Red Cross hospital had a 'Buddhist' godshelf at its entrance, and chanting monks had been invited in to 'cleanse' a new ward. A growing number of foreigners now sported Buddhist amulets around their necks. Even the 'Kruu Khmae', spirit mediums, with their black magic, were welcomed as 'indigenous healers', into wards run by the International Red Cross, to perform their incantations and 'cures' under the supervision of a Swiss social anthropologist. At this, even prominent Cambodian leaders in the camp balked, saying that this had never been permitted in hospitals even in Cambodia. These objections were dismissed by the foreign zealots and instant experts and diagnosticians of Cambodian culture as 'the prejudices of the oppressive classes'. It was an amazing spectacle to see western liberals for whom the word 'tradition' back home was a dirty word, something to be swept away, seeking to manipulate, compel and fossilise Cambodian society into some simplistic and idealised stereotype defined by them, the self-appointed guardians of Khmer culture.

It was a popular complaint by foreigners and Cambodians alike to bewail the crushing of Cambodian culture under the weight of some well-oiled Christian machine. The fact is that the Cambodian Christians ran their own affairs. Only one or two foreign Christians working in the camps could even speak the Cambodian language, and the activity of Christian workers was carefully watched by Thai Army and camp officials alike from whom passes to visit any border camp had to be obtained.

The Buddhists on the other hand outnumbered the Christians by at least twenty to one in the camp. They had the enthusiastic support of the leading international relief giants, and were surrounded by a sea of fifty-five million Buddhist Thai led by a devout and much-loved Buddhist king. The fact was, Thai Buddhists did little for the refugees in terms of any voluntary sustained physical or spiritual ministry. And within the camp, it seemed to me there were few Cambodian Buddhists prepared to seriously live and guide their people in the selfless spirit of 'the Buddha'. Instead, they increasingly came to represent the political and social forces of reaction, displaying a self-righteous siege mentality. Their principal patrons were foreign liberals and intellectuals. In Khao I Dang, it seemed that anything from Californian 'holistic healers' to Cambodian witch doctors were preferable to straightforward Bible-centred Cambodian Christians who simply wanted to pray for the sick and speak to them of Jesus Christ. The tensions, rivalries and disputes between the numerous strong-minded secular medical and relief agencies, with their various ideologies and philosophies, who came to Thailand after 1979 to 'help the Cambodian people' became inevitable as each zealously pursued what was right in their own eyes. Perhaps the only area in which they were united was their dislike of biblical Christianity, foreign and Cambodian.

One day in a 'freak' accident, the newly built Red Cross medical facility, recently blessed by chanting monks, exploded into flames and was completely destroyed. Miraculously, the fire did not spread to the rest of the camp of twenty-five acres of tightly packed dry bamboo and thatch huts. But all that remained of the expensive new hospital were the rows of blackened steel bedsteads, and the remains of one godshelf in a state of complete meltdown.

In some ways the Cambodian Christians, under the long-held but false assumption that all white people are Christians or at least sympathetic to the faith, naively stuck their heads into a number of nooses. Neither was it really possible or even appropriate, to protect them from all these dangers. They had to learn the hard way. Cynical journalists twisted their spontaneous, child-like testimonies, and purposely distorted their innocent statements out of context to create mischievous articles which showed the Christians in the worst possible light. A steady stream of visitors, photographed, filmed, and interviewed them, sometimes for their own publicity and fund-raising machinery. Others came bearing various kinds of gifts, some helpful, others burdensome. The bright yellow tee-shirts, for example, 'for Christians only' with 'Jesus in my heart' emblazoned in red, would show up on the backs of thieves and ne'er-do-wells apprehended in the camp jail, providing yet more colourful material for the media's campaign against the church. But to have aired my own misgivings would have brought down upon me not only the anger of the camera wielding donors, but the Cambodians themselves who needed new shirts!

Heads and hearts were easily turned by any clever con man or cult especially if they came with material goods and promises of sponsorship to the West. Total honesty was sometimes sacrificed on the popular altar of expediency when it came to interviews with embassy staff for emigration. Some thought that having a Christian baptism certificate in their file would enhance their chances of resettlement in the 'Christian' West. Embassy representatives were not impressed. The study and use of English in the church gradually grew in importance and prestige. A generous sprinkling of English words in the sermon was bound to impress. The preference for the external trappings of western Christianity, such as choir robes, western musical instruments, collars and ties etc over things indigenous, did nothing to dispel the universal belief among Cambodians generally that Christianity is a western religion and Cambodian converts had abandoned their culture to become second-rate western clones. Reports on numbers of 'converts' tended to be overstated rather than erring on the side of caution as some, perhaps too quickly elevated to leadership in the church, became puffed up with pride. Power politics and vainglory inevitably raised their ugly heads. But considering what a massive 'people movement' this was, and with so few mature and wise Cambodian Christian leaders surviving to pastor them, and with so many tares having been sown, the church at its height in 1980-82 conducted itself remarkably well. It was sometimes a temptation to want to stride in and rip out what looked like a harmful 'weed', even at the risk of uprooting the wheat. Spiritual collapse and falling away occurred later, after they had left Khao I Dang and moved to resettle in the 'well watered cities of the plain' of western civilisation.

What began as a 'holding centre' inevitably became a refugee camp like all the others with thousands being selected for settlement in a 'third country', and thousands more being left behind in limbo to become full-time refugees, dependent, indolent, the lassitude of the refugee sub-culture slowly taking over. Camps like Khao I Dang begin with a bang but end with a whimper. The nations came and took those they desired and left the others behind for Thailand, Malaysia and Hong Kong to worry about. By the end of the 1980s the 'party' was definitely over, and no one was really interested in the 'dregs' left behind. On the Thai border these 'unwanted', 'unchosen' ones would linger for another decade till they were all repatriated to largely Khmer Rouge controlled areas of Cambodia in 1993. In many cases their second state being worse than the first.

An expensive processing 'half way house' camp at Phanat Nikom, halfway down the road west to Bangkok, was constructed for the westward bound refugees. In Bangkok, several transit centres such as Lumpini, Suan Plu and Din Daeng housed multitudes more for final health and immigration clearance in the week or so before they finally boarded the great silver birds which would bear them up and away, thousands of miles from Cambodia physically and light years psychologically.

All the way down the line from border camp to transit centre, Christian missionaries and volunteers ministered to the refugees' physical, emotional and spiritual needs. YWAM[1] was one mission which sent scores of committed young Christian people out into refugee ministry in Thailand. These people were willing to do absolutely anything. And YWAM was never ashamed of the gospel or of boldly identifying with God's people, even if that meant being given the cold shoulder from other more accommodating and sophisticated groups.

I remember one occasion talking to some Cambodians in a transit centre when a group of YWAM youths emerged scruffily dressed from the latrines. They had been voluntarily cleaning out the absolutely foul camp toilets. (Toilet habits left much to be desired. Most of these rural folk were not used to modern toilets anyway and found the idea of sitting on a public toilet seat quite disgusting.) The refugees had little sense of pride in these crowded transit camps in Bangkok. The Cambodians seeing this international slop brigade were convinced that they must have all been criminals, probably drug addicts, who had been caught by the Thai and this was their punishment. They could not believe that a white man or woman would be doing such a filthy job otherwise. I told the Cambodians that these young people were not criminals, but Christians who were cleaning up 'your filth' in service to Jesus and in love for them just as Jesus had done.

Cambodians are not automatically impressed by or comprehend works of humble service and egalitarian gestures. On the contrary, they might more readily assume that such people are inferior, criminal or foolish, bereft of merit, to be despised in fact. There was a fine American Christian doctor who came to work for a while at the Aranyaprathet camp. Since no one else was willing to scrub down the dirty blood-spattered walls inside the ward, he appeared one day in blue jeans, rolled up sleeves and carrying a bucket of soapy water. He happily cleaned up the dirty ward himself. But when word of what he had done spread across the camp, some were horrified, and the conclusion was generally drawn that he must be a useless second-rate doctor if he had no more self-respect and dignity than that. Doctors were meant to look and behave like doctors, wear a white coat, give orders, leave the dirty work to lesser beings and turn the situation into some personal profit for their superior selves. Cambodians are very conscious of social and educational class, rank and wealth; even lightness of skin is seen as a mark of beauty and superiority. These attitudes are deeply entrenched. What we externally are and have denotes good or bad *karma*, the result of the good or bad we have done in previous incarnations. It therefore affects the way we are treated by others. One cannot ignore these clashes of philosophy and culture.

Alice Compain of OMF was probably the most well-known of the transit camp Christian workers as she orientated newer workers and helped thousands of refugees all through those traumatic and chaotic years of dislocation and resettlement. With her team of helpers, including Thai Christians, she clothed the refugees for European winters, and visited those left sick and dying in Bangkok hospitals or detained in prisons. She maintained a vast practical and pastoral correspondence with Cambodians and Christian contacts overseas and provided orientation on life for them for wherever they were going. She also gave wise spiritual counsel, linked refugees to relatives and supportive groups, opened her home for fellowship, liaised with Thai officials, organised special events, co-ordinated the printing of masses of Christian literature in various languages and performed a thousand and one other personal and domestic services for the Cambodian people she loved. But most of all, Alice will be remembered by most of us sitting calmly midst the bedlam of shrieking children, drying clothes, cooking pots, bedrolls, loudspeakers, and the accumulated noise of hundreds of restless refugees crowded into a stifling airless transit centre, playing beautiful melodies on her violin for a group of Christians sitting cross-legged around her with their Bibles and hymn books open before them.

It was here that Alice began noticing, collecting and sorting scores of new indigenous Khmer hymns and spiritual songs which certain gifted Cambodian Christians were composing, using their own musical heritage, and arising from profound experiences in their spiritual pilgrimage and in response to the Scriptures. In 1989, as a companion to the old Cambodian hymn book of translated hymns, a complete new Cambodian hymn book was published. It contained about two hundred of these wonderful Khmer tune hymns. Today, ancient and modern Khmer melodies are being enjoyed by Cambodian Christians all over the world from Cambodia to California. They are an inspiration for more Cambodian nightingales like Mr Sam Sarin, now settled in Australia, to put the timeless truths of God to the best of Cambodia's extensive classical and folk repertoire. Used by evangelists and radio broadcasters to Cambodia such as the Far East Broadcasting Corporation, this music will broaden the appeal of their programmes with a distinctive Khmer flavour, theology, and testimony. I am not convinced that the modern western charismatic choruses being translated and popularised in Cambodia today, any more than a previous generation of translated Moody and Sankey hymns, will be nearly as resonant in the ears of the millions of Cambodia's rural folk as the familiar sounds of their own rich musical heritage.

One of the most remarkable Cambodian refugees I discovered in the Lumpini transit centre in Bangkok was a former Lon Nol soldier named Sothy. He was completely blind having had his eyes burned out in a Khmer Rouge gas attack. He had been a typical wild-living young soldier, a womaniser, heavy drinker, and brawler as the scars on his head clearly showed. But now he was much humbled, and testified, 'The Lord had to take away my physical eyes in order to enlighten the eyes of my heart.' He was gifted musically and loved to play hymns on the traditional Cambodian two-string violin I had made for him by a craftsman in the Aranyaprathet camp. Wonderfully, he had a companion, Ham, about the same age but physically weak due to some injury he had received in Cambodia. When they went off to Germany together, Ham was Sothy's eyes and Sothy was Ham's arms: and both of them were complete in Jesus Christ.

By the second half of 1981, weekly flights from Bangkok had transported tens of thousands of Cambodians out of Thailand from the newer camps like Khao I Dang, and Sra Kaew II where only months before they had arrived close to death. As a result, the large Christian communities in these camps began to thin out and lose their dynamic early leaders and mature Christians.

The great harvest of wheat and tares garnered in the Cambodian refugee camps in Thailand beginning in 1975 and peaking in 1981 was now to be threshed and winnowed. It was gathered up, trampled over by many feet, and tossed to the four winds. Time and testimony would soon reveal the good seed sown by the Lord, and the tares sown by the world, the flesh and the devil.

CHAPTER 14

THE GLEANINGS

'Yet some gleanings will remain, as when an olive tree is beaten,
leaving two or three olives on the topmost branches, four or
five on the fruitful boughs,' declares the Lord, the God of Israel.

(Isaiah 17:6)

All through the decade of the 1980s, dust and ashes were settling over the brown stubble of the Cambodian harvest fields. It settled over the burnt-out battlefields of Vietnam's lightning invasion of Cambodia, and the scorched earth left behind by the fleeing Khmer Rouge. It settled over the Thai border and the refugee camps beyond where it had been kicked up in great clouds by multitudes of Cambodians who stampeded there for refuge in late 1979.

It was possible to walk through these two fields where the great harvests of 1970-75 in Cambodia and 1975-1981 in the refugee camps had been gathered in. Most of the grain from the first field had now fallen back into the ground and died. And most of the grain from the second field, with many tares in it, had been exported overseas to be winnowed on foreign threshing floors. But remaining in both the fields were gleanings, precious baskets full of grain still on the ground after the euphoria was over and the harvesters had left.

By the end of 1979 as tens of thousands of dazed Cambodians were returning to Phnom Penh, the few Christians remaining among them were meeting in five places in and around the capital: Bung Yipun, Duey Mec, the Old Market, at Tumnup Tik with Pastor Reach Yeah, and at Praek Talong near the former Bible School at Takmau with Pastor Siang.[1] There were in these five or six meeting places a total of two hundred or so Christian brothers and sisters, mostly old Christians and their families. These were the remnant, the precious gleanings, all that remained of the thousands of that earlier harvest.

As in former days, when they met, there were hymns, prayers, and Bible readings. Children would recite memorised texts, and small groups of singers presented special songs of praise. But most moving of all were the many testimonies proclaiming the Lord's provision and deliverance through the terrible Pol Pot years. The leader or pastor would teach from a passage of Scripture, and close the meeting with exhortations to forsake sin and faithfully follow the Lord.

In June 1980 for the first time in over five years there were baptisms in the Bassac River at Takmau. Early in the morning about fifty believers gathered for worship and the breaking of bread. Then they listened to the testimonies of the nineteen new Christians about to be baptised. It was a most joyous occasion reminiscent of the mass baptisms in those exciting and urgent days of 1974-75. But, as then, storm clouds of opposition were again gathering around them.

In mid 1980, the brief 'honeymoon' the church had enjoyed, as the new regime supported by up to 200,000 Vietnamese troops consolidated itself, came to an end. The vital breathing-space however had permitted the Christians to discover one another and assess the new realities. Clearly only a tiny percentage of the 1975 church had survived 'the killing fields'. The Christian community had been almost totally destroyed in Cambodia, but not quite. In terms of leadership, three pastors were still alive. One of these, Pastor Hom, had fled to Khao I Dang in Thailand with about forty of the Battambang Christians in November 1979. Another, Pastor Reach Yeah, would soon join them, escaping from Phnom Penh in June 1980 as pressure on the beleaguered remnant intensified. Even the ageing Pastor Siang felt it wise to leave for the Thai border and spent some months in Khao I Dang in the early 1980s. But later he returned home to his family who were still in Phnom Penh. This elderly pastor was therefore the only one of the active pre-1975 Khmer Evangelical Church pastors left in the country who didn't perish under the Khmer Rouge or emigrate.

It was a grave disappointment to Pastor Reach Yeah, when, after four years of total suppression under Pol Pot's *Angka*, this new regime began to crack down on their small Christian gatherings. Armed soldiers of the new pro-Vietnamese puppet government were dispatched to evening prayer meetings and Sunday worship services to order them closed as illegal and subversive meetings. What few Bibles they had were confiscated. They were told that they must stop believing in God and cease all Christian activity. One Sunday as Reach Yeah was teaching at Tumnup Tik on the subject of suffering from the Book of Acts, the place was surrounded by soldiers. The church meeting was forcibly closed. After this happened a second time, Reach Yeah himself was kept under constant surveillance and accused of being an agent of the CIA.

When a delegation of Christian elders went to the government seeking recognition and permission to hold meetings for Christian worship, this was refused absolutely. Once again, despite the danger, the Christians dispersed, hid their fragments of literature and met secretly 'underground' in homes and secluded gardens in groups of three to five people. Marriages, funerals and Christian festivals were maintained, but cautiously, and only in the company of those whom they knew and trusted. Infiltration, betrayal and arrest were ever-present realities. This pressure and uncertainty continued to a greater or lesser extent right through the 1980s.

The reasons, though baseless, for the government's hostility and suspicion towards the church are not difficult to understand. Firstly, successive Cambodian governments and the people at large had never really liked Cambodian Christians. The church all through its history had been regularly used as a handy scapegoat, particularly in times of trouble. And it never took much to stir up popular anger against Christianity among the Buddhist masses by scheming and corrupt politicians under the back-scratching slogan of Khmer nationalism. Why should this government, a communist one at that, be any different?

Secondly, the People's Republic of Cambodia was a totalitarian government, based theoretically on Marxism-Leninism and financed by the Soviet Union. Philosophically it was on a collision course with theistic Christianity. Indeed a number of its key leaders such as President Heng Samrin, Party Chief Chia Sim, and Prime Minister Hun Sen were until mid-1978 leaders among the Khmer Rouge. Can a political leopard really change its spots? Politicians, if they want to survive in power, invariably season their ideology with pragmatism, and this lot were no exception. There was recognition of minority Islam, and one sect of Buddhism as Cambodia's national religion, was enjoying a state-sponsored renaissance. But still, only elderly men were permitted to become monks. And with all the much politicised and gruesome mass graves and mountains of skulls now being unearthed across the country, a host of new shrines and altars were revitalising the powerful bedrock animism of the masses.

Thirdly, the regime still had many internal and external enemies. The re-grouped and re-armed Khmer Rouge, from their sanctuaries along the timber- and gemstone-rich Thai border were growing in strength, striking ever deeper and closer to the government's vital arteries. The Khmer Rouge-dominated anti-Vietnamese, liberation front set up in 1982 under Sihanouk was now supported by the United Nations, the 'West' and by ASEAN. It was not surprising that such a government, Marxist, isolated diplomatically, facing an economic blockade and pressurised militarily, looked with suspicion on western Christian aid workers who fraternised with a local Christian movement. The church was viewed as a potentially dangerous 'fifth column', a 'CIA conspiracy', definitely not to be trusted.

It was after three such westerners had visited the home of Sophiep[2] in Phnom Penh for a Christmas gathering in 1980 that this young Cambodian Christian leader was arrested, accused of being a CIA agent and imprisoned. Sophiep, formerly a Bible teacher with the Maranatha fellowship of churches, had begun discipling a small gathering of new and old Christians. One

Sunday evening, about 7.30 pm, as he was walking home, he became aware that he was being followed. They came upon him guns drawn, and with his hands in the air he was marched off to be interrogated.

'You are holding meetings in your home! How many have you held? What were they for? What was the one on December 24th all about?'

'We are Christians. We are meeting together to celebrate Christmas.'

'Why are you a Khmer celebrating Christmas? This is a western religion!'

'I am a Christian.'

Sophiep explained that he had been a follower of Jesus Christ these several years, and that it was his custom to pray every morning and evening, and on Sunday, the day of Christ's resurrection, to meet with God's people to worship him. He then went on to describe to his interrogator the full meaning and importance of Christmas. But the man was adamant:

'Will you confess this error?'

'No. I am a Christian.'

'You are working for the CIA.'

'No, I am a Christian.'

'Then you will be imprisoned! Have you anything more to say?'

'Nothing more.'

Sophiep was taken and locked in a small, dark and windowless cell and fed almost nothing. But as many other Christians have discovered in such circumstances, he was profoundly aware of God's presence with him there in the prison. He was filled not with fear but courage and joy. He was able to continue worshipping and praying. But as the months went by Sophiep's body grew weaker and weaker.

Among the other prisoners crowded into the filthy cell of that ancient and decaying prison was a very sick old man lying helplessly against a back wall. 'Which God is it that you cry out to?' the old man asked him one day. 'The living God, the Creator and Saviour of the whole world,' Sophiep replied, going over to talk with him. The young man was amazed how the Lord brought

Scripture texts back to him and spoke so wisely through him to the old man who was clearly dying. 'Come to me, you who are weary and heavy laden and I will give you rest. Take my yoke upon you and learn of me, for I am gentle and humble in heart, and you will find rest for your souls. For my yoke is easy and my burden is light.' Sophiep repeated to him the universal and unconditional invitation of Jesus to 'Come, follow me.' The old man accepted, confessing his sins and believing the gospel. Two weeks later he died. Sophiep thanked God for bringing him to the prison for this poor dying man's sake, and he rejoiced that now this old prisoner was finally free, with Jesus in glory.

More interrogations and threats followed, but Sophiep remained 'stubborn'. He was put in leg irons, in solitary confinement, and on starvation rations, but nothing would break his will. Sometimes he was questioned by Cambodian guards, sometimes by Vietnamese, and always his answer was the same: 'I am a Christian.' If they were determined to find him guilty of anything, then it would have to be for this confession alone.

He was now very thin and weak. When they found him lying one morning in his leg irons, eyes closed and still, he was taken to a hospital. 'He is dying,' he heard them say. It was in the familiar old Chinese Hospital that he now found himself with a bottle of serum dripping into his arm, and a guard sitting beside him.

The Cuban medic who attended to him was a young man of about twenty-five. He was unusually kind and attentive to Sophiep. One Sunday morning when they were alone, and the Cuban asked him how he was, Sophiep told him that he was here because he was a Christian. The young medic smiled, leaned forward and whispered, 'I too am a Christian and a child of God.' (Cubans were regarded as safe by the regime since Cuba was a friendly communist pro-Soviet nation also.)

From that day on, the young Cuban passed secret messages to Sophiep's wife and family and even managed to arrange a discreet visit. He delayed the return to prison for as long as he could, protesting that the patient was still too weak to return. But finally, back to prison Sophiep went, though it was to a cleaner cell and with improved food rations.

Sophiep, however, refused to eat. 'I am willing to die here if that is your will,' he prayed. 'Get him back to the hospital quick!' the chief prison officer ordered when he saw him a few days later. The following Sunday, in the hospital, his Cuban Christian friend found him. 'Can you walk?' he asked. 'Just about,' replied Sophiep. The medic gave him two bottles full of serum and told him to be ready when the guard left that evening for his dinner. Sophiep prayed hard all through the day. What was his brother planning? That evening there was a great storm which kept people off the streets. At seven o'clock the guard finally left. Then the Cuban appeared with a change of clothing and some food supplies for him. He led Sophiep to a door. 'This is the way out,' he said. 'Now, go quickly!' No one saw him leave. He went straight to a friend's house where he hid till all the family were gathered and ready for the long and hazardous flight to the Thai border. They had no other choice but to flee.

In 1981, several months after Reach Yeah, Sophiep also made it to the Thai border where I met him. Both these brothers and their families were eventually resettled in the United States. (Sophiep, after further theological studies, returned to minister once more in his beloved Cambodia in the 1990s, following the restoration of freedom of religion.)

* * *

The soldiers had been very angry at seeing a foreigner sitting in Reach Yeah's Christian assembly at Tumnup Tik in 1980. They assumed the pastor was working under the direction of this white man. When government officials came to Pastor Siang's group, the situation was the same. In January 1981, he was obliged to sign his name to an official banning order, terminating all public gatherings and activities of 'the Jesus religion' from that day forward. The directive had come down from the Central Committee of the Communist Party. It was a further blow to a church already fearful following the flight of former church president, Pastor Reach Yeah. 'From now on you must meet for worship under your mosquito nets,' Siang exhorted the believers at their final meeting together.

The old pastor, despite being imprisoned himself for a long time, was not daunted and continued to quietly visit the Christian homes and encourage his flock. He also travelled about the countryside looking for isolated believers, witnessing and preaching. On two occasions he even turned up at the sprawling Thai border settlements in search of Bibles and Christian literature. I was able to provide him and others with as much as they could carry on their bicycles, the several hundred kilometres back to Phnom Penh.

I recall one very memorable day when this border camp was abuzz with rumours that the Vietnamese were planning to gas the camp. All the foreign aid workers had left. But Margaret and I were determined to keep our planned rendezvous with the pastor and his entourage. Prayerfully, we searched the hushed and dusty squatter camp till we found him, smiling and jovial, wearing a weather-beaten trilby, patiently awaiting the Christian literature we had brought. Later, some German Red Cross staff working at the border were very angry when they saw that the literature was Christian, and they tried to confiscate it. But when their youthful Cambodian interpreters met the saintly old pastor they didn't have the heart to take away his precious cargo. He told them that this 'food and medicine' was of far more lasting efficacy than what they were dispensing. And anyway, the Cambodian youngsters had a deep cultural respect for this godly old man and could not understand what these foreigners were so upset about.

During this difficult time for the church in Phnom Penh, one of my former students from the Phnom Penh Youth Centre, a young woman who sold flowers in the market, would deliver important messages among the Christians, hiding them carefully in bunches of flowers which she would deliver to their homes.

While pressure on the church in Phnom Penh was intense, out in the provinces where Christians gathered quietly in small villages and provincial towns they were less troubled. In Siem Riep province, and in several Battambang villages, despite the departure of Pastor Hom and a number of key families, it was mostly faithful elderly 'aunties' and 'grannies' who kept the flickering fires of faith burning. They gathered the Christians together for fellowship in their homes to pray, sing and read the Scriptures. What they lacked in formal Biblical and theological knowledge, they made up for in prevailing prayer, childlike faith, and the joy of the Lord.

In other rural areas, the gleanings were very sparse and scattered indeed. A few small groups were meeting, though some dared not sing aloud or testify. In one village in Siem Riep province, the Christians were forbidden to meet. For the most part it was two or three families, mostly older Christians, gathering together in a home. In far-off places such as in Kampong Thom and Kratie there remained only one or two believing families. The church buildings in Kampong Cham and Battambang had been totally destroyed, as had Horeb and Sarepta Church in Phnom Penh. Occasionally, some of these provincial Christians travelled to Phnom Penh in search of their former Christian leaders, Bibles and hymn books.

For isolated Christians and secret believers cut off from the main body of Christians in Phnom Penh, the one-hour morning and evening Khmer Christian broadcasts over FEBC from the Philippines were a great encouragement. Now radios were allowed, and despite imperfect reception, limited resources, and a programme content which to begin with at least, lacked variety and relevance to Cambodians enduring the realities of a communist dictatorship, the broadcasts did provide a clear focus and teaching to the beleaguered church in Cambodia. It was especially heart-warming for some older rural believers because they could actually recognise the Cambodian voices they heard. The broadcasters were much-loved Christians from earlier days, like San Hay Seng (Lim Cheong), originally from Kampong Cham but now in California preparing taped material for broadcast to Cambodia; or the beautiful voice of Kim Ny, daughter of Kuch Kong, pastor of the Pailin church till he fled to Thailand and on to Texas in 1975. In the early 1990s, isolated groups of Cambodian believers were discovered who had never met another Christian before. They met around a radio set and did as they were instructed over the airwaves. They may have put up a cross in the home and they knew how to pray. They had been led to faith in the Saviour by radio evangelism and ministry alone.

Not only did the tiny remnant of the church in Cambodia face external threats, but internal problems also hampered its growth. Many of these surviving Christians were untaught, had been brutalised by the Khmer Rouge and, because of poverty, were vulnerable to temptation. The major pitfalls were greed and infidelity and the petty jealousies which arose as a result of well meaning gifts from overseas. It was no easy thing to live with integrity in a society where rampant bribery and corruption were a way of life. The problem of promiscuity and unfaithfulness, common enough in Cambodia at the best of times, was further exacerbated by the death of most of the young men at the hands of the Khmer Rouge. Huge numbers of widows remained, helpless and vulnerable, trying to raise their children and care for their aged relatives in these chaotic war-torn post Khmer Rouge years of the 1980s. With their lives in ruins, personal survival and security were all that mattered. With women outnumbering men by perhaps six to one, and so many widows and marriageable girls looking for husbands, men were in great demand. A man could literally sell himself to the highest bidder. Many moved from woman to woman with impunity. Unfortunately, some Christians also deserted their spouses and committed adultery. Others, backslidden, embittered, desperate, turned traitor or stumbled others. There was a tragic lack of biblical knowledge, teaching, and good example. The church had lost its institutional structure and leadership. New believers, too quickly elevated to leadership, became proud and careless. The problem of 'rice Christians' was inevitable given the grinding poverty. Despite the end of the Khmer Rouge extermination policies, these post 'killing fields' years were a very dangerous and precarious time for the church, 'harassed and helpless like sheep without a shepherd'. These weaknesses as well as the strengths which became rooted during the difficult 1980s, would continue to bear fruit in the 1990s.

What follows now is a selection of letters and reports from surviving Christians in Cambodia, some of whom we had known before 1975, which began reaching us in Thailand in 1979. Their own struggling words in English speak clearly for themselves:

Phnom Penh, February 1980

Dear Sister, [written to Alice Compain of OMF]

…We have been separated for a long time since the change of the late Cambodian government and the downfall of the Khmer republican regime on 17 April, 1975 on account of the Reds' attacks. During the time of suffering, I'm sure that, by Christian love, you would pray for Cambodian Christians… How much we Christians suffered during the black era of scarcity, famine, oppression and murder! The beginning of the Reds' ruling was the ending of our church attending. But as the matter of fact that event created subsequently an existence of 'a silent church' through our Cambodia… They destroyed the cross and burnt the Bible to let the world know that there was no church nor congregation there. They taught the people not to depend upon God but to love the Khmer Great Communist Party obeying and following its absolute platform. Eventually, we had no church nor Bible School to attend at all. You would know thus how hardly we Christians acted our responsibility toward God. In the location I lived in, I never saw a single Christian besides my wife. It came to reason that we were truly isolated. I communicated God personally and worshipped him silently without the sound of your violin being played and accompanied the chorus as before. I worshipped God early in the morning before going to my daily manual labour and agricultural practice. I worshipped God spiritually while I was ploughing and was harrowing the rice field. Sometimes I sang hymns while I was doing hard works such as carrying the seedling, transporting the manure by buffalo-cart, cutting wood and timber in the heart of the jungle, digging irrigation ditches, building canal systems, trail, causeway, dam, reservoir and so on…

I thanked God for changing the heart of the Reds' rural acting administrators and their detectives to never find faults with me during the period of my captivity. In as much as I got to my first chosen lodge in a never lived village called 'The fig tree', I was kept in a prison hidden in a jungle of Cambodian-Vietnamese eastern border in Prey Veng province, Eastern Region for 463 days. The guardian chief doubted my morning prayer and mealtime thanksgiving. Once, he asked me openly in an evening re-construction meeting in the presence of the Reds' quarter officials and members of Security Board for a certain answer. I was surrounded by the guards and the group of prisoners looking eagerly at me to hear my reply. 'I pray to a living God and I thank the God of mercy and loving kindness whose name is Jesus,' answered I. 'He's a Jesus believer!' they uttered their voice. I sat still down and waited for the moment of judgement. At that time I prayed God that my heart would be comforted unless they would neither oppose my will in believing God nor sent me out to an isolated square land. God knew my heart and answered my demand. The judge of the prison court didn't sentence me to death. On the contrary, he declared his statement as follows:

> The articles of our new constitution allow Cambodians to choose faith and religion for themselves as they want, but they are forbidden to follow an undeveloped religion at any case. You could keep on believing your God if it doesn't break our revolutionary ethic laws in everything you act. And we require and urge you furthermore to devote your energy largely to your duties toward our Communist Party in defending and building up our nation.

Under the shadow of the darkened waxing moon light, standing by the window of the cell, I in awesome wondered God's mighty handiworks and began to sing 'Then sing my soul, My Saviour God to Thee. How great Thou art, how great Thou art...,' while the drops of the rain were beating the roof and the ground. I liked to sing, 'Nearer, My God, to Thee' when came the time of weariness. I perceived that even though in captivity, God continually and abundantly poured down peace and assurance upon my heart. No one came to console me in the cell but Jesus could. Facing day after day worry, distress, suffering, famine and plague, two third of the prisoners couldn't endure living and subsequently died. I thanked God, my good shepherd for his loving care and satisfactory feeding in keeping me alive until now to tell you the evidence of his love and mercy which I experienced by myself in him in captivity...

...I had kept records of such strange and never seen things. On October 1978, I and my family were exiled to a hill village in Pursat province, North-eastern Region. There, many innocent men, ladies, young people, children and infants were seriously slaughtered without cause. Such crime and extermination were brought about as the result of strong, absolute and unfeeling decision of the Red's Chairman. My sister-in-law Bopha, twenty-one years of age, was killed with her troop of ninety young mobile girls while she was carrying paddy from the threshing floor to a granary and was buried in a bloody ditch alongside Svay Don Keo Riverbank. My brother-in-law Pong, nineteen years old was killed and buried in an abandoned stable on February 1979 while he was working in his jobsite of the construction of a trail. My mother-in-law and her youngest son were shot to death when they tried to escape from 'the people mobilisation' to the hill camps in Cardamome Range. At last my son Lyda, one-year-old-and-half was died in measle and dysentery. To be saved, both I and So, my wife decided to take a flight from that land of the deads. I left the exiled land and went downstream to the wilderness on the shore of the Great Lake. Few weeks later we continued our return trip eastward to Phnom Penh, on Friday, June 8, 1979. Walking about three hundred kilometres, we made out a return in a duration of forty-eight days. I came back in my search for my Christian friends. I searched Bethany Church for Bible and hymn book but I found nothing at all. It was changed to become the Campus of the RD Vietnamese Embassy. They took Takmau Bible School as a provincial hospital. Pastor Reach Yeah had come into Phnom Penh too. I met M S O, former Bethany Church helper and his wife, brother S and his family, some Bible School students and other Christians youth who are still alive. I thank the Lord again for keeping his children alive so that they endured the late Reds' government and finally could return safely from the shadow of death to their real fact of hope. They have formed a small church in the heart of sad Cambodia. They are gathering together to worship God, glorifying God, singing praises to God and praying God. They share their property to help each other even though they're not rich. Under the leadership of Pastor Reach Yeah, we, Cambodian Christians have made a motion to our today government to have freedom in worshipping God. We plan to open an evangelical church again. But up to now we have never received such an agreement from the Minister.

How much happy I am to hear hymn chorus and Khmer traditional Christian songs again in the tape sent from Thailand. Mr J has part in our congregation today. He has brought Cambodian Bible and hymn book and has distributed them to us in any way he could. The Bible had been mostly burnt few years ago, how glad and how happy we are to read it again! The Word of God never changes and his promises come true...I think that the activities and events which I keep tracks in this letter shall be an encouragement of faith to those who are in sorrow and distress. And I believe that it is better to share you some strengthening verses to memorise the grace and mercy the Lord Jesus has given to me when I was in captivity 'The Lord is my shepherd; I shall not want. Yea, though I walk through the valley of the shadow of death, I will fear no evil: for thou art with me; thy rod and thy staff they comfort me. Thou preparest a table before me in the presence of mine enemies... Surely goodness and mercy shall follow me all the days of my life.' Psalm 23:1,4,5,6... Tell Christian friends in Thailand that we, in Phnom Penh, rejoice tapes of songs and testimony from refugees' camps and churches very much. Bring them all my good wishes and my very familiar greeting in the Lord Jesus Christ.

If you meet N S whose nickname is Chhan, Mr T C's cousin, please let him know about me. Tell him that I got married to So, former girl member of Bethany Church. She brought birth to twin daughters whose name are Sisera and Temah. They are taken names after church attendants from two sub-clans, in the time that Ezra, the prophet came from Babylon to Jerusalem for the service in the Temple of God...

Is brother Andrew Way in Thailand? His works and good deeds are still remaining in my memory. As Bethany Church youth, I spent a fortnight to stay and pray with him before opening of OMF Youth Centre in the Khmer Republic. During Chadomuk Crusade 75 at National Conference Hall, I helped him as a guide and interpreter. I even translated his first teaching lecture 'Love and Obey'. I'm here missing him very much, thinking of him and praying for his works for the sake of the Lord Jesus Christ...

And you, sister, do you remember me? While you were playing your violin, I sang the top line. In the past, I sang 'Farewell, dear friends...' in Shalom but today I'm singing 'We'll meet again, may God bless you all,' is that OK? Pray for me that I will have no intention to quit my country but love my guilty nation with all my heart and serve my ignorant people with all my strength.

May the Lord be with you and his children in Thailand. May there be an increase in numbers of his church in all over the world.

With love in Christ Jesus!
Affectionately yours,
M S

Translated from Cambodian:
Phnom Penh, May 18, 1982

Information

…about the bodies of the Christians in Cambodia, who having left this world, were buried in the Kombole Cemetery, near Phnom Penh.

The Reds (Khmer Rouge) dug up all the coffins and strewed the bones all around near the opened graves. Every grave was vandalised. Our investigation showed not one coffin left in its grave.

As for the grave of Rev David W Ellison, it was dug open to great depth and the bronze coffin was taken away, though we found some of his bones. We have led some of the Christians in placing his bones back in his grave. As well as placing all of the bones of the Chinese, Vietnamese and Cambodian Christians back in their graves too.

We have not been able to mound all the graves yet. Only the grave of Rev David W Ellison has been completely remounded again, the one with the marker:

Acts 20: 27-32
David W Ellison
born 1898
left earth for heaven 1963

Pray for us as we take time out and lead the Christians in fixing up all these graves that have not been fully remounded…

Phnom Penh, Cambodia

…For a very long time now I have been living in much suffering and no Christians have known or heard about it yet. In 1975 I planned to walk straight to Thailand, to Surin, where I wished to serve God. But God did not allow me to go at the time when I started. It wasn't God's will. The boat sank in the Chatomouk river. Fortunately, God did not allow us to drown.

For my family travelling was difficult with my young children. In a short time they would be tired out. They could not go fast and needed a lot of rest. Then Pol Pot's army prevented us going on and made us live in their village and work for them. From 1975 to 1976 they separated husbands, wives and children and didn't allow them to live together. They were afraid that the people would escape to Thailand. They took me from my children and made me work on a dam at O-Lous with others at the edge of the forest, near the mountains. They made my husband work very hard. Their purpose was for him to die very soon. They made people all over Cambodia suffer a great deal.

Eventually two of my four children died without seeing my husband again, and then he died. While I had to work there, I had no feelings. I seemed to be living at the bottom of a well, where I couldn't see anything, just a wall around me. I didn't know the day or the month, just complete darkness as at night. Every day they forced me to work. I had hardly any rest. I ate only leaves mixed with rice soup and tapioca (these can both be poisonous, if you don't know how to make it properly). I never had enough food to eat. They forced me to work hard and obey their rules. I lived completely at their mercy with no liberty. If they had wanted to kill me, they could have done so, but I am thankful that God spared my life, and that now I have met with Christians again…

…After the Vietnamese came, the Pol Pot communists took all the people to hide. There was much suffering. I thank God for sending a Christian family to me for a short time in my sorrow. About ten days after that my mother and my younger brother came and took me and my children to live in Srok Koh, which is my birthplace. But there I did not feel comfortable as a child of God, to worship only a dumb statue, whereas I obey and fear God. Was it all right to live together? I decided that only three others should live with me; my mother and two children.

Some neighbours make a living by planting vegetables: long beans, cabbages, cucumber, turnips. They are the gardeners and give me their produce to sell. I exchange the vegetables for rice which I bring back to them, and they give me rice for myself and my children…

…The Christians and the teachers (meaning the teaching church leaders) are very sad because there is no church…

…Everyone is worried and cries until the tears come, and I cry too and pray to God to look upon me, for my flesh is weak but I always attend to my soul. If it pleases God and his Son, his people in Cambodia will not be totally destroyed.

Please spread this news and make it known to all the Christians. Please pray to God to help his servant who is taking the opportunity to spread the Good News and on 25th November 1979 saved the souls of nine people (seven old people and two young people) who believed. Thank God.

A few of God's children are alive here. Let us read God's Word and pray and praise him, singing loudly in our hearts with all the children of God.

In closing, may God be with you. I am sorry that I am sleepy and cannot keep my eyes open. My letter is at an end and I say goodbye to you.

K H[3]

Phnom Penh, 11th November 79

I really miss you and all of us pray every day for you and the missionaries. We should like to see you again. May God bless you and open the door of Cambodia and permit you to come here soon. I always remember your smiling faces and your good sermons. Would you please give my greetings to all the C&MA and OMF missionaries. Thank you. God bless you! Amen.

Love N

Phnom Penh, 2nd September 1980

The Lord gave me a good husband and now he has taken him back – he was always busy doing the Lord's work, and went to visit his family in Kratie after not seeing them for ten years. He was able to lead his mother, sister and brother to the Lord in the short time he was there. He returned to Phnom Penh to get Bibles for them, but on the return journey the ship sank, and his body was never found. The river was already high on 16th June when he went, but only the Bibles and his clothes were found. So he never met his family again. I am living with my parents and brothers at Tumnup Tik – please pray for us.

In Christ,
Srey Muey

Cambodia
Jan 1981

To brother Don,

'...I suffered for many years under the regime of Pol Pot. Because of the suffering I became stronger day by day. This is as I have read in Romans: 'And we rejoice in the hope of the glory of God. Not only so, but we also rejoice in our sufferings, because we know that suffering produces perseverance; perseverance, character; and character, hope. And hope does not disappoint us, because God has poured out his love into our hearts by the Holy Spirit, whom he has given us.' These verses helped to understand what is right and what is wrong, and how to choose the best way for my life. I have learned that the world is wrecked. Only 'the narrow way' is best for us, to follow God, even though that way is to suffer for his sake. I miss you very much...when we were together [in Phnom Penh], I was not good in God's sight. I only believed for food and money. Now I know that 'man does not live by bread alone, but by every word which comes from the mouth of God'...

Your brother, Sophan.

Sophan, who wrote the above, was one of the 'three bad boys', three likeable mischievous teenagers who came daily to the Youth Centre in Phnom Penh. The second of the trio, Hon, despite torture and long imprisonment, also survived. In May 1981, he was back in Phnom Penh, married, and working as a dock hand. In this way he was able to pass letters to friendly sailors from countries like Singapore on board the relief laden ships which tied up at the port in Phnom Penh. A Singaporean Christian navigator brought out a reply from him to an earlier note from me. Anticipating my concern for them, he reminded me of James 5:7-8:

Be patient, then brothers, until the Lord's coming. See how the farmer waits for the land to yield its valuable crop and how patient he is for the autumn and spring rains. You too be patient and stand firm...

He then went on to answer my urgent request for news of Setha, 'Little Brother', who had first taught me the Cambodian language, and as we were preparing to flee in 1975 had asked if he could have my potted plant.

Unfortunately, brother Setha is not seen anywhere in Phnom Penh. Sophan and I have been looking for him grievously. We have wandered far and wide searching for our faithful companion. We have buried our compatriots but we cannot stop thinking of them.

> How are the mighty fallen in the midst of the battle!
> ...I am distressed for you my brother.

By 1989, ten years after the overthrow of the Khmer Rouge and the installation of the Vietnamese-backed Heng Samrin government, it was obvious that much had changed for the better. On May 1, 1989, Hun Sen the Prime Minister announced a new constitution and another new name for the country: 'The State of Cambodia'. Buddhism was once again the official national religion. On September 26 the citizens turned out *en masse* to wave farewell to the departing Vietnamese occupation army. Phnom Penh was regaining something of her former beauty as gardens were recovered from their long neglect, and in the wide gracious boulevards, the avenues of trees flowered in a blaze of red yellow and lavender. Buildings were patched up. Citizens dressed in their colourful best, strolled once more down the water front esplanade and photographed one another at Wat Phnom and the Royal Palace. The roads were crowded with trucks, motorscooters, ox and pony carts, bicycles, and the traditional *cyclo-pousses*. Public buildings, libraries, museums, schools and government offices had re-opened. The markets were filled with consumer goods, mostly smuggled in by an army of intrepid entrepreneurs scurrying back and forth like ants from the Thai border. The Cambodian *riel* currency was back, and the markets were doing a brisk trade. The great unsightly mountains of rubbish and tangled barbed wire which had clogged roads and sewers were diminishing. Despite some shortages of rice, the spectre of famine no longer cast its grisly shadow. And over a hundred thousand busy citizens thronged the bustling re-born city, definitely aged and showing the wear and tear of her recent past, but clearly coping with her noisy and exuberant children after so long denied them. Phnom Penh in particular and the country in general had definitely come back to life. National reconstruction was under way. The Khmer Rouge, however, took the opportunity with the departure of the Vietnamese to seize vital timber- and gemstone-rich land along the Thai border including the strategic town of Pailin.

Among the first in after 1979, relief and development organisations like Oxfam, Christian Aid, Mennonite Central Committee and World Vision did a tremendous work in helping start rebuild the country's infrastructure. World Vision had built a Christian paediatric hospital which we saw completed in February 1975, only days before we were forced to abandon Cambodia. Now, five years later, it had finally opened. When World Vision leaders were given permission in 1979 to restore it, they were faced with an awesome task. Apparently, it had been used by the Khmer Rouge as a prison-torture chamber for students; perhaps some of those they cleverly duped into returning from France in 1976, for it was situated on the main road from the airport. It had been reduced to a stinking hole. They discovered a photo of two dead or dying men lying face down on a bed with their hands tied behind them. There were four other corpses in the photo. Blood and filth was spattered on the once spotless walls. But by 1980 it was once again a modern paediatric unit of seventy beds giving care to the most serious child illnesses endemic in Cambodia. The city was full of destitute orphans whose parents had perished under the Khmer Rouge. As a Christian hospital, it soon gained the reputation of the foremost hospital of its kind in Cambodia. While the expatriate medical staff, billeted in decaying hotels, and severely restricted in movement by the communist regime, were limited in what they could wisely say in terms of direct spiritual proclamation, there was no hiding the radiant Christian witness which through quality professional care and genuine compassion for these little ones, spread far and wide across the country and into the corridors of power.

The pressure had eased up on the church to the point where in July 1988, the Christians felt confident enough to hold a public Christian funeral service. The once small family cell groups meeting secretly in homes were expanding to larger groups of fifteen to thirty, forty, and fifty, drawing in friends and neighbours.

On June 18, 1989, hopeful that changes in the new State constitution would herald a new era of tolerance, the Christian elders meeting in a home, 'in a very friendly atmosphere of joy in the grace of the Lord', decided to draw up a provisional church committee. This committee once again made representation to the government for official recognition. Led by Pastor Siang, it comprised ten people, including four women elected to the positions of vice chairman, secretary and two treasurers. The Christians in 1988 were still an illegal body with no rights and certainly no church buildings. But it was clear that the climate had improved markedly since that bitter day in January 1981 when Pastor Siang had been compelled to sign the closure of his own church. A tacit unofficial recognition existed as large youth meetings went on unhindered, as also did the popular children's meetings, Sunday worship, personal evangelism, baptisms, weddings and funerals became increasingly more visible. A decade of patient and prayerful perseverance by the few who refused to be intimidated or discouraged was bearing fruit. Nevertheless in June 1989 the Council of Ministers still forbade the 'spreading of the Christian religion in the State of Cambodia'. But they did tolerate the 'reception of bibles, various religious books and material gifts from humanitarian organisations'.

In July 1989, the Cambodian church was invited to send delegates to the Lausanne II World Conference in Manila, Philippines. (Taing Chhirc and Son Sonne, now martyred, had been delegates to Lausanne I fifteen years earlier in Switzerland in 1974.) Unable under the present circumstances to attend personally they sent a report to the Conference delegates which began: '...We turn in confidence to the Almighty God who has not yet seen fit to make it possible for us to be present...' After a brief summary of the past ten years, the report listed eight meeting places in Phnom Penh with figures indicating that in the capital city of Phnom Penh a total of 207 people: forty-six men, eighty-six women and seventy-five children were regularly attending these 'house' churches. The largest was Reach Yeah's old base at Tumnup Tik with eighty and the smallest at Tuol Kauk with four. The figures reflected the great dearth of adult men in Cambodia after the Khmer Rouge killings, and the baby boom which had begun in 1979. Cambodia is a country of mostly widows and orphans and children. The report gave tentative figures for known Christians in six provinces totalling 182. Thus we have a conservative total for the entire country in 1989 of 389 church attenders, including the many children. These figures did not include all the 'secret' believers or emerging Roman Catholic groups. And the Lord no doubt had others 'hidden in caves' of whom they were not aware. These were the gleanings in Cambodia's fields at that time.

The Cambodian Church's report to Lausanne II concluded:

Dear Delegates of the Conference,

We meet with very many difficult problems which we are not able to solve, as follows:

- We have no proper church in which to meet. In the houses only a few people can gather together, and many do not dare to open their doors.
- The meeting places are scattered. This causes problems in relating to each other.
- We lack Bibles and hymn books.
- We lack instruments for teaching hymns to the Youth group and the Children's group.
- The Church has not a precise knowledge of the Word of God for lack of teachers.
- There are times when the church faces difficult problems, as, for example, when we are discriminated against because of our faith in the Lord Jesus and pushed out of the family dwelling.

Therefore we would ask the Conference to help pray for us as we face the problems mentioned above, that our hearts may be full of courage to carry our cross and follow the Lord, and that we may be faithful watchmen till the day when the Lord comes to set up his Kingdom on earth. (Psalm 118:27)

We have great hope that Lausanne II with 4000 Christian leaders gathering together will pray for us that the Lord of peace will grant peace to our country quickly. Please pray that we will soon receive rights concerning our belief in the Lord Jesus Christ and that the Lord will soften the heart of the Government towards us, that we may have permission to have a church in which to meet and worship him.

In closing, we pray that the Lord will bless Lausanne II, and in his grace give victory and peace.
Phnom Penh, 20th June, 1989
Signed by the Pastor, Chairman and Secretary of the Group of Elders.

Wonderfully, the prayer for official recognition of their 'rights concerning (our) belief in the Lord Jesus Christ, and that the Lord will soften the heart of the (Cambodian) government towards us...' was answered when ten months later on April 7, 1990, the Cambodian Government (The Council of the United Front for the Reconstruction and Defence of the Motherland of Cambodia) formally announced its recognition of the Christian Church (Protestant). An excerpt from the official document read:

> The Ministers of the Politburo fully authorise the opening of the Christian Church in the State of Cambodia ... and issue the decree regarding this permission to open the Christian Church and the church administration in Cambodia, according to the principles of the Politburo and the laws of the country. The Christians will execute this decree according to the doctrines of the Holy Scriptures and assure the welfare of social order.

It was signed by Party President and strongman, Chia Sim, and widely broadcast over Cambodian radio and television. Finally the Christian Church was once again officially recognised. The Cambodian government's Official Declaration on Christianity also accepted among other things that:

> The weight of destruction through the genocidal regime of the Pol Pot – Ieng Sary clique on that religion was particularly violent and vehement. The principal churches and other places of worship, especially in the city of Phnom Penh, and the book of the Bible, which is the law and directive of this religion, were utterly devastated. Priests, pastors and Christian believers, already few in numbers, were violently killed in the countryside and almost entirely obliterated.

The document also observed, no doubt as a result of a decade of meddlesome police surveillance:

> ...there has been no church building for the Christians in which to know God. However, depending on the number of Christians and also their means, active expression of worship of the Christian faith has generally found a clear outlet in the homes of individual Christians...

This liberating news after fifteen horrific years of persecution and harassment, opened the way for the many opportunities and initiatives which followed in the decade of the 1990s. It was the start of a new season of ploughing and seeding the blood-red killing fields and minefields of death, that they might become, once more, golden harvest fields of life.

A week later on April 14, in the presence of government representatives from the Front, in Phnom Penh's largest auditorium, over 1,500 Christians, both Evangelical and Catholic, Cambodian and Vietnamese, came together around the Lord's table in the joy of Christian freedom. The unity of the church would be sorely tested in the new heady freedom which followed.[4]

If the feeling in Cambodia in 1990 among the Christians was one of thankfulness and expectancy, the feeling in the Thai border camps was one of abandonment and hopelessness. But what gleanings could be found there from the harvest of wheat and tares earlier in the decade, most of which had now been exported around the world?

In 1990, ten years after the massive migration of Cambodians to the Thai border in 1978-80 for refuge, for food from 'the landbridge', for trade on the black-market, for emigration to America 'where you are paid for not working, and paid to have babies', about 350,000 (half were under sixteen and knew no other life) still remained stuck in the dead end no man's land of these border camps. Only about 20,000 of them were in UNHCR camps. The remainder were clustered in the forested border regions under the control of one of the three factions which made up the UN recognised tripartite 'Liberation Front'. The Khmer Rouge, militarily by far the most powerful, controlled 100,000 people at 'Site 8'. The Khmer Peoples' National Liberation Front (FNLPK), founded in 1980, a centrist grouping led by the ageing former Prime Minister of the late 1960s, Mr Son Sanne controlled another 150,000 at 'Site 2' and Sok Sann camps. And thirdly the Sikanoukists loyal to the ex-King and Front President, Prince Sihanouk, controlled another 60,000 at Site B under the FUNCINPEC party led by Sihanouk's son and heir (and future co-Prime Minister in 1993) Prince Ranariddh.

The Khmer Rouge-controlled areas were mostly to the south of Aranyaprathet, near to where in October 1979 defeated Khmer Rouge soldiers herded their skeletal captives, and the world press raised the cry of 'Holocaust!' Perhaps as many as 100,000 Khmer Rouge fighters and civilians were living here in areas under Khmer Rouge control in 1990. Camp figures are difficult to verify and were very fluid as people were constantly moving in and out of Cambodia.

'Site 8' was the biggest of the Khmer Rouge border settlements and had in its midst a community of Christians. Not surprisingly, surrounded by Khmer Rouge, the believers faced considerable persecution and intimidation. Two dozen or so met to worship in the home of Auntie M, including orphans, amputees from the minefields, the handicapped and the infirm. Others were forbidden to attend by the Khmer Rouge leadership and were, anyway, too fearful to make their faith public. Some had been led to faith in Christ earlier by Christians at Khao I Dang Camp where serious medical cases from the border were sent for treatment. The Christians at 'Site 8' would sing hymns together and read the Scriptures, with the maturer ones taking it in turns to teach and lead discussion. Although baptisms were forbidden by the Khmer Rouge and the Christians' lives were in constant danger, this unique little gathering stood vibrant amidst the deadening ideology of Khmer Rouge Stalinism and UN spiritual indifference.

The most popular border communities however were those under the more benevolent control of the FNLPK, junior partner to the Khmer Rouge in the 'Front' seeking to overthrow the 'imperialist' Vietnamese puppet regime in Phnom Penh. These 150,000 more Cambodians occupied the border strongholds north of Aranyaprathet near the Thai villages of Nong Chan Nong Samet and Ban Sangae. Six different camps sprawled along eight kilometres of border scrubland were grouped under the official name of 'Site 2' in March 1985. This was for administrative and security reasons; in particular the purpose of protecting and caring for the large civilian population which came under regular shelling from the Vietnamese army over in Cambodia during annual dry season offensives against the border enclaves. Although the Vietnamese occupation army left Cambodia in 1989, fighting continued between the tripartite resistance movement based here on the border and the troops of Hun Sen's 'State of Cambodia' in Phnom Penh.

Many Cambodian civilians had been lingering on the Thai border for over a decade by 1990. Backed into a corner with no hope of moving on into camps in Thailand and resettlement overseas, and fearful of returning to the exigencies of life in Cambodia, 'they were there because they were there'. In the two non-Khmer Rouge camps there was little or no discipline or law and order, just a lethargic 'welfare' mentality, giving rise to lawlessness and corruption further fuelled by the black market. Rape, murder and armed robbery were commonplace. It is hard to believe that they would have been any worse off if they had remained in Cambodia.

By 1990 five church groups were established at 'Site 2'. Despite the many discouragements and pitfalls in such a place, the more serious among them were devoted to prayer, and had a hunger for the Word of God. No one doubted that all these Christians would sooner or later have to return to Cambodia. They were therefore a very strategic minority to be gathered for serious discipling in the way of Christ. It was hoped that these would become the good seed when later they were dispersed back into Cambodia's waiting fields.

The Sihanoukists only had one major settlement at the border, close to the old Praesert camp in Surin province. It was called 'Site B' and contained over 60,000 potential recruits for Prince Sihanouk's faction. Like everywhere else, more than half of them were children, fruit of the post-1979 baby boom. In this camp, when boys reach the age of fourteen and had completed some basic schooling they were drafted into Sihanouk's army to fight with the Khmer Rouge and FNLPK against Phnom Penh's forces still firmly holding power in Cambodia despite the withdrawal of their mighty Vietnamese protectors and the collapse of the Soviet Union, their paymaster.

Formal Christian activities and meetings here had to compete with all the other routines and demands of camp life. The vast majority were nominally Buddhist and a pagoda had been erected in the camp. But as usual the real practical heart religion of the people was animism and dependence on the *Kruu Khmae* (spirit mediums) for all spiritual direction and physical maladies. There was also a Muslim meeting place here for refugees from the Cham ethnic minority in Cambodia.

Those calling themselves Christians were divided fairly equally between the Roman Catholics and Protestant groups. The number of mature and consistently faithful among them was not many. Hundreds were Christian in name only. Campus Crusade for Christ held meetings and training sessions, instructing people in the use of their 'Four Spiritual Laws'. How much of a lasting impact in terms of Christian discipleship and church planting this evangelistic device popularised on American campuses had among Buddhist and animistic Cambodians whose culture has no concept of a personal transcendent God, only time will tell. But like the Christians under the Khmer Rouge at 'Site 8', and under the FNLPK at 'Site 2', these newborn Christians would have to endure life in these unnatural hot-house border camps for several more years yet. It was not until 1993, just prior to the UN sponsored elections for a new government in Cambodia, that the last of the Cambodians on the Thai border were bussed back across the border.

Finally, the UNHCR refugee camp at Khao I Dang which in 1980 had the largest Cambodian church in the world and whose twenty-five-acre field was the site of such an abundant harvest, a decade later also had significant gleanings to be numbered. About a hundred or so members (1990 figures) still gathered in that grand old church built back in 1980 to house thousands. Virtually all of these had now been resettled overseas. By 1990, fifteen years after the fall of Indo-China to communism, the world had wearied of these refugees. Those who remained were the ones no one wanted or who were now conveniently dubbed 'economic migrants'.

The church's thatch roof leaked and creaked now, and the woodworms had done their work, but the Spirit of God still moved in that place consecrated with such enthusiasm and expectancy to him in those busy and exhausting days of harvest. But Khao I Dang was like Grand Central Station with people regularly boarding buses for the first stage of a long journey to resettlement in America, France, Canada or Australia. Building a church in a bus station wasn't an easy task. No sooner were mature leaders in place, programmes under way, and classes scheduled, when all the key people suddenly vanished, leaving behind others pre-occupied with the fact that their turn had not yet come.

Characteristically with things Cambodian, the church's administrative structure, procedures and precedents established so precisely at the beginning had passed down unchanged from one generation of leaders to another. Being a faithful imitation of one's teacher was the virtue, not innovation and novelty. The lifespan of one of these 'generations' was sometimes as short as a few weeks. But with the slowing down of resettlement after 1985 and the loss of the energetic early leaders, this church's final years saw just a handful of faithful men and women struggling with fewer resources and assistance to keep up the standards and traditions of the past. But the vital task of evangelism throughout the camp was maintained, as was the strategic ministry in the camp hospitals.

By 1990, this camp at Khao I Dang, which once commanded the attention of the world's leaders, resources and media, had become a forgotten backwater, and for the Thai, a thorn in the flesh, a troublesome magnet of hope which they wanted to close down. The few thousand Cambodians living there had missed the gravy train, and for the remaining Christians it was a hard field, trodden over by many passing feet.

The era of the camps was about to end. All these Cambodian

refugees along with God's 'gleanings' among them were about to be gathered up and scattered back into Cambodia's fallow and waiting fields.

CHAPTER 15

THE FALLOW GROUND:
AN EPILOGUE

'Peacemakers who sow in peace raise a harvest of righteousness'
(James 3:18)

The long tortuous dry season of 1993 was finally at an end. Signs of a new season were all around them as the four men pressed down harder on the pedals of their passengerless *cyclors*, sending them rattling and jarring noisily over the water-filled potholes all along Monivong Boulevard. Perspiration shone on their faces and trickled down their backs, forming large damp patches ringed with the whitish stain of body salt on their faded shirts.

The men were rice farmers from the same district of Svay Rieng Province over against the south-east border with Vietnam. Like tens of thousands of others, they had come to Phnom Penh to earn cash to buy rice for their families back in the village. The few sacksful garnered from last year's meagre harvest were finished, and this year's harvest was months away. They also needed money for seed, for fertiliser to spread on the poor leached-out soil, for supplies to repair their ramshackle bamboo and thatch huts under constant attack from termites, and just now being battered by the daily monsoons whose rains were softening the brown fields of stubble.

It was time again to 'awaken the earth', plough up the fallow ground, prepare special beds for the nurture of the precious seedlings, repair ploughs, field embankments and water channels;

in the expectation of a harvest, a good harvest at season's end.

Riding just ahead, sitting tall on the high saddle of his *cyclor* was Tola, chattering loudly to old Mien who at fifty was just about at the age limit for this strenuous labour. Knotted veins coursed down his bare sinewy legs to muddied feet from which hung a pair of worn-out rubber thongs. A cigarette dangled from his mouth and the smell of cheap whisky lingered on his breath. The drink dulled the persistent ache in his old joints but consumed much of the money he earned too. While Tola was full of carefree confidence and in his prime, with a young wife expecting their third child in as many years, Mien was already a grandfather, though his wife had just weaned their eighth living child.

The four companions had grown accustomed to the raucous scramble of life thronging the capital's garbage-strewn streets. It was in such marked contrast to anything they had ever known before in the silent poverty and despair of the village. Phnom Penh had suddenly become a boom town, awash with construction projects, swarming with foreign entrepreneurs and development agencies. Since the signing of the Paris Peace Accords in October 1991 between Cambodia's four warring factions, twenty-two thousand UN soldiers of the three billion dollar international peacekeeping force UNTAC had arrived to administer the country, disarm the fighters (in 1992, the Khmer Rouge reneged on the agreements, refused to disarm and abandoned the peace process almost immediately), repatriate the several hundred thousand refugees stuck on the Thai border, and administer a countrywide democratic election for a national assembly in May 1993. The many thousands of coolies, beggars, amputees, ragged children and *cyclor* drivers eking out a living on the streets of this tawdry 'vanity fair', understood little of the devious machinations of their politicians, manoeuvring for power and self enrichment, but they saw the opportunity to milk this overpaid and underdisciplined army until it pulled out in 1994.

The opiates of drink, cheap women, and all-night gambling sessions with other drivers, squatting between their *cyclors* pulled up along the broken pavements, kept Mien's mind from dwelling too much on the anxiety and fear which constantly tormented him.

Worry for the future and guilt for the past waged war on his soul in a fearful pincer movement. When in January 1979, the Vietnamese juggernaut had driven the genocidal Khmer Rouge from his commune, Mien had fled westwards with them. He had been a quisling and to such were meted out savage justice from the angry and newly liberated people. He had informed on the pathetic 'new people' driven out of the towns, and on village neighbours he had known since childhood. He had crept about, listening to gossip, the murmured complaints of starving people, whispered conversations at night heard from behind walls of straw. Any complaint against the revolution, against *Angka*, he reported to the cadre. He did it to survive, according to the prevailing law of the jungle. He had a big family, a tendency to laziness, and a wife who always had to have more and better than those around her. The Khmer Rouge discerned and utilised such opportunity very effectively.

When the Vietnamese caught up with him, he was tortured and imprisoned in Phnom Penh. Later, he had skulked back home to live in guilty silence and uneasy truce with both conscience and neighbour. Passions had cooled. The people by now were absorbed solely with looking ahead to the needs of the moment. Moral absolutes, the rule of law, social justice, crimes against humanity and so forth – these were niceties for the affluent West to pursue.[1] For now, Mien would be silently despised but publicly tolerated. *Karma,* not the people, would determine his fate.

On reaching Sihanouk Boulevard the foursome swung, illegally, to the left, skilfully negotiating a way through the seething mass of angry, honking white cars, motos, trucks, *cyclors* and handcarts, caught in a monstrous tangled gridlock, oozing round the intersection. Khin and Chenda in the rearguard, steered close in behind their colleagues, eyes fixed straight ahead. To glance to left or right was a sign of weakness, a signal to others to cut in. In order to get ahead, the rule is to pay no attention to what lies behind you, or to the side, only to what lies ahead.

Impassive and inscrutable, the four figures moved steadily forward through the anarchy around them. Perched high on their ancient chariots of steel, they were possessed of a singular dignity and poise. Khin was darker than the others and wore his *krama* wrapped around his head, peasant style. He felt out of place in the flaky sophistication of this 'gold rush' town. He pedalled slowly and steadily, with broad feet calloused from years of treading the fields, upon which his entire life depended and found its meaning.

Though well into his thirties now, he was a youth when the Khmer Rouge assigned him to one of their deadly mobile work brigades, and about eighteen when the Vietnamese puppet regime press-ganged him into military service to fight the resistance groups along the Thai border. Three times he was sent and three times he absconded, sickened by the carnage on the minefields, the greed and corruption of the officers, and the appalling conditions in which the enlisted men lived and died. Besides, he had no heart to kill other Khmers, farmers, 'little people', like himself just trying to survive the madness of Cambodia's quarrelsome leaders. They were there because they were there; not from any deep conviction but by accident of location or the expediency of fighting for another Cambodian patron-warlord.

In 1979, the commune elders paired him off when he was nineteen. He just glanced up and nodded when a young girl was trotted out and shown to him, standing with lowered head on the other side of the field from where he sat gambling and drinking with the men. After the brief ceremony during which they never spoke or dared even to look each other in the face, she had been so terrified of him that for days she trembled violently whenever he tried to get near her.

As with his father before him, gambling with cards was Khin's addiction. He had become famous for it, especially when despite the cries of his wretched wife and brood of sickly children, he tore the thatch roof from his house to sell for gambling money. If his wife complained or whined too much, she was beaten. That was accepted practice.

Finally, behind the others, rode Chenda, a gangly youth with a winsome smile. Mercifully, he could remember nothing of the Khmer Rouge terror. This life, scraping a living off the streets of the city was all he had known. When he was a boy, his father had collapsed and died, falling from his decrepit *cyclor* onto the street.

Now, his mother, along with numerous others across the country, was slowly dying from TB, coughing her life away and wasting their hard earned money on quack cures and useless drugs. Chenda was sole breadwinner for the entire family who waited for the rolls of torn and grimy *riel* notes which he sent back with the men travelling between city and village in search of work.

Chenda was an example of that awesome, dogged spirit of the vast body of Cambodian peasantry who quite unselfconsciously and despite everything, just keep on going. At seventeen, illiterate and penniless, he was characterised by a profound depth of serenity and gentleness of spirit. He was guileless, unsullied by the evil which flourished around him.

With the Independence Monument looming ahead through the evening gloom, the four *cyclors* turned sharply to the right and free-wheeled through the scurrying half-naked street urchins and long-legged athletic chickens, down the incline of Street 51. On their left stood Wat Lanka, a temple named after the country from which missionary monks had come centuries before bringing Buddhism. Out of habit, they looked curiously at the gaping hole surrounded by black soot at the foot of the tall crematorium chimney. Ultimately, every one, great or small, was pushed into that black hole, and after a brief flurry of rancid grey smoke, was gone. Beginning to pedal again as the road levelled out beyond the silent temple, but with their heads still turned to the left, the foursome clattered past the neighbourhood brothel. New and prosperous, it was just beginning to come alive with strings of colourful fairy light twinkling in front of its darkened windows.

At Street 294, marked by a cluster of seedy wooden drink stalls on the corner, the riders slowly turned left, swinging wide across to the far side of the road, in order to avoid the worst of the ruts and potholes they knew lay hidden beneath the black sewage water which erupted daily from the clogged drains nearby, and settled there, fermenting in the sun.

They drew up at the large gates of an old but beautifully restored colonial villa. In pre-communist days, it had been the home of the mayor of Phnom Penh. He was said to have been executed here with his family in April 1975 when the Khmer

Rouge captured the city. But now it was a church, The Church of the Lord Jesus Christ Our Peace.

Outside the high security fence over which hung a profusion of flowering bourgainvillea, along the raised concrete sidewalk, the church security guards were out stringing up large plastic sheets. A number of other *cyclors* were already pulled up under this roofing, sheltering from the intermittent rain, their riders preparing to spend the night sleeping in the single passenger seat of their conveyances or on grass mats, squeezing as many as possible in under some torn and sodden mosquito nets. To this place of refuge, security and peace, Tola, Mien, Khin, and Chenda had now arrived for the night.

The Anglican Church of Christ Our Peace was just one of a growing number of visible and expanding young churches which opened in Phnom Penh in the early nineties. This followed the granting of religious freedom for Christianity in 1990, and the 1991 signing of the Paris Peace Accords and adoption of the Universal Declaration of Human Rights guaranteeing freedom of religion.

In March 1992, seizing the opportunity of this newly opened door, the new Archbishop of Canterbury, George Carey, encouraged by the leadership of Christ Church, Bangkok, Thailand, wrote a letter to the about-to-be-recrowned King Sihanouk, requesting registration for a 'Christian presence in your country'. To this, Norodom Sihanouk, first crowned Buddhist 'god king' in 1941 and 'master of earth and water' graciously replied:

You are aware of the importance that I attach to the defence and respect of Human Rights in general, and more particularly to the liberty of opinion, of expression, of belief and religion... With these sentiments, in my capacity as President of the Supreme National Council of Cambodia, I grant my consent to the free activity of the Anglican church throughout the Cambodian territory.

Following the acceptance of the Anglican-Episcopal Church of Cambodia which also involved the consent of all the four warring Cambodian factions, including the Khmer Rouge who had once desired to kill me, I was ordained and later priested by the Bishop of Singapore whose Diocese included Cambodia. On Palm Sunday 1993, kneeling in the rubble and sweat of a reconstruction project on a grubby pillow borrowed from a worker at the site, and with water from recently poured cement upstairs dripping down on our heads, I was made priest-in-charge of the first Anglican Church in Cambodia.

Eighteen years after fleeing for my life from Cambodia, I was suddenly back in Phnom Penh, commissioned to establish a new church among the hundreds of English-speaking expatriate professionals working to help rebuild the shattered nation, and, more especially, to plant an enduring church among the Cambodians. With me in Cambodia, likewise rejoicing in this new day of opportunity, were many other dear friends and colleagues from earlier days in Cambodia in the seventies, from the Cambodian refugee camps in Thailand in the eighties, and from the Diaspora. Together we had returned to Cambodia to join hands in the unfinished task.

The existing Cambodian house churches which had persevered so valiantly during the trials and uncertainties of the eighties, were further strengthened by the return of some discipled leaders and new believers recently repatriated from the Thai border camps, where they had fled from communist persecution. Other Cambodian Christian leaders from the Diaspora who began returning home for visits at this time, brought further encouragement and hope to a severely weakened, fragmented church, emerging from a fifteen year long crucible of anguish and torment.

My initial exploratory visit to Phnom Penh in May 1992 was a rude but necessary awakening. I was simply not prepared for the enormous changes which had taken place in Cambodia over the intervening eighteen years of war, holocaust, invasion, persecution and famine. Added to this, my thoughts and deep feelings about Cambodia and the beloved ones I had left behind so tragically in 1975, had become distorted and sentimentalised by time and anxiety.

What I discovered was a people so changed that I despaired, three days into my visit, of ever being able to love them again. Everything appeared so unlovely. I wasn't sure that I even wanted to complete my week's stay in this brave new Cambodia, and especially after my intestines were hit by one of Cambodia's vicious and notorious bacterial attacks!

The physical appearance of the city was almost unrecognizable. The place was in a state of ruin: filthy, broken down, strewn with stinking garbage, and it didn't matter. The people, rich and poor alike, seemed mesmerised, bewitched by a frantic pursuit of money. Along with guns, it was the only thing that was respected, the only thing that mattered. Something had been lost, an innocence, a childlikeness, a graciousness. Now they appeared rough, aggressive and ugly, their faces shadowed by some dark inner void, etched with hard lines of tension; their eyes averted, their minds preoccupied. And everywhere the corruption, all embracing and overwhelming.

I visited the Khmer Rouge Death Camp, Tuol Sleng. I had visited this place once before with 'Little Brother', nearly two decades earlier when it was a high school. I left in a state of deep shock, sickened by what I had seen, guilty at having walked past the rows of photographs of the victims, portraits of naked horror in a macabre gallery, without having looked carefully and thoughtfully at each individual one, precious with the mark of the *imago dei*. The surrounding buildings had been absorbed into this gruesome, evil complex of death presided over by Comrade Deuch, among them the former sanctuary of Bethlehem Church.

My hotel, named with the words for 'highest heaven' in Buddhist cosmology, was full of UNTAC soldiers from formerly communist eastern European countries. They were enjoying their new found liberty, for the place was full of shrill, painted young Khmer girls, prostitutes servicing the peacekeepers. (Many more of them were going to die of AIDS than from disease, warfare or accidents put together.) And I inwardly grieved for the room boy, fresh in from the country, who, with no trace of traditional reserve, began by showing me how to access the non-stop blue movies on the television set.

Fleeing 'Highest Heaven', in search of my Cambodia, I hailed a *cyclor*. At least they hadn't changed. I directed the driver to one place after another – places I had loved and dreamed of for years.

First, the Youth Centre – it stood dark and empty, hidden behind sheets of rusting corrugated tin, to keep out thieves I suppose. Stepping back, I found myself standing in an open latrine right there on the pavement where once we had laughed and talked with scores of young Christians, seeing them off on their mobilettes, laden with books for various ministries. The show piece waterfront before the Royal Palace was all overgrown and strewn with rubbish, and the magnificent view across the Mekong marred by huge hoardings advertising cigarettes and beer. The tranquil gardens, avenues and shady trees where we had often walked engrossed in conversation – spoiled; by night the haunt of drunkards, thieves and the ubiquitous prostitutes. Bethany Church was completely unrecognizable, having been taken over by ranking military. They had seized all the best properties in the empty city immediately after the Khmer Rouge had fled and the Communist Vietnamese army of occupation had finished loading up all the City's 'decadent' wealth, carefully accumulated by the Khmer Rouge in warehouses, and shipped it back to Vietnam. The Chinese Church, full of hostile soldier squatters and their families, had been used as a cinema for pornographic films. Laundry hung in the old baptistry. The Bible School at Takmau was now a hospital full of sick and wounded soldiers from the many battlefields and minefields across the country.

Finally, after a perplexed *cyclor* driver had pedalled me up and down Norodom Boulevard for some time, I realised that number seventy-two, the old Christian and Missionary Alliance Home, had been completely demolished. In its time it had been the nerve centre of all the early pioneer work since the twenties, when the likes of Rose and her husband Koeum had come here from Battambang to help Mr Hammond with the first translation of the Khmer Bible. And here too, much later, during the siege of Phnom Penh, I had attended those memorable praise and prayer meetings which never stopped, even when the lights went out and Khmer Rouge rockets whistled overhead, led by that outstanding missionary to the Khmer, Norman Ens. Norm now worships perpetually, in eternal light.

Phnom Penh it seemed had been transformed from a silent ghost town under the Khmer Rouge into a bizarre vanity fair where, ironically, Cambodians escaping the killing fields had come to morally self-destruct in this swirling cauldron of violence, corruption, sex, cigarettes, alcohol, and gambling. It was hard to reconcile all this with the popular image of a people clinging tenaciously to a religious philosophy emphasizing the quelling of desire and the prohibition of violence, sex, alcohol, lying and theft!

So where was Beth El, the household of God? Bethel Church was the only one of that trio of churches, Bethlehem, Bethany and Bethel, I had not yet sought out. I eventually found the place, still recognisable from its churchlike facade. Closer inspection soon revealed that it too had been vandalised and desecrated beyond description. Inside, it was dark and oppressive, full of squatters, the stench of stale urine, filled with smoke from the open cooking fires on the floor and joss sticks which burned along the walls to ward off evil spirits. The local government boss of the district, quick to seize an opportunity to sell off more state property illegally, offered to sell the place to me for 250 ounces of gold.

I looked across through the desolation to a door in the far wall. Through this door, from the humble quarters beyond, old Pastor Haum used to enter the sanctuary Sunday by Sunday to lead and instruct the worshippers who crowded into this church. For a moment, I could just see it all the way it used to be. Then the image faded and the present reality returned. Pastor Haum had been martyred and so had most of the saints who used to gather here. It had been beautiful in its time, but this was not Beth El, it was a filthy crumbling old building. The Cambodian Beth El I had been searching for was not to be found in these old places, among the ghosts of the past. It existed out there, alive, wherever his Cambodian people were gathered in his Name.

I silently thanked God for what he had done in this place. I told the bemused squatters sitting around me about the people who had once worshipped the living God here. And I turned to the government official and said, 'No thank you.'

Over the next several days, I was joyfully reunited with four of our old students from the Youth Centre. I listened to their harrowing accounts of what had happened since we last met. They were no longer 'young people'. They had matured not only physically but spiritually as well. I also discovered that Khuy Sy the zealot, was alive and well and serving as a very high-ranking officer in the Cambodian army, still fighting the Khmer Rouge along the Thai border.

On the fourth day, I was surprised by a visit from 'the mad hunchback'. He had heard by the grapevine that I was returning to Cambodia, and had made the perilous journey all the way from Battambang, just to thank me for the literature and medicines I had sent in to him by refugee couriers from the border back in 1979. I was meeting this amazing old man for the first time; another of Cambodia's true saints.

As fluency and confidence with the language returned, I realised what an enormous spiritual vacuum now existed in the hearts of the people, and how easy it was to befriend them and engage in conversation about life and death and eternity. People everywhere would ask me: 'Will you be my brother?' 'Will you be my father?' Beyond the more sinister motives of some for a western patron, a free language teacher, a status symbol, an iron rice bowl etc, all of which must be expected and carefully discerned, I had no doubt that there existed in most hearts, a deep human yearning for authentic relationship, love and direction. It thrilled me and it terrified me. The opportunity was there to selflessly introduce them to a relationship with their father God, or to egotistically patronise and exploit, all in the name of Christian mission.

Soon I was inundated with visitors, inquiries, and invitations to visit homes. The opportunities were legion. But I could see that Cambodia's greening fields were full of stones and the seeds of thorns germinating rapidly. Will this sense of need, this spiritual hunger, soon be stifled by growing addictions to inward lusts and outward things, and the openness be clouded again by the old beguiling fantasies?

Many Cambodians, both literally and metaphorically, are abused, deprived and orphaned children, suddenly let loose in a dazzling hall of mirrors, a market place of delights. As such they are at once adorable and deplorable. They will almost certainly break your heart if you are seeking to love them yourself or looking for something in return. But then the sooner our deceitful human heart is broken, the sooner we can begin to learn to love them responsibly and unconditionally with the love of Jesus.

Despite what they say, like most of us, they are not helpless but vulnerable. They are not incapable, but lacking in confidence and encouragement. They are not to be pitied but supported and enabled. By the time I boarded the plane back to Singapore, all my wild enthusiasm for Cambodia had evaporated. But I found myself praying for faith and strength for both Margaret and myself to be able to fulfil this call from God to return for another season of labour in these radically changed but strangely familiar fields of life and death.

Tola, Mien, Khin and Chenda, were among the dozens of Cambodians who first encountered Jesus Christ between 1993 and 1995 at the Church of Christ Our Peace, a new and very special Beth El. A visitor once described it as being 'like a bright star shining in the darkness'.

I had been taught by missiologists, and they had the textbooks to prove it, that the reason missionary-planted churches were so dominated by the poor and outcast, was that they only preached to the poor and outcast, and not to the middle and upper classes who would likewise respond if given the opportunity. It was food for thought but I felt instinctively that this was too rationalistic, and overlooked the teaching of Jesus that the poor and outcast have a unique ability, in poverty of spirit and humility, to see themselves the way God sees them – as essentially needy.

The unique ethos of this Anglican Church and the circumstances of its founding was a good test for this thesis. We were perfectly placed to attract the who's who of Phnom Penh, but they were too busy. They were not interested. They never came, even when they had said they would. But in a very short time of beginning the Cambodian language services, the church became known as 'the *cyclor* church', because the overwhelming majority of people who entered its doors week by week for Sunday worship and weekday small group discipling sessions, were poor *cyclor* drivers.

For some long-serving Christian missionaries in the city, burdened for this hard-to-reach, ever-moving people group, so despised by Cambodian society and beset with such ingrained bad habits, it was an answer to their prayers. As time went on, these labourers of the street brought their families and friends, even their passengers. By 1994, the congregation began to represent a far wider cross-section of society, with students, tradespeople, professionals and housewives, not to mention the scores of children who delighted to come and sing, pray and learn the Bible stories, and later join the Brigades. These children, like the *cyclor* drivers, came with simple, receptive hearts and empty hands. They had no image or status to protect. They were simply following their hearts' desires.

And yet these 'little ones' whom the Lord especially loves, are the most threatened people in the country today. Considering that over half the population of Cambodia is now under the age of eighteen, following the baby boom which started in 1979, children's and young people's work must be a ministry priority. And over 200,000 of them are orphaned and abandoned.

The opportunities are enormous. The consequences of doing nothing are unthinkable. One wonders how very different Cambodian history might have been if bright, nationalistic and reform-minded young men like Pol Pot, Ieng Sary and Khieu Samphan had encountered equally concerned and articulate Christians, rather than Marxists, when they went to the colleges and universities of Paris in the early 1950s. What will this energetic but disillusioned generation of tomorrow's leaders be encountering now?

Many of them by the time they leave school in today's Cambodia have become experts in the art of cheating and lying. They are well qualified to join the parasitical bureaucracy, the corrupt military and the generally arrogant professional class who hold the masses of rural poor in such contempt. It is hardly surprising that when power 'fell into the street' in 1975, the Khmer Rouge sought to destroy all these people and the 'evil cities' of greed and dissipation they inhabited. None of this should really surprise us. If the Khmer Rouge ever form a democratic party and contest elections, they will do very well despite the excesses of twenty years ago, which only the minority over thirty-five years old recall now anyway.

Many of Cambodia's youngsters are growing up in chaotic, undisciplined, traumatised, fragmented homes and hard-pressed single parent homes. The alarming rise in youth crime is an indicator of the terrible legacy from the abolition of the family by the Khmer Rouge, the use of violence to solve conflict, continued civil and political unrest, and the deepening poverty gap between the minority very rich and majority very poor.

Large numbers of children live in makeshift orphanages and still more are 'street children', prey for paedophiles, gangsters, and the massive prostitution market in Cambodia and in neighbouring Thailand and Vietnam. Because of the enormous HIV risk, very young girls fetch good prices. They are abducted on the streets and vanish into the cesspool. They are even sold by parents into the sex industry. A number of Christian organizations, notably World Vision, are reaching out helping hands to these street children.

It was after a beggar widow offered her children for sale through the fence that Margaret started some self-help projects for a few of these desperate women. The nation is full of them. We must support and pray for groups like Southeast Asian Outreach (originally Cambodia for Christ founded by Taing Chhirc in England in 1973 before he returned to Cambodia and martyrdom.) Then there is 'Tabitha', an organization set up by Janne Ritchel, a dynamic and capable Canadian woman, dedicated to helping hundreds of the poorest slum widows to self sufficiency, and dignity, not with handouts and pity, but by firm harnessing of their considerable potential.

Other Protestant development agencies working effectively to minister to the body and soul of the Khmer people are World Concern, Christian Outreach, and Food for the Hungry. All the Christian missions serving in Cambodia since 1990 have significant relief and development components to their overall strategies. This is how it should be.

There is enormous scope in Cambodia today for Christian

schools and colleges,[2] not only in Phnom Penh, which always receives the lion's share of development aid, but in the main provincial towns also. I speak of schools of academic and moral excellence where minds are shaped, characters moulded and consciences educated in the noble tradition of the best of those schools set up around the world by Christian foundations, missionaries, and teaching orders over the centuries. Schools which today are considered elite institutions, though sadly many have compromised their Christian integrity. This would be an enormous undertaking, but in the long term bear results of incalculable good. Do people who possess this kind of energy and vision for planting Christian schools exist today, or is it a thing of the past?

On a less expensive but no less important level, much needs to be done with Christian young people's movements. A start was made in 1995 to introduce the Boys' and Girls' Brigades appropriately into Cambodia. Well-established Brigade movements in Singapore and Malaysia have already responded positively to this challenge. With these kinds of things, money is usually not the problem but rather committed personnel. Khmer youngsters will respond very enthusiastically to a highly disciplined 'muscular Christianity'. They are searching for direction, belonging, and vocation.

Along with a number of other women missionaries, and mature Cambodian Christians, Margaret also became involved in the development of teaching materials for Sunday Schools and church-based Christian education programmes, along with teacher training. These workshops were very popular, drawing Cambodians from a very wide area, longing to know how to better motivate and teach their young people. In not a few cases I suspect these Sunday School teachers were better prepared for Sunday than their pastors.

In tandem with this there is that very exciting and popular area of the teaching of music: instruments, voice and theory. OMF especially have gained experience and proven expertise in the area of indigenous Khmer Christian music. This must be encouraged on a national scale to enhance evangelism, discipleship and worship.

Like those four farmers, Uncle Has, Uncle Moeung, Grandfather Pum and Grandfather Bou, heading for Battambang market to hear the Good News seventy years earlier, Tola, Mien, Khin and Chenda were likewise drawn happily to Christ, because they were characterised by those same vital qualities of simplicity and childlikeness. The point is, such as these are the essence of Cambodia. They endure, they remain. They are the vast Cambodian peasantry.

They are waiting, hoping, looking for something better. They are only too willing to trust and follow. They are waiting for someone to declare the gospel to them clearly in their own language. And when they see it, many will say 'Yes', because it will make complete sense to them. And then they will say, 'Why didn't you come and tell us this before? Why did you take so long?'

For generations the Khmer people have been like pawns before powerful kings and queens, knights and bishops. For hundreds of years their greedy, inept and quarrelsome leaders from 'divine' monarchs to 'democratic' marxists have been more concerned with staying in power and destroying the opposition than actually leading the people towards something better. All have wrapped themselves in the banner of Khmer nationalism even to the point of racism and xenophobia, and outdone one another in claiming to champion 'the little people'. But all have championed only their own ends.

The Khmer people have to be among the most manipulated and abused peoples in the world. The masses are basically feudal in their politico-economic psychology. Their loyalty will flow up to where patronage flows down. Their loyalty is not to any moral absolute or objective ideal but permissive, determined by the exigencies of shifting pragmatics and situational expediencies.

The one exception to this is their fixed devotion to the land and the mystery of the waking earth, to the fields where the harvest of life-sustaining rice is produced season by season. I never ceased to be amazed at their perennial optimism when the rains came and it was time to 'awaken the earth'. And the sheer energy and excitement just before the harvest.

Disaster from drought and uncontrolled flooding is now more

likely than ever, given the devastation of the forests and the destruction of the hydrological system. When I questioned the very poorest farmers concerning the high cost of preparing the fields, hiring draught animals, buying fertiliser, time and energy expended and so on and the pitiful return, even in a good year; and then suggested that perhaps it might be better for the time being just to leave the fields fallow and work for hire in the city, they were incredulous. It was inconceivable that they should not plough up the fields and sow the seed when the time came. It had to be done. Whether the harvest was good or bad was not the point. The fields could not be left unsown whatever the cost, whatever the risk. And when corralled in those dreary refugee camps in Thailand, there was nothing the Cambodian farmers missed more than the fields, especially when the rains began to fall following the hot season.

The point I was making is that it is all too easy for the church to become just another petty feudal lord with its vassal Christians providing their homage. Like the entrenched 'caste' system sociologically, this 'feudal' system psychologically is extremely difficult to transform. I do not think any of us who have worked in Cambodia would say we have succeeded in this. Khmers, fearful when there is no 'father' king enthroned in the Royal Palace in Phnom Penh, need to know that Father God is their Lord and King. He is the master of earth and water who is permanently on the throne of heaven. And our relationship with him is a sacred and eternal covenant sealed with his blood. A careful teaching of the neglected Old Testament Scriptures will help instil an understanding of these relationships and responsibilities.

Only a liberating self-awareness in the knowledge of God will free the Khmer people from these cycles of deception and misery and lift them out of despair. Buddhism perfectly portrays their plight, for it is anti-human and a gross overkill, quintessentially a philosophy of despair and negation, promising many lives of misery and suffering till all natural desire is vanquished, and culminating in eternal non-existence. Here lies the counterfeit of authentic Cambodian self realization and full salvation.

Tola the farmer and *cyclor* driver saw this. He was moved by

God's words set to the ancient Khmer melodies which everyone loves, for these are an affective people, aesthetically and emotionally driven. He described it as an awakening by a bright light shining in his heart, illuminating everything. Several years earlier, when he had entered the monkhood for a season before marrying, he had seriously sought answers to those eternal questions which arise in every heart. But when he asked the abbot how and why all things originated, he was met with silence. Tola was a lively evangelist in the days soon after his conversion. But like all of us he faced a hard struggle with deeply-ingrained sin, as well as the chronic depression and self-doubt which often afflicts extroverts like him in particular, and post 'killing fields' Cambodians like him in general.

Good pastoral counselling is a vital skill urgently needed but not widely exercised in Cambodia. In this Cambodian pastors are best advised to work with their wives or in same sex situations. The intensity of the trauma of recent years, the breakdown of family and community, huge numbers of widows and orphans, handicapped and unwanted, widespread male promiscuity and unfaithfulness, over half the population under age, rampant child and wife abuse and demographic imbalances which have led to massive emotional stress, make it hard to imagine how church leaders are coping seriously and effectively with the horrendous discipline problems and past nightmares every new believer potentially brings into the church. It is vital that Cambodian pastors spend most of their energies in prayer, in study, internalizing and teaching the Word of God, discipling their people and giving spiritual direction.

The job is made harder by the fact that Khmers do not have a sense of guilt so much as a sense of shame and sorrow at being found out. Generally speaking, girls are raised more firmly and taught to be responsible and moral. Boys are too often spoiled and expected to be playful, macho and self-indulgent. More and more women today are realizing that they must break with past tradition and become economically self-sufficient. With the final responsibility of caring for the children and the old people, and no laws or social safety net in place to protect them, it is just too precarious for women to depend any longer solely on men who are either dead or have absconded.

Mien was transformed, not surprisingly, by God's promise of personal and unconditional forgiveness, and lucid words of Jesus repeated week by week in the liturgy which seemed to him the only hope for the kind of just society the Khmer Rouge only talked about.

> The first commandment is this: 'The Lord our God is the only Lord. You shall love the Lord your God with all your heart, with all your soul, with all your mind, and with all your strength.' The second is this: 'Love your neighbour as yourself.' There is no other commandment greater than these.

Mien knew that no man could have come up with wisdom like this. It was completely other worldly. Hearing the Word of God is always the most effective means of evangelism because it is the primary means through which the Holy Spirit desires to speak to us.

I have come to believe that the church in Cambodia, lacking leadership, semi-literate and fragmented, could benefit from the creative introduction of liturgical forms of worship. These would provide a much needed framework and direction to church services which are often *ad hoc*, unprepared, and downright chaotic. Struggling lay leaders of little churches emerging all across the countryside are unsure what to do week by week. Liturgy would also help counteract the propensity to egotism, demagoguery, and personality cults among some pastors who model their leadership style on that of local politicians.

While allowing appropriate space for the spontaneous, the extempore, the immediate need etc, inclusion of a definite time for general and personal confession at the beginning of the service is good, preferably kneeling or prostrated on the ground as Cambodians would instinctively want to do. This might follow recitation of the Ten Commandments or a reading of Scripture. Along with the Lord's Prayer and the Apostles' Creed, every believer would then have committed to memory that great paradigm prayer, the fundamental ethics of the faith, and a succinct statement of what the Christian believes.

Credal statements should be allowed to evolve further, articulating the distinctives of Khmer theology, polemics and apologetics; distilling their beliefs in the context of prevailing dualism, reincarnationism, fatalism, merit making, and so on. The creed could state for example when referring to Jesus Christ that he is the one who has made all the merit necessary for salvation. The experience of the Thai church is an excellent resource for Cambodian Christians, given the similarity in their cultures, and geographical proximity.

All these things can be said, or better still chanted or sung using the great wealth of indigenous music for this purpose. Every Khmer knows and loves these evocative melodies. They always respond positively and immediately to this music because it is their own. Having memorised these songs, they will continue singing them as they go about their lives, imparting them to others.

A suggested lectionary would ensure that the entire Scriptures are systematically read: Old Testament, New Testament, psalms, gospels, epistles. The ancient responses of the church are a wonderfully natural and spontaneous means of affirming, exhorting, recognising, participating, encouraging, teaching and memorizing truth:

'The Lord be with you.'

'And also with you.'

'Christ is Risen.'

'He is risen indeed.'

The more variety, the more senses employed, the more participation can only enhance the worship and keep the attention of a people unused to sitting and listening for long periods of time. And sermons should be short and sweet, little and often, carefully prepared, emphasizing one main point with good illustrative material, not degenerating into a stand up comic gig or a long ramble from Genesis to Revelation week by dreary week as in too many Cambodian churches.

As with the responses, so with the singing, choose carefully and distribute throughout the service, rather than an exhausting vocal marathon at the beginning as is popular today. And be Cambodian, for example having men and women singing antiphonally, the way their folk songs are sung, with a man's voice alternating with a woman's. This is lively, interesting and inclusive.

Order and due reverence have to be taught. Over the past two decades traditional Cambodian decorum and modesty have been lost. (At Buddhist temples people are not expected to be worshipping in a personal way or even to pay attention, but just to be present.) Cambodians are by nature conservative, deferential and respectful. They do not expect to come before a King in informality and familiarity. And I believe that ultimately we live up to the clothes we wear and the postures we adopt.

Tithing is weak everywhere in Cambodia. For most it is better to receive than to give, unless some merit is to be gained from it. Responsible tithing needs to be understood if the Cambodian church is ever to come anywhere close to being self-supporting. The way the offerings of the people are handled and integrated into the public act of worship has to be considered carefully. It is often quite misunderstood by Christians and non-Christians (who should not be required to participate) alike. Cynicism and false assumptions arising from Buddhist 'almsgiving' can only be overcome by teaching, and with transparency and accountability in all the financial affairs of the church. With sex and money offences as the two major causes of grief in this church, prevention is better than cure.

While sensitive to the dangers of superstition and idolatry, I have come to believe that Khmer Christians are to be helped by appropriate symbols and indigenous Christian art which illustrates and dramatises biblical truths constantly before their eyes; symbols which appeal to the emotional-artistic instincts and sensitivities of this people, rather than our deadening post-modern western preference for vocalising, rationalising, and utility.

It is good to see more Khmer forms and customs being incorporated now into weddings, dedications and funerals. But much more needs to be done to develop a profoundly Christian alternative to all those everyday community needs which Khmers look to monks and mediums to fulfil. I speak of healings, exorcisms, love and marriage counselling, fear, conflict resolution, childbirth, crop protection, house cleansing, sickness, death, and so on.

These all illustrate how very real the supernatural is to the Khmer people. Unlike us, they understand all things in spiritual terms. This is why the introduction of our contemporary revivalistic, pietistic and essentially narcissistic spirituality will in the end only be a halfway house to nowhere. Having weaned them away from the old ways we give them nothing lasting in return, leaving them high and dry before the rising tide of secularism, materialism and eroticism.

More days for Christian festivals and celebration should be added to substitute for the former ones, as well as in spiritual response to their unique pilgrimage and experience. In the light of its history, for example, the church might well remember to give thanks for that great cloud of witnesses who have suffered and been martyred for the faith. One recalls Taing Chhirc, just days before his martyrdom, identifying so totally with the weeping Jeremiah. Suffering is a powerful motif in the Cambodian church experience. It is a bearing from which to chart the future which will not suddenly be so very different from the past. And yet I am not aware of a single memorial to any Cambodian martyr or giant of the faith anywhere in the country. It is so important to inculcate memory in the church, a solidarity with the best of the past. Amnesia and the denial of pain in the contemporary Cambodian church are not healthy signs.

Khin, the third of our *cyclor* drivers, was at first very uncomfortable being with so many people he didn't know, and embarrassed because of his illiteracy. In church, he would pretend to be able to read, noisily leafing through the pages. At heart, he hated himself, especially for the shame and suffering he had brought upon his family. And he figured that everyone else must despise him too, which of course they did. He was convinced he could never understand anything which came out of a book. The gospel had to impact him not as something vocalised, but something actualised.

Late one evening, when I went outside the gate to talk with all the street people gathered for the night, I discovered Khin asleep, sitting up in the seat of his *cyclor*, wearing only a pair of shorts. His one set of clothes was hanging to dry on the fence. His entire body was covered by swarms of bloodsucking mosquitoes. I applied repellent cream to his body and thought no more of it. But unbelievably to him, I had also applied it to his feet. No one had ever touched his feet like this before. Cambodians regard the feet as the lowest and most socially unclean part of the body. Feet must never be allowed to touch anybody, and stepping over someone, or their things, is the height of rudeness. When sitting, the feet shouldn't even be allowed to point towards another person but be kept tucked away. And I had taken his very dirty and very lowly labourer's feet into my hands, and gently rubbed them all over with ointment.

In very formal Khmer, traditionally used when speaking to the king, the word for 'I' means literally 'the one with the top of my head lower than the dirt on the soles of your feet'. I had unconsciously treated him like a king by putting myself – including my head – lower than the dirt on the soles of his feet. He felt at once honoured and mortified. Did he have worth after all?

A month later another *cyclor* driver I was riding with told me that Khin had been lying slumped in his *cyclor* along the roadside for a long time. He was too weak to work and had no money for food or to get himself home. In fact, though seriously ill, he had recently left home and returned here to the city to pedal his *cyclor* in desperation for food and money for the family. Lifting the *krama* from his face I could see that he was barely conscious and seriously dehydrated.

I took him to rest for a week in the beautiful grounds of the church. With prayer, medication and rest, he recovered. Towards the end of his stay, during one of our long talks, he told me he wanted to know the God who could love even him like this. To those denied value and respect for as long as they can remember, even the smallest gesture of love in Christ's name is revolutionary. Such is the dearth of the love of one's neighbour in Cambodia, that God's love dramatised and exegeted in this way can change lives for eternity.

But the real challenge is not so much doing these things

ourselves, but getting the Khmer Christians to 'go and do likewise'. The gospel can very soon, in the prevailing religious climate in Cambodia, degenerate into religiosity, legalism and ideology. This is not the way of Jesus. In the West, we have made a virtue out of informality and egalitarianism; busting traditions, toppling heroes, being vulgar, are all very acceptable. But for Khmers, things are different. Even the poorest Khmer will rarely do an act of selfless love for a fellow Khmer. They are afraid people will take advantage or that they will lose status. It is always better to pass by on the other side. When two Khmers meet, the first thing to be established (and it is done quickly and routinely) is who has status over whom. What is the pecking order? The entire nature of the relationship is determined in this way, including the language they use to address one another.

Spontaneous acts of Christian love by Khmers (they expect us to be strange; we can afford to be) throw these ingrained cultural protocols into total chaos. They begin to create a counter culture. This is costly in a culture where unquestioning conformity is the expected norm. In Cambodia, a Christianity which is applied beyond the comfortable pew and purview of the missionary, a Christianity which is actualised in the secret places of family relationships and marketplace ethics, has yet to take root. Touching the untouchable, loving the unlovely, forgiving the unforgivable in a consistent spirit of Christ-centred selflessness is the difficult transformation the majority in the church have yet to experience. So the church tends to be self absorbed, encultured by prevailing social norms, compromised, and powerless.

This situation should cause us to consider the model of the early church when the small hard-pressed Christian community set in the decadence of Rome perceived itself as a living polemic, as a radical witness-martyr to Jesus Christ. Later, through the Middle Ages, whenever the church was beset by a spirit of accommodation, dynamic lay orders emerged. Their members, fleeing the corruption, consecrated themselves to God with vows of simplicity, sexual purity, and godly obedience.

What a powerful witness such a lay order would have in Cambodia – uncloistered, living devotedly by these vows in the 'cell' of their family units and communities, ministering to needy people, especially given Cambodia's own long tradition of monks and nuns. And just about every Khmer man traditionally becomes a monk for at least one rainy season in his life.

And again, what about the historical monastic reading method of *lectio divina*. This was the monks' daily discipline of reading the Bible aloud, slowly and softly, the way Khmers tend to do anyway, and listening to the words of the page, integrating and internalising them in a kind of listening and learning by heart. The monastics understood the texts of Scripture on four levels: the literal meaning, the figurative meaning, the ethical meaning, and the heavenly meaning. Based on the kinds of questions Khmer Bible students would ask me if we read together, I would say that they too were inclined to sense and interpret the text in this kind of way, not in a logical, analytical, grammatical way at all.

Many times I have thought of the medieval monks as I watched a group of *cyclor* drivers pulled up outside the church, Bibles open before them and reading aloud with such concentration that they are not aware of the other person reading beside them, or the roar of the traffic going by. How much superior this is to reading solely with the eyes, the heart engaged miles away.

These are some of the ways in which the Khmer church can grow out of the rut of second-hand 'do it yourself' spirituality which never did us much good, so why pass it on to them? And, besides, Khmers prefer to do things together.

As for Chenda, I'll leave him to tell his own story in the following translated testimony:

My name is Chenda. I am nineteen years old having had the misfortune to be born in the second year of the Pol Pot era. I have three younger brothers and sisters. When I was still a small boy, my father, a poor farmer from Svay Rieng province, fell from his *cyclor* and died there on the street in Phnom Penh. I think he was worn out from worrying how to earn enough money to support us. I heard later that he was a heavy drinker and gambler.

Since as long ago as I can remember, I followed my mother to Phnom Penh where we lived and worked on construction sites and on the streets of the city. We always did this between the planting and harvest seasons to try to earn money to buy rice and pay the endless debts. I attended the village temple school for only a few months. There wasn't any money to buy books and clothes for school, and mother needed me to work. Now my mother is too sick and weak with tuberculosis to leave the village, so I am working hard to support all the family as a *cyclor* driver in Phnom Penh like my father and grandfather.

One evening last September, during the rainy season, another *cyclor* driver from my village took me to the Christian Church where Pastor Don teaches. Along the road outside the church fence, plastic sheets were erected every night so that we street people could sleep in a dry place. We were happy to rest in the 'shadow' of this holy place of God. Every evening, 'Grandfather Don', as every one in our village calls him, came out to talk to us.

But now I call him Teacher because I am one of his students in the church. I am learning about the God who is the Creator and Saviour of the whole world. I can almost keep up with the singing now if it is not too fast. I am also learning to read and write Khmer every evening at the church. I still tie my mosquito net to the church fence before I sleep.

The church helped me with a loan to buy my own *cyclor*. So instead of paying one dollar every day in rent to the *cyclor* boss, I repaid the church. Now I own my own *cyclor* and can save a dollar each day to send to my mother to buy food. Last month when I went back to harvest the early rice I bought three hens. Now I am saving to buy a small pig ($14) and then a cow ($90), so we do not have to pay back almost half our crop to rent a cow for ploughing. Pastor Don encourages us to save, and stop all our old bad habits like smoking and gambling which wasted our money. He looks after our savings till we go back home.

Now that I have believed in the Lord Jesus I am happy because light has come into my heart and hope into my life. We go to singing practice every Saturday morning and to study the Bible with Pastor on Tuesdays. Every Sunday we park our *cyclors* outside the church and go in to pray to God, sing hymns, and learn more of God's truth. Last Sunday we celebrated the birth of Jesus the Saviour. We were all very happy and the church was so beautiful. I enjoyed the coconut shell dance and the songs by the Boys' Brigade best. Now I understand how Jesus was born into our world.

One thing I am worried about is that my mother burns incense sticks every day on a shelf in our hut in the village. This is for the ghost of my grandfather who was murdered by the Khmer Rouge and whom she trusts to protect our place. My mother is not very strong. I hope that one day she will trust in Jesus the Saviour too. On Sunday December 31, I am going to be baptised.

Christmas 1994 marked the twentieth anniversary of that last memorable Christmas of 1974 in Phnom Penh before the night fell. The numbers of Cambodians attending churches on this day in the capital and in provinces around the country is difficult to determine. But it must have been approaching the number of twenty years earlier: about 5,000 Christians.

What happened at the Church of Christ Our Peace was typical of many other churches all over the country. Christmas 1994 was the joyful culmination of a year which had seen steady spiritual growth and expansion of the gospel from this church. The message on the lips of *cyclor* drivers and other peripatetic labourers was being gossiped and rumour-mongered into far-off villages. The Khmer Christians, many of whom were celebrating Christmas for the very first time, threw themselves into it with great enthusiasm, displaying the distinctive creative talent too long suffocated under decades of violence and privation.

The warmth and brightness of Christmas 1994 dawned midst the 'cold midwinter' of drought and the failure of the annual rice harvest, poverty, political insecurity, widespread violence and stifling corruption. The church was a blaze of colour and light. Every evening leading up to Christmas Day, '*cyclor* songsters' gathered outside to sing their haunting Khmer hymns and carols, and practise their parts for the Christmas pageant. *Cyclor* driver shepherds, like the original shepherds considered among the dregs of society, jauntily shuffled up and down the church forecourt. 'Wise men from the East' including former Khmer Rouge, alcoholics and monks, moved reverently back and forth to the music, heading towards a home-made crib filled with straw and a doll swaddled in a traditional Khmer *krama*. The Khmer congregation leaders worked and reworked the drafts of their devotional messages. In all, about half the Khmer congregation were involved in this Christmas presentation, the meaning and significance of which they themselves had only just begun to discover.

No sooner was the morning English language service over when the guards came in and transformed the place into a cattle stall, complete with fresh cut bamboo fronds, sheaves of straw, old stools, baskets and other assorted things strewn around.

By 2.00 pm about eighty excited neighbourhood children had filled the church to watch our regular Sunday School youngsters sing carols and perform a Christmas play with considerable flair and enthusiasm.

The drama began with one of the children dressed up as the aged prophet Isaiah, foretelling the nature of the Saviour's birth. The children were transfixed as the story unfolded. Virtually all were seeing and hearing it for the first time. Two Sunday School teachers put hours of work into this event. But because time was short, with the adult programme scheduled for 6.00 pm, the children were given bags of treats at the gate rather than the planned picnic in the garden.

As the light began to fade from the sky, we switched on the many coloured lights hung in the trees and flowering shrubs around the giant spotlighted Christmas banner and at all the entrance ways. At a squeeze the church can hold about eighty thin Khmers. But by the time the adult programme got underway, that many again were crowded all around the doors and out beyond the fence, all trying to catch a glimpse of what was happening. And the sound of joyful singing drew still more onlookers from the street.

For me the high point of the evening was one of the Bible School students singing a Khmer Christian lullaby, accompanied by the plaintive strains of a two-stringed Cambodian violin, as 'Joseph' and 'Mary' worshipped in wonder at the manger, compelling everyone's rapt attention.

When it was over, the whole assembly poured out into the illuminated church grounds for refreshments. The atmosphere was as it should be: joyful, friendly, in total contrast to that of a typical dark night in Phnom Penh beyond the church fence.

Pausing to watch and consider for a moment from the guardhouse gate, I reflected on my first Christmas in Cambodia in 1974, exactly twenty years earlier, and just weeks before they were swept up into the darkness and terror of the Khmer Rouge revolution, the 'murder of the innocents'. All but a small remnant who celebrated at the final Christmas before 'night' came, fell like grains of wheat into the blood-soaked 'killing fields'.

Twenty years on, everything had changed. And yet nothing had changed. The names and faces were different but the people were the same. Many of the young people around me had not even been born then. Now they were energetic young adults like those in 1974 had been.

And tomorrow, I thought, *when all this is over and the decorations come down and the manger is put away, they must head out to their villages and fields to glean a few bushels of rice from the wasted landscape, avoid ten million land mines and the ever-lurking menace of Khmer Rouge killers and Royal Cambodian Army bandits. They will be worried about how they are going to feed their families, pay their debts, and raise enough cash to start again. They must deal with a parasitical bureaucracy and a corrupt ruling elite whose ineptitude and indifference will ensure they remain mired in poverty.*

All this awaits them beyond the lights over the guardhouse gate, I thought. *It is no less difficult to be a Cambodian Christian today than it ever was. But, similarly, the inner strength and courage which so characterised the Khmer Church in 1974 is no less available to Christ's Cambodian people today. For he is no more the baby in the manger, but the risen and glorified Lord, alive forevermore. And he will go with them as he promised, out through the gates of this church into the darkness beyond which still awaits the brightness of their coming, as bearers of that light which came at Christmas.*

In early 1995, the churches in the capital received a letter from the Ministry of Religion stating that all Protestant churches must organise themselves into a united body, headed by a council through whom the government could liase with the church. The government could identify the Buddhists, Muslims, Roman

Catholics, and their leaders. But when it came to the numerous Protestant organizations: denominational, para-church, independent, humanitarian and so forth, they were viewed uneasily as a pot-pourri of squabbling foreign lackeys.

While the initiative was welcome, it was an indictment of the Protestant church's inability and repeated failure to come together in a common unity, despite the diversity. There was really no good reason why this could not happen. All shared a common biblical and evangelical faith. It was a scandal that a Buddhist government had to order a unity after patiently waiting for the Christians to stop quarrelling and get their act together.

Apart from those groups considered to be cults, such as the Mormons, Jehovah's Witnesses, New Apostolics and others, the dissenting voices in the Protestant community seemed to be coming from two areas.

First there were those who, feeling themselves to be of the one true Spirit-filled church, could not join with others who did not preach a 'full gospel'. It was clear that they would have to have their own separate training schools, and even start their churches where another church already existed.

Second there were some Cambodians who had returned to Cambodia from the United States as missionaries with big para-church organizations, and who seemed to be under no constraint from their sending bodies to cooperate with the national church movement, or be accountable to anyone but themselves. These *prima donnas*, like their Cambodian political counterparts, seemed intent on building personal empires, and putting personal ambition before the national good.

It was a sad fact that few of the Khmers returning from overseas were able to get along with each other at all, due primarily to mistrust and jealousy. Unless this attitude changes, the Cambodian Christian diaspora, much of which has practised its Christian faith only in a western context, will have little to contribute to the church in the Motherland, except more heartache. All missionary agencies are advised to apply the same stringent screening, supervision and accountability to their Cambodian candidates as they would to any others.

Out of the debate arising from this government directive, some encouraging steps have been taken. Foremost among them is the setting up of the Evangelical Fellowship of Cambodia (EFC), which would like to link up with the World Evangelical Fellowship. For this to happen, the EFC must demonstrate that it does indeed represent the overwhelming majority of evangelical Christians in the country. Herein lies the rub. The government, pliable, inconsistent and open to persuasion, unfortunately decided to register several umbrella groups. The reasons for this are not clear, possibly as a weapon for when it serves their purpose to divide and rule. The Ministry of Religion has made no secret of the fact that if the Christians get out of hand (that is, become too numerous), they have contingency plans to deal with them. There is nothing new under the Cambodian sun!

All this has left the door open for strong, independently minded denominations and para-church groups to register separately as national Protestant bodies. The outcome is still not clear. The new EFC Khmer leadership, made up of the same busy people with so many responsibilities already, will have to prove itself by holding together under all the strains and stresses, jealousies and bitter memories of the past, and seek to be a practical help to the church and not just another layer of bureaucracy to be financed, and another meeting to be attended.

One vital role a strong and respected EFC can fulfil is to make representation to the Government in Phnom Penh regarding the plight of many rural churches seeking legal registration. They find themselves in a 'catch 22' situation in that they are illegal gatherings on the one hand, but on the other hand prevented from acquiring the documentation they need by all the various levels of corrupt and hostile bureaucrats demanding exorbitant fees for their signature. Of course, in reality, the officials are not going to be bothered with harassing unregistered churches unless there is a good reason to do so. And if the churches were registered and there was a good reason to harass them, they still would anyway. These rural groups of believers who face far more persecution from superstitious and lawless villagers and police than do churches in the towns are advised to be patient and not be in a hurry to erect 'churches' (that is, buildings). Rather, they should meet together in homes.

It must be understood, however, just how important it is to the Khmer Christians to have their own 'temple', their place, which they can identify. While they may appreciate theologically that it 'doesn't matter', emotionally they know that to their non-believing neighbours, their poor homeless God, worshipped under houses,[3] and thus under foot with the pigs and the chickens, is not a God highly esteemed, so the Christians prefer it otherwise. Many older Christians, due to past bitter experiences, do not trust the government and are reluctant to register names and details about their churches.

Just how such issues facing the Cambodian church in the late 1990s will be resolved is clearly beyond the scope of this book, and the jury is still out on what has happened to the Cambodian church since 1990. What seems significant now may well prove to have been of no consequence, and what is not worth mentioning now may well later prove to have been of great significance.

Following the release in Phnom Penh in 1993 of the New Testament in an urgently needed new translation of the Bible in modern Khmer, readable and culturally sensitive, the translation team led by the dedicated and hard working Sokh Nhep Arun[4] and Khmer scholar and priest Père Ponchaud[5] under the auspices of the United Bible Society, pressed on with the Old Testament. The entire Bible in this new translation should be in circulation as this book is published.

But just as many in the West believe the 1611 King James Bible to be the only acceptable translation, so inevitably there are those who insist that only the first Khmer translation (from the King James Bible) completed by American missionary, Arthur Hammond,[6] is acceptable. This new translation is seen by some Cambodians as 'the devil's Bible'. While Christians will be free to use either Bible, sadly there are those prepared to stir up such fierce controversy over it even to the point of trying to start an opposition Cambodian Bible Society, and leading the government to believe that the Protestants are now quarrelling over two different Bibles, rather than two translations.

Some of the Cambodians who had risen to leadership in the Khao I Dang Refugee Camp Church a decade earlier, and who had now received theological training in the United States, were also returning to Cambodia. In 1992, Sythan, backed by inter-denominational Cambodian groups in America and generous Chinese patrons, started the Phnom Penh Bible School in a leaky tumble down old house in the heart of Phnom Penh. Working tirelessly with the enormous responsibility, he soon had scores of bright and enthusiastic young Christians packing the place out, some from distant provinces.

The newly-constituted Chinese Church also first met here for services, only a block away from their original beautiful old church which was being denied them by the armed soldiers who were occupying it, and demanding more money to leave than the building was worth.

Now the Bible School has moved to better premises near the Olympic Market. With staff and resources from missions, and from the local evangelical community, such a school has the potential of becoming a vital research and training centre for the whole church.

Another Cambodian returnee and his family from among the 200,000 strong diaspora is Kong Chon. Despite the overwhelming odds against him, Chon has graciously persevered in encouraging unity and cooperation among the churches. With him in this are two or three very gifted local pastors[7] who have come up through the Cambodian 'school of hard knocks' over the past two decades.

One of the outstanding Cambodian Christian women who has returned to serve her people well is Miss Solina Chy from Canada. A bright young woman with a promising future, from a comfortable home in Battambang, Solina lost everything at the hands of the Khmer Rouge. Her mother, recovering from recent surgery, died in her arms on the road during a rainstorm in the early days of the forced exodus from Battambang in April 1975. Solina suffered indescribable torture under the Khmer Rouge. But they could not break her spirit.

Alone in Battambang's 'killing fields' she would stand and watch the sun sinking in the west, and wish with all her heart that she could just tie a string to it and be pulled over the horizon to freedom. Wonderfully, she did make it to freedom and a new life in Canada where she was loved and nurtured by Canadian Christians and the Cambodian church in Ottawa. Despite the terrible memories, she returned to Cambodia in 1995 with the Far East Broadcasting Corporation to prepare Christian radio programmes for Cambodia, visit and encourage those who write in to the programmes for help, and distribute radio sets to groups of believers for whom the Christian *Voice of Love* broadcasts aired from the Philippines are a lifeline.

Whatever uncertainties lie in store for the continued freedom of the church in Cambodia, these strategic radio broadcasts will continue to impact thousands with the Good News, especially those isolated in far-away parts of the country. Good quality Cambodian material is always needed for these daily broadcasts.

April 16 1995, the eve of the twentieth anniversary of the fall of Cambodia to the Khmer Rouge was also Easter Day. I was asked to address the open air sunrise service of about four hundred people gathered on a field behind the Australian Ambassador's house in Phnom Penh. It seemed that by now we should have reached some great landmark in the long march of the Cambodian church. And yet despite the ending of the reign of terror and communism, and the return of religious freedom, it was as if we were just starting all over again.

The following evening I wrote this reflection in my journal:

April 17, 1995 marked the twentieth anniversary of the fall of Cambodia to the Khmer Rouge in 1975, plunging Cambodia into the madness which was *Ankga*, 'the Organization', and which turned the country into a nation-wide death camp and left it a physical and spiritual wasteland.

What was most significant about the passing of this anniversary was that for the majority of Cambodians it was a non event. It was the expatriate community which did most of the remembering. Virtually nothing was said by the local media. Cambodians were incredulous at the foreigners' obsession with the events of twenty years ago. 'Let's just forget it' was the general response. Indeed, there seemed to be little appetite for remembering the past, documenting it, or seeing justice done to those who committed such horrendous crimes against their own people.

The American-financed 'Cambodian Genocide Project', 'to investigate crimes against humanity committed by national Khmer Rouge leaders' has now started its work in Cambodia led by Dr Etcheson of Yale University. Already they have documented the existence of over 8,000 mass graves (the final number could be close to 20,000) and suggest that at least 1.5 million Khmers may have been executed, with hundreds of thousands more dying from starvation and disease.

Someone once wisely pointed out that a people who refuse to remember and learn from the mistakes of the past are doomed to repeat them. And looking at the social-political-economic scene in Cambodia, on April 17, 1995, one could be forgiven for concluding that nothing has changed and Cambodia has learned nothing from the events of April 1975!

Corruption in the government, the civil service, police and army is worse than it ever was. Wealth still gravitates to the cities, and the rural masses continue to be mired in poverty with only lip service and token relief coming their way. As in 1975, the military hospitals are swollen with young soldiers, arms and legs having been blown away on the battlefields and minefields of the north-west. The conditions in these so-called hospitals are appalling. The soldiers are uncared for, unpaid and largely ignored by government, military chiefs and people alike who appear to treat such tragedy with fatalistic indifference. Too many military chiefs continue to grow rich as they always have, pocketing the salaries of their 'phantom armies', smuggling the country's dwindling timber resources to Thailand, and selling arms to the enemy. For them the ongoing civil war is very profitable business.

The Khmer Rouge are as insane as ever, like a mad dog chasing its own tail. Though corrupted, divided, and ideologically bankrupt, they still broadcast their familiar litany of racism, hate, lies, and killing which thrills them the most. They thrive on the selfish greed of unscrupulous Thai businessmen and military along the common border with whom they also trade in timber and gemstones. They thrive as they always have on the rampant corruption and class conscious arrogance which exists throughout Cambodian society. They continue to capture and murder westerners who pose no threat to Cambodia but have come to serve the people and enjoy their hospitality.

Their furious scorched-earth policy all across the north-west has inflicted endless suffering on the very 'little people' they purport to champion. Another dry season has passed with the demoralised Royal Army making little impact against them despite the enormous loss of life and resources. A political solution and healing for Cambodia's deep woundedness is as elusive as ever.

What rules in Cambodia today is not the rule of law but the rule of guns and money. If you have guns and money then you are the law because everything has its price, everything is measured in dollars: people's lives, state assets, natural resources, justice, morals etc. Everything and almost everyone can be bought off. Money is the only security there is and so people are out to make as much of it as possible by any and every means.

To the three big growth industries of sex, cigarettes and alcohol, we can now add a fourth – gambling. A magnificent floating casino has anchored at the water front. The government is encouraging gambling in a big way as a means of earning money. The 'high rollers', mostly Chinese from the region, are rolling in along with all the other evil elements which thrive in such a climate: Triad gangs, drug barons, money launderers and prostitution.

At the same time as all this is happening, the government is lamenting the loss of cultural and moral values in Cambodia and is calling on the people to return to traditional ethics and standards of conduct. An enormous full-blown AIDS time bomb is set to explode at any moment (experts estimate 40,000 dead by the year 2,000). But the show, the traditional Khmer shadow play, goes on. The amazing ability to keep truth and illusion in two separate compartments of the mind is a mental gymnastic which is perplexing at best and socially disastrous at worst.

A big question mark hangs over King Sihanouk's health. (He is in his mid-seventies.) He remains as perhaps the only enduring, though increasingly uncertain 'centre' in Cambodian society. When he dies that will be gone and perhaps the very institution of the monarchy itself will fall into decline. There will be much squabbling over the succession.

In the midst of this chaos and darkness the Cambodian people continue to seek a new 'Centre' around which to rebuild their shattered lives. They search seemingly in vain for hope, for light, for role models, for direction. One would like to say at this point that the Body of Christ, the church, is providing that light in the darkness, that salt in the corruption. But with the exception of some notable Christ-like examples this is in general not the case.

And so I must end this reflection with a call for a deep heart repentance in the fear of the Lord to all of us who bear the name of Christ in Cambodia. For the Cambodian church's light is dimmed and its savour tainted by its divisions, distractions, quarrels and petty jealousies which continue to tear it apart, make it a laughing stock to the government and an irrelevance to the masses.

Cambodians do not yet see much evidence that the Christians here are disciples of Jesus. Like the rest of Cambodian society, the church too has failed to learn from the past. It has become enculturated by the 'vanity fair' around it. Pride has triumphed over humility, pragmatism over godliness, and empire building over self-forgetfulness. This is the greatest scandal, the greatest tragedy of all. It is a time for weeping and heart searching; a time for us to return to the Lord in penitence and faith.

Don Cormack Phnom Penh. April 17, 1995.

It is especially encouraging to see the traditional long-term and experienced church planting missions increasing their teams, strengthening their leadership and cooperating together in Cambodia. By the end of the century there should be a whole new generation of fluent Khmer speaking missionaries from both Asia and the West working in Cambodia. The commitment to language acquisition and cultural awareness is long and costly but indispensable to responsible church planting and discipling in a country like Cambodia.

Foremost among these missions are the American Christian and Missionary Alliance who pioneered evangelical church planting in Cambodia and persevered alone here for fifty years, and the interdenominational OMF International[8] who joined in partnership with the Christian and Missionary Alliance in 1974 at the invitation of Taing Chhirc.

They have had to face the reality for better and for worse that now many other groups, good, bad and ugly, have arrived in Cambodia to work also. The situation is no longer as simple as it was in the 'good old days' prior to the 1970s when there was just the Khmer Evangelical Church *à la* Christian and Missionary Alliance. An independent American couple arriving in 1973 precipitated the first cleavage with the establishment of the 'Maranatha' churches, led mostly by pastors diverted from the existing Evangelical church.

The American Southern Baptists have long had an interest in Cambodia and performed a wonderful work among refugees in Thailand. These three major missions have always worked in close cooperation in this field.

Another hardworking group who carved themselves a reputation on the Thai border for being willing to do absolutely anything for the sake of the gospel and with great enthusiasm was Youth With a Mission. While traditionally a movement for young people for short-term service they are now developing mature church planting teams with a well-integrated social component.

No one who has seen the work or met the servants of Servants of Asia's Poor can be anything other than deeply impressed at the recovery of the Christ-centred call to simplicity and service to the poorest of the poor. Here is an international fellowship of faith which 'being found in human form' has humbled itself, 'taking the form of a servant' to become obedient even to the extremity of death to self.

Another smaller organisation Inner Change, based in California, is recruiting serious, thinking young people, dedicated to the long haul of excellence in language and cultural understanding, and willing to explore ways both old and new to bring the Cambodian people into a living relationship with Jesus Christ. Such organizations as these deserve our total support for they are going to be working alongside Cambodian Christians in the years ahead to plant enduring churches in Cambodia's fields.

I do have strong reservations about the prevailing obsession with short-term 'trips' to mission fields. That they have a lasting impact for good is, I believe, a costly delusion: a distraction, a drain on the resources needed to support serious projects and on missionaries whose time they take up. Cambodia is a popular resort for such Christian tourists. The 'fields' are criss-crossed with their well worn paths. They are often associated with some

English teaching programmes since there is little else they can safely do without the national language. Let me not be misunderstood. Short-termers are fine if they are well supervised and have a focused and definable project to fulfil. Some of the longer established organizations screen candidates well, and accept only those who are seriously committed to world mission in the longer term. For them the time away can be spiritually enriching, broadening, rewarding. But it is always a 'preliminary' and more properly seen as being for the benefit of the *person* rather than for the church they spend time in. Short-term trips are never a substitute for long-term preparation and planning, nor for nurturing and harvesting. And neither do the 'fields' benefit much from the constant parade of researchers and surveyors pausing endlessly to take the pulse of the victim who has fallen among thieves, before passing by on the other side.

Unfortunately, many Khmers have come to associate Christianity entirely with English language learning. Today if you tell a Cambodian on the street that you are a Christian working with a church, the chances are the first thing he will ask is, 'May we come and learn English with you?' One organization even had the words 'English language' written on a cross on their vehicles. Now does this help combat the widely held stereotype that Cambodian Christians are just self-seeking western clones? English may well be valuable to Cambodians including Cambodian Christians. But it is best kept out of the church and confined to language schools where it belongs. All through its history the Cambodian church has been mesmerised and stumbled by this aberration.

I have not referred much to the Christian development agencies, though there are a number of excellent ones in Cambodia. The important thing for these to learn from Cambodian church history is the danger of lassooing the local church or its leaders for its own agenda. Neither must we risk compromising Cambodian Christians hired by Christian humanitarian organizations who receive considerable state funding from their home countries, and may directly or indirectly serve their strategic interests. Too often by offering attractive salaries, the Christian development groups encourage the 'apostles' away from ministering the Word of God to 'waiting at tables'. These are very sensitive issues and they must be very carefully considered.

And surely the most important priority for a development organization which calls itself Christian and campaigns for money from the Christian community, is that it be consistently Christian, even when sitting in the counsels of the ungodly, and under pressure to hire nice people who are humanitarian but not Christian. This is potentially very confusing for young Cambodian Christians who trust these groups and look to their staff as role models.

Finally, it must always be remembered that western medicine only heals their bodies. It doesn't answer nagging internal questions about the theology of suffering. Cambodians link all things together, especially health and the supernatural. The native healers offer them answers, but do we?

Apart from a growing maturity in faith and in knowledge of the Word of God, nothing will encourage that elusive unity in the Cambodian church more than a closely united and prayerful spirit among the missionaries of every stripe. This willingness to work together recognising that the beliefs which unite us far outweigh the trappings which differentiate us is one of the best gifts we can give to the national church.

Cambodia has suffered too much already from squabbling leaders, and we are hypocrites if we go to Cambodia bearing the Name of Christ while harbouring a divisive party spirit. The situation is precarious. The time is momentous. Cambodia has become the garbage dump of the world, a place to send all the trash: inferior goods, banned chemical fertilisers, out of date drugs; third rate for the third world. As Christians, let us send our best, our tried and tested, those willing to fall into the Cambodian fields and die for the one who said, 'As the Father has sent me, so I send you.'

In November 1994 an American healer launched an ambitious but ill-advised crusade at the Olympic Stadium in Phnom Penh accompanied by days of massive nation-wide advertising. Thousands of desperate rural Khmers poured into the city bringing their sick and dying amputees and handicapped. Some had even sold land and livestock, believing this powerful Christian shaman from America would grant their heart's desire.

In the stadium terrible rioting and panic broke out as people worked into hysteria mobbed the platform, frantically thrusting their sick ones towards the healer. As he fled for his life and a gloating Cambodian military made arrangements for him to be secretly whisked out of the country, the angry people were destroying everything they could find associated with this man. They broke into groups and began prowling the streets shouting 'Christians are liars!' and stoning and vandalizing nearby churches.

It was a day of great shame for the Cambodian Christians. They learned how close to the surface is hostility towards the church, and that not everything suggested to them from the outside, even if accompanied by great expense, is helpful or appropriate. It would take a long time for the church to recover from this tragedy.

The Cambodian church must be allowed, under the direction of the Holy Spirit, to discover its own cultural identity and calling. It needs great wisdom to know how to help the Khmer people confront their illusions and fantasies. Above all, the church must comprehend the meaning of the cross of Christ. A Christianity which is loud and triumphalistic, which parades itself provocatively down the streets trumpeting the benefits and blessings of the Christian life, desperate to make God look good and successful is surely not the way ahead. I pray Cambodia will be spared...

We must remember that this is still an 'early church' aged three score years and ten. It has just passed through its 'Neronian' persecution. More will doubtless follow. The past does provide clues to the future. Its first generation of leaders are dead. As it confronts the post-modern world of designer religion, materialism, secularism, violence and eroticism, it must be developing firm biblical and theological underpinnings for itself, based squarely on the foundations of the prophets and the apostles with Jesus Christ himself as the chief cornerstone. This is the only way to authentic spiritual unity which is its strength.

Like the Roman world of our western early church, and indeed much modern western civilization today, the world inhabited by the Cambodian church is crumbling and passing away. It has lost its centre and is collapsing in on itself. It is adrift. It will buy more time selling off its resources and mortgaging its future; it will numb its pain with the opiates of materialism and dissipation. It will be increasingly dominated by other more powerful and disciplined peoples in the region. Leaders may well emerge briefly from the chaos wrapped in the banners of ancient Buddhism and Khmer ultra nationalism, calling the nation back to its roots and glorious Angkorian past. These people will persecute the church, and even more so if it is permeated by the stench of 'western decadence'. But the Cambodian church is there to be light in the gathering darkness and salt in the all-pervasive corruption. It is called to give the Khmer people back their authentic Khmerness in place of the counterfeit, and portray before them how they might appear in eternal glory with all God's people from every tribe, tongue and nation.

My impressionist brush strokes on the portrait of the Cambodian church are finished. I have tried to depict all that my eyes, ears and heart observed, using Cambodian motifs and hues. Others must further refine the contrasts of light and shadow, sharpen the lines of focus and points of perspective, and add more colour and detail where the canvas is muted and sketchy. The portrait, still unfinished, is of a wide landscape of Cambodian fields, stretching towards the vast dome of the sky arching overhead, and in which the planting of heaven is taking place through the seasons of earth – the planting of the Lord:

> 'They are the shoot I have planted,
> the work of my hands,
> for the display of my splendour.'

Isaiah 60:21b

AFTERWORD to the 2000 edition

In 1975 Khmer Rouge seized control of Cambodia. That was when life was stopped and wrenched violently back to primordial chaos and darkness. The nation was plunged into a radical, blood-drenched experiment in social engineering. All were to be remade into egalitarian peasants in an instant socialist utopia, or perish in the process. As the world remembered 2000 years after the coming of the Lord, Cambodia's survivors remembered twenty-five years after Pol Pot.

The words *killing fields*, synonymous with that odious regime, have now entered the English language. They provide a simple and fitting epitaph for the dying century, plagued with wars, weapons, holocausts, cleansings, terrorists, tyrants and abortions – Killing Fields, 1901-2000, RIP.

In Cambodia, a generation has passed since that most evil of all the violent twentieth century's rabid political ideologies. The Organization on High (*Angka*), the Khmer Rouge and their revolution, have all but passed into the pages of modern history, along with Hitler, Stalin, Idi Amin and a host of others. But the Christian church, which they sought so diligently to destroy, is stronger now than at any time since the gospel was first proclaimed in Cambodia.

Two names in particular come to mind when we think of the horrors of that time: Pol Pot, the mastermind of the revolution, and Duch, its chief executioner; two notorious, condemned men,

435

malefactors who committed massive crimes against the Cambodian people. In 1998, in a jungle hideout, the former died, alone, bitter and unrepentant; the other chose life, turned in faith to the crucified Saviour and said 'remember me'. As they dumped his remains on a bonfire, Pol Pot's erstwhile comrades in arms cursed his memory, 'Just burn, burn.' Duch, imprisoned in Phnom Penh, where he awaits trial for his terrible crimes, has heard the promise of Jesus, 'You shall be with me in paradise.'

In turbulent Cambodia, where the risen Christ is drawing thousands of men, women and children to himself at this time, the vision of Jesus lifted up between two thieves is palpable. Their Year 0 has been caught up into 2000 Anno Domini. The dawning of a new millennium is giving rise to new hopes of a better future. Above the lamentations of the killing fields, the eternal hymn is sounding, heralding the new creation.

Duch's tormented and hungry spirit heard it plainly, through the lips of a fellow Cambodian, members of whose family he had killed along with thousands of others who suffered an agonising death at the stroke of his pen. At the Tuol Sleng extermination centre Duch reigned supreme, head of the national security apparatus of which Tuol Sleng was the epicentre, a vast web of interrogation, torture and death camps all across the country. He personally participated in the torment and abuse of *Angka*'s victims. His personal signature is everywhere, 'Kill them all.'

The Cambodian evangelist who baptised Comrade Duch was one of those hundreds of thousands who fled from the killing fields and crossed the border into the refugee camps in Thailand. Here he heard the gospel. Like many others, after being brought to maturity in Christ in the United States, Australia or one of several other countries of resettlement, he has returned to his bereaved motherland with Good News.

In January 1979, after destroying as much incriminating evidence as he could, including the remaining prisoners at Camp S-21, Tuol Sleng, Duch fled before the Vietnamese *blitzkrieg* with the rest of the Khmer Rouge to the Thai border. He became a refugee in Site B Camp, Thailand, being cared for by the UN who at that time were fully supporting his blood-stained regime's seat at the UN in New York. Now, ironically, they are desperately trying to get the Cambodian authorities, under Prime Minister Hun Sen, whose government in Phnom Penh through the 1980s they refused to recognise, to bring Duch and other ageing arch-criminals to justice.

For twenty years, after slipping deftly through the hands of the occupying Vietnamese army, Duch remained hidden in Khmer Rouge areas of western Cambodia along the Thai border, studying English, French and involving himself in humanitarian work. It was during this time that his wife was killed by a bandit and he was injured. Having changed his name to Hong Pin, in 1993, he abandoned the revolution he had sacrificed his youth to serve and returned to teaching. This is how he was remembered by some, as a brilliant young mathematician in Phnom Penh in the sixties, before his arrest by Sihanouk's police, imprisonment as a communist activist and subsequent flight to the Khmer Rouge jungle bases. He might still be working for the Christian missionary and humanitarian agencies among Battambang's rural poor had he not been tracked down in April 1999, by journalists from the Far Eastern Economic Review (6 May 1999 issue, p.23). He made it very clear to them that he was now a changed man. He had become a Christian on Christmas Day 1993, surrendering his life to God. From that time on he had begun to study the Bible seriously and grow as a disciple of Christ under the guidance of Cambodian Christian workers from California.

Duch discerns the parallel between himself and the apostle Paul, a 'chief of sinners', who once slapped the face of God by persecuting his church and committing terrible atrocities against his creatures. He was baptised on 6 January 1996 in the Sangke River in Battambang; his sole desire is to grow in faith and knowledge of God, plant churches and bring relief to his suffering people.

Duch is unique among the old Khmer Rouge leaders such as Khieu Samphan, Ieng Sary and Nuon Chea. All these have generally denied the excesses of the revolution and their participation in the genocide. They have come to a classic Khmer 'understanding' and defected to the government side in return for quiet obscurity in Pailin on the Thai border; a kind of semi-autonomous zone, rich in timber and gemstones and controlled by ex-Khmer Rouge cadre growing rich on trade with Thai military and business interests.

Ironically, his candour, his revelations, potentially so dangerous to many still in power in Cambodia today, from King Sihanouk, Prime Minister Hun Sen, cabinet ministers, police and military and on down through the ranks, have forced the authorities to arrest him for his own safety, and charge him with genocide. Outspoken honesty is not a welcome commodity in Cambodian politics with the vast graveyards of skeletons in many closets.

In detention in Phnom Penh, along with the notirous Ta Mok, he awaits trial and an uncertain future. He has a Bible with him. The wait promises to be a long one given the simmering cauldron of political intrigue in Phnom Penh and the vagaries of Cambodian criminal law. He has become a key pawn, a useful gambit, in a very complex political chess game which involves the international community as well. Duch's life and testimony will be proclaimed to the world.

And unlike the others again, it is he who is actually free, and, under God, forgiven. In the spirit of Christ, he appears to have relinquished all concern for his own ego, safety and future. His future is now entirely in God's hands. Wisely, he has pleaded guilty and thrown himself upon the mercy of the Judge of all men. 'Whatever happens to me now that you have come,' he told the journalists, 'it is God's will.' An encounter with the overwhelming love and unconditional forgiveness of God in Christ crucified is what has transformed the heart of even a man like Duch. This should not really surprise us. It is such single-minded zealots as these that the Lord delights in arresting from self and bringing captive to himself.

It is news like this, reminding us of the powerful good of the gospel that gives reason for hope amidst the rapacious poverty, predatory crime, institutional corruption and endemic disease among Cambodia's ten million (and rising fast) people today. Indeed, apart from the transforming gospel of Christ, there is no real hope for Cambodia.

The church continues to multiply in every province, with the number of Christians nationally reaching beyond 20,000 in up to a thousand churches, sacred places, springing up across the Cambodian fields. With an increasing number of missionaries growing in fluency and understanding of the language and culture, and a newly-translated modern Khmer language Bible, there is growing hope for fields once filled with the stench of death to become fragrant with new life.

A new millennium gives rise to new hopes and fears. King Sihanouk, in his Monthly Bulletin of March 1999, recognised that his reign over Cambodia had been usurped by insidious and voracious forces of destruction: 'In today's Cambodia, the God of Impunity reigns side by side with the King of Corruption.' A shadow of absolute evil, even more virulent than that of the Khmer Rouge twenty-five years earlier, rooted and flourishing in the hearts of her people, threatens the very soul of Cambodia.

The Khmer Rouge sought to root out evil and injustice in society in the way they knew best; by killing all who offended against the revolution. It was as if they believed they could reinstate some pre-fall utopia which existed before class and racial enemies came and spoiled everything. In less than four years they were well on their way to killing most of Cambodia, including endless purges of their own ranks. In the end, weakened and divided, they were overrun by the Vietnamese forces of occupation.

The remaining veneer of Buddhism in Cambodia, with its anaesthetising fatalism, has little to offer in the face of the rising tide of evil because it is not interested primarily in this flesh and blood world, but in transcending it through the denial of passion. This teaching in predominantly Buddhist Cambodia seems to have had quite the opposite effect, with unbridled and inordinate passion let loose at every hand. Lists of rules and dogmas seem only to exacerbate the problem of human nature. People eventually rebel against the shackles of mere religiosity and ritual.

Neither will the familiar promise of education and modernisation, void of any moral absolutes or reference to God as it is in its politically correct form, and the inevitable march of secularism, illuminate the moral landscape any more than it has done in the West. And the much vaunted Information Super-highway, the Internet, which will impact Cambodia in the coming years will, I fear, prove to be just another feeder to that wide and spacious road to destruction, full of hidden viruses and increasingly clogged with the polluting traffic of deadly addictions.

Down through the heart of Cambodia flows a great river, the source of Cambodia's fertility and fruitfulness. The mighty Mekong springing far away in the mountains of Tibet brings a floodtide of life and fecundity to this land. And through all the changing seasons it flows on, itself unchanged, forever covering and bearing away in its waters the sins of a people, the bodies of Cambodia's slain, the rising tide of a nation's sewage. This river is a parable of the church of Jesus Christ in Cambodia in the new millennium: lifegiving, refreshing, radiant, cleansing, unceasing. And the wellsprings of this river of life are the prayers of the saints and their attentiveness to God, the Word of God internalised and the Spirit of Holiness actualised in a people, crucified and cruciformed; a counter-culture flowing through the heart of the nation.

A great deal of millennial excitement gives rise to millennial fantasies and elusive dreams. We awaken no different on 1 January 2000, or even mathematically correct 2001, from how we are when we go to bed on 31 December. The harsh realities of Cambodia will not be spirited away by lofty sentiments and visions of what the church might be. Hope for the Kingdom of God in the Kingdom of Cambodia in the new millennium cannot be sustained by our predictions and resolutions, our faltering goals and visions, but only by the conviction that the sovereign Creator and Redeemer God is Lord of time and space. And he saves us by stepping right into the fray of human life, illuminating our personal darkness, turning us round and rescuing us from ourselves and this stifling, darkening, siren world.

He himself is the hope for Cambodia; release for a people imprisoned in an endless cycle of life and death, reaching for comfort from the opiates of vanity fair. He is the hope who never disappoints, who gathers up and fulfils beyond all our wildest dreams.

Duch, searching for absolution and purpose, and thousands of other ravaged Cambodian lives, have reached out of their darkness to the undeviating God of hope, who, in Jesus, first reached out to them; not only from throughout the new millennium where he dwells already, but from the far side of eternity and the place of our heart's desire, the hope to which we are daily being called.

Don Cormack
Christmas 1999

APPENDIX 1

This address (edited) was delivered by the Rev Don Cormack at The Church of Christ Our Peace, Phnom Penh at a special remembrance service for 'VJ Day' on August 20, 1995. Later, it was printed in Cambodia's daily newspaper *The Cambodian Daily*. It ends with an appeal for peace in Cambodia.

'Half a century ago on August 15, 1945, all across this vast Asian continent, the guns fell silent. The most bloody and devastating war ever fought in the history of mankind, a war which for six dreadful years had claimed the lives of tens of millions of human beings all over the world, came to an end.

'And it was brought to its definitive end in no less violent a way than it had been fought; with the dropping of the first and then a second atomic bomb on Japan... And only then, finally, over the crackling airwaves, was heard the sombre voice of the Japanese Emperor, announcing Japan's unconditional surrender. And the people of Asia were at last able to enter into the joy of peace. A peace which their European compatriots had already known since the surrender of Germany in May 1945, three months earlier.

'All that was fifty years ago, and we have come here today to look back on these events in sober remembrance and reflection, in order that we might better go forward, not in the arrogant self-confidence which too often characterises post-modern technological man with his short memory, nor with any anger still burning in our bones, but in wisdom and in a spirit of humility and forgiveness, reconciliation and peace.

442

'A wise person once observed that "Those who refuse to remember the mistakes of the past are doomed to repeat them." There is no virtue in the platitude, "Oh let's just forget about all that and get on with the future." These are back-scratching words, but they are a delusion, because we cannot forget. We must not forget. We must recall and remember, so as to learn and grow.

'It is only cleansed wounds that heal. Old wounds covered over with anodyne sentiments and panaceas only fester on and break out again and again. This is Cambodia's dilemma, isn't it? She has yet to deal seriously with her past. A catharsis is what Cambodia has yet to experience, in dealing thoroughly, honestly, justly and uncompromisingly with the past decades.

'Thus the nation continues to repeat over and over again the mistakes of the past, continuing along a path of self-destruction as it has been doing now for at least half these fifty years since the end of World War II.

'The safest place to deal with our past, to experience authentic catharsis, is in the presence of our creator-redeemer God, before whom all of us are equal and before whom each one of us is ultimately accountable; before whom all fantasy, distortion and darkness is cleared away.

'The ancient Israelites had a custom every fiftieth or Jubilee year. Every fifty years, no matter what had happened in the intervening time, everything was returned back to the way it was. All the injustices, all the traffic which had moved back and forth between a man and his neighbour was returned to the perfect pattern of God's original blueprint. It was a time when everyone agreed to simply start over again, hopefully a little wiser than before. May August 1995 be the start of such a Jubilee year for Asia: a time to start over again, a time to rebuild, a time to forgive old debts, release all the slaves, set free all the prisoners and move forward armed with the confidence and wisdom which comes from remembering.

'One day Jesus Christ climbed to the top of a hill overlooking the Sea of Galilee, and with his disciples and a great multitude of people around him, he invited us to become members of a radical new community; a community drawn from every tribe and tongue and nation; a counter-culture whose values, summed up in the eight statements he made, are the complete antithesis of the values of our permissive and quarrelsome world.

'The seventh of these sentences, describing the beatific life of authentic heavenly mindedness fleshed out in the here and now is this: "Blessed are the peacemakers, for they will be called the children of God." Well, I guess we all had a bellyful of this world's costly peacemakers when we were inundated with thousands of overpaid and under-disciplined UNTAC soldiers a few years ago, cramming the bars and brothels of Phnom Penh. No, these were not the kind of "peacemakers" Jesus had in mind. He was speaking of people who are in a state of peace with their God and with their neighbour, through faith in Jesus Christ, the Saviour of the world.

'The Word of God makes it clear that the only secure ground for genuine "Shalom" is complete reconciliation, the absence of all hostility between former enemies; not *d'étente* or peaceful co-existence, containment or empty political slogans. All the king's horses and all the king's men will not be able to put the Cambodian Humpty Dumpty back together again.

'Only the risen Prince of Peace, with scars in his hands and feet can reconcile man with his God, man with himself, man with his neighbour, and man with his environment. This is the essence of the gospel. And it is very, very costly. Just look at that cross up there. It is the cruellest instrument of torture and death ever devised by man in all his sadistic ingenuity. So what is it doing here in a place of worship? Doesn't it belong more appropriately over in a place like Tuol Sleng?[1] No, it belongs here before our eyes, in church, to remind us of the costliness of peace. Because peace requires the ultimate in self-forgetfulness and self-sacrifice.

'And after he was raised from the dead, Jesus appeared to his terrified and despairing disciples hiding behind locked doors. He greeted them with the words, "Peace be with you" and then immediately it says, "He showed them his hands and his side." Peace is costly! Is Cambodia, I ask, in particular her leaders, prepared to pay the ultimate price for genuine peace in terms of selfless service, personal integrity and transparency, righteousness, justice and accountability? Real peace can come in no other way!

'Wonderfully, we see in Cambodia today, Chinese and Japanese, British and Germans, former enemies fifty years ago, now all working together to bring peace and development to a nation unique in the region for its insatiable appetite for killing its own, pursuing revenge and greed, and squabbling among its leaders. The heart of the Cambodian problem is the problem of the Cambodian heart. This is a universal fact. These things have to be said today. They cannot be ignored, because I find it a hard thing to be celebrating peace in a land where there is no peace; where there has been for so long now only suffering and fear.

'I want to end this VJ Day address with an appeal for peace, for God's "Shalom" here in Cambodia. I call urgently upon all the leaders of the various political groupings, in the government and in the Khmer Rouge, to search your hearts before God, in the hope that you might discover there a revulsion for death and destruction, and a deep desire for reconciliation and peace; a desire to cast out all the corruption, greed and pride which has brought Cambodia to the brink of destruction, to the delight of her enemies but to the utter dismay of her long-suffering people. For most of these past twenty-five years of conflict I have been with the Cambodian people. I have watched two generations of young Cambodians being killed, maimed and torn apart by violence. It is enough!

'Is there yet a desire finally to beat all those "swords into plough shares"? A desire to see all the killing fields and all the minefields transformed into harvest fields? I say to you, in the name of God, and in the name of the ancient Khmer people, stop the killing, stop the destruction of Cambodia! Be reconciled to one another in the name of God, your ultimate destiny, and in the name of Cambodia your present destiny. AMEN.'

Don Cormack

APPENDIX 2

HISTORICAL TIME CHART OF CAMBODIA

300 BC	Megalithic Age (Samrong Sen).
100 AD	Indian expansion into Cambodia brings Brahminism to mix with the indigenous animism.
200	The Funan Period.
550	The Chenla Period.
800	Empire of Angkor (ruled by Brahmin priest kings). Dawn of the Khmer Golden Age.
900	King Yasorvarman.
1000	King Suryavarman I.
1100	King Suryavarman II (Angkor Wat built).
1200	King Jayavarman (The Bayon and Angkor Thom built). Buddhism now the dominant religion.
1400	The fall of Angkor and collapse of the Khmer empire. The Thais sack Angkor in 1431.
1500-1900	Era of decline as the Khmer Kingdom is torn apart by palace intrigue, disintegration and domination by Thailand and Vietnam.
1500	A new capital is established at Ang Chan (Lovek).
1555	Roman Catholicism first introduced by Portuguese Dominicans from Malacca.
1568	A former Buddhist priest, converted and baptised, is the first Christian martyr.
17th C	French Roman Catholic priests establish their church in Cambodia.

1643	Dutch Calvinists trying to establish a branch of the East India Company are massacred in Phnom Penh.
1700-1800	Vietnamese invasion and occupation.
1724	King Satha II is converted to Catholicism, but to avoid trouble, delays baptism till his death-bed.
19th C	Thailand and Vietnam threaten to swallow up Cambodia altogether. French Catholic priest Marie-Joseph Guesdon translates passages of the Gospels into Khmer for the liturgy.
1863	King Norodom places Cambodia under the protection of France to avoid being annexed by Thailand or Vietnam. Catholic missionaries now have complete liberty throughout the Kingdom.
1921	Christian and Missionary Alliance missionaries see conversions among the *Khmer Kraom* in neighbouring South Vietnam. They begin to translate Bible portions, Luke and Acts.
1923-1925	Two American Christian and Missionary Alliance (C&MA) couples, the David Ellisons and the Arthur Hammonds, are permitted to enter Cambodia. The Ellisons, based in Battambang, begin a Bible school with five men (1925) for the training of pastors for the first village-based evangelical churches in Cambodia. The Hammonds, based in Phnom Penh, begin translating the Bible into the Khmer language. A number of Khmer Christians from South Vietnam start to settle in Battambang, NW Cambodia. These *Khmer Kraom* believers are the result of C&MA work in S Vietnam prior to the door to Cambodia opening. The reign of King Sisowath (1904-1927).
1928-29	King Monivong (1927-1940) issues a royal edict against evangelism. Bible school students are imprisoned. Missionaries forced to leave Kratie province. A street chapel opens in Battambang town.
1933	Arthur Hammond completes the translation of the New Testament.
1940	The Old Testament translation is completed, but the

Khmer Bible cannot yet be published.

1941   The Vichy French have the eighteen year old Prince Sihanouk crowned King of Cambodia.

The Imperial army of Japan occupies Cambodia and encourages the Thai to take over the north-western provinces of Battambang and Siem Riep. Some missionaries are interned.

1945   Japanese defeated, French return, Thailand returns the provinces of Battambang and Siem Riep to Cambodia.

1945-1952   Anti-French *Issarak* (freedom) uprisings, especially in the north-west, inspired by Thailand and the Vietminh communists. Many Catholics killed. At this time the first Protestants are martyred. (The *Issaraks* surrender in 1954.) In 1949 the Bible School leaves Battambang and relocates at Takmau, on the Bassac, just south of Phnom Penh.

1950s   Saloth Sar (Pol Pot), Ieng Sary, Khieu Samphan and other Khmer intellectuals studying at French universities in Paris on French scholarships undergo a political conversion to Marxist political philosophy.

1953   Cambodia is granted independence from France and becomes The Kingdom of Cambodia (till 1970).

The Khmer Bible is published and a specially bound copy is presented to King Sihanouk.

1955   King Sihanouk abdicates in order to seek real political power. The throne goes to his uncle, King Norodom Suramarit.

1960   King Norodom Suramarit dies. Sihanouk is appointed Head of State.

The Workers' Party of Cambodia, later to become the Communist Party, is started secretly in Phnom Penh by twenty-one radicals including Saloth Sar (Pol Pot) and Ieng Sary.

1963   Leaders of the Workers' Party including Pol Pot and Ieng Sary flee to the maquis from Sihanouk's deadly secret police. Khieu Samphan and others follow in 1967.

1965   All American Protestant missionaries are forced to leave

Cambodia as a result of Prince Sihanouk's anti-American, anti-CIA crusade. After forty years of work the Khmer Evangelical Church has a membership of less than a thousand.

1970   Prince Sihanouk is overthrown in a pro-American, anti Vietnamese right wing coup led by military strongman Lon Nol. Many of the Vietnamese community are massacred or flee to Vietnam. The country's name is changed to 'The Khmer Republic'. Sihanouk goes into exile in China where he becomes Head of the Khmer Rouge dominated front to 'liberate' Cambodia. He is supported by Prime Minister Chou En Lai and Chairman Mao Tse Tung.

Foreign missionaries of the C&MA return to find a church numbering about three hundred.

1970-1975   Vietnamese communist forces supporting the Khmer Rouge sweep into Cambodia capturing vast areas of the countryside, capturing the villages and surrounding the towns. The Khmer Rouge (Cambodian communists) grow in strength especially as a result of having Sihanouk as their leader and the unpopularity of the corrupt military regime of Lon Nol. Large numbers of Cambodians flee as refugees into the major cities for relief.

A lay-centred movement into scores of new 'house churches' multiplies across the city and significant church growth is seen in provincial centres also.

1973   Large evangelistic crusades in the crowded capital, Phnom Penh, raise the profile of the church and result in thousands of 'decisions'. Christianity begins to appeal to students and intellectuals. A massive Christian relief operation is under way among the city's burgeoning refugee population.

Taing Chhirc leaves his studies in the UK and returns to Phnom Penh, appealing for prayer and missionaries for Cambodia.

Missionaries from the Summer Institute of Linguistics begin working on the languages of several of the tribal peoples of Cambodia. Work begins on a new translation of the Bible (this work is lost in the ensuing chaos).

The Khmer Rouge are strong enough to fight the forces of Lon Nol without Vietnamese military assistance.

In August the Americans halt their bombing of Cambodia.

1974   The Overseas Missionary Fellowship (OMF), in response to Taing Chhirc's urgent request, send in a team of five missionaries who work alongside the established national Khmer Evangelical Church.

1975   Phnom Penh is surrounded by Khmer Rouge forces and completely cut off except by air. A massive American financed airlift of supplies keeps the besieged city alive till April when the Americans pull out.

The missionaries make a 'reluctant exodus'. The total number of Christians in Cambodia stands at around ten thousand.

On April 17, the Khmer Rouge march victoriously into Phnom Penh and immediately begin driving everyone into the countryside. This is repeated throughout the nation. The pogroms against the nation's leaders and educated classes begin immediately. Church leaders and pastors are soon martyred.

Prince Sihanouk returns to Phnom Penh as nominal head of the new regime for a few months after which he is imprisoned in his palace.

1975-1979 The years of the genocidal Khmer Rouge 'reign of terror' led by Pol Pot, Brother Number One. The country, transformed into a vast forced labour camp, is ruled by *Angka Loeu*, 'The Organisation on High'. Cambodia is renamed 'Democratic Kampuchea'.

At least two million of seven million Cambodians, including virtually all the Christian leaders and ninety percent of the church, are killed or allowed to die of starvation and disease. Tens of thousands flee to refugee camps in neighbouring Thailand and Vietnam.

A constitution banning 'reactionary religion' is passed in January 1976.

Sihanouk 'resigns' in April 1976. More mass movements of the people take place. Fearful of Vietnamese influence, the Khmer Rouge begin a nationwide campaign of internal purges in all regions.

1977   The Khmer Rouge begin bloody raids into Thailand and Vietnam claiming that they are restoring Cambodia to its glory and size during the Angkor Period.

1979   Led by the Vietnamese army, the 'Khmer Front for the Liberation of the Motherland', mostly former Khmer Rouge cadre who fled to Vietnam from Pol Pot's internal purges of the Eastern zone cadre in 1977-78, sweep across Cambodia and in a few weeks drive the Khmer Rouge out. Along with hundreds of thousands of desperate and dying Khmers they flee for sanctuary to the Thai border. The new leaders in Phnom Penh are Heng Samrin, Chia Sim and Hun Sen. Sihanouk along with Khmer Rouge leaders escape to Peking, flown there by their Chinese patrons. Cambodia is now 'The People's Republic of Cambodia'.

1979-1990 Hundreds of thousands of Cambodian refugees flee to camps and an uncertain future in Thailand. The Khmer Rouge are rebuilt by Thailand and China to wage guerrilla war against the 'Vietnamese puppets' in Phnom Penh.

About two hundred thousand Cambodians are resettled overseas forming a worldwide Diaspora (sixty percent go to the United States). Most will remain at the border under the control of various 'liberation armies' till repatriation in 1993.

An enormous church of several thousand emerges in the Khao I Dang camp in Thailand. Christian relief and development groups and a few missionaries work in these camps.

A massive Cambodian 'baby boom' is under way by 1980.

In Cambodia the new Soviet-Vietnamese backed communist regime struggles under a world economic embargo, and a new civil war in the north-west with the 'liberation armies' based in Thailand.

The church in Cambodia numbering less than a thousand is kept under surveillance and survives underground. Its remaining leaders flee to the Thai border. A few Christian relief organisations are permitted to operate in Cambodia but are kept under close scrutiny. Some Cambodian Bibles and other Christian literature are permitted in, but evangelism is forbidden.

1989   With the collapse of communism in Europe and under severe international pressure, the Vietnamese army of occupation leaves Cambodia.

The government in Phnom Penh under Prime Minister Hun Sen changes its name to The State of Cambodia. Buddhism is reinstated as the national religion.

1990   Christianity is once again formally recognised by the government after fifteen years of suppression. All the former church buildings, both Catholic and Protestant, have been desecrated and destroyed, or taken over for other purposes.

Christian relief and development agencies and missionaries from various denominations and parachurch groups, as well as a number of cults, begin to enter Cambodia.

1991   In October the Paris Peace Accords are signed by the three liberation factions based in Thailand and the Phnom Penh government to form an interim Supreme National Council headed by Prince Sihanouk. Cambodia is placed under the mandate of the United Nations Transitional Authority in Cambodia (UNTAC), and an international force of twenty-two thousand peacekeeping soldiers arrives to disarm the four factions, repatriate the refugees and organise elections.

Cambodians from the Diaspora begin to return for visits in large numbers including a number of Christians desiring to minister to their people. The C&MA and OMF and other missions all have workers resident in Cambodia again studying the language.

1992   The Khmer Rouge faction refuses to disarm or allow

UNTAC into their zones, effectively pulling out of the peace process.

They launch cruel attacks on the UN peacekeepers, on vulnerable rural communities and on the Vietnamese minority.

The Phnom Penh Bible School starts with about thirty full time students. A team of translators under the auspices of the United Bible Society are working on a new translation of the Bible in modern Khmer.

1993   The first Anglican-Episcopal church opens in Phnom Penh. Over three hundred thousand Cambodians are repatriated from Thailand. Cambodians turn out enthusiastically to vote for a National Assembly in May elections despite intimidation from the Khmer Rouge. There is no clear winner, but of the four main parties, FUNCINPEC, led by Prince Ranariddh, son and heir of Sihanouk, win most seats. The Cambodian People's party of Hun Sen, the incumbent party in Phnom Penh for the past fourteen years, come in a close second. Feeling cheated of victory they form a secessionist movement to split the country in two. A coalition government is finally agreed to with both Prince Ranariddh and Hun Sen as co Prime Ministers.

The Khmer Rouge continue to war against the government from their bases along the Thai border, well financed from sales of timber and gem mining concessions to Thai businessmen and military. In September, Sihanouk, aged seventy, is recrowned King, and his wife Monique is Queen. 'The King reigns but does not rule.' A new constitution is approved by the National Assembly enshrining freedom of religion. The country's name is again The Kingdom of Cambodia.

In October the New Testament portion of the new Cambodian Bible is released in Phnom Penh at a large Christian worship service attended by the Minister of Religion. The Bible Society in Cambodia is established under Khmer leadership.

1994   The Protestant church has now grown to about five thousand with churches in every province of the country. The church is seriously divided and far from self-supporting. It also lacks theologically trained and experienced leaders.

The government is rocked by an attempted right wing coup. Ill-conceived dry season offensives by an inept and top heavy military against Khmer Rouge enclaves fail. Hospitals fill with wounded and amputee soldiers.

King Sihanouk's health deteriorates. He spends time in Peking undergoing treatment for cancer.

1995   Instability in the government deepens due to rampant corruption, internal divisions in all the parties, an intimidated National Assembly, and a judiciary very much under the control of the Cambodian People's Party leader Hun Sen whose people still run most of the country.

The devastation of the remaining rain forests and environment in general continues apace as the nation's resources are sold off to foreign companies, mostly Chinese, from countries in the region. Flooding and drought plague the countryside where most Khmers live a subsistence lifestyle.

Some Khmer journalists investigating government corruption are killed, imprisoned or put out of business.

Cambodia is granted observer status by ASEAN. (Vietnam has full membership.)

The American financed Genocide Project begins its investigations into the war crimes of the Khmer Rouge. Thousands of new mass graves continue to be discovered all across the land.

Millions of land mines remaining in Cambodia kill and maim daily. There are over 50,000 amputees.

HIV is spreading at an alarming rate particularly among the army, police and large population of prostitutes.

The Khmer Rouge abduct and kill more expatriates.

1996   The coalition government begins to fall apart. The KR are seriously fragmented and corrupted by the lucrative timber and gemstone trade with Thailand.

The Protestant church continues to grow and a serious effort is made to heal its divisions with the formation of The Evangelical Fellowship of Cambodia. About sixty per cent of Cambodians are under twenty-one.

1997   The Pailin-based KR led by Ieng Sary break away and are granted amnesty from the King. The remaining KR at Anlong Veng turn on each other resulting in the execution of Son Sen and family, the overthrow and humiliation of Pol Pot, and a takeover by Ta Mok. In July, Hun Sen violently ousts Co-Prime Minister Ranariddh who flees to France, turning the clock back back to 1989 when he ruled unopposed as a military strongman. A FUNCINPEC rump assisted by Ta Mok's KR resist from the northern jungle outpost of O'Smach. Cambodia's UN seat falls vacant, ASEAN application lapses, and massive financial assistance is halted. In October, a despairing King orders no celebrations for his seventy-fifth birthday because 'Khmers are again killing Khmers'. He speaks much of abdication and retreats frequently to China.

1998   April 17th, the world hears that Pol Pot, this century's cruellest despot, dies suspiciously of a heart attack in the last KR jungle hideout, abandoned and unrepentant.

In July, Hun Sen's Cambodian People's Party wins the disputed national election which is followed by weeks of demonstrations and violence. Hun Sen is now undisputed leader of Cambodia.

The last Khmer Rouge stronghold of Anlong Veng collapses and the remaining leaders, Khieu Samphan and Nuon Chea (Brother Number Two, after Pol Pot) defect to the Phnom Penh side. They are permitted to live in the semi-autonomous zone of Pailin with Ieng Sary and other ex-cadre.

1999   In March, Ta Mok, the last Khmer Rouge leader at large who has not defected, is captured and imprisoned in Phnom Penh to await trial.

At Easter, a delegation of Christian leaders presents a

specially bound copy of the newly-completed translation of the Cambodian Bible to King Sihanouk in an audience at his palace in Siem Riep. He tells them that he will not put it away in his library, but keep it near him.

The notorious Comrade Duch, commandant of *Angka*'s S-21 Extermination Camp at Tuol Sleng, is tracked down by journalists in western Battambang where he has been working unrecognised, with Christian humanitarian organisations among the rural poor, under the name Hong Pen. Having left the Khmer Rouge in 1993, he became a Christian, was baptised in '96 and has been quietly ministering ever since. Although aware of his whereabouts, it is now expedient for the government to arrest him and charge him with genocide. Along with Ta Mok and with his Bible, he begins the long wait for trial, in detention in Phnom Penh. He is the only former Khmer Rouge leader to admit to the terrible atrocities he has committed.

The church in Cambodia now exceeds 20,000, about .02 per cent of the population. The number of local churches nationally, spreading across every province, is in the region of 1,000. Bible Colleges in Phnom Penh and Battambang are training new pastors and future leaders. Along with the national leadership, the church is served by a growing number of returning Cambodian Christians from the diaspora and an international community of expatriate missionaries fluent in the language.

In contrast with the grim socio-political scene of rampant corruption, intrigue, and impunity, the church is growing in strength, maturity and unity, and looks poised for increased opportunity and growth.

NOTES

Prologue

1. The *cyclor* or *cyclo-pousse* (in French) is a type of trishaw which was first used as a cheap mode of transport in Phnom Penh in the 1930s. It is a three-wheeled conveyance with a seat in front for the passenger who is pedalled along by the driver, seated behind and steering with a bar along the back of the passenger seat. Most *cyclor* drivers are poor farmers from the countryside.

Chapter 1 – The Fallow Ground

1. Ethnic Khmers account for over 90% of the people of Cambodia. Others are Chams, Chinese, Vietnamese and tribal. The word 'Khmer' therefore is virtually synonymous with 'Cambodian'.

Chapter 2 – The Implanted Seed

1. Cambodian houses are typically built on stilts.

Chapter 4 – The Pestilence, Drought and Destroyer

1. The *krama* is an all-purpose piece of chequered cotton cloth. It is wrapped around the head, around the waist when bathing, used as a sling for carrying babies, possessions, as a shade from the sun, as a mat for sleeping out, and as a covering. Its uses are limitless and all rural folk have one wrapped around them somewhere. The Khmer Rouge made these symbols of peasantry, red and white check *kramas*, a part of their uniform, wearing it like a scarf with their black pyjama-like clothes.

457

Chapter 5 – The Late Rains

1. Far Eastern Broadcasting Corporation.
2. Some names of surviving Christian leaders still in Cambodia have been changed.
3. This story is told in detail in chapter 11.

Chapter 7 – The Fields White unto Harvest

1. The mission has now dropped its full name and is known simply as OMF International.
2. How can one simply say farewell, and fly to safety knowing that many of the Cambodian Christians who must stay behind will die? Emotionally, it is surely the most painful thing for a missionary to have to do. And then to find oneself, as we did within minutes, transported into the noisy, glaring, ephemeral and disinterested world of Bangkok. Such is the enigma of missionary life, and the identity crisis which sooner or later every missionary must face. Unless our identity, our sense of personhood and self-worth is rooted firmly in a vocation of obedient sonship and service, we shall eventually be driven to despair.

Chapter 9 – The Seed Falls into the Ground

1. Haing Ngor, who received an academy award for his part in the film *The Killing Fields*, was murdered in Los Angeles in February 1996.

Chapter 10 – The Seed Dies

1. After the Vietnamese takeover in 1979, the remnant of Christians who returned to Phnom Penh lovingly gathered up Mr Ellison's bones which had, along with those of other Christians, been dug up and scattered, and remounded the grave once more, leaving his remains 'to await in peace', they wrote, 'Christ's triumphant return in glory.'
2. The history of Roman Catholicism in Cambodia, not within the scope of this book, is far far longer than that of Evangelical Protestantism. It reaches back to the sixteenth century and the Portuguese traders. It can be read in an excellent book by Fr François Ponchaud entitled *The Cathedral of the Rice Paddy: 450 years' history of the Church in Cambodia* published by Librarie Artheme Fayard, Paris 1990.
3. It was a scaly anteater called in English a pangolin, *manis javanica*. This animal has such a reputation for shyness, that Cambodians will

call a shy person by its name. When disturbed, or fearful, the pangolin curls itself up into a tight ball which it is believed even an elephant cannot break open.

Chapter 11 – The Scent of Water

1. UNHCR: The United Nations High Commission for Refugees.
2. The Association of South East Asian Nations originally included the five nations of Thailand, Malaysia, Singapore, Indonesia, and the Philippines. It was first set up as a security coalition against perceived Vietnamese communist expansion. In 1995, however, Vietnam was granted full membership in ASEAN and Cambodia observer status. Economic and political co-operation is its main objective.
3. 1 July 1979.
4. I married Margaret Lockhart at Chefoo, Cameron Highlands, Malaysia in 1979. We had met there in 1972 when working as teachers. Margaret was born in Chengdu, Sichuan Province, China, where her parents John and Jean Lockhart were working with the China Inland Mission (now OMF International). After fleeing China in 1951 as a little girl, she grew up in the Philippines where her parents then served under OMF. Later she went to school in England and Alberta, Canada. We worked together in the Cambodian border camps and when the opportunity opened for a return to Cambodia, we went there together in March 1993. We have three daughters studying in England: Elizabeth, Margaret-Grace and Katherine.
5. One *rai* equals ten square metres.
6. One *hun* is equivalent to a gram.
7. A cart pulled by a motor cycle.
8. About one US dollar.

Chapter 13 – The Harvest of Wheat and Tares

1. Youth with a Mission.

Chapter 14 – The Gleanings

1. Name changed.
2. Name changed.
3. K H was married to Serey, the Bible School student who spent a year as an intern at the Christian Youth Centre with OMF missionaries. (See Chapter 11.)
4. One hopes that a new spontaneous unity, glimpsed that day, not

organizational but spiritual, built on a common faith and love in the Lord Jesus as revealed in the Holy Scriptures, might also be possible. This spirit of unity has prevailed in the subsequent Bible Society project to translate a new modern Khmer language Bible for the whole church in Cambodia.

Chapter 15 – The Fallow Ground: An Epilogue

1. I believe that eventually we shall see the Khmer Rouge master criminals accepted back into the mainstream of social and political life with royal amnesties, red carpets and broad smiles. The blame, if any is to be apportioned for 'the killing fields', will most likely be laid at the feet of that familiar Cambodian scapegoat, the Vietnamese.
2. I would also mention the great need and potential for Christian clinics, small teaching hospitals and specialist hospitals.
3. Cambodian houses are typically raised on stilts, and so Christians meeting on ground level, in the open area under the floor of the raised house, are beneath the feet of anyone in the house above.
4. Arun studied theology and became a Cambodian church pastor in France following his long and difficult escape from Cambodia and the Khmer Rouge.
5. Author of that outstanding book *Cambodia Year Zero* Penguin 1978.
6. Arthur Hammond worked with the Christian and Missionary Alliance.
7. Best not to give names.
8. Until recently known as the Overseas Missionary Fellowship, formerly the China Inland Mission.

Appendix 1

1. Tuol Sleng is the name of the notorious Khmer Rouge death camp in Phnom Penh where tens of thousands were liquidated. Today it is a museum and contains a number of the cruel instruments of torture once used there.

INDEX

English-Speaking OMF Centres

AUSTRALIA: PO Box 849, Epping, NSW 2121
Tel (02) 9868 4777. Freecall (outside Sydney) 1800 227 154
email: omf-Australia@omf.net *www.omf.org*

CANADA: 5759 Coopers Avenue, Mississauga ON, L4Z 1R9
Toll free 1-888-657-8010. Fax (905) 568-9974
email: omfcanada@omf.ca *www.omf.ca*

HONG KONG: PO Box 70505, Kowloon Central Post Office,
Hong Kong
email: hk@omf.net *www.omf.org*

MALAYSIA: 3A Jalan Nipah, off Jalan Ampang, 55000, Kuala Lumpur
email: my@omf.net *www.omf.org*

NEW ZEALAND: PO Box 10-159, Auckland
Tel 09-630 5778
email: omfnz@compuserve.com *www.omf.org*

PHILIPPINES: 900 Commonwealth Avenue, Diliman,
1101 Quezon City
email: ph-hc@omf.net *www.omf.org*

SINGAPORE: 2 Cluny Road, Singapore 259570
email: sno@omf.net *www.omf.org*

SOUTHERN AFRICA: PO Box 3080, Pinegowrie, 2123
email: za@omf.net *www.omf.org*

UK: Station Approach, Borough Green, Sevenoaks, Kent, TN15 8BG
email: omf@omf.org.uk *www.omf.org.uk*

USA: 10 West Dry Creek Circle, Littleton, CO 80120-4413
Toll Free 1-800-422-5330 *www.us.omf.org*

OMF International Headquarters:
2 Cluny Road, Singapore 259570.